LETTER OF TRANSMITTAL

SMITHSONIAN INSTITUTION,
BUREAU OF AMERICAN ETHNOLOGY,
Washington, D. C., May 9, 1938.

SIR: I have the honor to submit the accompanying manuscript, entitled "Archeological Remains in the Whitewater District, Eastern Arizona, Part I: House Types," by Frank H. H. Roberts, Jr., and to recommend that it be published as a bulletin of the Bureau of American Ethnology.

Very respectfully yours,

M. W. STIRLING, *Chief.*

Dr. C. G. ABBOT,
Secretary of the Smithsonian Institution.

SMITHSONIAN INSTITUTION
BUREAU OF AMERICAN ETHNOLOGY
BULLETIN 121

ARCHEOLOGICAL REMAINS IN THE WHITEWATER DISTRICT EASTERN ARIZONA

Part I. HOUSE TYPES

By FRANK H. H. ROBERTS, Jr.

UNITED STATES
GOVERNMENT PRINTING OFFICE
WASHINGTON: 1939

For sale by the Superintendent of Documents, Washington, D. C. - - - - - - - - - Price 50 cents

CONTENTS

	Page
Foreword	XI
Introduction	1
Remains of structures	17
Group No. 1	21
Structure 1	21
Structure 2	33
Structure 3	46
Surface house and brush shelters near structures 1, 2, and 3	53
Structure 4	58
Structures 5a and 5b	62
Structures 6, 7, and 8	67
Structures 9, 10, and 11	81
Surface house B and granaries	98
Group No. 2	102
Structure 12	102
Structures 13a and 13b	116
Structure 14 and dance court	124
Shelter and granaries	130
Structure 15 and associated granaries	135
Structure 16 and associated granaries	149
Additional pit remains	160
Structure 17	160
Structure 18	166
Unit-type structures	170
Unit No. 1	171
Unit No. 2	194
Unit No. 3	227
Great Pueblo ruins	244
Summary and discussion	253
Literature cited	267
Index	271

ILLUSTRATIONS

Plates

	Page
1. Map of Whitewater district	2
2. *a*, Looking across Whitewater Valley toward Puerco River. *b*, Arroyo in bottom of Whitewater Valley	2
3. *a*, Interior of structure 1. *b*, Main framework for restoration of structure 1	28
4. *a*, Brush and bark covering over framework, restoration of structure 1. *b*, Completed structure showing rounding dome and smoke hole-hatchway entrance	28
5. *a*, Interior view of portion of restored structure. *b*, Pillar left in excavating pit, structure 1	28
6. *a*, Masonry wall resting on slab foundation. *b*, Pilaster in structure 2	28
7. *a*, Compartment side of structure 2. *b*, Plaster pilaster behind wooden roof support	54
8. *a*, Fire pit beneath wall of surface structure. *b*, Opening into pit oven	54
9. *a*, Stone ventilator aperture in structure 6. *b*, Fire pit above floor in fill of structure 6	54
10. *a*, Ventilator side of structure 9. *b*, Portion of structure 11	54
11. *a*, Pillar left from fill in pit for structure 10. *b*, View across structures 9, 10, and 11	104
12. *a*, Floor in structure 12, showing ladder holes, deflector, ash and fire pits. *b*, Plastered-over depression in floor of structure 12	104
13. *a*, Pillar from fill, fire pit in fill, and logs on floor of structure 12. *b*, Pit for structure 13a	104
14. *a*, Floor of structure 13b. *b*, Portion of floor area structure 13b	104
15. *a*, Structure 14. *b*, Upper end of ventilator shaft for structure 14	128
16. *a*, Dance court as seen from end of Great Pueblo ruin. *b*, Portion of structure 14 underlying dance court and dais	128
17. *a*, Burned roof timbers in pit of structure 15. *b*, Series of slanting side poles for roof of structure 15	128
18. *a*, Bowl below roof timbers in fill of structure 15. *b*, Jar containing carbonized ears of corn lying on top of roof debris in structure 15	128
19. *a*, Pit and floor of structure 15. *b*, Compartment wall and ventilator of structure 15	158
20. *a*, Granaries and remains of shelter, structure 15 group. *b*, Pit and floor of structure 16	158
21. *a*, Double burial beneath granary floor in structure 16 group. *b*, View across Developmental Pueblo village	158
22. *a*, Second unit in Developmental village. *b*, Wall construction in portion of second unit	158
23. *a*, Stone step and wall construction in room 8. *b*, Corner bin in room 11	198
24. *a*, Corner of building outside room 11 and bin. *b*, Original floor in Kiva B	198

VII

ILLUSTRATIONS

	Page
25. *a*, Holes for slanting side poles at back of original bench top in Kiva B. *b*, Katcina niche in wall of Kiva B	198
26. *a*, Subwall storage box in Kiva B. *b*, Ventilator openings in Kiva B	198
27. *a*, Surface structure in third unit. *b*, Clearing debris from kiva for third unit	232
28. *a*, Wall construction in bench of third unit kiva. *b*, Holes for wainscoting poles at back of bench in third unit kiva	232
29. *a*, Floor in kiva for the third unit. *b*, Mound covering large building in Great Pueblo group of ruins	232
30. *a*, Portion of Great Pueblo ruins, corner of building below and to left of standing figure. *b*, Arroyo cut through refuse mound	232

TEXT FIGURES

1. Group 1 pit and surface remains	22
2. Plan of structure 1	24
3. Diagram of pillar left from fill in structure 1	28
4. Plan of structure 2	36
5. Plan of structure 2a	40
6. Plan of structure 3	47
7. Postulated reconstruction of cribbed roofing erected over pit of structure 3	51
8. Plan of surface building A	54
9. Plan and section for pit oven	56
10. Sections through surface remains A, pit oven, and structure 3, and shelter and structure 1	58
11. Plan of structure 4	60
12. Plan of structures 5a and 5b	63
13. Surface remains B and associated pit remains	67
14. Plan of structure 6	70
15. Plan of structure 7	74
16. Plan of structure 8	79
17. Section through structures 6, 7, and 8	80
18. Plan of structure 9	82
19. Plan of structure 10	86
20. Plan of structure 11	90
21. Section through structures 9, 10, and 11	92
22. Diagram of test pillar from fill in structure 10	94
23. Postulated reconstruction of timber arrangement in superstructure erected over pits 9, 10, and 11	99
24. Surface remains B in first group	100
25. Group 2 pit and surface remains	103
26. Plan of structure 12	105
27. Diagram of positions of burned timbers on floor of structure 12	107
28. Postulated reconstruction of superstructure erected over structure 12	109
29. Diagram of pillar left from fill in structure 12	111
30. Structure 13a, plan and section	117
31. Plan of structure 13b	121
32. Plan of structure 14	125
33. Plan of dance court	127
34. Plan of brush shelter	131
35. Sections for structure 12, dance court and brush shelter	134
36. Plan of structure 15	136
37. Plan of structure 15 group of house, granaries, and shelters	146

		Page
38.	Plan of granaries A and B and shelter in no. 15 group	148
39.	Plan of structure 16 house and granary assemblage	150
40.	Plan of structure 16	153
41.	Plan of granaries A and B of the no. 16 group	157
42.	Plan of structure 17	161
43.	Plan of structure 18	167
45.	Plan of Kiva A	181
46.	Plan of brush shelter	208
47.	Plan of Kiva B, upper floor level	210
48.	Plan of Kiva B, original floor level	213
49.	Sections through portions of first and second units	219
50.	Plan of the third unit	228
51.	Plan of kiva for third unit	234
52.	Sections through portions of third unit	238
53.	Plan of large ruins of Great Pueblo period	246

FOREWORD

The data furnishing the basis for the following report were obtained during the field seasons of 1931, 1932, and 1933. In the summer of 1930, while the writer was engaged in investigations at the Village of the Great Kivas on the Zuñi Reservation in western New Mexico,[1] Mr. J. A. Grubbs, of Houck, Ariz., reported the existence of a large group of ruins south of Allantown, Ariz. Upon completion of the project near Zuñi in September of that year a general reconnaissance was conducted in the region bordering the Arizona-New Mexico boundary line between the Zuñi Reservation and the Puerco River of the West. During the progress of this survey Mr. Grubbs pointed out the ruins in question. In addition, many scattered small village remains were noted in the immediate vicinity of the principal cluster. The possibilities for securing valuable information on the growth and development of one component of the prehistoric sedentary Indian culture pattern were so apparent that permission was obtained from Mr. Grubbs, who had acquired the land upon which they are located, to carry on a series of excavations. Work was started in May 1931 and continued through to the end of September. During the 1932 and 1933 seasons the investigations were conducted in the months of June, July, and August.

At the end of June 1931 the Laboratory of Anthropology at Santa Fe, N. Mex., joined with the Bureau of American Ethnology and throughout July and August the work was carried on as a joint project. Four graduate students in anthropology assisted in the researches during the time the Laboratory cooperated in the undertaking. They were holders of fellowships granted by the Santa Fe institution, for training in archeological field methods, and came from the departments of four universities. The men were: Carl F. Miller, University of Arizona; Solon T. Kimball, Harvard University; Ralph D. Brown, University of Minnesota; and Dale S. King, University of Denver.

The work of the 1932 season was carried on solely by the Bureau of American Ethnology, while that of 1933 was mainly under the auspices of the Laboratory of Anthropology, the writer being on leave of absence from the Bureau during the months of July and August. The personnel of the party for the third season consisted

---

[1] Roberts, 1932.

chiefly of graduate students, also holders of Laboratory fellowships. These men were: Erik K. Reed, Harvard University; Joe Finkelstein, University of Oklahoma; Sidney J. Thomas, University of Texas; and Harold E. Cooley, University of Minnesota. Deric Nusbaum, Harvard University, joined the party during July and August as a volunteer worker.

Linda B. Roberts supervised the cleaning and cataloging of specimens all three seasons. Secretarial work was performed by Ruth R. Butchart. Robert Kneipp, of Washington, D. C., assisted in the excavations and around camp during the 1931 season. Similar duties were performed in 1932 by David Jones, Jr., of Gallup, N. Mex. Carl F. Miller was also a member of the 1932 party and assisted in the preparation of maps and plans of the ruins. He devoted considerable time to a study of the timbers used in the structures and by means of the Douglass tree-ring chart determined the cutting dates of many of the beams. From this evidence it is possible to give approximate dates for the construction of the houses. Workmen employed in the digging were Navajo and Zuñi Indians. The hearty cooperation of all concerned aided the advancement of the researches in no small degree.

The main ruins have no name. The Navajos simply refer to them as "The Ruins." They were unknown to the Zuñis and the white settlers in the vicinity do not have any particular designation for them. Up to the time this report was written no work had been done on the large Pueblo structures, consequently there is nothing about these buildings to suggest a name.

Information and materials accumulated during the three seasons of investigations are so extensive that it is necessary to issue the report in two parts. In this, Part I, house types and antiquities pertaining to that phase of the subject are discussed. Lesser objects of the material culture, pottery, bone and stone implements, and other artifacts, are described in Part II, which will be published at some subsequent date.

The writer wishes to take this opportunity to express his personal appreciation, as well as that of the institutions concerned, to Mr. Grubbs for his generosity in permitting excavations on his land and for his cooperation in the promotion of the work.

ARCHEOLOGICAL REMAINS IN THE WHITEWATER DISTRICT, EASTERN ARIZONA

PART I. HOUSE TYPES

By FRANK H. H. ROBERTS, JR.

INTRODUCTION

The main site, where most of the investigations described and discussed in the following pages were conducted, is located on the ridge of mesas to the south of the Puerco River of the West and west of Whitewater Creek, an intermittent tributary of the Puerco. It is 3½ miles (5.633 k) south of Allantown, Ariz. (pl. 1). Specifically, it lies in the southwest quarter of sec. 34, T. 22 N., R. 30 E., Gila-Salt River meridian, Apache County, Ariz. The other excavated ruins are situated along the foot of the escarpment, below the principal group, at the west side of the valley.

Topographically, the district is characterized by comparatively broad valleys and flat-bottomed washes, and is cut by deep, narrow arroyos or ravines. The remains of horizontally laid sandstone beds, generally bordered by cliffs, form the high points.[2] Inasmuch as there is a variety of colors in them, these sandstone cliffs constitute one of the scenic attractions of the region. There are a number of shades of red, ranging from dark to light, interspersed with layers of white. The brightness of the rocks contrasts with the diverse hues of the valley bottoms and the slopes of the mesas.

The region is a part of the major topographical division called the Colorado Plateau. According to one classification the archeological site is located just south of the southwestern end of the Manuelito Plateau subdivision, only a short distance east of the mouth of Black Creek, called Bonito Valley and Defiance Creek on some of the older maps, that forms the dividing line between the Manuelito Plateau and Defiance Plateau provinces.[3] Another clas-

---

[2] Gregory, 1916, p. 26.
[3] Gregory, 1916, map, pl. 1.

sification places it in the southern part of the Navajo section of the Colorado Plateau, an area characterized by young plateaus with smaller relief than the canyon lands section to the north, a region marked by recent erosion and retreating rock scarps.[4] In general it may be said that the topography in the immediate vicinity of the ruins consists of gentle valley slopes and comparatively flat mesa tops (pl. 2, *a*, *b*). The valleys are dotted with some sagebrush, greasewood, rabbit bush, and many kinds of weeds. Extensive grazing in recent years has thinned the grass and forage plants to a marked degree. The mesas are covered with cedar, pinyon, and some yellow pine trees. The latter are more prevalent on the higher elevations north of the Puerco than they are along the southern mesas. In the open spaces on the mesa tops there is much more brush than in the valley bottoms.

Animals present in greatest numbers are the rabbit and prairie dog. There are some coyotes and porcupines, and a few fox and wildcat. Deer and antelope formerly roamed the countryside and the bear was not unknown. There are not many kinds of birds in the vicinity, although the raven, nighthawk, hawk, a sporadic eagle, the pinyon jay, owl, dove, and swallow are observed. At one time the turkey was plentiful, judging from the bones found in the refuse mounds. Insects are common and there are several kinds of snakes, although the latter do not occur in large numbers.

The soil in the valley bottoms and on the mesa tops, where there has not been too great a sand drift, is capable of producing good crops when there is sufficient rainfall or where water is available for irrigation purposes. If the many ruins scattered throughout the district may be considered as a criterion, it at one time supported a rather numerous population. It is possible that prior to the cutting of the deep arroyo channel in the bottom of Whitewater Valley (pl. 2, *b*), as well as that of the larger Puerco, the whole flats could have been devoted to fields for corn, beans, and other agricultural products such as the pre-Spanish occupants of the region raised. The run-off from the higher slopes could have been used for flood-water irrigation, thus providing, in addition to that normally falling on the fields in the form of rain, sufficient moisture to insure good crops. There are no evidences of definite irrigation ditches or reservoirs.

Tradition and the memory of Indians is at best doubtful evidence with respect to conditions in the past, but a number of aged Navajo in this district insist that when they were boys there was no arroyo in Whitewater Valley and the Puerco flowed, during the periods when it carried water, in an ordinary stream bed and not in a deep channel such as it occupies at the present time. If such was the case

---

[4] Fenneman, 1928, p. 342, map.

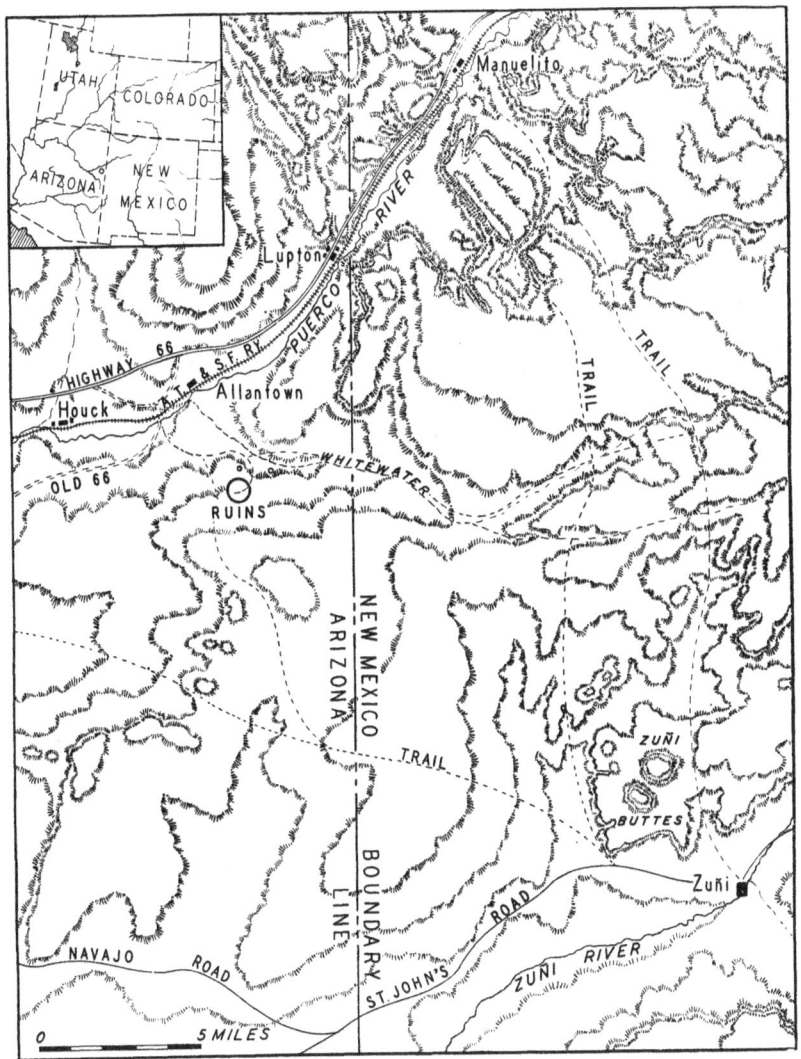

Map of the Whitewater district. Inset shows location of ruins with respect to general southwestern area.

a. Looking across Whitewater Valley toward Puerco River.

b. Arroyo in bottom of Whitewater Valley.

when the site under investigation was occupied, the flats below the ruins would have provided an ample food supply. In this same connection it is interesting to note that reports by early explorers in the region do not mention deep-cut stream beds. It was only after the Whipple Railroad Survey party reached the district beyond Navajo Springs, 25 miles (40.234 k) west from the Allantown neighborhood, that reference is made to an arroyo of any depth.[5] There is a notation that a bridge would be required at that place if a railroad was built along the Puerco. Lieutenant Simpson crossed the Puerco of the West in 1849 en route from Canyon de Chelly to Zuñi. The crossing took place in the vicinity of the present settlement of Manuelito (pl. 1) and his diary contains a reference to the stream bed which was bordered by a few cottonwood trees.[6] No mention is made of the height of the banks but it may be assumed that it could not have been very great, since elsewhere in his journal Lieutenant Simpson always takes care to state the amount of work necessary to make deep gullies traversable for wagons and artillery. Had conditions at that time been similar to those existing today he undoubtedly would have made some mention of the fact, because in the entry for that date he specifically describes the labor which would be involved in making other portions of the route accessible.

The problem of the water supply for the various villages whose remains occupy the immediate vicinity south of Allantown is one which has not yet been satisfactorily solved. There are a number of springs along the course of Whitewater Creek, but these are at a considerable distance from the groups of ruined houses. If the supply was no closer during the period of prehistoric habitation the situation would have necessitated the transportation of water for a distance of about 2 miles (3.219 k). Some of the older maps indicate springs and pools along the course of the Whitewater in locations much nearer to the main archeological site than those now in existence. The filled-in remnants of old depressions suggestive of former ponds and places which probably were rather swampy may be seen along the banks of the arroyo. At the head of a small gully terminating at the base of the low cliffs forming the edge of the mesa about one-quarter of a mile (0.402 k) from the main site are indications of the former existence of a spring. There are large quantities of potsherds scattered about at this place and in every instance the fragments noted were from large jars such as were used for water and storage purposes. This suggests that the onetime occupants of the now ruined houses obtained a portion of their water supply at that place, an occasional container being broken in the process. It is likely that the cutting of the deep arroyo in the bottom of the valley lowered

---
[5] Whipple, 1856, pt. II, sec. V, p. 28.
[6] Simpson, 1850, p. 112.

the water table of the region sufficiently to cause the drying up of numerous springs located along the bordering cliffs. Furthermore, drifting sand may have buried such sources as had not previously dried up.

At present the climate is marked by considerable variations. The winters are cold and the summers quite hot, but despite the heat of the summer sun the nights are as a rule chilly. Due, no doubt, to the 6,300 feet (1,920.238 m) altitude. Some winters are accompanied by unusually heavy snows; others are exceedingly dry. During the summer season, particularly in the months of July and August, there normally are heavy rains which frequently flood the country and fill the generally dry stream beds with raging torrents. A second short rainy spell usually occurs in September. Throughout the remainder of the year, it may be said, precipitation is deficient. Under average conditions, however, there is sufficient moisture for the growing of such crops as are necessary to sustain life. Over a long period of time the Indians of the uplands area developed types of corn, beans, pumpkins, and melons which germinate, flourish, and reach maturity during the short growing season which the region provides, and except in periods of drought or when hordes of insects descend on the fields, the yield is ample. There is nothing to indicate that there have been any pronounced climatic changes between the time of the first occupation of this district by the Indian peoples and the present and it seems logical to suppose that they coped with conditions not unlike those of today.

The cultural remains present at the sites where the investigations were carried on represent a number of stages in the development of the sedentary peoples of the plateau region. At the local of the main cluster of ruins there are vestiges of three or four distinct and sequent phases. In order that there may be a better understanding of the significance of the various finds, a brief summary of the present status of southwestern archeology is advisable. Continued research in the ruins of the Southwest during the last 80 years has brought to light many data concerning the history of the region. Investigations since the termination of the World War have been especially productive and the period since 1927 has been marked by a tremendous increase in knowledge. At the present time archeologists group the remains located in the States of New Mexico, Arizona, southwestern Colorado, Utah, eastern Nevada, western Texas, and northern Mexico into two major divisions characterized by differences in material culture, topographical environment, and geographical distribution. One division or province had its location in the uplands or plateau portion of the area; the other centered in the desert region. The uplands group is called the Anasazi, a Navajo name for the peoples who built and lived in the ruins which dot the plateau, and those in the lowlands are referred to as the Hohokam, the name used by the Pima to denote the ancient ones inhabiting the desert precincts. What may eventually prove to be a third and lesser province is one which hitherto has been thought to represent a regional variation of the Anasazi. There is a possibility that it may emerge as a subpattern resulting from a fusion of very early Hohokam and Anasazi in a peripheral area, but at present it is regarded tentatively as a separate entity and is called the Mogollon. The name is taken from a prominent range of mountains in the district where the remains are found. There are peripheral precincts where the patterns are not clear-cut. In these outlying reaches many features common in the nuclear districts are missing and there is a progressive fading of the basic patterns in proportion to the distance from the central portions of the provinces. These marginal regions are generally referred to as the "eastern, northern, western, and southern peripheries." They may in time be set apart as minor subdivisions, but at present they are considered as local variants of the major divisions. Developments in the two major provinces followed somewhat parallel lines, but until comparatively late horizons were for the most part seemingly independent. In the lesser, tentative third province the unfolding of the cultural pattern progressed through a series of stages broadly synchronous with those of the main two, but on the whole was more closely related to the Anasazi than to the Hohokam.

The Anasazi remains are found in the regions of the San Juan River, the Rio Grande, the Upper Gila and Salt Rivers, the Little Colorado River, most of Utah, and a portion of eastern Nevada. The uplands of this plateau area with its rugged mesas, narrow canyons, and broader valleys furnished the setting for an interesting cultural florescence. From a very simple beginning the people who inhabited the region passed from a nomadic hunting existence to a relatively highly advanced mode of life. To simplify the study of this development the various stages through which the people passed have been grouped under two main headings, names better known than that of the main designation Anasazi, called Basket Maker and Pueblo. Each of these major divisions has been separated into a number of minor groups. The Basket Maker, which evidence has shown to be the older, has two, although until recently it was listed with three. The Pueblo, which followed and owed much to the Basket Maker, has five. The growth and development of the various stages did not follow a smooth and ordered progression, but advanced intermittently with periods of quiescence during which there was little change. It is the material from the intervals when conditions were static that furnishes the picture for each typical horizon. The boundary lines between periods are often vague and there is an overlap of characteristics which sometimes tends to be confusing. These occurrences generally may be explained through careful consideration of all of the factors involved. While the progression of stages in the culture sequence implies a certain degree of contemporaneity between sites of the same horizon, it does not imply necessarily that they will fall within identical chronological dates. There may have been, and no doubt frequently was, a difference in actual years in which objects were in vogue in various districts. For example, during a certain stage in one portion of the area a particular style in ceramic art may have been very popular, so popular, in fact, that it spread into other sections. Like groups of objects found at two widely separated ruins would indicate a degree of similarity in age between two sites. In a broad sense they belong to the same stage of progression and yet in actual years may have been separated by an appreciable interval. This tendency to a chronological discrepancy in direct proportion to the distance from a center of origin is well illustrated in our own culture. During the era prior to the development and improvement of the motion picture and radio, the styles of the day in New York were the styles of two and three years later in the more remote sections of the country. The popular music of Broadway did not reach the farthest corners until long after it had been forgotten in the music halls where it was introduced. This lag in cultural traits was even more marked in earlier times. Failure to consider this tendency has in the past caused some confusion in the minds of southwestern workers and students and for that reason is emphasized here.

During the decade following the first conference of southwestern archeologists and workers in related fields, held at Pecos, N. Mex., in the latter part of August 1927, the classification adopted by that group was widely used by writers on the subject. The Pecos Classification listed three divisions for the Basket Maker, denoted by the name and numerals I, II, III, and five for the Pueblo, again using the name and numerals I to V. Because of some confusion arising from the implications of chronology embodied in the numerical qualifiers, the writer suggested a new terminology in an article in the American Anthropologist [7] and added one additional name in a subsequent review of southwestern archeology appearing in American Antiquity.[8] Inasmuch as this later classification has been accepted and used by a number of investigators it will be used in this report. It was developed by the substitution of descriptive names, terms suggested by the characteristics of the period, for the numerical designations. Some of these names were provided as alternative titles at Pecos, others were used by certain workers prior to the first conference, and

---

[7] Roberts, 1935.
[8] Roberts, 1937.

three were the writer's own choice. They were applied to a modified form of the Pecos Classification published in a number of the writer's previous reports in the bulletin series of the Bureau of American Ethnology. Thus at present the period designations and their earlier counterparts are as follows:

Pecos Classification	Bulletins 96 and 111	Revised nomenclature
Basket Maker I	Basket Maker I	Omitted.
Basket Maker II	Basket Maker II	Basket Maker.
Basket Maker III	Basket Maker III	Modified Basket Maker.
Pueblo I	Pueblo I	} Developmental Pueblo.
Pueblo II	Pueblo II	
Pueblo III	Pueblo III { phase a / phase b	Great Pueblo. / } Regressive Pueblo.
Pueblo IV	Pueblo IV { phase a / phase b	} Renaissance Pueblo.
Pueblo V	Pueblo V	Historic Pueblo.

Basket Maker I was wholly postulated, no remains attributable to it having been found, and for that reason it has been dropped from the list. Hence all that was needed in making the change was to drop the II and retain the name Basket Maker, a term that typifies the outstanding characteristic of the stage. Changing Basket Maker III to Modified Basket Maker indicates that basically the complex is the same, although sufficiently altered in traits to warrant a separate designation. The combining of Pueblo I and Pueblo II under the single heading Developmental Pueblo shows that the culture was in the evolutionary stages leading up to the maximum development and avoids difficulties caused by the fact that one or the other was missing in some sections, a feature particularly noticeable in peripheral precincts. The use of Great for Pueblo III tersely describes the characteristic of the period. The term Regressive applies to the stage when there was a definite subsidence from the cultural peak of the great period accompanied by a short-lived era of instability and flux. This interval includes a portion of the latter part of Pueblo III and some of the early IV of the Pecos Classification, all of Pueblo III, phase b, and a portion of IV, phase a, of the synthesis in Bulletins 96 and 111. Renaissance explains the nature of Pueblo IV in a general way and includes most of phase a and all of phase b. The significance of these features will become more apparent in the discussion of the general growth of the cultural pattern in ensuing pages. The Historic Pueblo denotes the period extending from the era of Spanish colonization to the present.

The first traces of the Anasazi thus far found in the plateau province are those of the Basket Maker, a semihunting, semiagricultural group. Archeologists postulate that in the beginning the region was thinly populated by a widely distributed, simple nomadic hunting people. Their food consisted of game and such wild fruits and vegetable products as could be found. On occasions they may have erected flimsy brush shelters against the vagaries of the weather, but more probably relied on caves for such temporary protection from the elements as they deemed necessary. In the course of time they took up agriculture, having obtained corn (maize) and a knowledge of how to plant and cultivate it. Whence this product came or how it reached them is not known, although it is supposed that it was introduced from the Mexican area to the south. Eventually their crops became more abundant and as a consequence the people adopted more sedentary habits. Bountiful harvests mean a surplus of food which can be stored against future needs. Well-stocked granaries require a certain amount of protection which can not be provided if the owners wander too far afield. Hence small communities assembled around the storage-bin nucleus. It is at this point that there is first definite knowledge of the people. The hypothetical series of events leading up to this stage constitute the Basket Maker I of the Pecos Classification, the conjectural stage omitted from the present revised nomenclature.

Basket Maker granaries were small pits dug in the floors of caves and were lined with large stone slabs. They were covered with funnel or domelike superstructures of poles, brush, bark, and mud plaster. Little is known of the dwellings of this period, as only a few ruins, possibly attributable to it,[9] have been noted and information obtained by excavation is not available. Numerous caves containing granaries and other remains have been investigated and no houses found. Impermanent brush shelters which have left no traces may have been used in some cases. There is evidence that slab cists lined with grass and bark were sometimes used for sleeping places, but these hardly could be called houses. The main objects of the handicrafts of the period which have been preserved are excellent baskets, sandals, ropes, nets, twined and woven bags, and robes made from fur cloth. There was no true pottery, although at about the end of this stage unfired clay vessels with grass or cedar bark binder made their appearance. The idea of making clay vessels probably came from the south, but the development was entirely local. The main weapons were an S-shaped club and a short javelin, the latter thrown by means of an atlatl or spear thrower.

Modified Basket Maker is characterized by some additional features. True pottery with painted decoration was developed. Semisubterranean dwellings of a comparatively permanent nature were erected. Several kinds of corn were grown where previously there

---
[9] Hargrave, 1935, p. 42.

had been but one. Beans appeared in the list of agricultural produce. Robes made from feathers were occasionally employed. Sandal types were changed and baskets became less important in the complex. The bow and arrow began to replace the spear thrower as a weapon. This feature probably correlates with another factor, one which had a marked influence on subsequent developments. Namely, new peoples were drifting into the area and it is possible that they were the bearers of this different kind of weapon, although it seems to have preceded them as a diffused cultural trait. This new group did not sweep over the plateau as an invading horde, but made a gradual penetration in successive small bands. Their arrival is recorded by differences in skeletal remains. The Basket Makers were long-headed or medium long-headed, while the newcomers were possessed of broad skulls. The latter are found only in burials made toward the end of the Basket Maker era. These immigrants seemingly brought little with them beyond the bow and arrow, possibly the grooved ax, and a capacity for cultural development. They took over, changed, and adapted to their own needs the material culture of the older inhabitants and launched the second major stage in the history of the Anasazi, that of the Pueblos.

There were many changes during the course of the Developmental Pueblo stage. These were not brought about immediately, as the earliest phase was one of transition and instability. Eventually new features appeared and the foundations were laid for future developments. Cotton and materials made from it became one of the important items in the industry of the people. Pottery was more extensively made and the ceramics took on definite features typical of the period. Fur-string robes or blankets were replaced to an even greater degree by those made from feathers. The wild turkey was domesticated; previously the dog was the only tamed creature. The grooved ax became an important tool. Apparently cradling practices were changed as crania from the graves of this and subsequent periods show an occipital flattening. Broad skulls found in association with Modified Basket Maker remains do not have such a deformation. In the nuclear parts of the province the single-room, semisubterranean dwellings gave way to structures with only slightly depressed floors instead of pits. The major portion of the house was above ground and had several contiguous rooms. In some cases the walls were of pole and plaster (jacal) construction, and in others horizontally laid stones were employed. These were replaced by masonry houses erected entirely above ground. Buildings of this nature were a single story in height, had flat roofs, and contained four, six, eight, sometimes even more, rooms. The rooms were placed in a long single row, a shorter double row, an L-shape, or in the more highly developed forms in the shape of a rectangular U the wings forming an enclosed court at one side of the building. This kind of dwelling is called the single-clan or unit type. In the peripheral districts semisubterranean houses continued in use for some time, although in modified form. Pits for the underground portion were dug deeper and entrance to the chamber was by means of a ladder through the smoke hole in the roof instead of by an entryway at one side. The latter was retained, however, in reduced and altered form and functioned as a ventilator. These structures eventually were abandoned in favor of others approximating the unit type. These new dwellings did not reach as high a degree of excellence as those in the nuclear districts. In the south and west, pole-and-mud houses and buildings consisting of irregular agglomerations of rooms whose walls were formed from large quantities of adobe mud and unworked boulders constituted the living quarters. In the Flagstaff, Ariz., area rectangular semisubterranean houses prevailed to the end of this horizon.

The new-type dwellings necessitated some provision for a place in which to hold the religious rites and ceremonies that had previously been performed in the old circular domiciles. Instead of changing the rituals to meet the requirements of the new houses, each group provided one of the old style structures. It generally was placed at the south or southeast side some distance from the dwelling. Eventually these special chambers became more formalized and developed into what is called the kiva. They did not become as highly specialized in the peripheral districts and in some sections the circular form is entirely missing, yet its purpose was served by analogous rectangular structures.

During the period when these changes were taking place the people lived in small villages scattered throughout the province. Then a new trend set in. The population began to concentrate in large urban centers and the Great Pueblo period was at hand. Extensive terraced houses, several stories in height and containing many hundreds of rooms, were built on canyon floors, in the caverns in cliffs, and on mesa tops. The ceremonial chambers were included in the main block of the building and their former subterranean character was simulated by filling with earth the spaces between their circular walls and the rectangular ones enclosing them. Pottery forms and styles of decorations crystallized and became so highly specialized that each center had its own characteristic wares. The rise of these urban centers was more the result of an ever-growing tendency on the part of the people to abandon the outlying small houses and concentrate in various communities than to a sudden and marked increase in population. What caused this movement is not known. It probably was induced by a combination of factors. Severe droughts occur periodically in the Southwest and such an occurrence may have made some districts so unproductive that the occupants were forced to join their kinsmen in sections where conditions were less rigorous. In order not to encroach too much on tillable land the dwellings were consolidated and evolved into the typical pueblo or apartment house of the period. At the same time there was a constantly increasing pressure from the nomadic tribes of the borderlands. Drought conditions would make marked inroads on the supplies of seeds, nuts, wild fruits, even on game, and small unprotected villages with reserves of corn and beans would be tempting plunder. That raids did occasionally take place is indicated around the peripheries of the province by the remains of unit structures which give evidence that they were pillaged and their inhabitants slain. For this reason the desire to gather in populous centers as a means of defense may have been an important element in the trend of affairs.

The large towns thrived for a time and then began to decline. The Regressive period was setting in. In some of the centers the people, although reduced in numbers, carried on. Other communities were abandoned. There was a pronounced withdrawal from the more northern districts and a definite drift toward southern portions of the area. Causes for this phenomenon have not been determined. Unquestionably there were several. Encroaching and plundering nomads evidently became troublesome during this period, as many large ruins show that attempts were made to fortify the villages. Internal discord and factional strife may have arisen and as a result large groups moved out to settle elsewhere, a thing that has happened in historic pueblos and no doubt did in earlier times as well. Then there were recurring droughts. A series of prolonged crop failures may have reduced the resistance of the people to such an extent that they gave up the struggle and started off in search of better locations. Irrespective of what the actual causes were, there was a marked recession from the former cultural peak and the era was one of instability and migration. The northern part of the province, that traversed by the San Juan River and its tributaries, ultimately was deserted. New villages and communities developed along the Rio Grande and the Little Colorado River. After these were established the arts and industries took on new life and the Renaissance was under way.

Outstanding in the Renaissance period was the growth of various centers along the Rio Grande and the Little Colorado River. The highest stage of development in these two regions was attained during this stage. It, like preceding horizons, had certain typical features in pottery types and other objects of the material culture that provide criteria for identification. The arrival of the Spaniards in the latter part of the period, 1540, served as a check on the progress of the native culture, but the full impact of European influence was not felt until after the revolt, reconquest, and complete capitulation of the Pueblos in 1700. The Historic period begins then and continues through to the present. It is the era of the modern villages. The stage in general shows the gradual replacement of the Pueblo culture pattern by traits introduced by the white man, a process continuing with marked acceleration at the present time.[10]

Several diagnostic traits are used in identifying the various stages in the Anasazi pattern. The same traits apply whether the Pecos Classification or the revised one discussed in preceding pages is used. Skeletal material is thought significant for the two major groups, Basket Maker and Pueblo, although elements in the material culture are so well differentiated that they probably furnish a more reliable criterion. Indicative components in the complex are: House and village types, architectural features, textiles, baskets, sandals, pictographs, stone and bone implements, kinds and styles of ornaments, and pottery. Pottery is considered to furnish the most abundant, convenient, and reliable criterion, with the culinary or utilitarian wares the simplest for sequence determinations. The reason that pottery plays so important a part is that it is characterized by easily noted differences in style and form and it was an exceedingly sensitive element from the standpoint of variations in both time and place. These are factors, however, that will be discussed in greater detail in the second part of this report, that dealing with the artifacts, and need not be considered further here.

The sequence of the several stages outlined in the foregoing pages is based on evidence obtained mainly from excavations. The most important type of proof was that of the stratigraphic relationship between different forms in the complex. In places undisturbed layers of deposits containing objects of a particular form and style were found overlying other layers in which similar objects exhibited different characteristics. There was no question but that those from the upper level were more recent and the variation in objects furnished a definite standard by which to gauge their relative ages. In addition, changes and developments in articles of the same type were demonstrated. Modified Basket Maker remains have been found above those of Basket Maker in so many sites that there can be no doubt of their sequence. Elsewhere ruins of Pueblo structures have been noted resting on mounds covering the remains of Modified Basket Maker houses, and Developmental Pueblo dwellings have been discovered beneath the foundations of Great Pueblo buildings. Correlations between sites and districts were worked out through study of trade

---

[10] For a more detailed discussion of the evolution and growth of the Anasazi (Basket Maker-Pueblo) cultural pattern and a review of the archeological progress culminating in the Pecos Classification see Roberts, 1935. For references and examples of ruins and sites belonging to the various periods see Roberts, 1932.

objects and their positions in local sequences. The entire structure of Anasazi history was erected on this foundation. That it is essentially correct has been shown by the development of a new method for determining not only relative age but actual dates. This new aid to the archeologist is dendrochronology, the tree-ring calendar discovered and perfected by Dr. A. E. Douglass. Dates obtained through this medium demonstrate that the stratigraphically determined sequence is true in its main outline and that the relative ages of numerous large ruins and village sites, even of remains in different districts, were correctly deduced by the archeological method.

Dr. Douglass, of the University of Arizona, in studying sun spots and their effects on climatic conditions, turned to the growth rings of trees in an effort to obtain evidence on the occurrence of drought periods and the intervals of moisture. In doing this he discovered that definite ring patterns, as distinct as human fingerprints, recorded specific year groups and as a consequence developed a system whereby he can tell the year when a log was cut from a living tree. Beginning with trees whose actual cutting date was known, he has been able to devise a type ring chart going back to the beginning of the Christian era. To secure evidence to substantiate his own theories he was forced to resort to timbers from ruins for material antedating living trees and thus furnished the archeologists with a valuable time scale.[11] When beams are found in ruins it is possible to check their rings against the type chart and, provided the outer surfaces have not been damaged or removed, tell the year of their cutting. The timber may not have been placed in a house immediately after it was cut and occasionally a log was reused, but such factors can be checked by the archeological aspects of the site and a date is assured which approximates closely the year or years when the dwellings were erected.

Explanations for certain features noted in the cultural pattern are also furnished by dendrochronological studies through information on the occurrence of drought and periods when conditions were more favorable. Dates for a number of the droughts correspond to definite phenomena in Anasazi history. One dry period correlates with the trend toward concentration in urban communities at the end of the Developmental period. Another was undoubtedly an important factor in the abandonment of some of the centers at the end of the Great Pueblo stage. The greatest expansion and growth in one of the leading centers of the Great Pueblo era took place in a 20-year period when conditions were favorable. When more dates are available and additional information has been obtained from several districts that are not too well known at present, an inter-

---

[11] Douglass, 1932, 1935.

esting study of the effects of weather on the movements of peoples can be developed. Present evidence only hints at the possibilities.

There are no Hohokam remains in the Whitewater district, hence only a summary mention of the general character of the desert cultural pattern is necessary. According to present information there were six main stages in the Hohokam. They are called Pioneer, Colonial, Sedentary, Classic, Recent, and Modern. Although the two patterns overlapped to some extent along the hazy boundary line between the two provinces, the Hohokam and Anasazi were quite distinct until about the year 1000 A. D. After that date Anasazi from southern parts of the plateau began to drift into the Hohokam province and establish communities there. The two seemingly lived side by side for a time and then the northern group withdrew and returned to the uplands. During the Developmental Pueblo period there was a northward thrust of Hohokam into the periphery of the plateau province in the Flagstaff, Ariz., region.

There are no dendrochronological dates for the Hohokam. Timbers used in house construction were of varieties of wood not adapted to tree-ring studies. The determination of periods depends in large measure on pottery types. Some dates can be suggested on the basis of trade objects, as in the case of the Anasazi penetration, but on the whole the status is much the same as that of the Anasazi prior to the perfection of the tree-ring calendar. The time factor is largely postulated. Present evidence is that the Pioneer stage was roughly contemporaneous with Modified Basket Maker and the beginnings of Developmental Pueblo, Colonial with Developmental and early Great Pueblo, Classic with late Great Pueblo and Regressive, Recent with Renaissance, and Modern with Historic.

The main differences between the Anasazi and Hohokam may be summarized briefly. The Hohokam practiced cremation; the Anasazi, in all stages, buried their dead. The Hohokam built rectangular single-unit houses of pole, brush, and plaster construction during all stages; while the Anasazi progressed from circular or rectangular single-unit dwellings of poles, brush, and plaster to multi-storied communal houses built of stone. The Hohokam progressed from floodwater irrigation to extensive canal systems for supplying their crops with water; the Anasazi depended mainly on floodwaters but in some sections did employ series of small ditches. The Hohokam had extensive carving in shell, which was rare in the Anasazi pattern. The Anasazi domesticated the turkey; the Hohokam apparently did not. Pottery made by the two groups differed in certain respects. The coiling method was used in both cases but the finishing processes varied. The Anasazi smoothed the surfaces of their vessels with scrapers and polishing stones; the Hohokam completed theirs by em-

ploying a paddle and anvil. The Anasazi painted wares over a long period were of the type with white background and black designs, followed by a series of polychrome forms; Hohokam painted vessels had red designs on a buff background, a factor that was responsible for the name first used to designate the group. Earlier papers call the pattern the Red-on-Buff Culture.[12]

The Mogollon pattern seems to center in the San Francisco and Mimbres River valleys in southwestern New Mexico, although traces of it are found extending in all directions for considerable distances. The basic feature is that of a sedentary agricultural-hunting complex, the hunting aspect being more pronounced than in either the Anasazi or Hohokam. Several stages are recognized in the pattern. These are called Georgetown, San Francisco, Three Circle, Mimbres, and Animas. Chief characteristics of the Mogollon are that it had rounded semisubterranean houses followed by rectangular semisubterranean structures, then Pueblo type dwellings. Pottery was made by the coiling process with the scraper and polishing stone as finishing implements. The dead were buried as a rule, but there was some cremation. The atlatl and bow and arrow were used for weapons. In the beginning the people were a roundheaded group with low skull vault. They did not practice cranial deformation. Later a roundheaded group with high skull vault and deformed occiputs appeared in the area. As is to be expected in peripheral districts, there were local adaptations of borrowed elements, developments peculiar to the region, and some lag in the appearance of certain features.

Because of the abrupt change in house types, as well as marked differences in some of the minor elements in the material culture, it is thought that there may be a break between the Georgetown and San Francisco stages. Perhaps there is a period which thus far has not been recognized or for which evidence has not been found. The true Mogollon pattern is included in the Georgetown and San Francisco. The beginning of Anasazi and Hohokam influences are noted in the Three Circle. These culminated in the Mimbres when the pattern became a coalescence of Mogollon-Anasazi-Hohokam traits. At the end of the Mimbres stage the people deserted the province, seemingly moving south into northern Chihuahua where they fused with other groups. Subsequently another group appeared in the province. They apparently came in from the north and west and were fully developed at the time of their arrival. They were Anasazi and this stage is the one called the Animas.

Timbers from a number of Mogollon houses have been dated and this makes correlation with the Anasazi easier than with the Hohokam. It has been suggested that basic Mogollon, as yet not

---

[12] For detailed information on the Hohokam (the Red-on-Buff) consult the reports of the Gladwins and E. W. Haury.

clearly defined, was contemporaneous with Modified Basket Maker, Georgetown and San Francisco with Developmental Pueblo in its earlier stages and Three Circle with its later phase, Mimbres with Great Pueblo, and Animas with Renaissance. On the whole the Mogollon shows closer affinities to the Anasazi than to the Hohokam and numerous Mogollon traits penetrated into some sections of the Anasazi province.[13]

At the main archeological site south of Allantown three periods in the growth of Anasazi pattern are represented. There are traces of Modified Basket Maker, Developmental Pueblo remains are numerous, and the large ruins belong to the Great Pueblo era. In view of this association the location is an important one from the standpoint of information on the transitions between the several periods. Fortunately all of the occupants of the site did not build on the same spot. A series of trenches dug in various places along the ridge where many of the remains are located demonstrated that in the early stages the people lived in straggling settlements of single family houses. As time went on the domiciles were placed in more compact groups and a certain system of arrangement developed. The first structures were semisubterranean in form. Later this type was given up and small buildings, with several contiguous rooms, were erected above ground. Ultimately two large communal houses, sheltering many families, two and three stories in height and containing more than 100 rooms evolved. These last structures occupied only a small portion of the area covered by the older horizons. As a consequence it is possible to obtain representative remains of the separate stages without first excavating those of more recent date. There is definite stratification in a number of places, however, which establishes the proper sequence for the different forms of structures and types of associated objects. Complete excavation of the site should give valuable information concerning the changes which took place during the closing days of Modified Basket Maker and the beginnings of Developmental Pueblo, together with data on the growth of the cultural pattern through Developmental and Great Pueblo. The data covering the remains to the end of the Developmental stage are helpful and interesting. As no work was done in the Great Pueblo ruins knowledge of their character is meager. For some reason as yet undetermined the location was abandoned during the Great Pueblo stage and never reoccupied.

The small ruins scattered along the valley bottom represent different periods. Inasmuch as a number belong solely to one single horizon they furnish opportunity for valuable checks on the data obtained at the main site. The unavoidable mixing of objects over

---

[13] Detailed discussion of the Mogollon will be found in Haury, 1936, a, b.

a long period of occupation sometimes produces a certain amount of confusion in the evidence and clear-cut material from representatives of a single phase serves to clarify such complications.

REMAINS OF STRUCTURES

Activities during the summer of 1931 and most of 1932 were confined in the main to the outer fringes of the main site, to the excavation of pit remains and accompanying surface ruins, and the trenching of nearby trash mounds. Toward the close of the 1932 season attention was turned to a small unit-house of the fully established Developmental Pueblo type located 1 mile (1.609 k) up canyon, to the east, from the main site. This was done for the purpose of singling out and establishing definitely the characteristic Developmental traits in the district so that they could be recognized more quickly in the material from the main site. The 1933 work consisted of a complete and thorough investigation of a small Developmental village situated on the talus at the foot of the escarpment just below the main ruins. This place was chosen for two reasons. First and foremost was the desire to give the graduate students as wide an experience as possible in the several phases of an excavation. Second, and not inconsequential, was the fact that available funds were not sufficient to warrant an attempt to excavate the large ruins on the main site. The work of the two previous years carried the investigations to the point where that was the next logical step. Complete excavation of the large stone remains would require an extensive budget and rather than start something that could not be continued through to a proper conclusion it was deemed advisable to leave the mounds undisturbed. At the main site the subterranean portions of 18 pit structures were cleared of the debris that accumulated in them during the interval since they were abandoned and fell into ruin, and 2 more were excavated at the nearby places where additional work was done. Fire had destroyed several of these structures and the charred remnants of their superstructure timbers were lying on the floors in positions clearly indicating the type of roof construction. This evidence, in addition to that furnished by the pits, makes it possible to reconstruct an accurate picture of the semisubterranean structures prevailing during the early stages in the occupation of the site. The general term of structure is used in preference to that of dwelling because in one or two examples there is a question as to whether or not the function was ceremonial or domiciliary. One in particular suggests that it might have served first as a dwelling and then, after a lapse of time during which it was untenanted, was remodeled for a religious chamber.

The remains probably represent places of habitation in a majority of cases. The structures were rather crude, but they no doubt served their purpose to a degree highly satisfactory to their builders. They had consisted of a circular, oval, or rectangular excavation roofed over with a pole, brush, bark, and plaster superstructure. The earth walls of the pits were faced with a coating of plaster made from adobe mud in which there was a slight admixture of ashes. Two examples varied from the others in that the walls were lined with large stone slabs set up on edge. Resting upon and rising above the top slabs in one were several courses of masonry formed from rough stones. The stone facing of the walls in these cases was covered with plaster and to the casual observer the interior would not have differed in appearance from the other structures. The pits varied in depth from 2 feet (60.96 cm) to 6 feet (1.828 m) and from 10 to 20 feet (3.048 to 6.096 m) in diameter.

Four upright posts set in the floor close to, or a short distance from, the walls supported the superstructure over the pits in all but two of the groups of remains. In one there were four posts and one masonry pillar, all placed against the wall, and the other exception had five posts. The upper ends of the main supports were forked and sustained cross beams. Tree trunks with suitable crotches were secured for the purpose. The latter formed a rectangular framework against which rested the upper ends of small timbers, their butts placed on the ground some distance back from the edges of the pit. These slanting poles constituted a major part of the roof, in the form of a sloping ceiling. The rectangular space at the center was flat. Near the middle was an opening that served both as smoke hole and entrance. The entire framework was covered with reeds or grass, then strips of cedar bark, brush, and leaves. A thick layer of adobe plaster was spread on top of this and over all was a thin coating of earth. The structure with four posts and a masonry pillar had a different type of covering, a cribbed roof. This superstructure was like those generally found in later-day kivas or ceremonial chambers. The timbers were laid from post to post, each succeeding row above being placed nearer the center of the room, the logs cutting across the corner of the series below, etc., until the framework rose into a kind of dome. The area near the center, bordering the smoke hole and entrance, was usually flat. The framework was covered with bark, leaves, and plaster. The tops of the roofs, both types, were only elevated above the ground level sufficiently to provide for drainage. In most cases the structures were placed along the top of a ridge or on the side of a hill so that the run-off of surface water would be facilitated. A village consisting of houses of this type would not be striking in appearance. All that would be visible would be a series of low, rounding mounds with the ends of ladders projecting through rectangular openings in their tops.

The interior features were usually simple, although an occasional example was characterized by a large variety of basins or cache pockets in the floor. Near the center of each chamber, directly under the opening in the roof, was a fire pit. A second depression, close to the fire pit and generally at its southeast side, served either as a rest for the lower end of the ladder used in gaining access to the room, or as a depository for ashes. In one instance entrance had not been through the roof and there was no central ladder, although one was employed to reach a short passageway leading into the chamber. Various small holes or pockets scattered about in the floors probably served as depositories for implements of stone and bone or other minor objects. There were some examples of storage recesses in the walls. Where these were present they were on or extended slightly below the floor level; none were placed above it.

An aperture in the wall at the east or southeast side of the room opened into a small tunnel. The latter led to a vertical shaft whose outlet was on the ground level some distance from the edge of the roof mound. This feature has been termed the ventilator because a constant supply of fresh air was drawn down through the shaft and the tunnel by the circulation of air in the main chamber. An upright slab of stone was generally, although not always, set in the floor at the base of the ladder, between the opening in the wall and the fire pit. This stone has been termed the deflector, since it prevented inrushing air from blowing directly on the fire, and diverted it around the walls of the room. The draft through the ventilator seems at times to have been so strong that it was necessary to stop the opening completely and well-worked, oval-shaped slabs of stone were provided for the purpose. When a number of the pits were excavated these cover stones were in position in front of the openings.

The structures in general showed a marked similarity to the widespread semisubterranean type of house built in many sections of the Southwest. They are particularly comparable to pit dwellings in the Chaco Canyon, in northwestern New Mexico,[14] and at the old Long H Ranch in eastern Arizona, about 30 miles (48.280 k) southwest from the present location.[15] There were individual differences and variations such as may be expected in any group of ruins, but in their main essentials the structures exhibited a marked similarity.

One feature brought to light by the excavations was peculiar to this site. The structures in two different groups were connected.

---
[14] Roberts, 1929.
[15] Roberts, 1931.

There were no partitions at the sides where they joined and long, narrow houses resulted. One of the examples had two connecting chambers, the other three. Each of the rooms was complete in itself, but because of the absence of a separating wall, became an integral part of a larger structure. Another of the groups had three adjacent chambers, although they were not connected. The significance of grouping of structures by threes is not known. A comparable situation was found at the Long H Ranch where three pit houses were built close together. Each was distinct in itself, although there was a small opening between two of them which had a definite purpose, that of a ventilator.[16] Another example of a row of three placed in juxtaposition was reported from southern Colorado by Martin.[17] In this case there seemed to have been no opening between any of the chambers. Perhaps the best example of pit dwellings placed in a contiguous row, although not in series of threes, is in Harrington's Pueblo Grande in Nevada. The houses at that site, however, differ considerably from the pit structures at this location.[18]

The pit remains at the main site were associated with some surface ruins and all features were investigated as the work progressed. The pits were numbered consecutively, although they occurred in two main groups. The first cluster was located south of the mounds enclosing the Great Pueblo ruins and consisted of 12 pits, a pit oven, 4 brush shelters, and the remains of 2 surface masonry structures (fig. 1). The latter appeared at a later stage than some of the pits, but the oven and several of the brush shelters apparently were part of the older horizon. The second main group was located north of the large stone ruins and included 6 pits, some surface remains, and a dance court (fig. 25).

The various trash mounds or refuse heaps were trenched for the purpose of obtaining stratigraphic evidence on ceramic changes and also for the purpose of locating burials. They were situated at the southeast side of the house groups. Their relation to the latter is shown on the plans.

The 2 additional pit remains were located on the floor of the valley. One was at the site of the fully developed unit-type structure of the late Developmental period and the other was included in the early Developmental village. To preserve unity in consideration of the pit type of structure, they are numbered as continuations of the main sequence and discussed in that order.

---

[16] Roberts, 1931, fig. 1, pp. 19–43.
[17] Martin, 1930, pl. VII, fig. 2, pp. 27–33.
[18] Harrington, 1927, p. 264.

Group No. 1

STRUCTURE 1

The first of the pit remains uncovered consisted of a roughly rectangular excavation with rounded corners. The structure seemed to have been one of the oldest in the first group. This was evidenced both by the potsherds found on its floor and by the rings in the charred beams from its burned roof. The floor had a great variety of pockets and basins in it, but in the main the interior features were quite comparable to the general type of pit house found throughout the plateau region. The pit had been dug into the native earth and the face of the excavation covered with a mud plaster to make the walls of the room. There was no encircling bench of the type frequently found in such cases, but the equivalent of such a feature had been obtained by setting the lower ends of the slanting poles of the superstructure back some distance from the top of the wall. The ground level at the time when the house was built was a sandy surface which could have kept the sloping timbers from sliding without the necessity of a bench. As a consequence the builders may have decided that the actual construction of such a feature was unnecessary. The roof was supported by four posts and the charred timbers lying on the floor demonstrated that the superstructure had been of the general type described in a preceding paragraph.

Near the center of the room was a circular fire pit and adjoining it a pit like those in the majority of houses where the lower end of the ladder rested. In this particular example it must have had some other purpose because the ends of the upright pieces of the ladder had been embedded in the floor a few inches from the edge of the second pit. It is possible that the occupants first made use of the pit and then discarded it in favor of a second form of ladder base. There was nothing to show that this had been the case, however. This pit was practically filled with wood ashes when the debris was cleared from the structure. There were no indications that a fire had burned in it and the ashes must have been removed from the true pit and placed there. The secondary pit was possibly a special provision for the depositing of ashes. Several of the houses at the site had similar features and it may be that in some of the structures in this locality there was a definite shift in function from ladder box to ash pit as a correlative of embedding the lower ends of the ladder posts in the floor.

The ladder provided for gaining access to this structure was undoubtedly of the two-pole-and-rung type. The lower ends of the side timbers were still in place in the floor between the basin, that would normally be considered the ladder rest, and the deflector stone. The remains of the posts sloped at just the angle which the ladder would have required in order to pass over the fire pit to the smoke hole and entrance in the roof above. Indications in early forms of houses in the Southwest are that the runged ladder was employed practically

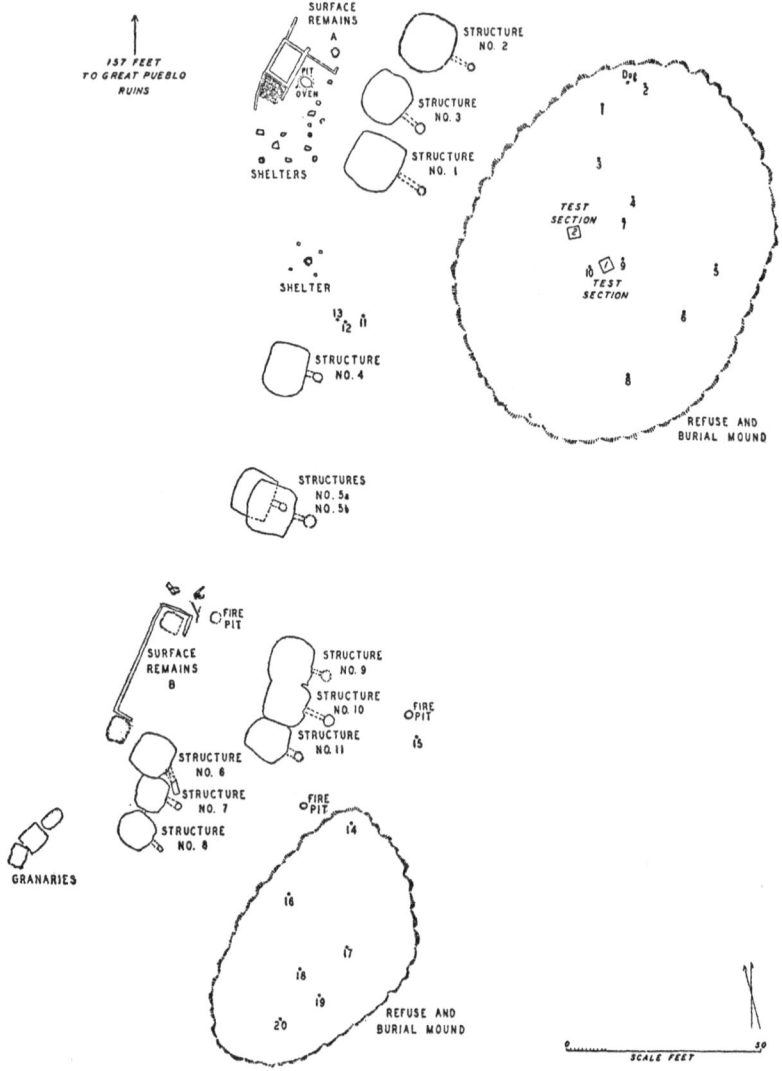

FIGURE 1.—Group 1 pit and surface remains. Numbered dots indicate location of burials.

from the beginning of the use of pit structures. Traces of their presence were found in pit dwellings at the Long H Ranch [19] and a number of the structures excavated in 1931 and 1932, in addition to No. 1, gave unmistakable evidence of their use. It is not possible, of course,

[19] Roberts, 1931, pp. 33–34, 55.

to determine just how these ladders were made. Examples found in Pueblo ruins of later horizons have consisted of two upright poles with the rungs lashed to them. In other cases the long timbers were notched and the rungs fastened in the notches with cords made from hide or yucca fibers. Somewhat similar methods of construction were no doubt used in the ladders in earlier times but until one is found intact their exact nature will not be known.

The large number and variety of holes or pockets in the floor of No. 1 are indicated on the plan (fig. 2). It is not possible to determine what all were used for, although most of them no doubt served as depositories for small objects employed in household industries. Bone and stone implements were recovered from a number of them. Objects of this type would easily be misplaced unless special efforts were made to provide them with a container. A simple solution of this problem would be to make a pocket in the floor or wall. For some reason or other the latter seems rarely to have had such a feature at this site. The floor furnished all the space needed for such purposes.

The larger basin-like depressions (fig. 2, c, d, w) possibly served as places in which baskets or jars were set, although there was no indication that such had been the case. What function the curiously shaped depression e may have been intended to fulfill is a question for which no answer has been found. At the time when the remains were excavated a small pitcher of the culinary variety of pottery was sitting in the end toward the ventilator side of the room. Several who saw the house suggested that loom sticks may have been placed across the depression in the arm-like projections at each side of the central portion. In view of weaving practices in general, as they are known throughout the Southwest, this does not seem to be a good explanation. There was nothing about the depression itself to furnish a clue.

The hole marked h, figure 2, corresponds in its general size and position to similar ones found in most pit houses and in many present-day kivas. In the kivas or ceremonial chambers the feature is called the sipapu, because the modern Pueblos use that name or a close variation of it to designate the hole. According to them it symbolizes the mythical place of emergence through which their ancestors are supposed to have passed in their journey from the inner portions of the earth, where they were created, to the surface of the world upon which they now live. Whether a similar interpretation was made in the past or not is a matter of conjecture. The belief is so firmly implanted in Pueblo mythology, however, that it may with considerable justification be assumed that the prehistoric people regarded the feature in the same light. A further support for this theory is derived from the clear evidence that the later kivas represent definite survivals of the old subterranean house.

At the base of the ladder an upright stone was set in the floor midway between the fire pit and the ventilator opening in the wall (fig.

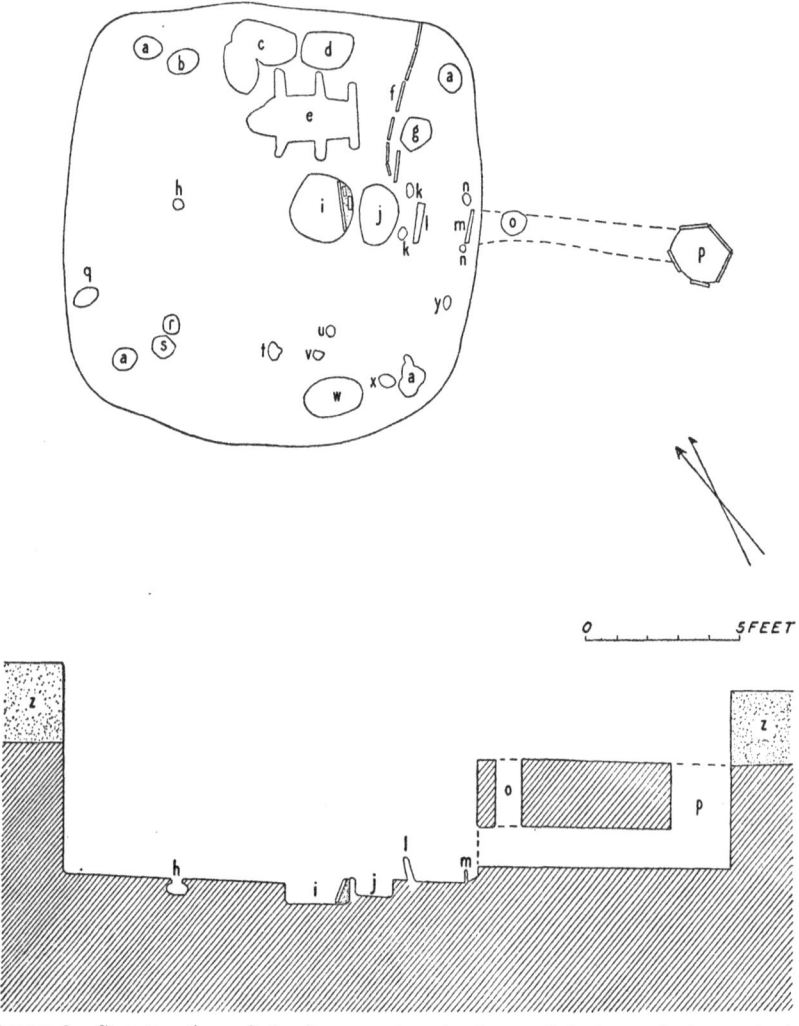

FIGURE 2.—Structure 1. *a*, holes for support posts; *b*, *c*, and *d*, storage basins; *e*, basin in floor; *f*, wall forming compartment; *g*, basin in floor; *h*, sipapu; *i*, fire pit; *j*, ash pit; *k*, ends of ladder poles; *l*, deflector; *m*, stone to protect ventilator opening; *n*, pole placement; *o*, small shaft in ventilator; *p*, main ventilator shaft; *q*, pot rest or storage hole; *r*, *s*, *t*, *u*, *v*. *w*, *x*, and *y*, storage holes and basin; *z*, sand accumulation above old ground level.

2, *l*). This is an example of the deflector. It was so placed to prevent air, coming through the ventilator aperture, from blowing directly on the fire.

One interesting feature in this structure consisted of a row of seven stones forming a bin-like enclosure at the southeast corner of the room (fig. 2, *f;* pl. 3, *a*). One of the typical interior elements in Modified Basket Maker houses consists of a low wall of stone slabs separating the ventilator or, as was the case in many of the dwellings of that period, the entrance side of the chamber from the rest of the room. Sometimes the partition wall extended entirely across from support post to support post. Then again it was broken by a doorway in front of the passage opening into the wall. Occasionally a house is found that only has corner bins at that side of the room.[20] The enclosure in one corner of No. 1 is very suggestive of the more complete examples found in the Chaco Canyon houses and possibly represents a survival in the houses of a later day of a characteristic common during a previous stage in house development. The purpose of such compartments is not known. Two metates or grinding stones were found in the present example. This would suggest that the enclosure may have served as a mealing bin for the house. On the other hand it is quite possible that the stones were placed there during intervals when they were not in use, since one was leaning against the partition and the other against the wall. The bin may have served solely in the capacity of a storage place. Firewood, jars containing surplus food and other items connected with the daily life of the people could have been placed there where they would not interfere with the general trend of affairs in the main part of the structure. Somewhat comparable enclosures in the earth lodges of some of the Plains Indians, dwellings which in many ways bear a strong resemblance to the pit houses of the Southwest, despite the fact that they were largely surface structures, were employed for storing the supply of firewood in winter.[21]

In a previous discussion of the partitioned-off portion of the pit house, the theory was advanced that the compartment may have had some ceremonial significance in addition to its utilitarian purposes. Persons not taking part in such religious observances as were performed in the main portion of the room may have gathered in the compartment where they could witness but would not intrude upon the rites. An analogous situation is described in a report on a council held in an earth lodge at the mouth of the Platte River in 1833. The writer, J. T. Irving, observed that the passage was completely crowded with women and children watching the progress of events within the structure.[22] When it is recalled that the ventilator unquestionably was derived from and represents a modified survival of an older passageway entrance, the parallelism becomes more apparent. In the

---
[20] Roberts, 1929, figs. 4, 5, 21, 22; pls. 4, 6, 7 *a*.
[21] Bushnell, 1922, fig. 8. Coues, 1897, vol. 1, p. 337. Maximilien, 1843, vol. 3, fig. 4, facing p. 36.
[22] Bushnell, 1922, p. 117. Irving, J. T., 1835, vol. 1, p. 234.

same connection it has been suggested that the so-called spectators' bench in the regular kivas of the Hopi Indians may represent a modified survival of the compartment.[28] It should be pointed out, however, that there is no chronological hiatus between the modern and early forms, since many of the circular kivas of the Developmental and Great Pueblo periods have deep recesses or niches above the ventilator which apparently fit into the compartment-spectators' bench sequence. There is no reason why the pit-dwelling compartments could not have functioned in all of the ways outlined. They undoubtedly had utilitarian value in the beginning, or they would not have been incorporated in the structure. In the later ceremonial chambers the modified survival may well have served only a ritualistic function.

The ventilator at the southeast side of the chamber consisted of a passage and shaft. The horizontal portion was dug through the earth as a tunnel. In some cases it was the custom to run a trench for the passage and then cover it over with poles, brush, and earth. In this particular instance the more difficult method was followed. The aperture from the room into the tunnel was oval in shape and was finished with a coating of plaster. Around the edges of the opening was an offset in which a cover slab could be placed. This was in position when the remains were excavated. The sill of the opening was some distance above the floor level and consisted of a thin slab of stone. The ventilator passage was practically horizontal; there was no upward slant at the outer end as is frequently found in structures of this type. The shaft was roughly circular in contour and was faced with large stone slabs. The ventilator for No. 1 was not large enough to have functioned as an actual entrance, hence it must have served purely as a means for bringing fresh air into the chamber.

The ventilator had one feature not commonly found. This consisted of a small vertical shaft which rose from the ceiling of the passage, just back of the main aperture into the chamber, and opened in the top of the pseudo bench just in front of the sloping superstructure poles (fig. 2, *o*). Just what reason motivated the construction of this shaft is not clear. It may have functioned for ventilating purposes by distributing incoming air at a higher level than the ordinary opening in the wall did. Experiments with the two openings showed that one or the other had to be closed before the air would circulate properly. The aperture in the wall had a cover stone for that purpose and there was a thin slab over the top of the shaft. With one of these in place and the other removed the air passed through the uncovered opening in an appreciable draft. When both openings were left uncovered no movement of air

---

[28] Roberts, 1929, p. 89.

could be felt. Since this was the only structure in the entire group which had such a feature it is possible that some individual peculiarity in the house necessitated the arrangement. No other reason can be advanced for its presence in No. 1 when similar construction was absent in the other structures.

The structural details of No. 1 were so clearly shown that the superstructure was restored in order that visitors to the site might see just what domiciles of that type were like. In doing this it was necessary to use new timbers because the original posts, beams, and poles were too greatly damaged by the fire which destroyed the structure to permit their reuse. Every effort was made to follow the plans of the first builders, although in two factors it was necessary to deviate from them. One of these was in the matter of the use of reeds on top of the slanting wall poles. At the present time there is no source for such material in the general vicinity. Where the prehistoric inhabitants secured their supply is not known. It is possible that the occasional small ponds and marshy places in the valley bottom, referred to in the introduction, furnished places where reeds grew. The second variation consisted in the placing of two heavy beams in such a position that they rested on the earth at each side of the pit rather than on the support posts. This was done as a precautionary measure so that there would be no likelihood of the roof caving in when a number of visitors stood on it or when domestic animals belonging to the nearby Navajo chanced to cross it, factors which the early people did not have to consider.

The preliminary framework of upright posts and beams for the flat portion of the roof is shown in plate 3, *b*. The sloping side poles of the superstructure were then put in place and covered with brush and cedar bark as illustrated by plate 4, *a*. The hole was then covered with earth and took on the appearance of a low, flat mound (pl. 4, *b*). A view of one corner of the completed interior is illustrated by plate 5, *a*. The weathering qualities of such a roof were well tested by the winter of 1931-32 when unusually heavy rains and snows fell throughout the district. For a period of several weeks more than 3 feet (91.44 cm) of snow covered the house. Only a small amount of moisture penetrated to the interior during the melting period and a slight amount of repair was all that was necessary in the late spring of 1932. Had the structure been occupied and the usual amount of upkeep provided by the tenants, it would have come through the winter with practically no damage.

When the debris of accumulation was removed from the interior of No. 1 a 3-foot (91.44 cm) square pillar was left near the center of the pit (pl. 5, *b*). This was done wherever practicable in order that a careful study might be made of the fill and that a stratigraphic test could be made of the potsherd material contained within such sections. Considerable information of interest was obtained in this way. The pillar for No. 1 was 6 feet 6 inches (1.981 m) from top to bottom. In making the study of the material which it contained the earth was removed stratum by stratum and put through a screen. The top 6 inches (15.24 cm) consisted of a recent accumulation of sand with a slight admixture of ashes (fig. 3, *a*). There was not a great amount of material, such as chips of stone and bone, in this layer and there were no potsherds. The contents indicated a wind deposit which probably was subsequent to the Indian occupation.

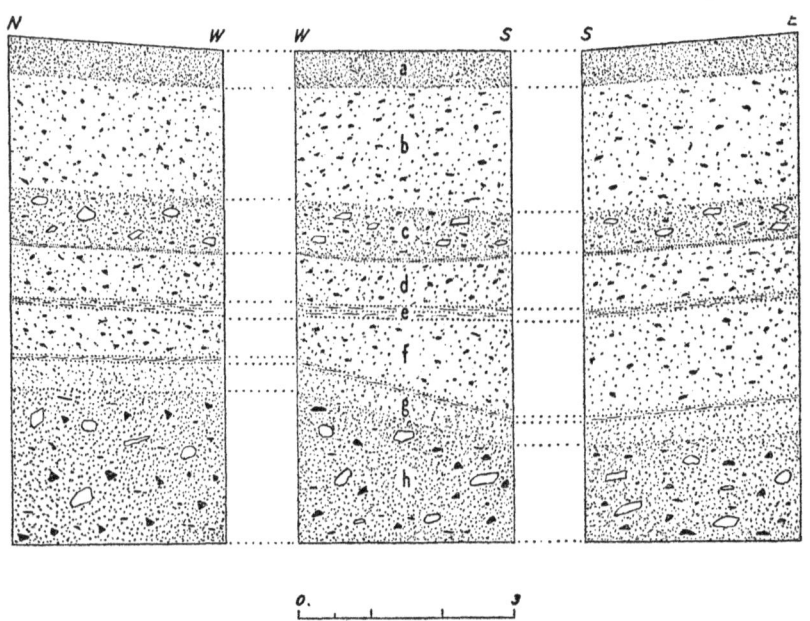

FIGURE 3.—Pillar left from fill in structure 1. N, W, S, and E, indicate north, west, south, and east corners. *a* to *h*, Strata in fill.

The second stratum (fig. 3, *b*) was considerably thicker than the first. It was 1 foot 6 inches (45.72 cm) from top to bottom. The main content was blow sand and ashes with some charcoal. Toward the lower half there was a marked increase in the number of potsherds present. In fact there was only one other layer in the entire pillar which contained more. This would suggest that there was considerable activity around the site at that time and the remains of many broken vessels found their way into the abandoned pit. The stratum did not give distinct evidence at this point of having typical refuse material in it and it does not seem that it can be attributed to house sweepings and other waste matter being dumped there. Rather would the character of the fill at this point suggest a more or less natural gravitation of objects into a depression.

a. Interior of structure 1.

b. Main framework for restoration of structure 1.

a. Brush-and-bark covering over framework, restoration of structure 1.

b. Completed structure showing rounding dome and smoke hole-hatchway entrance.

a. Interior view of portion of restored structure.

b. Pillar left in excavating pit, structure 1.

a. Masonry wall resting on slab foundation.

b. Pilaster in structure 2.

The third layer (fig. 3, *c*) was 8 inches (20.32 cm) in depth and consisted of sand, ash, large fragments of charcoal, rocks, and broken stone implements. This stratum unquestionably recorded the deposition of debris and waste material from a habitation, since there was a large showing of potsherds and broken animal bones.

The layer immediately below (fig. 3, *d*) was also 8 inches (20.32 cm) thick. It was separated from the one above by a fine streak of water-washed sand. Although insignificant in itself this mere line of deposit was of importance because it marked the old ground level. Everything above this line, both in the fill and beyond the borders of the house, represents an accumulation subsequent to the occupation level when the pit was dug. The relation of this accumulation to the ground level around the pit is illustrated by the section through the house (fig. 2, *z*). The layer just below the sand streak consisted of ashes, charcoal, sand, broken bones, stone chips, and potsherds, typical refuse-mound content.

Next below this deposit in the pillar (fig. 3, *e*) was a 2-inch (5.08 cm) streak of water-washed sand. It contained no objects of stone, bone, shattered pottery, or charcoal. The deposit recorded a heavy amount of precipitation with the attendant washing of material into a depression.

The sixth layer from the top of the pillar ranged from 6 inches (15.24 cm) to 1 foot 3 inches (38.1 cm) in thickness (fig. 3, *f*). The content consisted of sand and charcoal, which again suggested a typical refuse deposit. There were large numbers of stone chips, spalls, broken bones, and potsherds. The next two layers were sterile as far as any traces of human occupation were concerned and have been combined in the diagram (fig. 3, *g*). The first of the two was 1 inch (2.54 cm) thick and was composed entirely of water-washed sand. This again indicates either a heavy rain or a deep fall of snow. The melting of the latter could easily carry such material into a pit. The 4 inches (10.16 cm) immediately below consisted of clean wind-blown sand. The 5 inches (12.7 cm) of these combined strata evidence a comparatively long interval in which there was little activity around this portion of the site. It is quite possible that it may even have been abandoned for a time.

The next layer was the bottom of the pillar (fig. 3, *h*). It measured 2 feet 1 inch (63.5 cm) in thickness and comprised burned roofing timbers, plaster from the roof, broken stones, ashes, and the general debris which follows a conflagration. The greatest number of potsherds in the entire pillar came from this level. Some of them were on the floor, but the majority were high enough in the fill to suggest that their presence was due to the use of the pit as a dump immediately following the fire.

The general significance of the fill in pit No. 1 may be summarized briefly as follows: The structure was destroyed by fire and immediately thereafter was used as a dumping place for refuse from other nearby habitations. Then for some unknown reason the site was abandoned for an interval sufficiently long to permit an accumulation of 4 inches (10.16 cm) of clean sand. On top of this layer an additional inch (2.54 cm) of sand was deposited by water. People again began to move about and dwell in the immediate vicinity and evidence of their presence is to be found in the charcoal, ashes, and potsherds deposited there. This record is broken by the evidence of another interval of marked precipitation when only clean sand was washed into the pit. Following this there was a considerable period when refuse was deposited in the pit. The accumulation settled and became compressed into a deposit 8 inches (20.32 cm) thick and the pit was completely filled. A thin sheet of sand was then swept across the top by water, possibly the run-off from a heavy rain. Everything above this line probably represents deposits that accumulated through a combination of factors. Material no doubt drifted down from the ridge above and mixed with that collecting as a result of human activities. Ultimately the entire site was abandoned and the topmost layer resulted from action of the elements, wind and surface water depositing material at the spot where the house once stood. The significance of the potsherds from this section will be considered in detail in the second part of this report under the subject of pottery.

Despite the large amount of charred roofing material obtained from the floor of No. 1, it has not been possible to determine the cutting date of the timbers by the Douglass method.[24] A number of beam fragments from this house gave a good series of rings, but when this report was written they could not be fitted into the major chronological chart. The work on the beam material was done by Mr. Carl F. Miller under the supervision of Dr. Douglass.

The diameter of the pit portion of No. 1 was 13 feet 5 inches (4.089 m) on the sipapu, fire pit, ventilator line. At right angles to this measurement it was 13 feet 8½ inches (4.177 m) from wall to wall. There was no true bench to the structure but the poles forming the sloping part of the superstructure were set back from the edge of the wall an average of 1 foot 6 inches (45.72 cm), forming to all intents and purposes what might be called a bench. The depth of the pit varied somewhat from side to side. The wall opposite the ventilator was 4 feet 1½ inches (1.257 m) above the floor. At the ventilator side of the chamber the top of the wall was only 3 feet 8½ inches (1.130 m) above the floor. This difference is due to the

---

[24] Douglass, 1932, 1935. The method of obtaining dates from the growth rings in the beams found in prehistoric houses is described by Dr. Douglass in these articles.

fact that No. 1 was placed on the side of a hill so that there was a certain amount of slope in the top of the wall.

The holes for the support posts varied somewhat in size and in their distances from the wall. That at the north corner of the chamber was oval in shape with diameters of 11 inches (27.94 cm) and 9 inches (22.86 cm). It was 9 inches (22.86 cm) from the wall at one side and 1 foot 3½ inches (39.37 cm) at the other. Its depth was 2 feet (60.96 cm). The hole at the east corner had diameters of 9 inches (22.86 cm) and 10½ inches (26.67 cm). It was 4½ inches (11.43 cm) from one wall and 11½ inches (29.21 cm) from the other. It measured 2 feet 2 inches (66.04 cm) in depth. The hole at the south corner of the room was irregular in outline because of the fact that it had been formed by the use of two supports. It is likely that the original post placed at that corner may have needed reinforcing, so a second one was placed there. Due to the irregularity, it is not possible to give the exact measurements of each segment. It will suffice to give the total length and greatest breadth. Across the long diameter it measured 1 foot 3½ inches (39.37 cm). At its widest section it measured 9 inches (22.86 cm). The wall at this part of the room had more of a curve than for the two previous corners, so that the edges of the hole were about equidistant from it. The average distance was 7 inches (17.78 cm). One segment of the hole had a depth of 1 foot 10 inches (55.88 cm) and the other 1 foot 7 inches (48.26 cm). The west post placement was more nearly circular than the others with diameters of 8½ inches (21.59 cm) and 9 inches (22.86 cm). It was 1 foot (30.48 cm) from the wall and had a depth of 2 feet (60.96 cm).

The fire pit was roughly circular in form with diameters of 2 feet (60.96 cm) and 2 feet 1½ inches (64.77 cm). Its depth averaged 10 inches (25.4 cm). The oval depression which functioned as a depository for ashes was 2½ inches (6.35 cm) from the fire pit. The depression had diameters of 1 foot 3 inches (38.1 cm) and 1 foot 10½ inches (57.15 cm). Its average depth was 7 inches (17.78 cm).

The deflector stone stood 7 inches (17.78 cm) from the oval depression adjacent to the fire pit. The stone was 1 foot 3½ inches (39.37 cm) long and ranged in thickness from 3 inches (7.62 cm) to 2 inches (5.08 cm). It stood 1 foot 3 inches (38.1 cm) above the floor. The second stone placed upright in the floor 3½ inches (8.89 cm) from the ventilator opening suggested a secondary deflector. It was not high enough, however, to have functioned in such a capacity and probably was placed there to protect the sill of the opening. This stone had a length of 1 foot 1 inch (33.02 cm) and a thickness of 1½ inches (3.81 cm). It rose 5 inches (12.7 cm) above the floor. At each end of this stone was a small hole in the floor which had contained a post, possibly so placed to aid in closing the ventilator opening. These holes were 1 and 2 inches (2.54 and 5.08 cm) from the ends of the stone. Their diameters ranged from 2½ to 4 inches (6.35 to 10.16 cm). They were 4 inches (10.16 cm) deep. The sipapu was 3 feet 6 inches (1.066 m) from the fire pit and 3 feet 5½ inches (1.054 m) from the wall at the side opposite the ventilator. The sipapu had diameters of 3½ and 4 inches (8.89 and 10.16 cm). The hole was not cylindrical but jug-shaped (fig. 2, h). As a consequence the diameter below the floor level was 8½ inches (21.59 cm). The depth of the sipapu was 6 inches (15.24 cm).

The various holes and pockets in the floor had a considerable range in size and depth. The hole b, figure 2, had diameters of 1 foot ½ inch (31.75 cm) and 9 inches (22.86 cm). The average depth was 10 inches (25.4 cm). The odd-shaped depression c had two parts. The larger was 2 feet 1½ inches (64.77 cm) long and 1 foot 3 inches (38.1 cm) wide. The second had a length of 1 foot 9 inches (53.34 cm) and a width of 1 foot 1 inch (33.02 cm). The average depth of the entire depression was 4 inches (10.16 cm). The basin d, figure 2, had a length of 1 foot 8 inches (50.8 cm) and a width of 1 foot 2¼ inches (36.19 cm).

The curiously shaped pit with arms (fig. 2, e) had a length of 3 feet 7 inches (1.092 m) and a width of 1 foot 5½ inches (44.45 cm). The arms ranged in length from 5 inches (12.7 cm) to 10 inches (25.4 cm). The average depth of the main portion was 10 inches (25.4 cm) and of the arms 2 inches (5.08 cm).

The five-sided depression in the floor within the compartment formed by the row of upright slabs set between the east wall and the ladder had a width of 9 inches (22.86 cm) and a length of 1 foot ½ inch (31.75 cm). Its depth was 3 inches (7.62 cm). The holes where the ladder posts were placed had diameters of 3 to 4 inches (7.62 to 10.16 cm) and 3½ inches to 4 inches (8.89 to 10.16 cm). One had a depth of 3 inches (7.62 cm) and the other 4 inches (10.16 cm). The holes at either end of the stone in front of the ventilator opening, n, figure 2, had diameters of 2½ inches to 4¼ inches (6.35 to 10.79 cm). Their depths were 3 inches (7.62 cm) and 2½ inches (6.35 cm).

The oval-shaped hole q, figure 2, had diameters of 10½ inches (26.67 cm) and 6½ inches (16.51 cm). Its average depth was 3½ inches (8.89 cm). The hole r had diameters of 6 and 7 inches (15.24 and 17.78 cm) and a depth of 5 inches (12.7 cm). The one immediately next to it, s, measured 9 inches (22.86 cm) by 8½ inches (21.59 cm) on two diameters and was 10 inches (25.4 cm) deep. The irregular hole t measured 5½ inches (13.97 cm) and 6½ inches (16.51 cm) on two diameters. It was rather shallow, having a depth of but 3 inches (7.62 cm). The hole marked u on the diagram was covered with a small, thin stone slab when found. The cover was square with rounded corners and had been carefully worked. The hole was practically circular with diameters of 3½ and 4 inches (8.89 and 10.16 cm). Its depth was 5 inches (12.7 cm). The hole v had diameters of 3½ and 4 inches (8.89 and 10.16 cm). The depth was 6 inches (15.24 cm). The oval depression w near the south support post had a long measurement of 1 foot 10½ inches (57.15 cm) and a short one of 1 foot 2 inches (35.56 cm). The average depth was 4½ inches (11.43 cm). The hole x had diameters of 5 and 7 inches (12.7 and 17.78 cm). Its depth was 2 feet 2 inches (66.04 cm). The oval hole y measured 5¼ inches (13.34 cm) on its long diameter and 2¾ inches (6.98 cm) across the short way. Its depth was 4 inches (10.16 cm).

The enclosure formed by the row of stones f measured 5 feet 1 inch (1.549 m) by 3 feet (91.44 cm). The stones used to form the compartment varied in size from one measuring 5 inches (12.7 cm) long to one which was 1 foot 1 inch (33.02 cm) in length. Their average thickness, from which there was only a slight variation, was 1½ inches (3.81 cm). There was also a difference in height. The tallest was 1 foot 11 inches (58.42 cm) and the shortest 11 inches (27.94 cm). At the time when the house was in use, however, such discrepancies in height would not have been noticeable as a heavy coating of plaster extended along the tops of the stones and made a level rim.

The opening into the ventilator measured 1 foot 2 inches (35.56 cm) wide at the sill and 1 foot (30.48 cm) at the top. The opening was 1 foot 3 inches (38.1 cm) high. The sill was 3 inches (7.62 cm) above the floor. The offset into which the cover slab fitted had an average width of 3 inches (7.62 cm) and a depth of 2 inches (5.08 cm). The small shaft rising from the ceiling of the tunnel and opening just inside the sloping roof poles was 8½ inches (21.59 cm) from the aperture in the wall. This shaft had a diameter of 10 inches (25.4 cm). The tunnel of the ventilator from the opening in the room to the main shaft at its outer end measured 6 feet 2½ inches (1.892 m). The tunnel had a width of 1 foot 1 inch (33.02 cm) where it opened into the shaft and was 1 foot 3 inches (38.1 cm) high. The shaft was slightly oval in contour with diameters of 1 foot 9½ inches (54.61 cm) and 1 foot 7 inches (48.26 cm). Its depth below the ground level at the time of occupation was 3 feet 3 inches (99.06 cm). It is 7 feet 8 inches (2.336 m) below the present ground level.

STRUCTURE 2

Structure No. 2 was one of the few in the entire group that had a pit lined with large stone slabs. The use of slabs to form a facing for the walls of the excavated portion of pit houses was a widespread practice during the Modified Basket Maker and early Developmental Pueblo periods. In some sections, however, the builders were content to cover the earth walls with a heavy coating of adobe plaster. This treatment would have been entirely satisfactory where the quality of the ground was such that the sides of a pit would hold their form. Where there was considerable sand and the likelihood of crumbling, some reinforcement was required and this generally took the form of large stones. In some districts material that could be used in this manner was not available and it was necessary to place a wainscoting of poles around the walls before the plaster was applied, or else to depend entirely upon the retaining capacity of the plaster itself. Just why there was so little use of slabs in this group of pit structures is not known. The low cliffs bordering Whitewater Valley a few hundred feet from the house remains would supply a limitless number of such stones. Furthermore, the soil has a heavy sand content and walls of pits are prone to slump unless held in place by some other material. The plaster used on the walls of most of the houses was unusually thick and it is quite possible that the builders found that it was sufficient.

The pit portion of No. 2 was roughly oval in form. One wall was almost straight but the others had a slight curve to them and the corners were rounded. The slabs used to line the pit varied in height. Some were low while others extended to the ground level. To compensate for the discrepancy, the spaces above the shorter slabs were filled in with a rough form of masonry (pl. 6, *a*). The use of horizontal masonry in this manner had a fairly early inception in the Southwest. Guernsey found examples in some of his Modified Basket Maker houses,[25] and a number of those in the Chaco Canyon exhibited the feature.[26] It is quite possible that the idea of building structures of coursed stones, which became one of the outstanding characteristics of Pueblo architecture, had its beginning in this way. With improved methods of laying stone and the development of the mason's technique it became progressively a simple matter to erect structures entirely above ground and eventually to increase the number of stories in the buildings.

Structure 2 was of unusual interest because it gave evidence of two different occupations separated by an interval of some length of time. There were two distinct floors with a fill 1 foot (30.48 cm) in depth lying between them. This fill for the most part suggested material requiring an appreciable period to accumulate. Lying on the original floor was a deposit of charcoal several inches deep. This layer

---

[25] Guernsey, 1931, pl. 8, lower; p. 11.
[26] Roberts, 1929, pl. 2, *a;* p. 15.

also included ashes, potsherds, broken stones, bones, and other refuse. Above this the fill consisted of clean sand. The second floor was laid on top of this material. The upper surface of the sand layer had not been level, as was shown by the presence at several places of lenses of refuse representing intentional fills of dump-heap rubbish so placed that a smooth, flat base was provided for the plaster. As a part of the work of remodeling and to compensate for the lessened depth of the pit resulting from the new floor level, it was necessary to increase the height of the wall. This was accomplished by adding several courses of rough masonry to the top of the original wall, as is shown in plate 6, a, beginning at the 4-feet 2-inch mark on the measuring rod. The more recent courses did not exhibit as careful workmanship as the original ones.

The floor plans were somewhat different. The upper was more elaborate than the lower. The two levels will be discussed separately. In excavating the house remains the second floor, or in other words, the more recent, was first uncovered. The various features of this level are shown by the diagram (fig. 4). The superstructure had been supported by four upright posts as shown by the holes in the floor (fig. 4, a). The position of these holes suggests that the roof was of the truncated type with flat center and sloping sides.

Associated with the support at the south corner of the room was a feature of marked significance insofar as it offers a plausible explanation for the development of a structural element common to the kiva or ceremonial chamber of later cultural horizons, namely, the pilaster or stone pillar used to support the roof. A pillar of stone and adobe mud had been placed between the main support post and the wall at that side of the chamber, presumably as a brace for the timber (fig. 4, i; pl. 6, b). This was possibly necessitated by the roof shifting out of alinement at that side of the room. The stones and plaster were fitted around the pole and its impression was still to be seen in the face of the pillar. It would be an easy step from a piece of construction of this kind to one slightly more elaborate in which the masonry could support the main roof beams and the upright timber be omitted entirely.

The evolution of the pilaster, on the basis of the foregoing evidence, might be postulated as follows: In the earliest of the semisubterranean structures the main support posts for the roof were set in the floor some distance from the walls of the chambers. As time went on, the posts were placed almost, but not quite, against the wall. A tendency for the weight of the superstructure to push one of the posts out of alinement, toward the wall, led to reinforcing it with blocks of stone and mud plaster. From the first attempts to construct such a brace a fairly good pillar was evolved and then it was discovered that the pillar itself was fully capable of supporting the roof and that the wooden upright posts were not necessary. When circular dwellings of this type were no longer occupied as habitations but were present in the village only in the form of a survival

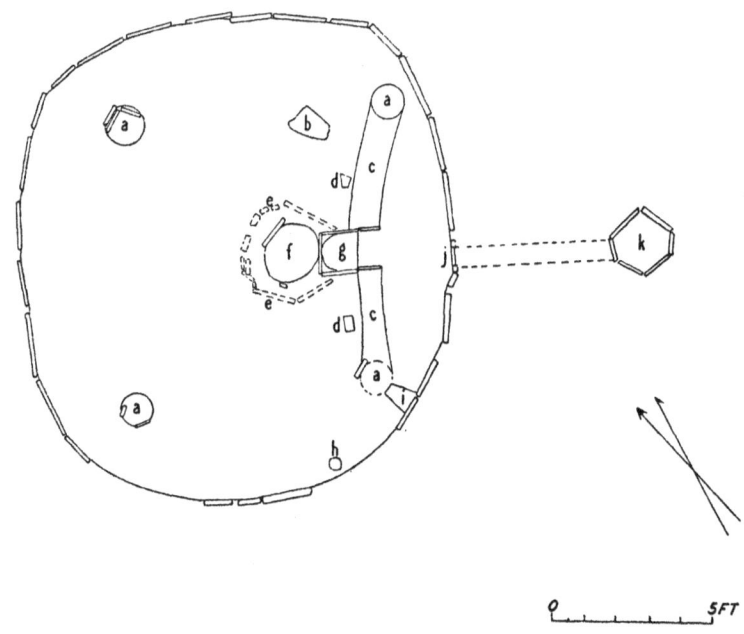

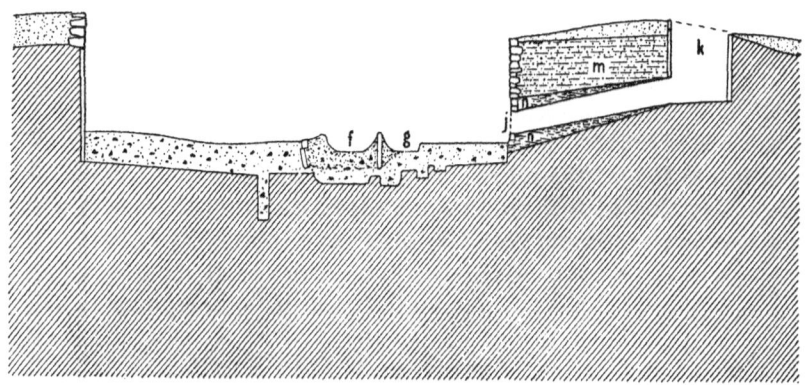

FIGURE 4.—Structure 2. *a*, holes for superstructure posts; *b*, stone embedded in floor; *c*, compartment walls; *d*, stone posts; *e*, subfloor slabs reinforcing fire pit; *f*, fire pit; *g*, ladder box and ash pit; *h*, storage hole; *i*, pilaster behind support post; *j*, ventilator opening; *k*, ventilator shaft; *m*, fill over ventilator passage; *n*, plaster used to reduce passage size.

in the ceremonial chamber, the roof supports were made of stone. Had No. 2 been the only structure in which this feature was present it might be attributed to an individual effort to remedy a weakness in one particular pit house. Another one, however, gave evidence of a similar piece of construction and in addition had a pilaster with no upright timber in front. This will be considered in greater detail in the discussion of that structure, No. 3, and further comment is not necessary in connection with No. 2.

The fire pit in the upper floor was roughly oval in shape and its lining was mainly of plaster. A small section of the periphery at the north side had a stone slab placed in it and there was one small stone along the western arc, but the remainder was entirely of plaster. The pit was reinforced, or it might be said was built up, by a series of slabs set in the fill which rested upon the original floor. The tops of most of these stones were covered with plaster and were not in evidence until the work of removing the upper floor was started. The stones are indicated in the drawing, figure 4, e. The fire pit on this floor level had not been used throughout the entire occupation of the chamber. It had been allowed to fill with ashes and charcoal. This accumulation was then overlaid with a sheet of clean sand upon which two small stones rested. The entire fill was then hidden by a coating of plaster. The fires lighted in the structure during the last days in which it was inhabited were laid in the rectangular box that is generally considered as the ladder pit or depository for ashes. The secondary pit in this instance was faced on three sides with large stone slabs. The fourth, that toward the ventilator, was finished with plaster. When the debris was cleaned from this structure the rectangular box was partially filled with wood ashes containing some bits of charcoal. The stone and plaster sides showed clearly the marks of burning from the fires that had been kindled there at various times.

This floor was not broken by many holes or cache pockets. There was no sipapu and only one hole that might have functioned for storage purposes. This single example was located near the south corner of the chamber (fig. 4, h).

At the ventilator side of the room there was a suggestion of a compartment such as those described in the discussion of No. 1. The inclosure in this case, however, was not formed through the erection of a wall of upright slabs, but consisted of horizontally laid blocks of stone set in large quantities of adobe mortar. The plaster portion of the partition was not well preserved and in places large chunks had been broken out (pl. 7, a). The relation of these low walls to the support posts and fire and ladder pits is illustrated by the diagram, figure 4, c, and needs no further description. The walls themselves rested upon the floor and showed clearly that they were erected after it had been laid down.

Close to the low walls forming the compartment were two rectangular-shaped blocks of stone placed in upright positions about midway of each partition. The stones were set in the floor in the main part of the chamber a few inches from the inclosure (fig. 4, *d;* pl. 7, *a*). What their purpose may have been is not known. Such features were rare in structures of this type previously excavated and how extensively they occurred cannot be determined until more remains have been uncovered. The suggestion that two pieces of wood were used in similar positions was noted in No. 9, discussed in later pages of this report. None of the other structures, however, seem to have had them.

At the east side of the pit a large irregular slab of stone was placed flat in the floor. Its upper surface was flush with the floor level and it constituted the only piece of paving in the entire chamber (fig. 4, *b;* pl. 7, *a*). There was nothing to indicate what its significance may have been. A similar stone was embedded in the original floor in practically the same position and there seems little question but what they had a definite purpose. Other structures of this general type at various locations have also shown comparable stones in the floor. Two suggestions may be offered as to their function. One specifically concerns the ceremonial side of the people's life; the other, based on some evidence, concerns a more prosaic utilitarian phase. The suggestion from the ceremonial standpoint is that when the chamber was employed for religious observances a drum or basket functioning as a drum may have been placed there. Some of the kivas in the modern pueblos have such a feature. The other explanation is that a milling stone or metate may have rested upon the flat slab. The stone was incorporated in the floor to prevent such wear and tear as a heavy object, like a metate, would cause. In one structure located elsewhere [27] and in Nos. 5a and 15 at this site, grinding stones were found on the floor in the same relative positions as this slab occupied. In one case the metate rested upon such a stone, but the latter was not embedded in the floor.

During the remodeling process in No. 2 the ventilator opening was reduced in size and the passage made correspondingly smaller. The method employed in restricting the aperture was that of placing a frame of stones inside the original opening. Two blocks were set upright along the sides. A new lintel was placed on them and a sill was set in at the bottom. All were covered with plaster to complete the frame of the opening. A new floor level for the aperture and passage was made necessary by the fill above the first level of occupation. This is shown by the drawing of a section through the chamber and ventilator in figure 4. The reduction in the size of the passage

---

[27] Roberts, 1931, p. 47.

was accomplished through the use of thick layers of plaster. The relation of the remodeled passage to the original one is also illustrated by the drawing. Figure 4, *n*, shows the extent to which it was found necessary to apply the adobe plaster.

Very little change was required as far as the shaft at the outer end was concerned. The only alteration made in it was the addition of a row of stones around the northern arc. This was essential, as sand had drifted over the old ground level to such an extent that some means for preventing its falling into the shaft had to be provided. This was accomplished by setting additional stones on top of the slabs that had lined the original shaft. The passage for the ventilator was first constructed by means of the trench-and-cover method. It was not tunneled as in the case of No. 1. To make it, a deep trench was dug from the side of the house to the shaft. The excavation was covered with poles and slabs of stone and brush, and the space to the ground level was filled in with rubbish from a refuse mound.

The original floor in No. 2 was similar in most respects to the one just described. There were some differences, however, as the plan (fig. 5) shows. The same holes were used for the main support posts for the structure; as a matter of fact it is not at all improbable that the same posts may have been in service in both occupations. The presence of the lower level was discovered when the post molds were being cleaned out. The old floor line was so plainly marked that the removal of the upper level was decided upon.

The fire and ladder pits occupied practically the same position as on the later level. As previously noted, a stone was embedded in the floor at the east side of the fire pit. The bin or compartment feature at the ventilator side of the chamber was not as pronounced in the earlier structure as it was in the remodeled form. Instead of a low wall separating the ventilator portion of the room from the remainder of the chamber there was a ridge of adobe running from the base of each post at that side of the room to the ladder pit. Ridges in the floor in this position are quite common in Modified Basket Maker houses and also are present in structures belonging to the Developmental Pueblo phase. Where an actual compartment is absent, one frequently is indicated in this way. It was a not uncommon practice, in certain sections, to incorporate logs of wood in these ridges.[28] There was no evidence of timber having been used in such a way in No. 2; the plaster alone sufficed. In this the ridges corresponded to the type present in the Chaco Canyon.[29]

The fire pit in the first floor tended to an oval shape with one side slightly flattened. No stones were used in it and the lining was

[28] Judd, 1926, p. 113, fig. 29.
[29] Roberts, 1929, pp. 51, 57-58, 59.

entirely of plaster. The ladder box was a long rectangle in shape. The ends were abraded in such a fashion as to indicate clearly that the base of a runged ladder had rested there. In this floor one

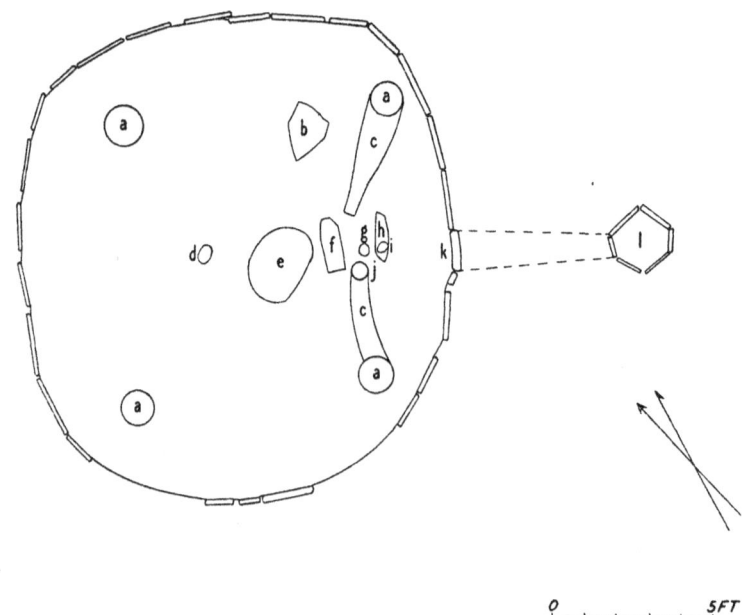

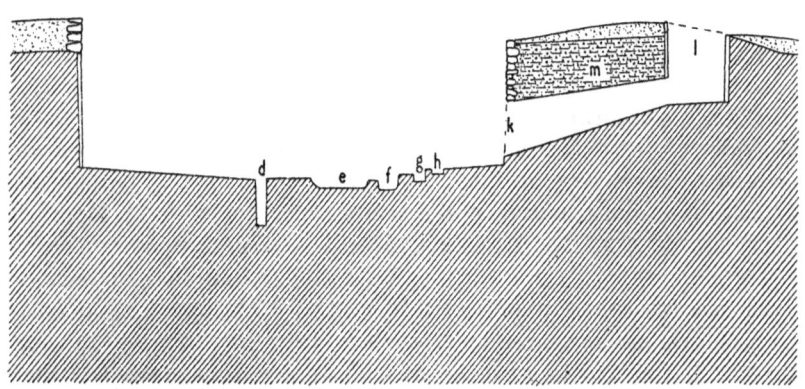

FIGURE 5.—Structure 2a. *a*, holes for main support posts; *b*, stone embedded in floor; *c*, adobe ridges forming compartment; *d*, sipapu; *e*, fire pit; *f*, ladder box; *g*, storage hole; *h*, groove in floor; *i*, pole mold; *j*, storage pit; *k*, ventilator opening; *l*, ventilator shaft; *m*, fill above ventilator passage.

feature was present that was lacking in the later level, namely, a sipapu (fig. 5, *d*). In addition there was a second trench, similar to the ladder pit, in the floor just inside the compartment (fig. 5, *h*).

At the bottom of this groove, near one end, was a hole whose sides bore the imprint of a pole. The only explanation which suggests itself for this feature is that there may have been a plaster deflector reinforced by a single upright bit of timber. Pole and mud, or wattle and plaster deflectors have been found at various places in the Southwest and it is possible that this structure may have had one. The floor around the edges of the depression indicated an upward slope as though plaster had extended up over some object. It is possible that the remains of such a deflector were removed when the second floor was placed in the pit. There were two holes in the floor at this place in the chamber (fig. 5, g, j). Both were carefully plastered and possibly served for storage purposes. The ventilator during this stage of occupancy was larger than in the subsequent one. Its features were sufficiently described in the discussion of the upper floor to obviate need for further comment.

No. 2 was located at the end of the ridge upon which the first group of structures was built. It was not as deep as the others and as a consequence the pillar left in the center of the room when the debris was removed from it was not as tall. This condition was augmented by the fact that the pillar rested upon the upper or second floor level. It was 4 feet 6 inches (1.371 m) high and like the one discussed for structure 1, 3 feet (91.44 cm) square. The strata were not as clearly marked as they were in No. 1 and for that reason an arbitrary 6-inch (15.24-cm) level was adopted as the best means for studying the material. The earth and ashes were removed every 6 inches (15.24 cm), put through a screen, and all of the objects found therein saved and tabulated.

The general character of the fill from top to bottom in the pillar was sand with a large ash and charcoal content. The first layer or 6-inch (15.24-cm) level was composed in the main of sand and ashes. No charcoal was present. Other material, however, included potsherds, broken bones, and fragments of implements made from that material. In addition, there was some broken stone in the form of spalls and chips.

The second stratum contained a large proportion of charcoal, numerous chalcedony chips, and other fragments of stone. There was not as much bone as in the first, but quite a few fragments were recovered. The showing of potsherds was not as marked in this level; in fact there was a decided diminution in the number present. On the other hand, this layer yielded material which was absent from the first stratum, namely, obsidian flakes.

More charcoal was present in the third layer than in the second. There was approximately the same amount of broken bones, a slightly smaller number of stone chips, although the latter contained a good percentage of obsidian flakes, and practically the same quantity of potsherds. The fourth level showed little change in the content of charcoal and bone in comparison with the third. It differed from the latter, however, in that the number of stone chips decreased. There was a sharp upturn in the amount of potsherds in the deposit at this point. In fact they doubled in number in the fourth stratum.

The fifth level again remained consistent in the amount of charcoal present. There was an increase in the number of broken animal bones and also the quantity of stone chips. The potsherds diminished, however, and there were only half as many in this layer as in the one above.

In the sixth level from the top there was an increase in the charcoal content accompanied by a decrease in the amount of both bone fragments and stone chips. The potsherds were more numerous than those found in the level above but did not reach the peak of those in the fourth stratum. The sixth layer also contained large quantities of building stone and spalls from such material. This was the first stratum in the fill where objects of this nature were present.

Layer No. 7 contained an amount of charcoal equal to that present in the sixth. Furthermore, it showed a marked increase in the number of building stones and ordinary chips. The bone content was the same as that in 6 but the quantity of potsherds was sharply diminished.

A somewhat smaller percentage of charcoal was observed in the eighth level than in the two above it. There was an increase in bone fragments and stone chips. The number of potsherds was also larger in this layer than in the one immediately above.

The charcoal content in the ninth stratum was more plentiful than in the eighth; as a matter of fact this layer corresponded to the sixth and seventh in that respect. The amount of bone material in the ninth was the equivalent of that in the eighth. This was also true for the bone fragments and stone chips. There was a marked decrease in the number of potsherds.

There are several points of significance in the data from the stratigraphic section. The greatest number of potsherds occurred in the first and fourth levels. The peaks in the quantity of bone fragments occur in the first, third, fifth, and last levels. The flint chips were found to occur in greatest numbers in the second, fifth, and eighth levels. The last two peaks coincide with those of the bone fragments. The presence of obsidian was confined to the second and third layers. The only shell obtained came from the seventh layer. The greatest amount of charcoal appeared in the sixth, seventh, and ninth strata. The first had none at all and the remaining levels were about equal in their content.

The material thus outlined may be considered to indicate two distinct intervals when considerable refuse was deposited in the pit. One of these occurred near the top of the pillar and the other about halfway between the top and the upper floor. There was a slight increase just above the floor, but the amount of refuse did not correspond to the larger deposits at higher levels. The gap between the moderate showing of refuse at the lowest level, on top of the later floor, and midway of the pillar was quite pronounced. That between the midsection and top of the pillar was not so evident. The data in general may be interpreted as indicating that for a short time after the house was abandoned it was used as a dumping place for refuse. Then for a considerable interval there was only a natural accumulation of material. Following this, refuse was again deposited in the depression. After a considerable amount of this rubbish had been dumped there, another interim of natural accumulation occurred. The duration of this process was comparatively short and it was immediately followed by another round of active deposition of refuse that was even greater in proportion than the preceding one had been. This stage was succeeded by a gradual tapering off in the amount of refuse thus disposed of and the top layer again seemed to be one resulting from natural accumulation. Just what the intervals when only slight amounts of refuse entered into the fill may indicate is problematical. They possibly may be interpreted as representing periods when there was little activity about the site. Perhaps, as was suggested in the case of structure No. 1, the inhabitants may have moved away for a time. In the first of the intervals this was of longer duration than in the second. The evidence furnished by the potsherds collected from the different levels has some bearing on the problem, inasmuch as a certain progression in form is noted. This will be discussed at some length, however, in connection with the subject of pottery and need not be brought forward at this place.

The charcoal fragments from the fill above the second floor in No. 2 gave the dates 814 and 815, placing the second occupancy well along in the development of the Pueblo Pattern. Material from the fill between the original and upper floor levels could not definitely be dated. It apparently belongs to the cycle occurring about the middle of the eighth century. This would indicate that considerable time elapsed between the abandonment of the structure in its original form and the remodeling and reoccupation which took place in the ninth century.

The pit for No. 2 had a diameter of 13 feet 3½ inches (4.051 m) on the fire pit, ladder, ventilator line. At right angles to this diameter the chamber measured 13 feet 11 inches (4.241 m) from wall to wall. The depth varied at different points around the chamber.

This probably was due to the fact that the structure was built on a decided slope. For the upper floor at the ventilator side of the room the height of the wall was 3 feet 2 inches (96.52 cm); at the opposite side it was 3 feet 6 inches (1.066 m). At the west side of the chamber the wall was 4 feet 1 inch (1.244 m) above the floor and at the east 2 feet 9 inches (83.82 cm). The latter was in part attributable to the slope of the ground and to some extent to the weathering away of the surface at that point.

The holes for the support posts averaged 1 foot 1 inch (33.02 cm) in diameter. Their depth varied from 1 foot 6 inches (45.72 cm) to 2 feet 3 inches (68.58 cm). Their distances from the wall were 1 foot 8 inches (50.8 cm) for the north hole, 4½ inches (11.43 cm) for the east post, 10 inches (25.4 cm) for the south, and 1 foot 6 inches (45.72 cm) for the west.

The fire pit for the upper floor had diameters of 1 foot 8 inches (50.8 cm) and 1 foot 10 inches (55.88 cm). It was 6¼ inches (15.87 cm) deep. The rectangular pit measured 1 foot 1½ inches (34.29 cm) by 1 foot 1 inch (33.02 cm). It had a depth of 5¾ inches (14.61 cm). There was no sipapu or deflector on this level. The only hole in the floor, in addition to the places where the posts had been set and to the fire and ladder pits, was the small circular one (fig. 4, *h*) at the south side of the room. It had a diameter of 5 inches (12.7 cm) and was 7 inches (17.78 cm) deep.

The low walls which formed the binlike compartment at the ventilator side of the chamber varied in width. That at the north side of the ladder pit averaged 1 foot (30.48 cm), while that at the south ranged from 8 inches (20.32 cm) to 11 inches (27.94 cm). The height also varied. That at the north end averaged 7½ inches (19.05 cm) and the one at the south 10½ inches (26.67 cm). It is possible that there was not as great a discrepancy between the heights of the two at the time when the house was occupied because there were clear indications that a portion of the top of the north wall had been broken off. The north partition at the end next to the support post was 9 inches (22.86 cm) from the wall, and in front of the ventilator was 2 feet 2 inches (66.04 cm) from it. The south partition was 1 foot (30.48 cm) from the wall of the chamber at the end next to the roof post and 2 feet 2½ inches (67.31 cm) separated it from the ventilator opening. The stones which formed the ends of the partitions near the ventilator opening had heights of 7 inches (17.78 cm) for the north one and 6½ inches (16.51 cm) for the south. That at the north side had a thickness of 1⅞ inches (4.76 cm), while the south stone measured 1¾ inches (4.45 cm).

The pilaster erected behind the support post at the south side of the room was 10 inches (25.4 cm) thick. Along the wall it measured 8½ inches (21.59 cm) and where the post stood 4 inches (10.16 cm). Its height at the time when the room was excavated was 2 feet 8 inches (81.28 cm). There was sufficient material in the debris at the base, however, to indicate that it had originally risen to approximately the height of the wall.

The ventilator opening was 7 inches (17.78 cm) wide at the bottom and 6 inches (15.24 cm) at the top. The aperture was 8 inches (20.32 cm) high. The sill was 4 inches (10.16 cm) above the floor level. The passage from the opening in the wall of the chamber to the base of the shaft was 5 feet 1 inch (1.549 m) long. The opening into the shaft was 10 inches (25.4 cm) high and 9 inches (22.86 cm) wide. The shaft had a diameter of 1 foot 9 inches (53.34 cm) on the passage line and 1 foot 10 inches (55.88 cm) at right angles to it. The shaft was 2 feet 6 inches (76.2 cm) deep at the tunnel side and 2 feet (60.96 cm) at the other.

The wall heights for the original occupation of No. 2 were 3 feet 9 inches (1.143 m) at the ventilator, and 4 feet 2 inches (1.270 m) at the opposite side of the chamber, 3 feet 9 inches (1.143 m) at the north, and 4 feet 10 inches (1.473 m) at the south side of the room. The latter measurement was taken from the top of the wall at its present level, which is that of the second occupation of the structure. Making allowances for the additions to the wall when the second floor was placed in the chamber, the original height above the floor at that side was 4 feet (1.219 m).

The floor features associated with the first level of occupation had different measurements from those on the later one. The fire pit had diameters of 2 feet 4 inches (71.12 cm) and 1 foot 8 inches (50.8 cm). It was shallower than the upper pit and had a depth of only 3 inches (7.62 cm). The ladder pit was 3½ inches (8.99 cm) from the fire pit. It had a length of 1 foot 7½ inches (49.53 cm) and a width of 7 inches (17.78 cm). On the fire pit side it had a depth of 3½ inches (8.89 cm) and on the side toward the ventilator was 5 inches (12.7 cm) deep. This difference was due to the fact that the floor level in the compartment was higher than that throughout the rest of the chamber.

The rectangular depression just inside the compartment, which it was suggested might represent the place where the deflector had stood, measured 1 foot 6 inches (45.72 cm) long and 4¾ inches (12.065 cm) wide. It had an average depth of 1½ inches (3.81 cm). The oval-shaped hole near one end of this groove (fig. 5, *i*) had diameters of 4 inches (10.16 cm) and 3 inches (7.62 cm) and was 2⅝ inches (6.67 cm) deep.

The hole in the floor between the ends of the compartment ridges (fig. 5, *g*) had diameters of 3½ inches (8.89 cm) and 4½ inches (11.43 cm). It had a depth of 3¼ inches (8.26 cm). The sipapu was

1 foot 3 inches (38.1 cm) from the fire pit and 5 feet 5½ inches (1.663 m) from the wall. The hole had diameters of 6¾ inches (17.15 cm) and 4½ inches (11.43 cm). It was much deeper than the average with a measurement of 1 foot 4½ inches (41.91 cm) from the floor level to its bottom.

The adobe ridges which formed the compartment at the ventilator side of the chamber were more irregular in width than the walls to the similar inclosure on the upper level. The ridge at the north side was 1 foot 1 inch (33.02 cm) wide at the base of the support post and tapered down to a width of 4½ inches (11.43 cm) at the end in front of the ventilator opening. The average height of this ridge was 3 inches (7.62 cm). The south ridge was 8½ inches (21.59 cm) wide at the base of the post and 6 inches (15.24 cm) across at the end in front of the ventilator. There was a circular hole in the floor at that end of the ridge which had a diameter of 6 inches (15.24 cm) and a depth of 4⅛ inches (10.48 cm). The average height of the south ridge was 3 inches (7.62 cm).

The ventilator opening in its original form was 1 foot 3 inches (38.1 cm) wide and 1 foot 8 inches (50.8 cm) high. The sill was 3 inches (7.62 cm) above the floor. The passage had the same length during this occupation as it had for the later one. The width of the tunnel where it entered the shaft was 9½ inches (24.13 cm) and its height 10 inches (25.4 cm). There was no difference in the diameters of the shaft between this stage and the later one. There was some variation in depth at the side where the tunnel opened into the shaft. During the original occupation this was only 2 feet 2½ inches (67.31 cm) instead of 2 feet 6 inches (76.2 cm) as recorded for the later inhabitation. The depth at the side opposite the tunnel opening was the same.

STRUCTURE 3

Structure No. 3 was located between Nos. 1 and 2, as shown on the ground plan (fig. 1). No indications of this ruin were observed on the surface and it was not until after Nos. 1 and 2 had been cleared completely of their accumulated debris and a trench was run between them that the third pit was found. The excavated portion of No. 3 was roughly D-shaped (fig. 6). The wall along the ventilator side was flattened to some extent and produced this form. The structure is of particular interest because it gave distinct evidence of having been covered with a cribbed roof. It was the only one in the entire group which appeared to have had that type of covering erected over the pit. The roof had been destroyed by fire but the timbers were only partially consumed and as a consequence most of them were lying on the floor in positions which clearly indicated the manner in which they had been placed in the framework.

The superstructure was supported by four posts set in the floor and one pilaster or masonry pillar. Two of the support posts had been braced with mud plaster placed between them and the wall in the same fashion that the post in No. 2 had been buttressed (pl. 7, *b*). One curious factor in this connection is that in both Nos. 2

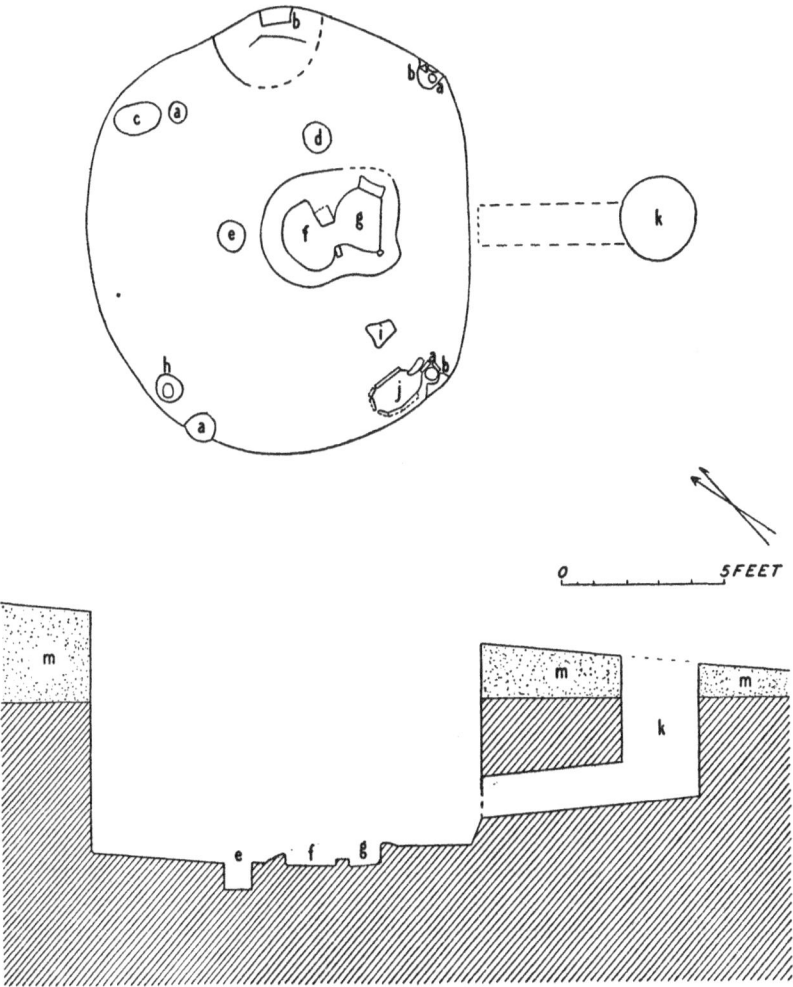

FIGURE 6.—Structure 3. *a*, support posts for superstructure; *b*, pilasters; *c*, storage basin; *d*, storage hole; *e*, sipapu; *f*, fire pit; *g*, ladder box; *h*, storage hole; *i*, stone embedded in floor; *j*, secondary fire pit; *k*, ventilator shaft; *m*, sand accumulation above old surface.

and 3 one of the same posts, that at the south corner of the room, had been braced. Whether this was a "happenstance" or had some marked significance is not known. It seems rather curious that posts in the same position in different houses would have needed bracing, although it is possible that the superstructure in each case may have been forced out of position as the result of winter snows resting upon the north side of the roof for a longer period than on the south. While this explanation is a plausible one there possibly was some other reason more specifically responsible, but what that may have been can not be stated.

The cribbed portion of the roof conformed to the general type that has been observed throughout the northern portion of the Southwest, the plateau area. Logs were laid from support post to support post, including the masonry pilaster, around the wall of the chamber, forming a pentagonal framework. None of the beams passed over the center of the room, as in the case of those forming the main frame in the type of superstructure described for the other structures, but followed the periphery. In this example of cribbing, the timbers were placed in pairs, possibly because they were rather small, although single beams were frequently employed in building roofs of that type. Each succeeding row of logs was placed so that the beams cut across the corners of the preceding series. Each new set also formed a smaller pentagon and approached nearer to the center of the chamber until the framework had been built up into a kind of dome (fig. 7). The portion above the central part of the room generally had a flat surface bordering the smoke hole and entrance hatchway. The proportion of cribbing to flat construction varied from structure to structure. In some a large area constituted a flat ceiling while in others the covering was almost entirely dome-shaped. In the case of No. 3 there probably was more of the cribbing, although it cannot be definitely so stated. Indications suggested such a condition but the evidence was not clear enough to warrant a positive assertion to that effect.

As was mentioned in the introduction to the subject of houses, it has been thought that a cribbed roof was characteristic of kivas or ceremonial chambers. When No. 3 was in the process of excavation the belief was that it represented another structure similar to Nos. 1 and 2 which appeared to have functioned as dwellings. After the roof timbers were found on the floor in positions showing definitely that the roof construction had been of the cribbed type, the question was raised as to whether or not this structure had functioned primarily as a domicile or as a ceremonial chamber. After all of the debris had been removed there was little in the pit to suggest a dwelling. Furthermore, indications were that it was much later than either of the adjacent pits. This evidence was later substantiated by the date obtained from the timbers. The latter shows that No. 3 was erected 50 years after the remodeling activities in No. 2, at approximately 867 A. D. In view of this fact, and also of the similarity between pottery fragments found in this structure and those obtained from the nearby surface remains, it would seem that

No. 3 may have been the ceremonial chamber for the dwellers in that house (fig. 1, Surface Remains A). If this were true the presence of a cribbed roof can be explained on the grounds that it was kiva and true to type, although still in an early stage of development. On the other hand, it is possible that the pit-house builders adopted a crib style of roofing before the transition from semisubterranean to above-ground houses. As the structure under consideration represents a stage approximately coinciding with the period of change in this district it may qualify as an example of the evolution in roofing practices. The shift from house to ceremonial chamber is shown in other structures dating from this same horizon, but this is the earliest cribbed roof at the site.

There was no bench around No. 3. The sides of the pit extended from the surface of the ground to the floor without a break. In this the structure corresponded to those previously described. Interior features were simple. Near the center of the room was a sipapu (fig. 6, *e*), fire pit, and ladder box (fig. 6, *f*, *g*). There were two storage pits near the west and north support posts (fig. 6, *c*, *h*). At the base of the south post and extending along the wall of the chamber was a shallow depression lined with stone slabs (fig 6, *j*) that appeared to have functioned as a secondary fire pit. It had not been used to any great extent, however. This may possibly be attributed to the fact that it was so close to the support post that it would have been a decided fire hazard. Its position, also, was such that smoke from it would have tended to cling about the ceiling and would not have passed out through the smoke hole as readily as could be desired. One function which suggests itself is that the pit was not employed for actual fires but rather as a container for live coals from the main pit near the center of the room. In such a capacity it could have served as a crude form of brazier. Charcoal fires of that type are not known to have been prevalent in the Southwest, but they were in use in regions to the south and may have been employed occasionally in this district.

Embedded in the floor at the south side of the fire pit, about midway between it and the south support post, was a slab of stone the top of which was flush with the floor (fig. 6, *i*). Except for being placed at a different side of the chamber, this stone corresponded to those described for both levels in No. 2 and may have served the same purpose.

The fire and ladder pits in this structure (fig. 6, *f*, *g*) were combined in that they were surrounded by a rim of adobe plaster which inclosed both basins. Both were dug into the floor and were lined with plaster. A low ridge of the same material separated them. Two stones were set in the ridge and reinforced it. The ladder pit had a fairly large stone incorporated in it near the east corner and another at the south. The fire pit was rather shallow but its depth was increased to some extent by the bordering plaster. There were no ashes in the ladder pit and its bottom and end showed clearly the marks of abrasion caused by the ladder poles. There was no deflector between the ladder pit and the ventilator, but provision for shutting off the draft was made in the form of a small stone cover to place over the opening in the wall.

There was no bin or compartment at the southeast side of the chamber, not even an indication of one. The pilaster at the north side of the room (fig. 7, b) was constructed of large blocks of stone, but roughly shaped, laid in adobe plaster. The amount of plaster in proportion to the stone varied from course to course. In some cases it was quite thick; in others it barely separated the stone. The face and sides of the pilaster were not true. One stone in a course might project some distance beyond those immediately above and below, or another not extend to the edge of the pillar. This unevenness was lessened to some extent by the application of thick coats of plaster, so that when the structure was in use the pilaster had a fairly regular appearance. Despite its crude construction it seems to have functioned in a satisfactory manner so far as supporting the roof was concerned.

The ventilator was smaller than the average for such structures, although the shaft was comparatively large. The horizontal portion of the ventilator had been worked out by trenching. The aperture in the wall of the chamber was at a higher level than in most of the structures and had a sill of stone embedded in adobe plaster. The opening was reinforced with a rim of plaster, containing a slight offset in which the cover stone rested. There was an upward slant to the floor of the passage and the shaft at the outer end was almost circular in form.

No stratigraphic study was made of the fill in No. 3 because the pillar which was left in the center of the room collapsed before it could be removed and put through a screen in the usual way. Preliminary notes made during the course of the excavation, however, record the fact that most of the upper half of the debris in the pit consisted mainly of clean wind-blown sand. There was very little refuse or broken material in the remaining portion above the burned timbers of the superstructure. There was little indication of the pit having served as a dumping place. As a matter of fact the fill suggested that in the interval shortly after the structure was destroyed by fire there was very little activity in its vicinity and the material which collected in the pit was an accumulation due to the action of surface water rather than human agents. The timber salvaged from the floor of the pit was carefullly studied and gave

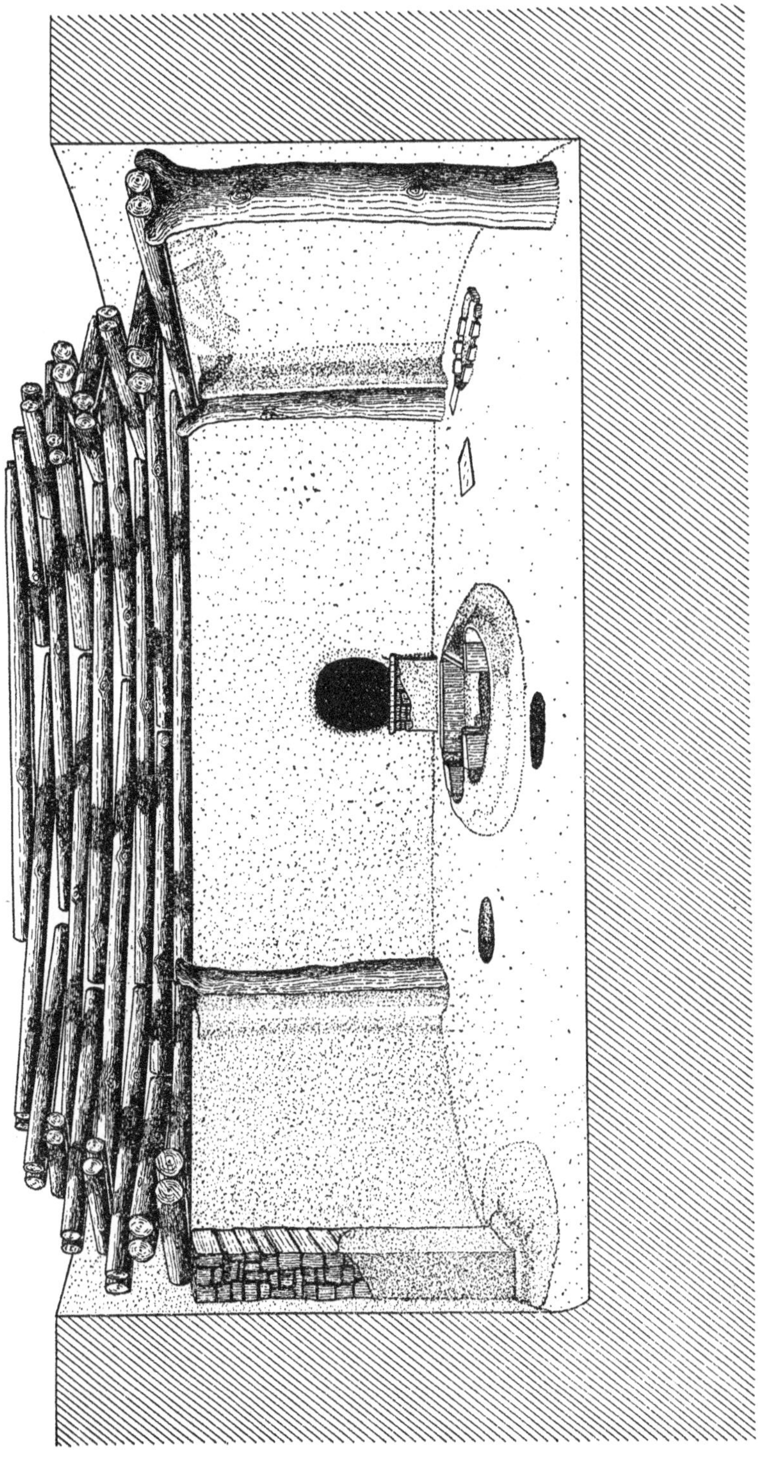

FIGURE 7.—Postulated reconstruction of cribbed roofing erected over pit of structure 3. One side removed to show method of laying timbers.

the dates 842, 852±5, and 867, which are from 38 to 52 years later than those obtained in No. 2.

No. 3 measured 11 feet 9 inches (3.581 m) in diameter on the line through the sipapu, fire pit, and ladder pit. At right angles to this line it was 13 feet 2 inches (4.013 m) from wall to wall. At the ventilator opening the wall was 4 feet 4 inches (1.320 m) high. The fill above the old ground level was 1 foot 8 inches (50.8 cm) deep, so that the floor when the structure was excavated was 6 feet (1.828 m) below the present surface. At the opposite side of the chamber the wall was 4 feet 6½ inches (1.384 m) high at the time of occupancy. When excavated the sand accumulation had increased the measurement to 7 feet 3 inches (2.209 m). The posts used in structure No. 3 ranged in size from 5 to 9 inches (12.7 to 22.86 cm). The charred ends of all of them were present in the floor. The north post stood 1 foot 4 inches (40.64 cm) from the wall. That at the east corner was 2 inches (5.08 cm) from it. The south pole was 3½ inches (8.89 cm) from the wall and the space between was filled with adobe plaster. The third post was partially embedded in the wall.

The pilaster at the east side of the chamber (fig. 6, *b*) measured 6 by 10 inches (15.24 by 25.4 cm). It was 3 feet 3 inches (99.06 cm) high when the pit was excavated. Around its base there was an adobe reinforcement over the floor. The edges of this feature started 1 foot 7½ inches (49.53 cm) from the base of the pillar at the north side, was 1 foot 10 inches (55.88 cm) from its face, and 1 foot (30.48 cm) from its south side. This reinforcement was flush with the floor at its outer edge and rose to a level 2 inches (5.08 cm) high at the base of the pilaster.

The fire pit had diameters of 1 foot 3½ inches (39.37 cm) and 2 feet ½ inch (62.23 cm). It had a depth of 4 inches (10.16 cm). The rim around the pit had an average width of 8 inches (20.32 cm) and was 2 inches (5.08 cm) high. It sloped upward from its outer borders to form a summit almost at the edge of the fire pit. The ridge separating the fire and ladder pits was 5 inches (12.7 cm) wide and 3½ inches (8.99 cm) high. The ladder pit measured 1 foot 7 inches (48.26 cm) by 1 foot 5 inches (43.18 cm). It was 7 inches (17.78 cm) deep at the side toward the ventilator. The adobe rim at the end of the ladder pit was 6½ inches (16.51 cm) wide and 1½ inches (3.81 cm) high.

The sipapu (fig. 6, *e*) was 6 inches (15.24 cm) from the fire pit. It had diameters of 10 inches (25.4 cm) and 11 inches (27.94 cm), and a depth of 9½ inches (24.13 cm). The hole at the east side of the fire pit, ladder pit combination (fig. 6, *d*) was 6½ inches (16.51 cm) from the adobe rim around the pits. The hole had diameters of 10½ and 11 inches (26.67 and 27.94 cm). It had a depth of 6 inches (15.24 cm). The oval depression between the north roof post and the wall (fig. 6, *c*) had diameters of 1 foot 5 inches (43.18 cm) and 11 inches (27.94 cm). Its average depth was 4½ inches (11.43 cm). The hole near the third post (fig. 6, *b*) was 2½ inches (6.35 cm) from the wall; it had diameters of 9 inches (22.86 cm) and 10 inches (25.4 cm) on the floor level. At the depth of 2½ inches (6.35 cm) below the floor a second inner hole with diameters of 5 inches (12.7 cm) and 3½ inches (8.89 cm) extended downward 4 inches (10.16 cm). The oval-shaped depression near the south roof post (fig. 6, *f*) had diameters of 1 foot 7 inches (48.26 cm) and 11 inches (27.94 cm); it was 4 inches (10.16 cm) deep.

The ventilator opening was 1 foot 2½ inches (36.83 cm) high and 1 foot 1½ inches (34.29 cm) wide. The sill of the opening was 8 inches (20.32 cm) above the floor. The ventilator passage had a length of 4 feet 9 inches (1.447 m). The shaft had diameters of 2 feet 3½ inches (69.85 cm) and 2 feet 5½ inches (74.93 cm). Its original depth was 3 feet 2½ inches (97.79 cm). At the time of the excavation the sand which had drifted across the top of this part of the site increased the depth to 4 feet 6 inches (1.371 m). The passage opening into the shaft was 1 foot 3 inches (38.1 cm) wide and 1 foot 3 inches (38.1 cm) high.

SURFACE HOUSE AND BRUSH SHELTERS NEAR STRUCTURES 1, 2, AND 3

Just west of the pit remains described in preceding pages were the ruins of a small surface house and three brush shelters. Only the foundations of the house and a few courses of stone remained (fig. 8). The structure appeared to have been one containing four rooms. Three of these were built in a row, while the fourth was erected at the north and projecting toward the east so that a small court was formed. A fragment of the wall south of this room extended on toward structure 3, suggesting to an even greater degree provision for a court. Only portions of the two inclosures at the north end of the building were present; the rest of the foundations presumably were washed away. The ruin was located on the edge of a slope whose surface gave indications of having been eroded to a considerable extent and there was sufficient wall material scattered over the slope to warrant belief that the walls necessary for the completion of the building once stood there. The probable extent of these walls is indicated in the drawing (fig. 8) by dotted lines. The chamber that formed the east wing of this small dwelling contained a fire pit. The room at the south end, that is the remaining portion of it, had a paved floor. The other two rooms had little of interest about them. The masonry in the walls was rather crude. Most of the stones employed in the construction were used in their natural state, little attempt having been made to shape them. The builders used a large amount of adobe mortar to compensate for the irregularity of the stones. There was very little fallen wall material on the surface around the house. This lack may be explained on the grounds that the builders of the later structure probably robbed the older ruin of its stone for use in the newer construction. At two places in the central room in the west tier the foundation and walls

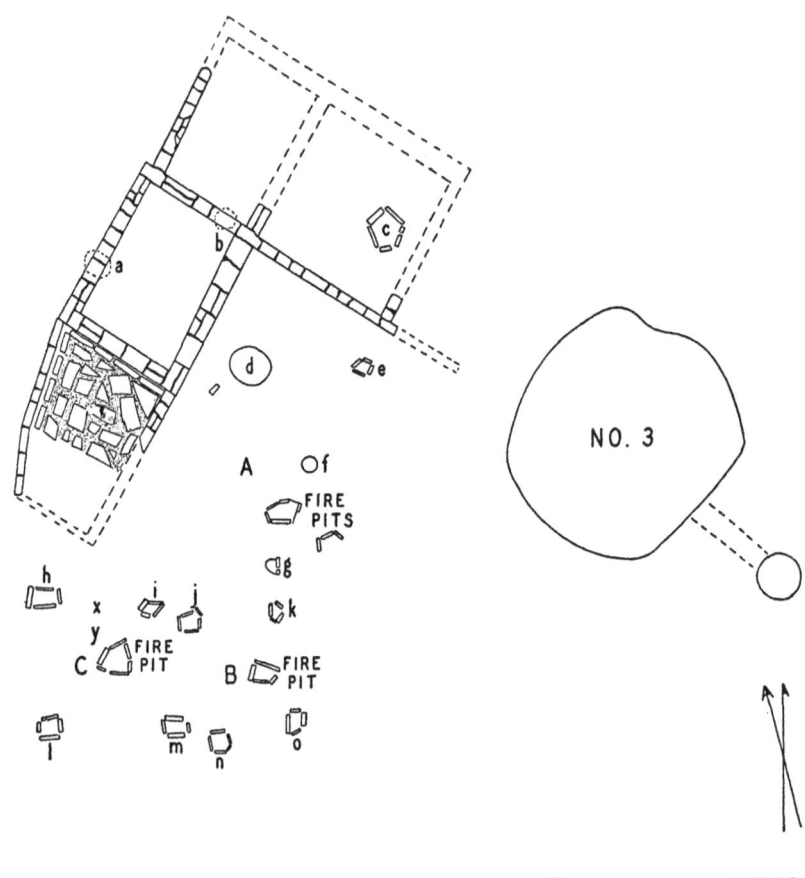

FIGURE 8.—Remains of surface building A. *a* and *b*, fire pits beneath foundations; *c*, fire pit in floor of room; *d*, opening into pit oven; *e*, *f*, and *g*, placements for portico posts; *h*, *i*, *j*, *k*, *l*, *m*, *n*, and *o*, placements for shelter posts; *x*, location of fragment of child's skull; *y*, location of black-on-white bowl.

extended across former fire pits (fig. 8, *a*, *b*). At the time the structure was built these pits were apparently on or just below the existing level of occupation. They were filled with stones and mud before the wall was carried across them (pl. 8, *a*). Another feature, that of a porch or portico, was indicated by the row of post molds or holes along the front of the structure. A similar feature was found near house 15 and inasmuch as the latter exhibited better the

a. Compartment side of structure 2.

b. Plaster pilaster behind wooden roof support in structure 3.

a. Fire pit beneath wall of surface structure A.

b. Opening into pit oven. Trowel indicates flue.

a. Stone ventilator aperture in structure 6.

b. Fire pit in fill of structure 6.

a. Ventilator side of structure 9.

b. Portion of structure 11.

nature of the construction, detailed discussion will be reserved for the section describing that dwelling. As was suggested in connection with structure 3, the latter may have been a ceremonial chamber. If it was a kiva for the small house, the combination would be a good example of an early form of the unit-type structure of the Developmental Pueblo period. Potsherds from the floor of the surface house are typical of the vessel styles associated with that era.

The pit oven in the court formed by the angle in the surface house did not belong to the same period as the house (fig. 8, *d*). The top of the pit was on the level of occupation corresponding to that of structure No. 1 and seemed unquestionably to belong to that horizon. Above the oven was a layer of clean sand on which there was a harder layer of adobe clay. The foundations for the surface structure rested upon this level, which showed conclusively that they were of a later date than the oven (fig. 10, upper section). The oven was of particular interest for two reasons: one was associated with the actual form of the pit itself and the other its similarity to an example found previously on the Zuñi Reservation in western New Mexico.[30] The distinctive feature of both of these pits was a flue extending from one side to the ground level. The pit was jug-shaped with a narrow opening at the top (fig. 9).

The interior gave evidence of hot fires having burned there until the plaster was baked to a bricklike consistency. The earth walls back of the lining were colored a distinct red by the heat. Just what ovens of this type were used for is not known. It is possible that they functioned in the same way as the pi-gummi ovens of the Hopi, in which a corn-meal mush bearing the same name is cooked. The latter ovens have been known for a long time but it is only recently that prehistoric examples have been found. In Mindeleff's description of the modern type he states that the flue was provided not, as might be expected, to increase the draft but in order that the fire burning in the interior might be poked and arranged from time to time.[31] Mindeleff also suggested that baking pits of this type probably were the stem upon which the domelike Spanish oven now found in all the pueblos was grafted. They are alike in principle and general form and it would be a simple step to shift from the one to the other. In general practice the methods of heating and of usage would be similar. The main difference, of course, is that one was beneath the ground level while the other was built above it. The custom was to light large fires in the pits and heat the walls to the desired temperature. The fire, charcoal, and ashes were then removed, the material to be cooked was placed inside, and the opening sealed.

[30] Roberts, 1932, pp. 44–46.
[31] Mindeleff, 1891, pp. 163–164.

There was a slight difference between the example found on the Zuñi Reservation and that uncovered at this location. In the Zuñi pit the flue was oval to circular in form. It sloped obliquely upward and its outer end opened on the surface some distance from the main aperture of the oven.[32] The flue of the oven in the court of Surface

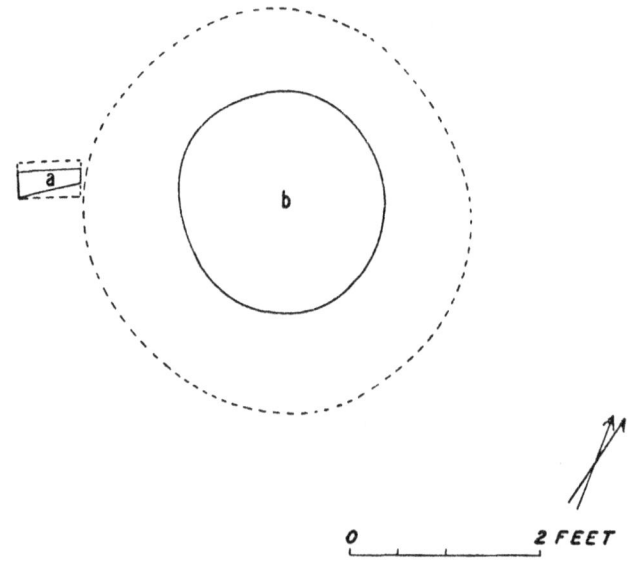

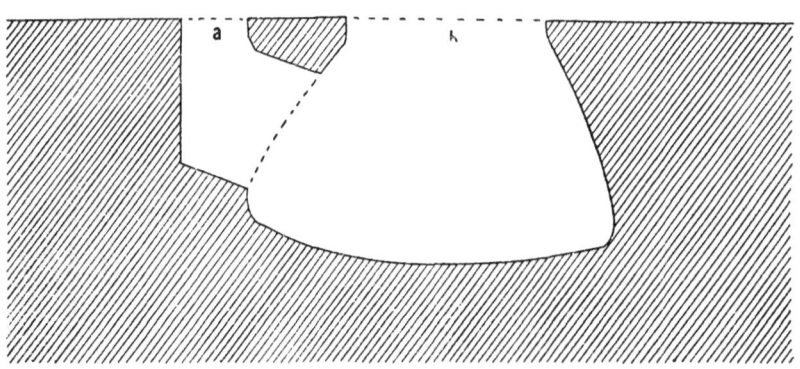

FIGURE 9.—Pit oven. *a*, flue; *b*, opening on ground level.

House A was a rectangularly shaped slit rising vertically from the main pit. The opening on the ground level was only a few inches away from the mouth of the oven (pl. 8, *b*; fig. 9, *a*).

The brush shelters were simple arborlike structures erected on the ground level. They consisted of four upright posts which probably

---

[32] Roberts, 1932, fig. 6.

supported flat roofs of brush. The framework may have been inclosed on two or three sides by poles and branches leaning against the framework, but there were no indications that side pieces had been embedded in the ground. The remains of these structures suggest that they were like the summer hogans and wickiups used by modern Indians in the region. The people may have lived in the pit structures in the winter and during the summer months spent most of their time on the surface outside. Evidence from early Pueblo villages in various sections has indicated that considerable use was made of such shelters or arbors, particularly for cooking and allied tasks. Harrington reports such remains in Nevada.[33] Hough found them near Luna, N. Mex.[34] Judd observed them in the course of his work in Utah,[35] and an example was found by the writer in his work in southern Colorado.[36] It is even possible that during the growing season similar temporary shelters were erected on the valley bottom below and the people lived there during the time when the crops were reaching maturity. After the harvest they could have returned to the hilltop location for the winter season. All of the brush shelters indicated on the plot near the surface remains were not contemporaneous. Two of them lettered A and B on the plan (fig. 8) were on the same level as the surface house. C, however, was on the level of occupation which corresponded to that of the pit oven and structure 1 (fig. 10, lower section). The shelter located some distance from the surface house group, southwest from structure 1, and midway between it and No. 4, figure 1, also dated from the early horizon.

The surface house had a total length of 25 feet (7.620 m) and a width at the north end of 15 feet 9 inches (4.800 m). Across the middle of the central room the total width was 7 feet 7 inches (2.311 m). The east room at the north end of the building had an east-west measurement of 7 feet 11 inches (2.413 m). The remaining east wall was 1 foot 5 inches (43.18 cm) long and that at the west 1 foot 11 inches (58.42 cm). The west room at the north end of the house was 5 feet 4 inches (1.625 m) wide and the remaining west wall was 5 feet 9 inches (1.752 m) long. The central room was 5 feet 8 inches (1.727 m) wide and 8 feet 5½ inches (2.577 m) long. The south room had a width of 5 feet 7 inches (1.701 m) and the west wall, which was the longest remaining, measured 9 feet 3 inches (2.819 m).

The opening to the pit oven was oval in shape. It measured 2 feet 7 inches (78.74 cm) on the long diameter and 2 feet 1 inch (63.5

---
[33] Harrington, 1927, p. 267.
[34] Hough, 1919, pp. 415–416, pl. 35.
[35] Judd, 1926, p. 29.
[36] Roberts, 1930, p. 72.

cm) on the short. The pit had a depth of 2 feet 6 inches (76.2 cm). At its bottom the diameter was 3 feet 11 inches (1.193 m). The flue was 1 foot 1 inch (33.02 cm) from the mouth of the pit. The flue measured 9 inches (22.86 cm) by 3 inches (7.62 cm). It was 2 feet (60.96 cm) long. The bottom of the flue was 6 inches (15.24 cm) above the floor of the oven.

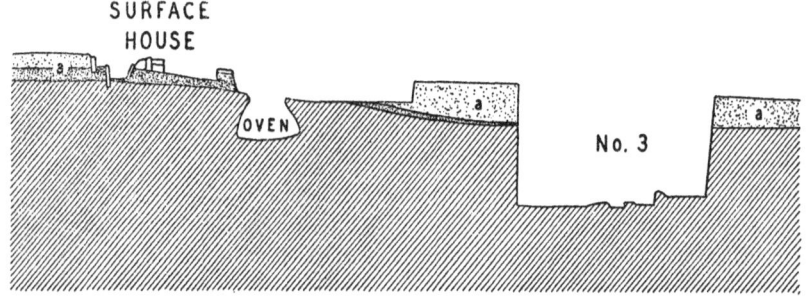

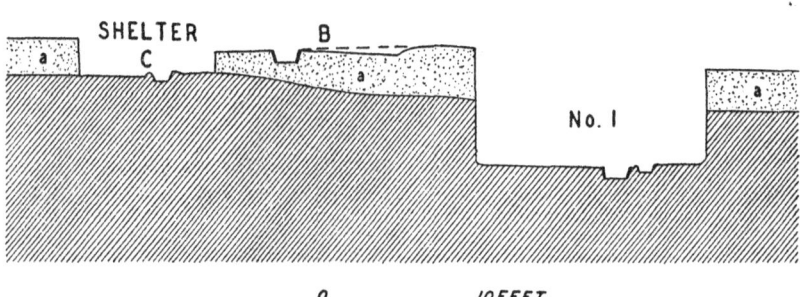

FIGURE 10.—Sections through surface remains A, pit oven and structure 3, shelter and structure 1. *a*, accumulation of sand above original surface of occupation.

STRUCTURE 4

Structure No. 4 stood alone and was placed in the earth along the ridge some distance from the group of three pits and surface remains discussed in preceding pages (fig. 1). It had a roughly D-shaped pit; two sides were curved and two were practically straight (fig. 11). The pit was excavated with straight sides from ground level to floor and had no bench. There were four holes for posts near the corners of the chamber, indicating that the superstructure had been of the flat-ceiling, sloping-side-wall type common in the majority of the structures at the site. None of the timbers remained, however, and only the holes where the main posts stood were left to show that they had been present.

The interior features of No. 4 were simple. There was a fire pit near the center of the room (fig. 11, c), a small irregularly shaped depression in the floor at the north side of the chamber (fig. 11, b), and between the fire pit and ventilator opening a deflector (fig. 11, e). The latter was flanked at either end by additional upright stones embedded in the floor (fig. 11, d, f). The latter suggested the beginnings of a bin or compartment. There was nothing to show that the ventilator side of the room had been completely separated from the remaining portions of the chamber, as in Nos. 1 and 2, hence, the two stones must be considered as augmenting the deflector rather than forming a compartment.

The fire pit was a simple depression in the floor and was faced with plaster. No stones were used in its lining. In the floor box at the north side of the room (fig. 11, b) stones were used to reinforce the sides. What this box may have been used for is not known. It probably functioned as a storage place, since there was no indication that fires had been laid in it. No traces could be found of a sipapu and there was no ladder pit. The surface of the floor between the fire pit and the deflector was roughened and abraded to some extent, suggesting that the base end of a ladder had rested there. Possibly the deflector stone itself kept the poles from slipping on the surface of the floor. The deflector consisted of an upright slab of stone. It is possible that the spaces between it and the other two stones (fig. 11, d, f) at one time had been filled with plaster, making the entire group one large deflector or fire screen, although no evidence of such plaster remained.

The ventilator simply consisted of a tunnel and shaft. The feature distinguishing it from the ventilators in the structures previously described was that of the shortening of the tunnel. It was quite small in comparison with the others. The shaft at the outer end was comparable to those previously described. The main difference was that in No. 4 the bottom of the shaft had a pronounced slope from front to back, while in the others it was practically level (fig. 11, section). The passage portion of the ventilator was tunneled through the earth between the bottom of the shaft and the chamber, and the floor of the shaft sloped slightly downward toward the tunnel.

The fill in No. 4 had nothing of significance to offer. The upper part of the pillar was clean sand and the lower was of sand slightly stained with ash. There were no distinct strata in it. Charcoal was largely absent and there were no potsherds. The pit unquestionably was never used as a dumping place. Furthermore, there was nothing to indicate the relationship between this and the other structures. The few potsherds on the floor were from culinary vessels of the Developmental Pueblo banded-neck type.

No. 4 had a diameter of 10 feet 4½ inches (3.162 m) on the line through the ventilator and fire pit. Across the other way it measured 12 feet 9½ inches (3.898 m) from wall to wall. At the ventilator side the original depth of the pit was 3 feet 5½ inches (1.054 m). There

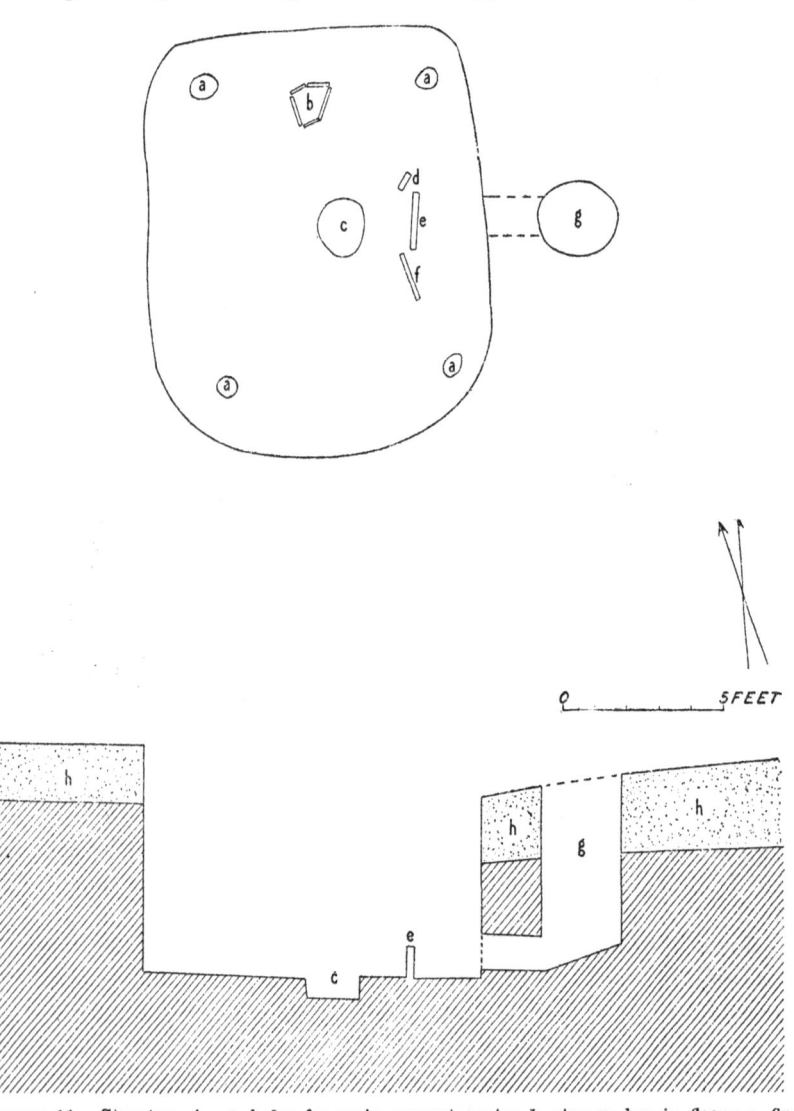

FIGURE 11.—Structure 4. *a*, holes for main support posts; *b*, storage box in floor; *c*, fire pit; *d*, standing stone; *e*, deflector; *f*, standing stone; *g*, ventilator shaft; *h*, sand accumulation above original surface.

were 2 feet (60.96 cm) of fill above the old level which gave the pit a total depth of 5 feet 5½ inches (1.663 m) when it was excavated. At the opposite side of the room the original wall rose 5 feet (1.524 m) above the floor level. The accumulation of sand above the original surface was only 1 foot 9½ inches (54.61 cm) deep. This, however, gave the pit a total depth of 6 feet 9½ inches (2.070 m) at the time when the debris was removed from its interior.

The holes for the posts varied somewhat in size but not to as marked a degree as in the case of some of the other structures. The hole at the northwest corner of the room had diameters of 8½ inches (21.59 cm) and 10 inches (25.4 cm). It was 1 foot 1 inch (33.02 cm) from the wall and was 1 foot 3 inches (38.1 cm) in depth. The hole at the northeast corner had diameters of 7½ inches (19.05 cm) and 8 inches (20.32 cm). It was 1 foot 5 inches (43.18 cm) deep and stood 10 inches (25.4 cm) from the wall. The southwest hole was more oval in shape with a long diameter of 9 inches (22.86 cm) and a short one of 6 inches (15.24 cm). It was only 1 foot 2 inches (35.56 cm) deep and was placed 7½ inches (19.05 cm) from the wall. The hole at the southwest corner was the smallest of the group and more nearly circular in contour; it had diameters of 7½ inches (19.05 cm) and the depth was 1 foot 7 inches (48.26 cm). From the edge of the hole to the wall measured 1 foot 3½ inches (39.37 cm).

The fire pit (fig. 11, c) had a diameter of 1 foot 5 inches (43.18 cm) on the ventilator line, and 1 foot 9 inches (53.34 cm) at right angles to it. Its depth was 6½ inches (16.51 cm). The slab-lined pit at the north side of the chamber (fig. 11, b) was practically midway between the two support posts at that side of the room. It was 2 feet 3½ inches (69.85 cm) from the northwest pole and 2 feet 7 inches (78.74 cm) from the one at the northeast corner. It was 1 foot 7½ inches (49.53 cm) from the wall and 2 feet 4½ inches (72.39 cm) from the fire pit. The box itself measured 1 foot 3 inches (38.1 cm) by 1 foot ½ inch (31.75 cm). The box was 6 inches (15.24 cm) deep.

The main deflector stone (fig. 11, e) stood 1 foot 6 inches (45.72 cm) from the fire pit. The stone measured 1 foot 9 inches (53.34 cm) in length, had a thickness of 2½ inches (6.35 cm), and stood 11 inches (27.94 cm) above the floor. A space of 4 inches (10.16 cm) separated it from the stone at its north end. This stone (fig. 11, d) had a length of 6½ inches (16.51 cm), a thickness of 2 inches (5.08 cm), and a height of 1 foot 4 inches (40.64 cm). The third stone in the group was 3 inches (7.62 cm) from the south end of the deflector (fig. 11 f). The stone had a total length of 1 foot 5½ inches (44.45 cm), was 1½ inches (3.81 cm) thick, and stood 1 foot 11 inches (58.42 cm) above the floor. From the edge of the deflector to the ventilator opening measured 2 feet ½ inch (62.23 cm).

The ventilator opening was 1 foot (30.48 cm) high and 1 foot 2 inches (35.56 cm) wide. The sill was 3 inches (7.62 cm) above the floor. The passage was 1 foot 10½ inches (57.15 cm) long. Where it entered the shaft it was 1 foot 1 inch (33.02 cm) high and 1 foot

2 inches (35.56 cm) wide. The ventilator shaft was oval in shape with a long diameter on the passage line of 2 feet 6 inches (76.2 cm) and a short diameter of 2 feet 2½ inches (67.31 cm). The original depth of the shaft at the passageway was 3 feet 4½ inches (1.028 m). The 2 feet 2½ inches (67.31 cm) fill of sand above the old ground level increased the depth to 5 feet 6 inches (1.676 m). At the time when the excavation was made at the back of the shaft the original depth was 2 feet 9 inches (83.82 cm), with a sand fill of 2 feet 4½ inches (72.39 cm). The depth was increased to 5 feet 1½ inches (1.562 m).

STRUCTURES 5A AND 5B

The remains of No. 5 were among the most interesting of the finds made during the season of 1931. Two structures had occupied practically the same position at different periods and for that reason were designated as 5a and 5b. Originally there had been a fairly large structure of the pit type located at that particular spot. After it was abandoned the pit became filled with refuse and debris to the ground level and a second structure was built. The pit portion of the second and later house was dug into part of the fill in the old structure. The remaining portion of the newer pit was excavated in undisturbed soil. The floor level of the second house was higher than that of the original. The ventilator and practically all of the east half of the room in the subsequent structure were in the fill of the first. The material in the pit did not provide a solid face for the walls of the second structure and it was necessary to reinforce them with stone slabs and wattlework.

The existence of the later and smaller structure was discovered while the workmen were cleaning the debris from the original house. The exploratory trench dug across the ridge at this point penetrated No. 5a at its southeast corner. The workmen then proceeded to follow the wall to the floor and were cleaning out the accumulation when the ventilator and east wall of No. 5b were discovered. Unfortunately the wall of the second structure which was in the fill of the first could not be left standing since all of the material that backed it had been removed. Its presence and relation to both structures was noted and measured, however, and the combination of two houses is shown in figure 12.

Because of the unexpected development of finding one pit house partially overlying and within the confines of another it was not possible to retain a pillar for stratigraphic study. The pillar left at the start of the work was found to consist largely of the ventilator of structure 5b and for that reason was of little value from the viewpoint of a study of the strata. Good stratigraphic evidence on the ceramic sequence was furnished between the two floor levels. Potsherds from No. 5a indicated an older, less developed ware than those from the floor of 5b. The walls of the pit of 5a were very irregular. The structure had a tendency toward a rectangular shape but some

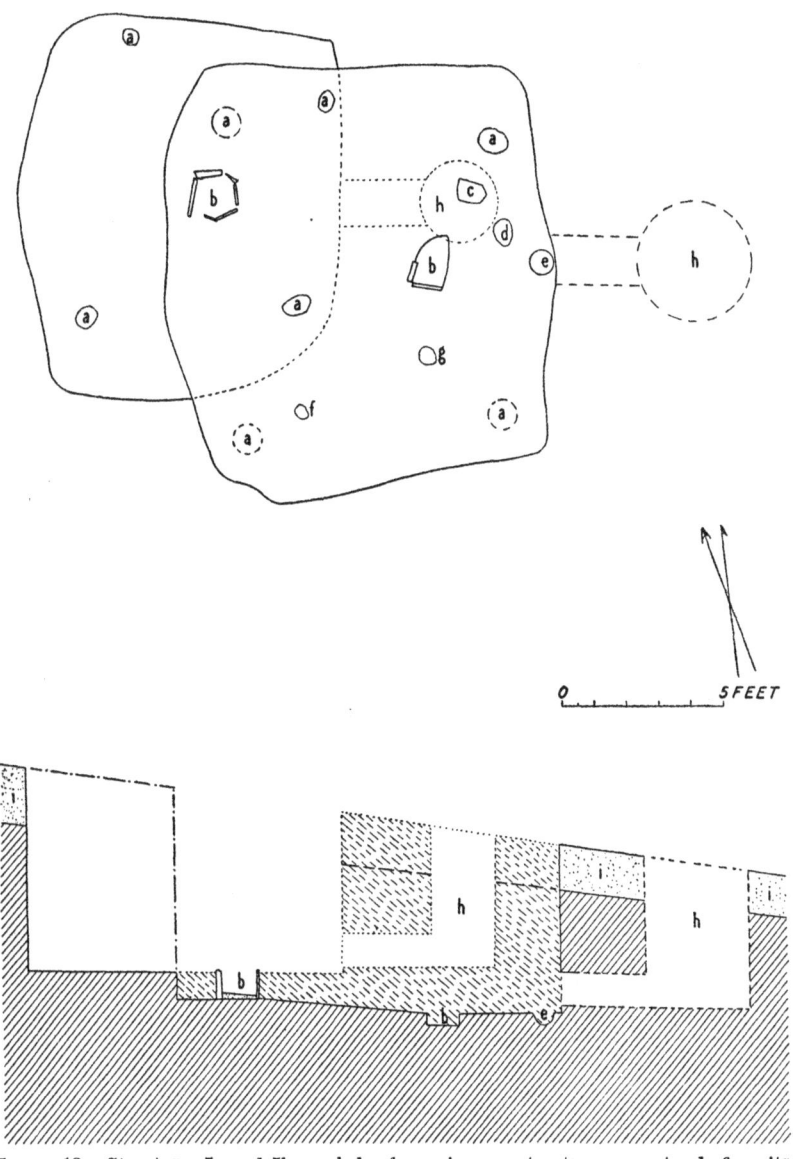

FIGURE 12.—Structures 5a and 5b. *a*, holes for main superstructure supports; *b*, fire pits; *c*, stone embedded in floor; *d*, basin in floor; *e*, hole in floor; *f* and *g*, storage holes; *h*, ventilator shaft; *i*, sand accumulation above old surface.

portions of the walls were concave and others convex, so that each side of the chamber was quite uneven. In its general features the structure had been comparable to the others previously described. There was no bench and the superstructure had been supported by four upright posts set in the floor at some distance from the corners. There was a fire pit near the center of the room (fig. 12, *b*). It was peculiar in shape, two sides and a portion of the third being practically straight. The fourth was a long curve. It really consisted of the fourth and part of the third sides combined. One end and a portion of one side had a facing of stone; the rest of the pit was lined with plaster. A stone was set in the floor, similar to those in No. 2, between the fire pit and the northeast roof post (fig. 12, *c*). Close to this stone was an oval pit (fig. 12, *d*). A circular hole was placed in the floor in front of the ventilator opening (fig. 12, *e*) and there were two additional small holes of the storage type at the south side of the chamber (fig. 12, *f*, *g*). There was no sipapu, no ladder pit, and no deflector. The floor between the fire pit and the ventilator opening was broken, however, and it is possible that there had been a ventilator stone that was pushed out during the reconstruction process associated with the erection of structure 5b. The stone in the floor between the fire pit and the northeast post probably served a similar purpose to that suggested for the stones in No. 2. All indications were that the smaller holes in the floor had served for storage purposes.

Just what the purpose of the depression in the floor in front of the ventilator opening (fig 12, *e*) may have been is debatable. A small hole is frequently found in such a position in houses of this type. Some investigators have expressed the belief that they represent a sipapu placed in a different position from that usually found. In some of the structures at the Long H Ranch holes of this type were observed in which there were indications that timbers had been set there.[37] In discussing this feature in the report dealing with those houses it was suggested that a pole had been embedded in that position to hold a cover stone in front of the ventilator opening. In the present example, however, the depression was more like a basin than a post hole and there was no indication that a piece of wood had been placed in it. What other purpose it may have served was not indicated. That it functioned as a sipapu does not seem logical inasmuch as that feature, if present at this site, was consistently in the portion of the floor between the fire pit and the wall opposite from the ventilator.

The ventilator in No. 5a was of the tunneled form with a short passage and rather large shaft. The exact limits of the passage and shaft could not be determined because there had been considerable weathering at that portion of the structure. They were approximately as shown in the drawing but may have varied a few inches from the size indicated.

---

[37] Roberts, 1931.

The interior of structure 5b was without extensive furnishings. The only different feature found was a slab-lined fire pit placed in the fill above the old floor. The four holes near the corners of the structure showed that the roof had been supported by four upright posts and indicated that the covering of the pit was similar in form to those already described. The ventilator, because of its position wholly within the fill in 5a, was of the constructed type. The passage was covered with poles and brush in order that the fill would not fall into it, and the shaft was reinforced with sticks and plaster. As will be seen from the diagram (fig. 12) No. 5b was smaller than 5a. The exact relationship of the two structures, from the standpoint of the position of one lying within a part of the other, is clearly shown by the section at the lower half of figure 12. It will suffice to say that the potsherds from the floor of 5b were Developmental Pueblo, while those from 5a were Modified Basket Maker. This indicates that an interval of some length elapsed between the abandonment and filling of 5a and the digging of the pit and erection of 5b, although in the general form of the two structures there is little variation to be observed.

On the fire pit, ventilator line, structure 5a measured 12 feet 1 inch (3.683 m) from wall to wall and at right angles to that line the room was 12 feet 6 inches (3.810 m) across. The wall height at the ventilator side of the chamber was originally 3 feet 8 inches (1.117 m). With the accumulated sand the depth at the time of excavation was 5 feet 1 inch (1.549 m). The exact wall height at the opposite side of the room could not be determined because it had been dug away to make the pit for 5b. The point where pits 5a and 5b coincided, however, near the southwest support post placement of 5a, gave a wall height of 4 feet 9 inches (1.447 m). This probably approximates the original height for the west wall of 5a. The accumulation of sand over the remains of the structure made the depth from the ground level to the floor 6 feet 5 inches (1.955 m).

When the debris was cleared from the pit the holes for the uprights for 5a showed that fairly heavy timbers had been employed to support the superstructure. The hole at the northwest corner of the room was practically circular in form with a diameter of 11 inches (27.94 cm). It was 1 foot (30.48 cm) from the wall and had a depth of 1 foot 6 inches (45.72 cm). The northeast hole was more oval in outline and had diameters of 11 and 9 inches (27.94 and 22.86 cm). It was 1 foot 3 inches (38.1 cm) deep. The distance between the hole and the wall was 9 inches (22.86 cm). The southeast support-post hole was 11 inches (27.94 cm) in diameter and 1 foot 4 inches (40.64 cm) deep. It was placed 11 inches (27.94 cm) from the wall. The southwest-post hole was circular in form with a diameter of 10½ inches (26.67 cm) and a depth of 1 foot 3 inches (38.1 cm). It was located 9½ inches (24.13 cm) from the wall.

The fire pit measured 1 foot 6 inches (45.72 cm) by 1 foot (30.48 cm) and was 4 inches (10.16 cm) deep. The hole in the floor (fig. 12, *d*) had diameters of 7 inches (17.78 cm) and 9½ inches (24.13 cm). It had a depth of 7 inches (17.78 cm). The basinlike depression in front of the ventilator opening (fig. 12, *e*) had a diameter of 8½ inches (21.59 cm) and a depth of 3½ inches (8.89 cm). The other two holes in the floor (fig. 12, *f*, *g*) had diameters of 4 inches (10.16 cm) and 5½ inches (13.97 cm) and depths of 8½ inches (21.59 cm) and 9 inches (22.86 cm).

The ventilator opening was approximately 1 foot (30.48 cm) high, and 1 foot 5 inches (43.18 cm) wide. Its approximate length was 2 feet 8 inches (81.28 cm). The shaft was roughly circular in form with a 3-foot 6-inch (1.066 m) diameter. The shaft had an original depth of 3 feet 3 inches (99.06 cm) and an accumulated depth of 4 feet 6 inches (1.371 m).

The pit portion of structure 5b had a diameter on the fire pit, ventilator line, of approximately 10 feet (3.048 m). This measurement may have varied slightly since it was not possible to determine exactly where the interior surface of the wall had been. Across the opposite direction the room was 11 feet 3 inches (3.429 m) from side to side. The depth of the ventilator side can only be approximated since a portion of the floor was removed before the measurements were taken. Roughly the wall stood 3 feet 3 inches (99.06 cm) above the floor at the time of occupation. The later accumulation of sand on the surface increased this depth to 4 feet 10½ inches (1.485 m). At the opposite side of the chamber the original ground level was 4 feet 5 inches (1.346 m) above the floor. The drifted sand increased the depth to 6 feet 2 inches (1.879 m).

The holes for the support posts were smaller than those in 5a. The northwest hole in 5b had a diameter of 6 inches (15.24 cm) and a depth of 1 foot (30.48 cm). The hole was 5 inches (12.7 cm) from the wall. The northeast post was set in a hole 6 by 7½ inches (15.24 cm by 19.05 cm) in diameter. A portion of the depth of this hole had been in the fill above the floor of 5a, so that when the measurement was taken only 7 inches (17.78 cm) of the total remained. This hole had been approximately 3 inches (7.62 cm) from the wall. The southeast post hole had diameters of 6½ and 11 inches (16.51 and 27.94 cm). It also had passed through the fill above the floor of 5a and only 5 inches (12.7 cm) of the total depth remained. The hole had been approximately 9 inches (22.86 cm) from the wall. The hole at the southwest corner of the room measured 7 inches (17.78 cm) and 8½ inches (21.59 cm) in diameter. Its depth was 1 foot 6 inches (45.72 cm) and its distance from the wall

1 foot 1 inch (33.02 cm). The fire pit measured 1 foot 3 inches (38.1 cm) by 1 foot 2½ inches (36.83 cm). It had an average depth of 8½ inches (21.59 cm).

Inasmuch as any measurements which might be given for the ventilator and ventilator shaft of 5b would be only a rough approximation of the original figures they will not be included in the report. The diagram (fig. 12) shows very nearly the size of each and its relation to the rest of the structure and this will have to suffice since the exact data cannot be presented.

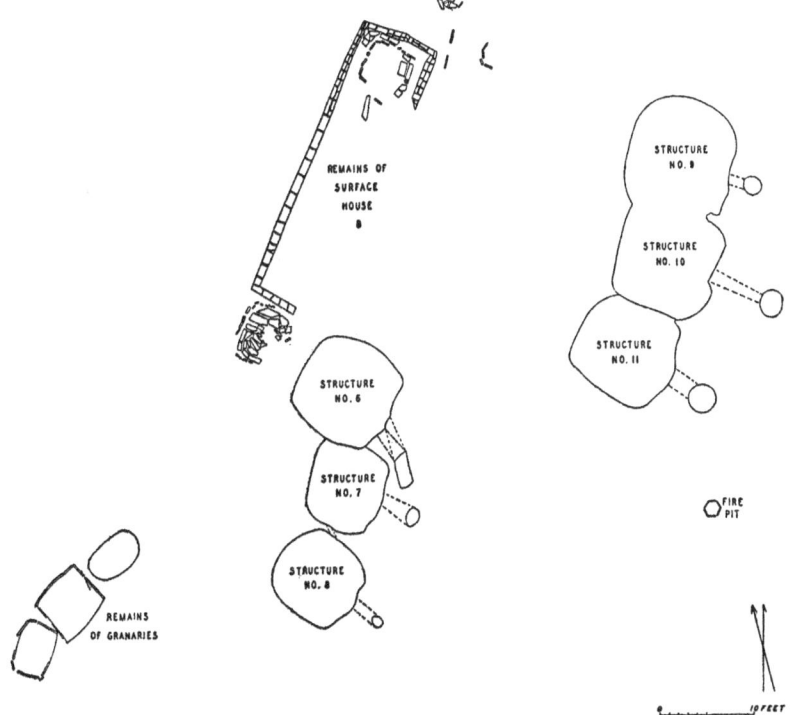

FIGURE 13.—Surface structure B and associated pit remains.

STRUCTURES 6, 7, AND 8

A short distance along the ridge southwest from structure No. 5 were the remains of surface house B and a group of pits numbered 6, 7, and 8. The remains of the semisubterranean structures formed one of the groups of three connected houses previously mentioned in the introduction (fig. 13). Two of them, 6 and 7, were actually parts of one large structure, as there was a fairly large opening between them. The third, No. 8, except for a narrow slitlike opening in the wall between it and No. 7, was independent of the other two. This opening was large enough to permit intercourse between the two chambers and it would have been possible to pass small objects from one to the other through it. The aperture was too small, however, to have permitted a person, or even a small child, to pass from one room to another. Anyone desiring to do so would have found it necessary to go outside by means of the smoke-hole hatchway from one and enter the other through the corresponding entrance. The structures, individually, corresponded closely to the general type of pit structure. Each constituted a unit and will be discussed as such.

Structure No. 6 had a roughly rectangular pit with slightly curved walls and rounded corners. The wall at the ventilator side of the chamber was more irregular than the other three. This was probably due to the fact that the original aperture had been blocked and a new opening made. Like the structure previously described, No. 6 had no bench. The sides of the pit extended perpendicularly from the floor to the ground level. There were four holes near the corners of the chamber, indicating that the pit portion had a superstructure not unlike those previously described.

The interior features were simple. There was a center fire pit, a ladder pit, sipapu, and storage hole in the floor (pl. 9, a). Between the ladder pit and the eastern support post a large slab of stone had been set in the floor to form a binlike compartment at that side of the chamber. In this respect the structure corresponded to No. 1 where, it will be recalled, there was a similar inclosure, although one that was more elaborately made.

No. 6 contained one feature which was not present in the structures previously described, namely, a niche in the wall opposite the ventilator side of the chamber (fig. 14, b). The location of the niche in the wall a short distance above the floor suggests the Katcina Kihu found in kivas of the more fully developed Pueblo periods. The Katcina niches were usually of two shapes, cylindrical and rectangular. The example in structure 6 was not of these forms. The section through the pit (fig. 14) shows the shape. The evidence was that while it was in the position usually occupied by the Katcina Kihu, in which ceremonial paraphernalia was usually kept, it should not be considered in the same classification because indications were that a brace for the superstructure had been placed there. It is probable that the main superstructure framework began to sag toward that wall and in order to check the tendency to collapse a brace was supplied and the niche b was the place where it had rested. The niche was not the only provision made for bracing the superstructure. In the wall at the east corner there was another hole where a brace had been set (pl. 9, a). The latter had a decided slant and suggested that a timber with a forked end had been embedded there. The crotch being placed against the upright at about the height of the main stringers would have braced the framework in an efficient manner.

The fire pit in No. 6 was roughly circular in form (fig. 14, *f*). It had been dug through the floor into the undisturbed soil beneath and the sides were plastered with adobe. Around its edges, on the floor, was a plaster ridge similar to the one discussed for structure No. 3. It differed from the latter, however, in that the rim did not include the ladder pit. The ladder pit was a shallow depression with carefully plastered sides and bottom. A small stone slab was set in it close to the edge on the ventilator side in such a way that the base of the ladder might rest against it and not mar the wall. The nature of this object is illustrated in the drawing (fig. 14, *g*). The stone may have served also as a step for persons using the ladder.

One of the interesting features in connection with No. 6 was that of the ventilator. As mentioned before, for some reason or other the original passage was blocked and a new opening into the chamber provided. The relationship of the new aperture and passage to the old is shown in the drawing (fig. 14). As a result of the construction of the passage that part of the ventilator was lengthened. What advantage a longer passage might have had over a shorter one is not known, but the builders must have had good reason for making the change. The aperture from the chamber passage was unique as far as the structures at this site were concerned, because it had a stone frame for the opening (pl. 9, *a*). The stone employed in this capacity was a metate which had been used until the trough portion became very thin. A rectangular hole with rounded corners was then pecked through the grooved portion of the stone and the ventilator opening thus provided. When the debris was removed from the interior of the pit a carefully worked cover stone was found in position over the opening. The use of stone as an aperture frame is not unknown in the Southwest, although examples of it are not common. In one of the kivas excavated at a site in Nutria Canyon, northwest from the Pueblo of Zuñi, New Mexico, a somewhat similar treatment of the ventilator opening was observed. In this case, however, the stone used was a large flat slab and not an old metate. Furthermore, the vent frame was cut in the shape of a horseshoe rather than in the form observed in house 6.[38]

Perforated stone slabs have been found at various sites, particularly in the Little Colorado region, but in most cases there has been little to indicate what their function may have been. Fewkes in some of his reports has suggested that they may have been built into walls of rooms to partially close the passageway, but he found no example in position. Most of those that he recovered were lying

---
[38] Roberts, 1932, p. 73, pl. 13, *a*.
68764—39——6

over burials. The explanation, or rather suggestion, made in this connection was that the hole was for the escape of the soul or breath body.[39] Hough during his investigations in the Milky Hollow district of Arizona, east of the Petrified Forest and southwest from the

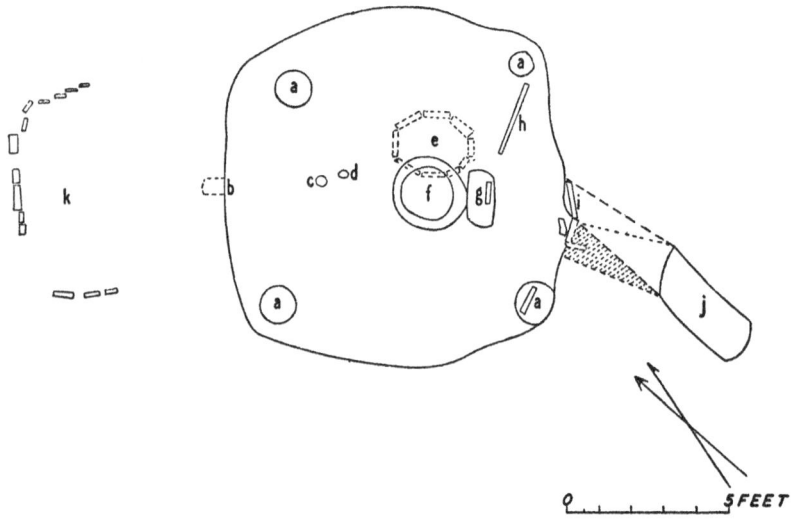

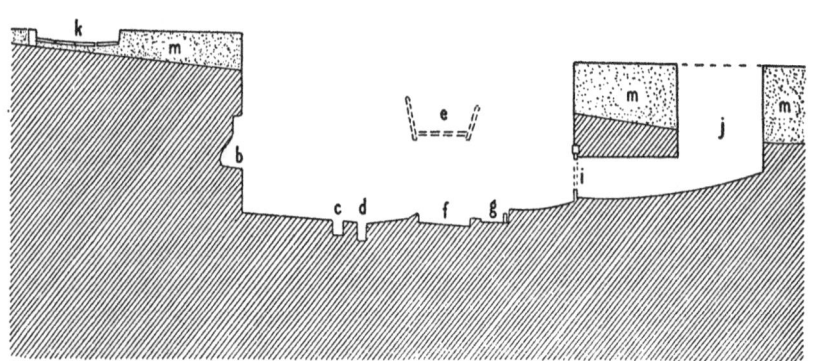

FIGURE 14.—Structure 6. *a*, holes for main roof supports; *b*, placement for roof brace; *c*, storage hole; *d*, sipapu; *e*, fire pit in fill; *f*, fire pit for 6; *g*, ladder pit; *h*, stone forming bin; *i*, ventilator stone; *j*, ventilator shaft; *k*, remains of granary; *m*, sand accumulation above old surface.

present location, discovered perforated slabs that were used as tops on fire pits.[40] Just north of the region where Hough made his discovery a group of students from Colorado College found similar

---
[39] Fewkes, 1904, pp. 106, 160–162.
[40] Hough, 1903, p. 230.

specimens. During the course of his work at the old Zuñi Village of Hawikuh, Hodge conducted some excavations in a small pre-Hawikuh site nearby and uncovered a perforated stone which was in position over the fire pit in a dwelling room. A similar find was also made in one of the early Hawikuh dwellings.[41] The preparation of such stones for use over fire pits may have suggested the use of similar objects as a frame for the ventilator opening in houses. The idea seems plausible, in the light of present knowledge on the subject, since the former have been found in larger numbers than the latter.

One curious feature about the ventilator for No. 6 was that the shaft at the outer end had an unusually large opening. In fact, the line measurement for the shaft was practically the same as the length of the original passage; the second one had been somewhat longer. Furthermore, this shaft was the only one in the whole group of structures excavated which had a rectangular form. Because of its size it suggests that its original purpose may have been that of an actual entryway rather than merely that of a ventilator. However, the shaft and tunnel could not have functioned as an entrance in the condition found when the chamber was excavated. The opening in the stone which framed the aperture was too small to permit the passage of a person other than a very small child. On the other hand, the original tunnel was large enough to have permitted its use as an entrance. Structure No. 6 may be an example of a dwelling occupied at the time when the change from entrance to ventilator was made and the means of gaining access to the house was through the smoke hole and down a ladder. Evidence from No. 6 suggests that the structure was built and occupied at about the stage when Modified Basket Maker was giving way to Developmental Pueblo. In view of this it would be quite possible for the ventilator changes to have been made as a part of the transition accompanying the readjustments occurring at that time.

In the fill at structure 6 was a fire pit dating from a later stage in the occupancy of the site (fig. 14, e; pl. 9, b). As far as could be determined from the general position of this fire pit, and the material in the fill, it belonged to the stage represented by surface house B. There was nothing unusual in any way about the pit itself. It was oval in outline, the sides were faced with stone slabs, and there was stone paving on the bottom. The pit was filled with ashes and charcoal and the stones gave evidence of considerable burning, so that it is probable that fires were lighted in it over a fairly long interval.

The pillar left in this structure for stratigraphic study showed that for an appreciable period after it had been abandoned and gone into

---
[41] Hodge, 1923, pl. XVI, p. 26.

decay there was little activity in its immediate vicinity. The first 1½ feet (45.72 cm) of fill above the floor was clean sand. From that point to the original surface the depression had been used as a dump and the material was typically refuse-mound deposit. It contained a large amount of ashes, bits of charcoal, broken bones, potsherds, and stone chips. From the top of the secondary fire pit to the present ground level the fill was largely clean sand, probably blown over the house after that portion of the site was abandoned.

Structure No. 6 measured 10 feet 6 inches (3.2 m) from wall to wall on the line through the sipapu, fire pit, and ladder pit. Across the opposite way it was 10 feet 8 inches (3.251 m) from wall to wall. The depth showed more variation than the foregoing measurements. At the ventilator side of the chamber the original ground level was 2 feet 8 inches (81.28 cm) above the floor level. Due to an accumulation of drift sand the depth at the time of excavation was 4 feet 2 inches (1.27 m). At the opposite side from the ventilator the wall from the floor to the original ground level measured 4 feet 3½ inches (1.308 m). The accumulation of drift sand added 1 foot 2 inches (35.56 cm) to this measurement, making a total of 5 feet 5½ inches (1.663 m) for the depth at the time of excavation.

The holes for the support posts showed some variation in size. That at the north corner of the room had a diameter of 1 foot 1 inch (33.02 cm). Its depth was 1 foot 7 inches (48.26 cm). It was 10½ inches (26.67 cm) from the wall. A smaller post was used at the east corner since the diameter of the hole where it was placed was only 9 inches (22.86 cm). The hole had a depth of 1 foot 3 inches (38.1 cm) and was 4½ inches (11.43 cm) from the wall. The post at the south corner of the room was set against the wall of the chamber. The hole in which it stood measured 1 foot 1½ inches (34.29 cm) on one diameter and 1 foot 3 inches (38.1 cm) on another. The hole had a depth of 1 foot 4 inches (40.64 cm). The post had not completely filled the hole as a stone slab was set in it to help brace the timber. The hole at the west corner of the room had a diameter of 1 foot 1 inch (33.02 cm), a depth of 2 feet 1½ inches (64.77 cm), and was 6 inches (15.24 cm) from the wall.

The fire pit (fig. 14, *f*) had a diameter of 1 foot 6½ inches (46.99 cm) on the ventilator line and 1 foot 6 inches (45.72 cm) at right angles to it. The depth was 3½ inches (8.89 cm). This measurement includes the adobe rim which had a height of 1½ inches (3.81 cm) above the floor. The rim ranged from 3 to 4 inches (7.62 to 10.16 cm) in width.

The ladder pit (fig. 14, *g*) was 10 inches (25.4 cm) wide and 1 foot 8 inches (50.8 cm) long. It had a depth on the fire pit side of 1½ inches (3.81 cm) which was provided in part by the plaster rim of the fire pit. At the opposite side, from the bottom of the pit to the floor level was 5 inches (12.7 cm). The small stone set in the floor of the ladder pit was 3 inches (7.62 cm) high, 8 inches (20.32 cm) long, and 1¼ inches (3.175 cm) thick.

The sipapu (fig. 14, d) was 1 foot 4 inches (40.64 cm) from the edge of the fire-pit rim. The hole had diameters of 3½ inches (8.89 cm) and 2½ inches (6.35 cm). Its depth was 6 inches (15.24 cm). The storage hole, or perchance a second sipapu (fig. 14, c), was 4½ inches (11.43 cm) from the sipapu. It had a diameter of 4 inches (10.16 cm) and a depth of 5½ inches (13.97 cm). This second hole was 2 feet 10 inches (86.36 cm) from the wall. The niche in the wall (fig. 14, b) measured 6 inches (15.24 cm) in width and 1 foot 7 inches (48.26 cm) from top to bottom along the wall. At the top it was 3½ inches (8.89 cm) deep. Midway between top and bottom it was 4 inches (10.16 cm) deep and at the bottom measured 8 inches (20.32 cm) from front to back. The bottom of the niche was 1 foot 4 inches (40.64 cm) above the floor. From the top of the niche to the original ground level was 1 foot 4½ inches (41.91 cm).

The ventilator stone (fig. 14, i) was 2¾ inches (6.985 cm) thick at the bottom and ¼ inch (0.635 cm) at the top. It was 13 inches (33.02 cm) wide at the bottom and top as it stood in the wall. The end embedded in the floor, however, tapered to a width of 8¼ inches (20.955 cm) at the bottom. The total height of the stone was 22 inches (55.88 cm), but only 16 inches (40.64 cm) rose above the floor when the stone was in position. The opening measured 8 by 10 inches (20.32 by 25.4 cm). The passage was 3 feet 9½ inches (1.156 m) long. It had a width of 1 foot 6 inches (45.72 cm) where it entered the shaft. At the room end it was 1 foot 2 inches (35.56 cm) high, and at the shaft 1 foot 1 inch (33.02 cm). The shaft measured 3 feet 5 inches (1.041 m) by 1 foot 5 inches (43.18 cm). Its original depth at the passage side was 1 foot 11 inches (58.42 cm), but with the sand accumulation measured 3 feet 10½ inches (1.181 m) from ground level to the floor. At the back side of the shaft the original depth was 9 inches (22.86 cm), but at the time of excavation measured 3 feet 2 inches (96.52 cm) from top to bottom. The original passage had a length of 3 feet 9 inches (1.143 m). At the aperture end its width was 1 foot 1 inch (33.02 cm), and where it entered the shaft 1 foot 6 inches (45.72 cm).

The fire pit built in the fill which accumulated in the room after it had been abandoned (fig. 14, e) was 2 feet 3 inches (68.58 cm) above the floor. The pit had diameters of 2 feet 2 inches (66.04 cm) and 1 foot 7½ inches (49.53 cm). Its depth averaged 1 foot 1 inch (33.02 cm).

Structure No. 7 was more irregular in shape than most of those excavated during the season's investigations. This was in part due to the fact that a segment of the north wall was cut by a portion of No. 6 which overlapped No. 7 at that place. The pit was dug into the ground and had no bench. Four posts were used to support the superstructure, as in most of other houses. One of these posts, however, that at the north corner of the room, was not actually in No. 7 but instead was placed in the floor of No. 6. The interior features for structure 7 were quite simple. There was a sipapu and a fire pit

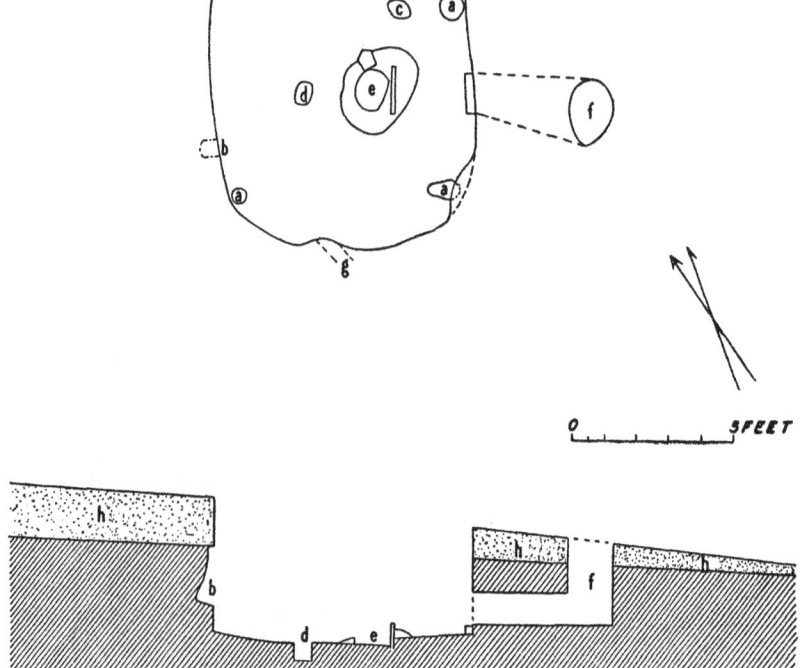

FIGURE 15.—Structure 7. *a*, holes for main support posts; *b*, placement for brace; *c*, storage hole; *d*, sipapu; *e*, fire pit; *f*, ventilator shaft; *g*, opening into 8; *h*, accumulation above original surface.

near the center of the chamber and at the north side of the fire pit a small storage hole (fig. 15).

The fire pit differed from those previously described in that it was both built up and dug into the floor (fig. 15, *e*). The floor level at the ventilator side of the chamber was somewhat higher than that throughout the remainder of the room. Consequently about half of the fire pit was dug into the higher floor level, while the other half was formed by a plaster ridge which encircled the pit. Only two stones were used in its construction. One was set in the adobe rim at the north side of the pit, its top flush with that of the rim. The other was placed at the ventilator side in such a position that it probably served as a deflector. This was the only example of a deflector stone actually incorporated in and forming a part of the fire pit.

The stone did not rise as high above the floor as in some of the other structures, but it was of sufficient height to have served such a purpose. There was no ladder pit, although the floor between the firepit rim and the ventilator opening was abraded to a degree which indicated that the base of a ladder had rested there.

The sipapu in this structure was almost rectangular in shape, a form not usually observed (fig. 15, *d*). The sides were practically straight, but the corners were rounded sufficiently to suggest the oval form. The inside and bottom were carefully plastered. Between the fire pit and the east support was a hole in the floor that was oval in outline (fig. 15, *c*). It contained no evidence to show what its purpose was. As in the case of similar features in other floors it is possible that it served as a depository for small objects.

A niche at one side of the chamber (fig. 15, *b*) was very much like that described for structure 6, the main difference between the two being that this example was not at the center of the wall but was placed quite close to the west support post. Its location and general form are shown in the plan and section (fig. 15, *b*). Like the previous one, it probably was the placement for a roof brace.

The slitlike opening in the wall between structures 7 and 8 started just above the floor level and extended almost to the top of the wall. The opening penetrated the partition obliquely as is shown in figure 15, *g*. The sides of the slit were carefully plastered, an indication that the feature was intentional and not an accidental break in the narrow section of earth between the two chambers.

The ventilator in No. 7 consisted of a simple tunnel and shaft. The passage had actually been tunneled through the earth and was not of the constructed type. The aperture was faced with plaster and the walls of the passage were treated in the same fashion. A single block of stone resting on the floor of the chamber served as a sill for the opening. The shaft at the outer end was oval in form.

Structure No. 7 measured 8 feet 1 inch (2.463 m) from wall to wall on the fire pit, ventilator line. From the point on the north wall where it coincided with No. 6 to the opposite side of the chamber was 9 feet 1½ inches (2.780 m). The wall at the ventilator side measured 2 feet 4 inches (71.12 cm) from the floor to the old ground level. The present ground level is 3 feet 3 inches (99.06 cm) above the bottom of the pit. At the opposite side of the room the floor was 2 feet 7 inches

(78.74 cm) below the old ground level. From the present ground level to the floor of the pit was 4 feet 1 inch (1.244 m).

The north support post was set in the floor of No. 6 and touched the edge of the floor of No. 7. The latter was 1 foot 3 inches (38.1 cm) higher than that of No. 6. The hole for the support post had a diameter of 7½ inches (19.05 cm). It was not very deep, however, measuring only 6 inches (15.24 cm) from the floor level to the bottom. It would seem that the builders had depended in part on the wall of the step between the two chambers for additional support. The hole for the support post at the east side had a diameter of 9 inches (22.86 cm) and a depth of 1 foot (30.48 cm). It was only 1 inch (2.54 cm) from the wall. The hole for the south support was broken out along one edge so that it had a long diameter of 1 foot (30.48 cm) and a short diameter of 7 inches (17.78 cm). Indications were, however, that it had originally been circular in form with an average diameter of 7 inches (17.78 cm). This post must have slanted somewhat, because the wall of the pit slightly overhung the hole and the top of the wall extended into the room 3½ inches (8.89 cm) beyond a vertical line from the point where the floor and bottom of the wall met. The hole for the post was 1½ inches (3.81 cm) from the wall at the floor level. It had a depth of 1 foot 2 inches (35.56 cm). The west support post seems to have been the smallest of the group because the remaining hole had diameters of only 5 inches (12.7 cm). It had a depth of 1 foot (30.48 cm). As in the case of the other support posts, this one was very close to the wall; there was only 1 inch (2.54 cm) between it and the edge of the hole.

The fire pit (fig. 15, *e*) measured 1 foot 2½ inches (36.83 cm) by 11½ inches (29.21 cm). It had a depth at the ventilator side of the chamber, where it was dug into the floor, of 6 inches (15.24 cm). At the opposite side, where it depended entirely upon the adobe rim for its depth, the measurement was 2½ inches (6.35 cm). The rim around the pit ranged from 5½ inches (13.97 cm) to 10 inches (25.4 cm) in width. At its inside edge, the highest part of the rim, it had an average height of 2½ inches (6.35 cm). Just back of the stone slab, set on edge in the position of a deflector, the height of the rim was 3½ inches (8.89 cm). The stone was 1 foot 5 inches (43.18 cm) long, 1½ inches (3.81 cm) thick, and rose 6 inches (15.24 cm) above the floor. The top of the stone was 9 inches (22.86 cm) above the bottom of the fire pit.

The sipapu (fig. 15, *d*) was 11 inches (27.94 cm) from the edge of the fire-pit rim. The hole measured 8 inches (20.32 cm) by 6 inches (15.24 cm) and had a depth of 5½ inches (13.97 cm).

The storage hole at the northeast corner of the room (fig. 15, *c*) was 10½ inches (26.67 cm) from the fire-pit rim and 11 inches (27.94 cm) from the east support post. This hole had diameters of 9 inches (22.86

cm) and 6½ inches (16.51 cm), and had a depth of 3½ inches (8.89 cm).

The niche near the west support post (fig. 15, *b*) was 6 inches (15.24 cm) wide and 1 foot 9½ inches (54.61 cm) high. At the top of the wall it was 2½ inches (6.35 cm) deep, and at the bottom the back was 6 inches (15.24 cm) from the face of the wall. It was 9 inches (22.86 cm) above the floor. The top was on the line of the old ground level. The aperture between Nos. 7 and 8 (fig. 15, *g*) was 8 inches (20.32 cm) wide and 2 feet 8 inches (81.28 cm) high. The wall between the two chambers at that point was 7¾ inches (19.68 cm) thick. The opening between 6 and 7 at the opposite side of the room was 4 feet 5 inches (1.346 m) wide.

The ventilator opening was 1 foot 2 inches (35.56 cm) wide at the bottom and narrowed down to 9 inches (22.86 cm) at the top. The aperture was 1 foot ½ inch (31.75 cm) high. The bottom of the passage was 3½ inches (8.89 cm) above the floor. The stone which formed a sill for the aperture was 3 inches (7.62 cm) high, 2½ inches (6.35 cm) wide, and 1 foot 2 inches (35.56 cm) long.

The passage was 2 feet 11 inches (89.9 cm) long. Where it opened into the shaft it was 2 feet (60.96 cm) wide and had a height of 1 foot 1 inch (33.02 cm). The shaft was oval in form with diameters of 2 feet (60.96 cm) and 1 foot 5 inches (43.18 cm). Its original depth was 1 foot 11 inches (58.42 cm) at the passage side and 1 foot 10 inches (55.88 cm) at the back. At the time when the structure was excavated this depth had been augmented by a 9½-inch (24.13-cm) layer of blow sand.

The third structure in this group, No. 8, was typical of the pit houses at this location. The subterranean portion was dug into the earth and no bench provided. Three of the sides were fairly symmetrical arcs but the fourth was very irregular and undulating (fig. 16). This was the ventilator side of the chamber and it is possible that the construction of this feature may in part have been responsible for the unevenness of the wall. The pit for this structure was somewhat shallower than in the case of some of those previously described. The tendency of the people in the earlier southwestern horizons to construct their pit houses on a slope is well illustrated in the case of the remains of No. 8. The ventilator side of the structure was much lower than the other and any surface water would have drained away from the house quite rapidly. This was also true of structures 6 and 7 and the sections in the several drawings illustrate this point better than could any extended descriptions.

The covering over the pit of No. 8 was supported by four main posts set in the floor close to the corners of the chamber. The roof probably was of the flat ceiling, sloping sides type previously described. The interior features were simple indeed, as they consisted solely of a sipapu and a fire pit. The only other item of consequence was the opening in the wall between this structure and house 7.

The fire pit was merely a depression in the floor with plaster sides and bottom (fig. 16, d). The sipapu was a roughly circular hole in the floor close to the fire pit (fig. 16, c). The sides and bottom of this hole were also plastered. The ventilator was of the simplest form. The passage was tunneled through the earth to the oval-shaped shaft at the outer end (fig. 16, e). The aperture in the chamber wall was larger than the remaining portions of the passage. The ceiling of the latter was practically horizontal but the floor had a decided upward slant to the bottom of the shaft. The ventilator as a whole was not large enough to have functioned in the capacity of an entrance and must have served only to bring fresh air into the chamber.

Structure 8 measured 9 feet 8 inches (2.946 m) from wall to wall on the fire pit, ventilator line. The diameter at right angles to the latter measurement was 8 feet 10 inches (2.692 m). At the ventilator side of the chamber the wall was 1 foot 11½ inches (59.69 cm) high. Above the original ground level was an accumulation of sand which increased the depth of the pit at the time of excavation to 3 feet 4½ inches (1.028 m). At the opposite side of the chamber the original wall height was 3 feet 2 inches (96.52 cm). This was increased to 4 feet 4 inches (1.320 m) by the accumulation of sand that drifted over the site after the abandonment of the structure.

The hole for a support post near the north corner of the room had diameters of 7½ inches (19.05 cm) and 9½ inches (24.13 cm). The hole was 1 inch (2.54 cm) from the wall and had a depth of 9½ inches (24.13 cm). The hole for the east post measured 9½ inches (24.13 cm) by 10½ inches (26.67 cm). Its depth was 1 foot 1 inch (33.02 cm). The hole was placed 1¾ inches (4.44 cm) from the wall. The hole for the south post had diameters of 9 inches (22.86 cm) and 8½ inches (21.59 cm). Its depth was 11 inches (27.94 cm). The hole actually touched the wall. The west-support hole was 8 and 7½ inches (20.32 and 19.05 cm) in diameter. Its depth was 1 foot (30.48 cm). As in the case of the hole at the south corner, this one also touched the wall.

The fire pit (fig. 16, d), with diameters of 1 foot 3 inches (38.1 cm) and 1 foot 7 inches (48.26 cm), was quite shallow, having a depth of only 4 inches (10.16 cm).

The sipapu (fig. 16 c) was 7 inches (17.78 cm) from the fire pit and 3 feet 11½ inches (1.206 m) from the west wall of the chamber. The hole had diameters of 3 and 2½ inches (7.62 and 6.35 cm). It was 5 inches (12.7 cm) deep.

The slitlike opening in the wall between structures 7 and 8 was larger in No. 8 than it was in No. 7. The width at the side of the wall was 9 inches (22.86 cm) and the height 2 feet 10 inches (86.36 cm). The greater height was made possible because of the fact that the floor of room 8 was 3½ inches (8.89 cm) lower than that in room 7.

The ventilator opening was 1 foot 1 inch (33.02 cm) wide and 1 foot 1½ inches (34.29 cm) high. The sill of the opening was 2½

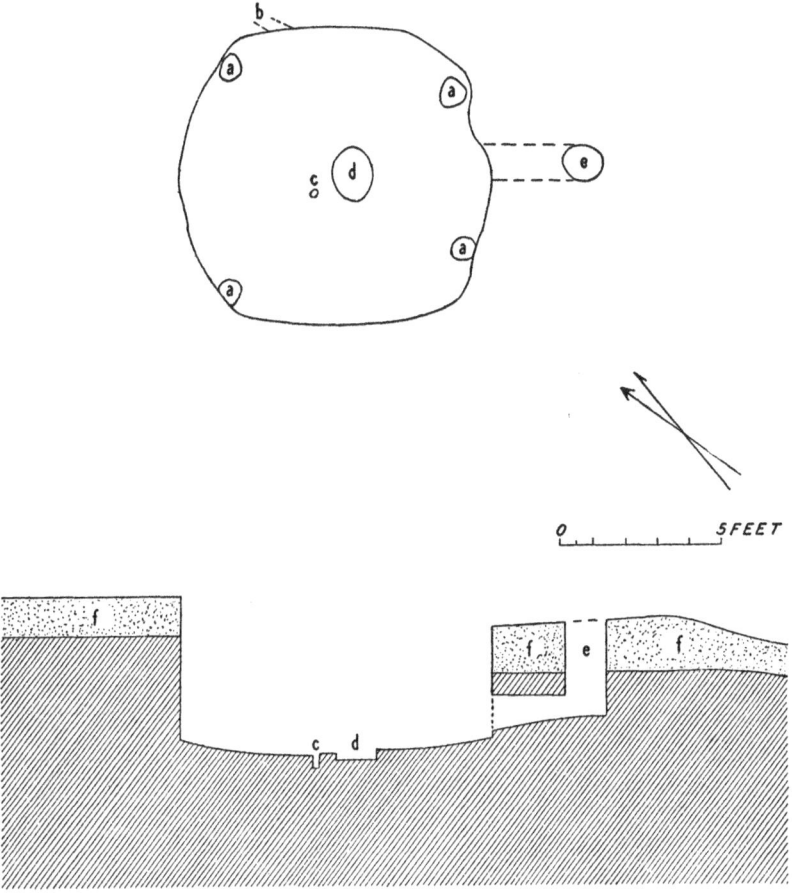

FIGURE 16.—Structure 8. *a*, holes for main supports; *b*, opening into 7; *c*, sipapu; *d*, fire pit; *e*, ventilator shaft; *f*, recent accumulation of sand above original surface.

inches (6.35 cm) above the floor. The passage was 2 feet 3½ inches (69.85 cm) long and where it entered the shaft was 1 foot 3 inches (38.1 cm) and 1 foot ½ inch (31.75 cm). At the passage side its original depth was 1 foot 4½ inches (41.91 cm), which was increased to 2 feet 11 inches (88.9 cm) by the sand drift. At the back of the shaft the original depth was 1 foot 4 inches (40.64 cm) and that at the time of excavation 2 feet 10½ inches (87.63 cm).

In the preceding paragraphs the three structures forming this particular group have been discussed as single units. They should be considered, however, from the standpoint of the series as a whole and the relationship existing between them. No. 8 stood sufficiently apart from the other two to constitute a single structure. Nos. 6 and 7 were so closely connected that, to all outward appearances, at the time when they were occupied they must have seemed to be a single building.

The coverings over these two pits were predominantly of the flat ceiling, sloping side wall type of roof. However, the section where the two houses opened into each other could not have had the slanting poles and in all probability the space where the opening occurred must have had a flat roof. This could have been provided through the use of timbers extending from one rectangular framework to the

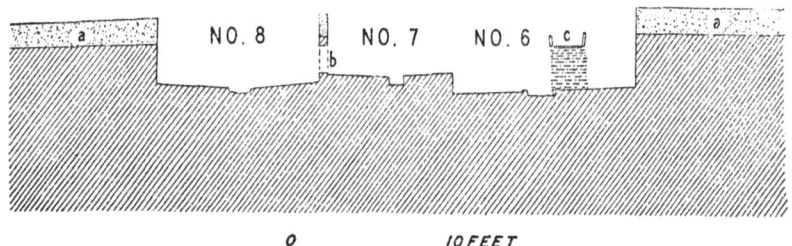

FIGURE 17.—Section through 6, 7, and 8. *a*, sand accumulation above original surface; *b*, opening between 7 and 8; *c*, fire pit built on fill in structure 6.

other, forming a continuous flat ceiling over that part of the pits. The sides could have been closed with no difficulty by using the customary sloping poles. The earth wall between Nos. 7 and 8 was sufficiently thick to have supported sloping timbers for each of the roofs. If the poles had been placed alternately one sloping to the framework in No. 7, the next to that of No. 8, etc., the sides for the coverings over the two pits would have been of the usual type and quite satisfactory. They would have met at the bottom in the form of a V which, if properly plastered, would have functioned as a gutter for drainage purposes.

Despite the large opening between No. 6 and No. 7 each chamber seems to have functioned as a separate unit because the evidence was that each had had its own smoke hole and ladder. When the pits were first being excavated it was thought that either No. 6 or No. 7 was the older and had been abandoned before the other house was erected. All of the evidence, however, pointed to a contemporaneity between the two. The fill extended from one through the opening into the other and fragments from the same pottery vessels were found on the floors of both. Consequently it was concluded that they must have been occupied at the same time. If more privacy than such an arrangement permitted had been desired it would have been an easy matter to hang a blanket or erect a brush screen in the opening, but there was nothing to show that any type of partition had been placed there.

The relationship between the floor levels of the three structures, 6, 7, and 8, is shown by the section (fig. 17). The drawing makes clear the marked change in level between Nos. 6 and 7 and shows that No. 8 was slightly lower than No. 7, although not in as pronounced a degree as in the case of the other structure. What the reason may have been for the break in levels between 6 and 7 is not known. Possibly the step was in the nature of a property line, inasmuch as there was no partition wall between the two chambers. It would have served to designate where one room left off and the other began, even though one was not completely separated from the other. A similar break in floor levels occurred between two of the structures in the group of three united rooms, discussed in following pages, and because of its presence there it is thought that there was some specific significance to the feature, even though no satisfactory explanation for it is forthcoming.

STRUCTURES 9, 10, AND 11

The group of three structures Nos. 9, 10, and 11 was located a short distance, 18 feet (5.486 m), east of structure No. 6 (fig. 13). This series of three was particularly interesting because while each was an individual unit complete in itself there were no partition walls between them, and all three formed one large structure. As in the description of the preceding group, each of the structures will be considered separately and then the group will be discussed as a whole.

Structure No. 9 was roughly D-shaped in outline, although one side was quite uneven (fig. 18). As noted in some of the other structures, the wall that was most irregular was the one where the ventilator occurred. The pit was dug into the native earth with practically vertical sides. There was no bench encircling it. The excavation was somewhat deeper than the subterranean portion of some of the other structures at the site, but in its general aspects was quite similar to them. The superstructure had been supported by four upright posts and in general seems to have been of the prevailing type. One side of the roof must have been an exception, because of the fact that there was no wall between this structure and the next, through the omission of the sloping poles. Timbers lying flat and extending from the rectangular framework on top of the main support posts in this house to that in the next probably covered the space at the south side, in the same manner as described for Nos. 6 and 7. This construction will be discussed more fully, however, in the consideration of the three structures as a single building.

The interior features in No. 9 were somewhat more elaborate than

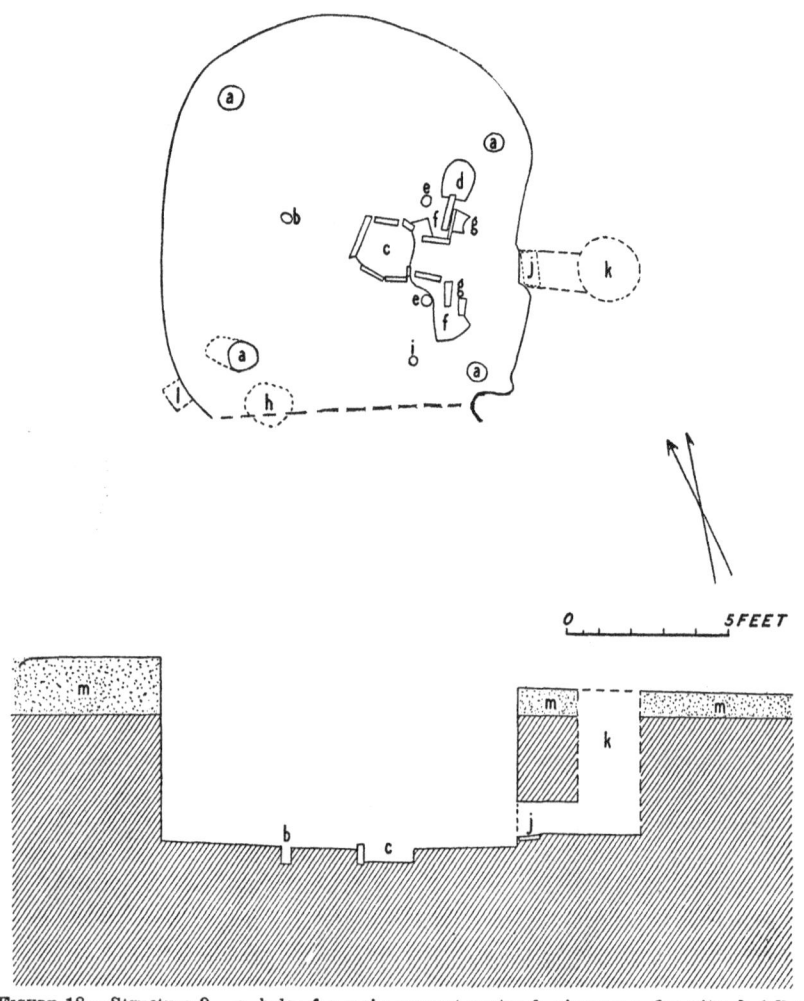

FIGURE 18.—Structure 9. *a*, holes for main support posts; *b*, sipapu; *c*, fire pit; *d*, fallen stone from compartment wall; *e*, holes for small poles; *f*, adobe plaster placement for compartment wall slabs; *g*, stones in compartment wall; *h*, location of support post for superstructure over 10; *i*, storage hole; *j*, ventilator opening and sill; *k*, ventilator shaft; *l*, placement for roof brace; *m*, sand accumulation above old surface.

those in the three structures forming the group described in preceding pages. Near the center of the room was a slab-lined fire pit. Between the fire pit and the ventilator a group of upright stone slabs were arranged in such a manner as to suggest the former existence of a compartment similar to the one in structure No. 1. All of the stones were not present when the house was excavated but a few of them were still in position and indications were that the low wall had extended from one support post to the other at that side of the chamber (pl. 10, a). There were several holes and depressions scattered about in the floor. One of these was the sipapu, placed about midway between the fire pit and the west wall of the chamber. Another was probably for storage purposes and two additional ones gave evidence of having had posts set in them.

The fire pit was not elaborately constructed (fig. 18, c). A hole of sufficient size was dug into the floor and the interior walls on three sides were lined with stone. The fourth side toward the ventilator opening was merely faced with a heavy coating of plaster. The bottom of the pit was also plastered. There was no ladder pit, although a small opening was present in the compartment wall between the fire pit and the ventilator aperture and there were two shallow depressions where the ladder ends probably rested. The opening in the compartment was flanked on either side by upright stones probably set in the floor, in the positions found, to protect the ends of the low wall from the feet of people ascending and descending the ladder.

Evidence that small poles were set in the floor in the main part of the chamber about midway of each partition wall (fig. 18, e) suggests that in structure No. 9 there was a similar feature to the upright stones set in approximately the same positions in No. 2. As was stated in the discussion of the latter, however, their purpose is not known. It is possible that they had some connection with the function of the binlike compartment at that side of the chamber, but what the relationship may have been is a problem still to be solved. In the case of No. 9 the small poles may have been incased in plaster and thus have presented about the same appearance as the stone examples. The compartment walls were not only of stone (fig. 18, f, g), but in addition a large amount of adobe plaster was used and the intervening spaces between the slabs was completely filled with that substance.

There was a niche in the wall of structure No. 9 like those described for Nos. 6 and 7. The niche was in the southwest corner, just back of the support post (fig. 18, l), and suggested that here also it was necessary to supply a brace to counteract a shifting of the roof framework. The niche in this case was higher in the wall than in the other chambers and more cylindrical in form. It appeared to have been dug in a shape that would conform to the contours of the timber.

The ventilator for No. 9 had a tunneled passage. The block of earth above the horizontal portion of the ventilator was of sufficient size and compactness to hold its form without extensive reinforcement and the pit was at a depth that would have required a considerable amount of digging had the passage been constructed by the trench and cover method. In view of this it would appear that the builders adopted the easiest method of procedure and simply tunneled a passage. The aperture had a stone sill (fig. 18, *j*) and a lintel of the same material. The sides of the opening were carefully plastered (pl. 10, *a*) at the outer end of the ventilator passage. The exact nature and size of the shaft was not determined because a large cedar tree was growing at approximately the place where it occurred and the information was not deemed of sufficient importance to warrant the destruction of the tree. The approximate location of the shaft was determined by cleaning out the passage and removing as much as possible of the debris that had collected in it. While exact measurements could not be obtained in this fashion the approximation was enough to suffice.

Only one pillar was left in removing the fill from the three structures. This was in the center of No. 10 and since the fill was the same in all three pits the material in the pillar will be discussed in connection with all of the houses as a single building.

Structure No. 9 had a diameter of 11 feet 1 inch (3.378 m) on the fire pit, ventilator line. Across the opposite way the distance from the north wall to a line drawn across between the two points that approximately designated the division between 9 and 10, was 11 feet 9 inches (3.581 m). At the ventilator side the original wall rose 3 feet 11½ inches (1.206 m) above the floor. Above this there was an accumulation of 10 inches (25.4 cm) of sand which increased the depth to 4 feet 9½ inches (1.460 m). At the opposite side of the chamber the wall was 3 feet 9½ inches (1.155 m) from the old ground level to the floor. The sand accumulation increased the depth of the pit to 5 feet 6½ inches (1.689 m) at the time of exacavation.

The poles for the support posts in this structure had a greater size variation than in some of the other chambers. That at the northwest corner of the room measured 8 inches (20.32 cm) and 9 inches (22.86 cm) in diameter. It had a depth of 1 foot (30.48 cm) and was 10 inches (25.4 cm) from the wall. The hole at the northeast corner had diameters of 6½ and 7 inches (16.51 and 17.78 cm). It was 9½ inches (24.13 cm) deep and was placed 10 inches (25.4 cm) from the wall. The diameters of the southeast hole were 6½ and 7 inches (16.51 and 17.78 cm). The hole was 4 inches (10.16 cm) from the wall and 1 foot 4 inches (40.64 cm) deep. The hole at the southwest corner was broken out on the floor level but near the bottom it was possible to obtain the diameters, which were 10 inches (25.4 cm) and 11 inches (27.94 cm). The hole had a depth of 1 foot 1 inch (33.02 cm) and it was 1 foot 6 inches (45.72 cm) from the wall.

The fire pit (fig. 18, c) measured 1 foot 7½ inches (49.53 cm) on the ventilator line and 1 foot 6½ inches (46.99 cm) in the opposite direction. The pit was 5 inches (12.7 cm) deep. The slabs which lined the three sides projected above the floor level from ¼ inch (6.35 mm) to 2 inches (5.08 cm). The probabilities are that when the structure was occupied the stones were covered with plaster and the discrepancies in their heights were compensated for by the plaster and the rim around the pit was practically level.

The sipapu (fig. 18, b) was 2 feet 1 inch (63.5 cm) from the fire pit and 3 feet 8½ inches (1.130 m) from the wall. The hole was oval in form with diameters of 4½ inches (11.43 cm) and 3½ inches (8.99 cm). It was 6 inches (15.24 cm) deep.

The storage hole in the floor south of the fire pit (fig. 18, i) had a diameter of 3 inches (7.62 cm) and a depth of 2½ inches (6.35 cm). The holes in the floor where small poles had been set near the compartment (fig. 18, e) had diameters of 3½ inches (8.89 cm) and a depth of 6 inches (15.24 cm).

The stones forming facings for the ends of the low compartment walls were approximately the same size. The one at the end of the north wall was 10½ inches (26.67 cm) long and 2 inches (5.08 cm) wide. That at the end of the south wall was 10 inches (25.4 cm) long and 2 inches (5.08 cm) thick. The one on the north wall was 5½ inches (13.97 cm) in height and the other was 4¼ inches (10.79 cm). The space between them measured 11 inches (27.94 cm). The stones used in forming the bin ranged from 6 inches (15.24 cm) to 1 foot 1 inch (33.02 cm) in length, from 5½ inches (13.97 cm) to 1 foot 7 inches (48.26 cm) in height, and 1 inch (2.54 cm) to 3 inches (7.62 cm) in thickness. The adobe ridge in which they were set averaged 5 inches (12.7 cm) in height. In front of the ventilator aperture the end of the north partition was 2 feet 2 inches (66.04 cm) from the wall, and that of the south, 2 feet 3 inches (68.58 cm) from the opening.

The ventilator opening measured 1 foot 1 inch (33.02 cm) in width and was 1 foot 1 inch (33.02 cm) in height. The sill was 3½ inches (8.89 cm) above the floor. The passage had a length of 1 foot 10 inches (55.88 cm), was 11 inches (27.94 cm) high, and 1 foot 2 inches (35.56 cm) wide where it entered the shaft. The shaft was approximately 2 feet (60.96 cm) in diameter.

Structure No. 10 had only two walls, one where the ventilator opened into the chamber and the other at the opposite side. Where the additional sides of the pit would normally have been the structure opened into Nos. 9 and 11. The division line between Nos. 10 and 9 was indicated by the juncture of the curving east-and-west walls of the two pits, but it was not a distinct boundary between the rooms.

The floor was continuous and showed clearly that it had been laid as a single operation, as it extended from one chamber into the other. In the plan (fig. 19) a boundary between structures 9 and 10 has been indicated by a dotted line. At the opposite side of the chamber there was a differentiation in rooms. The floor of No. 10 was

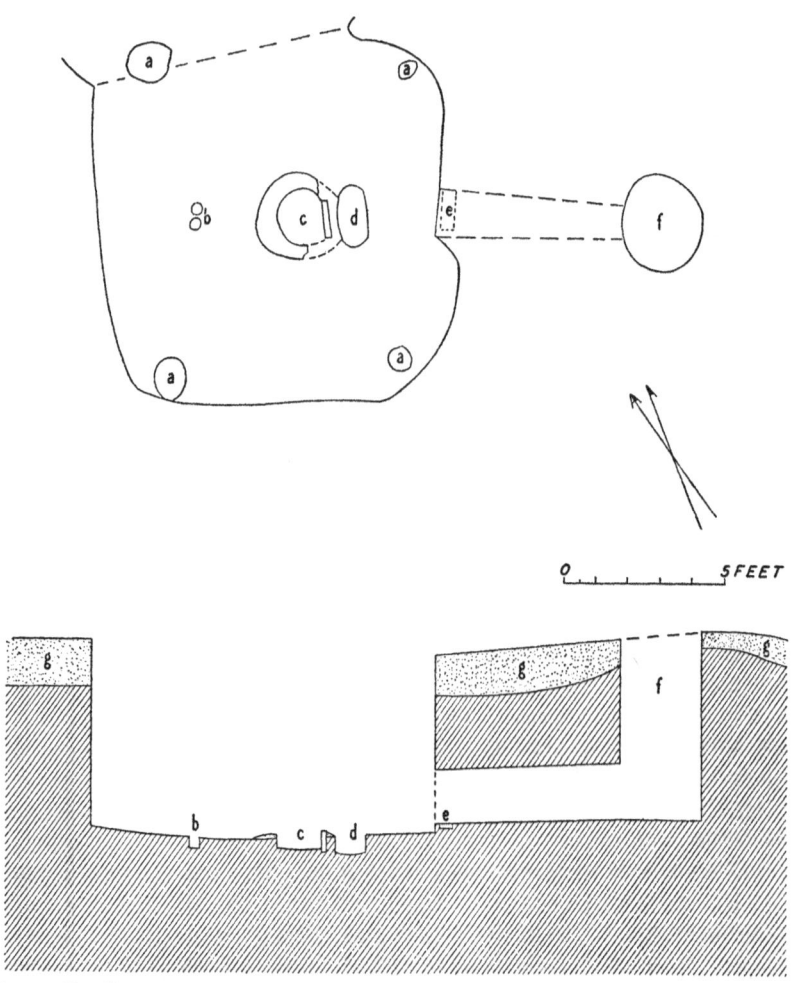

FIGURE 19.—Structure 10. *a*, holes for support posts; *b*, sipapu; *c*, fire pit; *d*, ladder box; *e*, ventilator opening; *f*, ventilator shaft; *g*, accumulation of sand above original surface.

distinct from that of No. 11 because the latter was at a higher level and as a consequence formed a line of demarcation between the two chambers.

The interior features of structure No. 10 were very simple. There were the four holes for support posts, one of which, that at the north, really fell within the limits of house No. 9. Near the center of the room was a fire pit and ladder box and two sipapu holes. There were no other depressions in the floor and there was no deflector in front of the ventilator opening. The superstructure supported on the four main posts probably had a flat ceiling and sloping poles on two sides. At the ends where there were no walls the roof was probably constructed in the manner suggested in the discussion of No. 9, namely, timbers were extended from the rectangular frameworks in each adjacent structure across the intervening space to the frame in No. 10 to form a flat ceiling above the sides where the sloping walls would normally have been. Small poles were undoubtedly slanted from these beams to the ground so that the superstructure presented an unbroken exterior surface.

The fire pit in the center of room No. 10 was roughly circular in form (fig. 19, c). It had been dug into the earth floor and its sides and bottom were faced with adobe plaster. Encircling it on the floor level was a rim of plaster that increased the depth and served as a coping to protect the edges of the pit. A stone slab was embedded in the face of the pit at the side toward the ladder box. This no doubt functioned as a reinforcement to prevent damage which might be caused by the ladder or people using it. At first it was thought that the stone originally was of sufficient height to serve as a deflector, but this did not seem to be the case. Had it extended some distance above the top of the adobe ridge it would have formed a deflector similar to the one embedded in the plaster rim around the pit in structure No. 7. That it had done so can not be assumed from the evidence in the pit, despite the fact the top of the stone suggested that it might have broken off.

The ladder box (fig. 19, d) was a simple oval-shaped depression adjoining the fire pit. Its sides and bottom were plastered. The bottom and one edge, where the base ends of the ladder poles had rested, were roughened and broken.

In the floor midway between the fire pit and the west wall of the chamber were two circular holes (fig. 19, b) occupying the position where the sipapu is normally found. It was not possible to tell which of the two had been intended for the sipapu. Both were carefully finished and there was little difference in their diameters and depths. Because of this both have been considered as sipapus.

The ventilator was similar to those previously described, although the passage was somewhat longer than in some of the other structures and the shaft at the outer end was nearly circular in form. The passage was of the tunneled type. Where it opened into the chamber a stone slab was embedded in the floor to form a sill. The floor of the passage sloped slightly upward to the bottom of the shaft. This slant was almost imperceptible to the eye and became apparent only when the section through the room was made with leveling instruments.

The pit of structure No. 10 measured 10 feet 6 inches (3.2 m) from wall to wall on the line passing through the ventilator, fire pit, and sipapu. Between the raised floor level separating Nos. 10 and 11 and a line drawn between the two points where the arcs of the walls for Nos. 9 and 10 intersected, the room measured 10 feet 5 inches (3.175 m). At the ventilator side of the chamber the pit had a depth of 4 feet 1½ inches (1.257 m) below the old ground level and 5 feet 4 inches (1.625 m) below the present ground level. At the opposite side of the room the floor was 4 feet 2½ inches (1.282 m) below the ground level at the time of occupation. From the present level to the floor was 5 feet 7½ inches (1.714 m).

The hole for the north support post had diameters of 1 foot 2 inches (35.56 cm) and 1 foot 4 inches (40.64 cm). The hole was 1 foot 2 inches (35.56 cm) from the point where the walls of Nos. 9 and 10 intersected. The hole for the east support post had diameters of 8 inches (20.32 cm) and 6 inches (15.24 cm). It had a depth of 1 foot 5½ inches (44.45 cm) and was placed 1½ inches (3.81 cm) from the wall. The hole at the south corner of the room had diameters of 9 inches (22.86 cm) and 8 inches (20.32 cm) and was 4 inches (10.16 cm) from the wall. The hole near the west corner of the chamber touched the floor of structure No. 11. It had diameters of 1 foot 3 inches (38.1 cm) and 11 inches (27.94 cm). It was 7 inches (17.78 cm) from the corner of the room and had a depth of 1 foot 4½ inches (41.91 cm).

The fire pit (fig. 19, c) in No. 10 had a diameter of 1 foot 5 inches (43.18 cm) on the ventilator line. At right angles to this measurement the pit was 1 foot 8½ inches (52.07 cm) across. At the ventilator side the bottom of the pit was 4 inches (10.16 cm) below the floor, and at the opposite side was 3 inches (7.62 cm) below that level. This depth, however, was increased by the adobe rim which encircled the pit. The average height of the rim was 1½ inches (3.81 cm). The width of the ridge varied from 5 inches (12.7 cm) to 8½ inches (21.59 cm). The stone set in the face of the pit at the ventilator side was 1 foot 1½ inches (34.29 cm) long, 2½ inches (6.35 cm) wide, and 8 inches (20.32 cm) high.

The space between the fire pit and the ladder pit was 5½ inches (13.97 cm). The ladder pit (fig. 19, d) was 1 foot 10 inches (55.88 cm) long, 11 inches (27.94 cm) wide, and 6 inches (15.24 cm) deep. From the edge of the ladder pit to the ventilator opening was 2 feet 2 inches (66.04 cm).

The sipapu, or rather two holes which may have functioned in that capacity (fig. 19, b), were 1 foot 9 inches (53.34 cm) from the edge of the fire pit rim and 2 feet 11 inches (88.9 cm) from the wall at that side of the chamber. The one at the north had a depth of 4½ inches (11.43 cm) and the other was 6½ inches (16.51 cm) deep. The holes were 1 inch (2.54 cm) apart.

The ventilator opening was 1 foot 3½ inches (39.37 cm) wide and 1 foot 7½ inches (49.53 cm) high. The stone slab which formed the sill for the opening was 1 foot 3 inches (38.1 cm) long, 5 inches (12.7 cm) wide, and 1½ inches (3.81 cm) thick. The passage had a length of 5 feet 9 inches (1.752 m). It was 1 foot 1 inch (33.02 cm) wide where it opened into the shaft and was 1 foot 8 inches (50.8 cm) high. The shaft had diameters of 2 feet 6 inches (76.2 cm) and 2 feet 10 inches (86.36 cm) at the passage side. The original depth was 4 feet 7½ inches (1.409 m) and the depth at the time of excavation was 5 feet 5 inches (1.651 m), the increase being due to sand accumulation on the surface. At the back of the shaft the original depth was 5 feet 2 inches (1.574 m) and the present depth 5 feet 8½ inches (1.739 m).

Structure No. 11 was somewhat more elaborate than No. 10 and in this respect corresponded better to No. 9. The pit was quite irregular in shape (fig. 20). The west wall was roughly crescentic in contour, but the east was decidedly uneven. The south side was comparatively straight, although of course there were rounded corners. At the north the chamber opened into structure No. 10. As in the case of the other rooms there were the holes for the four posts upon which the superstructure had rested. The covering was probably like that suggested for No. 9. It was typical of the flat ceiling, sloping-sided type except where it opened into room 10. As previously suggested, there possibly was a flat roof between the main frameworks of Nos. 10 and 11 and slanting poles were placed at either side to fill in the space between the ceiling and the walls of the excavation.

The interior features of structure No. 11 (fig. 20) were fairly complete. Near the center of the chamber was a slab-lined fire pit, and at the ventilator side were the remains of a compartment similar to the one described for Nos. 1 and 9 (pl. 10, *b*). At the center of the room were two holes in the floor, either one of which might have functioned as a sipapu. They were not in the same position, however, with respect to each other as those in No. 10. There was no deflector and no ladder pit in this structure.

The fire pit (fig. 20, *e*) had been dug into the surface of the floor to a depth which corresponded with that of the pits in other houses. The walls of this excavation were then lined with blocks of stone which were covered with adobe plaster. The plaster extended over the faces of the stone and down across the bottom of the pit. Both of the holes near the fire pit in the approximate position of the sipapu had been carefully plastered (fig. 20, *c*, *d*).

Only the stone portion of the wall which formed the compartment at the ventilator side of the room was in position when the house was cleared of the debris which had accumulated in it. Some of the slabs were found lying where they had fallen and grooves in the floor gave evidence that there had been additional ones. All of the plaster that had been placed between and over the stones had slumped away as a result of moisture. There seems little question but what there was a complete partition at that side of the chamber, except for a space at the center between the fire pit and ventilator opening where there was a doorway. A metate was in the north end of the compartment. In this connection it will be recalled that there were two

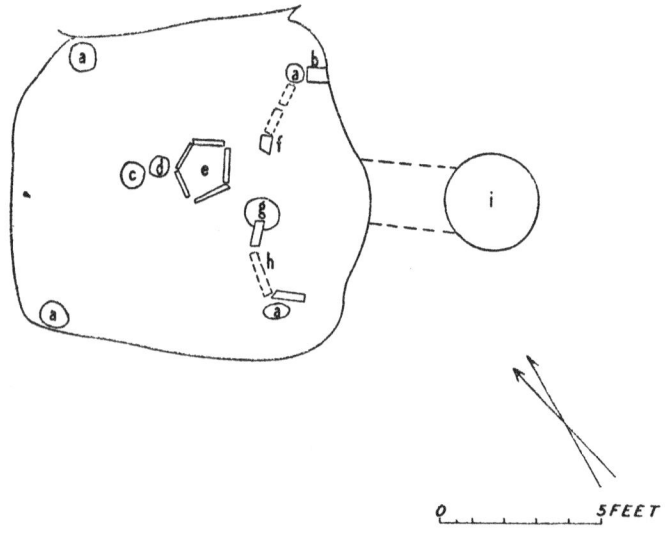

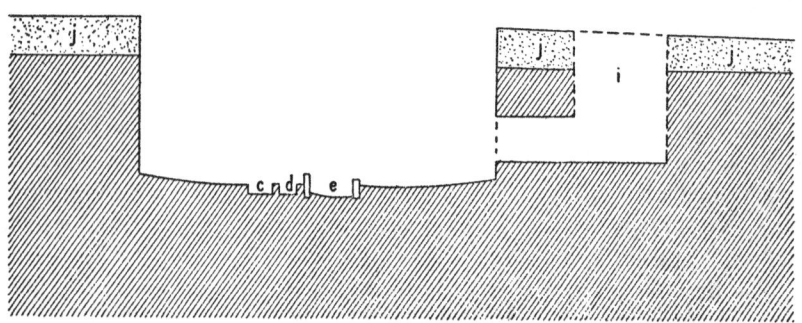

FIGURE 20.—Structure 11. *a*, holes for main support posts; *b*, stone in compartment wall; *c* and *d*, holes in floor in position of sipapu; *e*, fire pit; *f*, stone in compartment wall; *g*, storage basin; *h*, stone mold; *i*, ventilator shaft; *j*, accumulation of sand above original surface.

milling stones in the bin in structure 1. That in No. 11 had been placed against the wall of the compartment but the collapse of the latter had permitted it to fall to the floor.

The floor space for No. 11 was distinct from that of Nos. 9 and 10 inasmuch as it was at a higher level (fig. 21). In this respect it corresponded to the relationship between structures 6 and 7 where a difference in levels was also noted.

The ventilator was of the tunneled form. As in the case of some other examples there was a slight although almost imperceptible upward slant to the passage floor. The shaft at the outer end was damaged and it was impossible to obtain full information concerning its character. It apparently was almost circular in form and rather large when compared with some of the others, but beyond this nothing could be ascertained.

The pit for No. 11 measured 11 feet 1 inch (3.378 m) on the sipapu, fire pit, ventilator line. At right angles to this measurement there were 9 feet 10½ inches (3.009 m) between the south wall and the edge of the floor between Nos. 10 and 11. At the ventilator side of the chamber the floor was 3 feet 5 inches (1.041 m) below the old ground level and 4 feet 7 inches (1.397 m) below the present surface. At the opposite side of the room the pit had a depth of 3 feet 7 inches (1.092 m) below the surface at the time of occupation. The present ground level is 4 feet 9 inches (1.477 m) above the floor.

As was the case in some of the other structures, there was considerable variation in the size of the holes in which the main support posts were set. The hole at the north corner of the chamber had diameters of 11 inches (27.94 cm) and 10 inches (25.4 cm). The depth was 1 foot 4 inches (40.64 cm) and the edge of the hole was 2½ inches (6.35 cm) from the wall. The east hole had diameters of 6 inches (15.24 cm) and 7 inches (17.78 cm). It had a depth of 1 foot 3 inches (38.1 cm) and was 9½ inches (24.13 cm) from the wall. The south hole was decidedly oval in form, with diameters of 9½ inches (24.13 cm) and 5½ inches (13.97 cm). The hole was 1 foot (30. 48 cm) deep and was placed 1 foot 2½ inches (36.83 cm) from the wall. The west hole had diameters of 9 inches (22.86 cm) and 10 inches (25.4 cm). The depth was 1 foot 1 inch (33.02 cm), and the distance between the edge of the hole and the wall of the chamber measured 1 inch (2.54 cm).

The fire pit (fig. 20, *e*) measured 1 foot 4½ inches (41.91 cm) on the ventilator line. In the opposite direction its greatest width was 1 foot 7 inches (48.26 cm). The pit had a depth of 6 inches (15.24 cm).

The two holes in the floor at the west side of the fire pit were closer to the pit than ordinarily was found to be the case. The first, or one immediately adjacent (fig. 20, *d*), was only 2½ inches (6.35 cm) from the fire pit. The hole had diameters of 8½ inches (21.59 cm) and 7 inches (17.78 cm). The depth was 4½ inches (11.43 cm). The second hole (fig. 20, *c*), was 2 inches (5.08 cm) from the first, 1 foot 1 inch (33.02 cm) from the fire pit, and 3 feet 5 inches (1.041 m) from the wall of the room. It had diameters of

9 inches (22.86 cm) and 9½ inches (24.13 cm). Its depth was 3½ inches (8.89 cm).

The only depression in the floor, in addition to the fire pit and the two holes near it, was located at the north end of the south partition wall (fig. 20, *g*). The diameters of the hole were 1 foot 1 inch (33.02 cm) and 11 inches (27.94 cm). The depth was 4 inches (10.16 cm).

The stones employed in the construction of the low wall forming the compartment varied in size. The one standing between the east support and the wall of the chamber (fig. 20, *b*) was 8 inches (20.32 cm) long, 5 inches (12.7 cm) wide, and 1 foot 4 inches (40.64 cm) high. The space between the end of the slab and the edge of the hole for the post measured 1 inch (2.54 cm). The only slab remaining in position between the hole for the east post and the passage way between the fire pit and the ventilator opening (fig. 20, *f*)

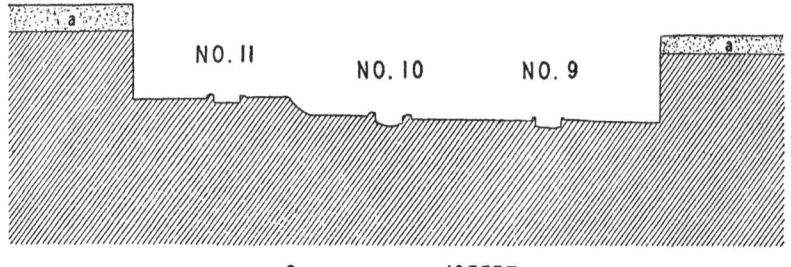

FIGURE 21.—Section through structures 9, 10, and 11. *a*, accumulation of drifts and above old surface.

was 6 inches (15.24 cm) long, 4 inches (10.16 cm) wide, and 1 foot 3 inches (38.1 cm) high. The stone that had stood between this one and the east support post had a length of 1 foot 9 inches (53.34 cm), a width of 7 inches (17.78 cm), and a thickness of 3 inches (7.62 cm). The opening in the center of the partition wall measured 1 foot 11 inches (58.42 cm). The north stone in the south portion of the partition was 9 inches (22.86 cm) long, 3½ inches (8.89 cm) thick, and its top was 1 foot 1 inch (33.02 cm) above the floor. The next stone stood 2 inches (5.08 cm) from the preceding one. It was the largest in the group, with a length of 1 foot 4 inches (40.64 cm), a thickness of 3½ inches (8.89 cm), and a height of 1 foot 7 inches (48.26 cm). This stone had slumped out of position but the place where it originally stood was plainly evident (fig. 20, *h*). The next stone in the group was separated from the one just described by a space of only 1 inch (2.54 cm). This slab had a length of 1 foot (30.48 cm), a thickness of 2½ inches (6.35 cm), and stood 1 foot 6 inches (45.72 cm) above the floor.

The ventilator opening was 1 foot 8¾ inches (52.71 cm) wide at the bottom. At the top it measured 1 foot 4 inches (40.64 cm). The height of the aperture was 1 foot 4½ inches (41.91 cm). The sill of the opening was 6½ inches (16.51 cm) above the floor. The passage was 2 feet 5 inches (73.66 cm) long. The shaft at the outer end was approximately 2 feet 11 inches (88.9 cm) in diameter. The original depth of the shaft was 2 feet 10 inches (86.36 cm), and at the time of excavation the floor was 3 feet 11 inches (1.193 m) below the ground level.

The pillar left in the center of structure No. 10 to facilitate a study of the fill in the pits had a height of 5 feet 2 inches (1.574 m). There were 8 distinct strata in the pillar and the material contained in each layer was quite dissimilar in character to that in the others (pl. 11, *a*). The first stratum at the top consisted of rather coarse, clean yellow sand that apparently had been carried into the pit by wind action. The layer was somewhat uneven, as the diagram (fig. 22, *a*) shows. A shallow ditch ran through the top of the fill along the line that approximately cut the group of three structures through the longitudinal center. This may be attributed to the fact that the pits were located on the side of the ridge where there was a double slope, one extending from the west walls of the chambers toward the ventilator sides of the structure and the other from No. 11 toward No. 9. The original ground level at the north side of No. 9 was somewhat lower than that at the south side of No. 11 (fig. 21). In addition, there originally had been a second ridge just beyond the series of ventilator shafts. At the time when the houses were occupied there was a small gully between the edges of the ventilator shafts and the slope of the second ridge. It no doubt carried away all surface drainage from around the structures. After they were abandoned, fell into decay, and the pits had become filled with accumulated debris, the wind shifted sand across the site and piled it up against the ridge to the east. As a result its western slope was extended until it covered the old ventilator shafts and shifted the drainage channel, for the small area involved, several feet. It then passed over the subterranean portion of the houses, cutting the gutter indicated in layer *a* in the central face in the group of three shown in the diagram (fig. 22). That this took place subsequent to the abandonment of the site was indicated by the fact that there were no potsherds, bone fragments, stone chips, or charcoal in the layer. Layer *a* varied in thickness from 6 inches (15.24 cm) at the center of the ditch to 1 inch (2.54 cm) at the corner of the pillar. The thinnest portion was at the east side where there was an upward slope toward the east ridge beyond the ends of the ventilators.

The second layer in the pillar (fig. 22, *b*) was composed of discolored sand mixed with a considerable amount of humus. This layer also appeared to be subsequent to the occupation of the site. Presumably there had been considerable vegetation on the surface of b for a fairly long period of time prior to the deposition of the top stratum of clean sand. This vegetation with the attendant decay of the plant matter was what gave the color to the sand and was responsible for the humus content. As will be seen from the drawing (fig. 22, b), this layer was somewhat irregular in outline. It was thickest on the west side and as in the case of the upper layer sloped upward toward the east. The stratum ranged in thickness from 6½ inches (16.51 cm) to 1 foot (30.48 cm).

Stratum c was of interest because it was not continuous throughout the course of the three pits, in an east-and-west direction. It occurred as a lens extending from north to south along the east

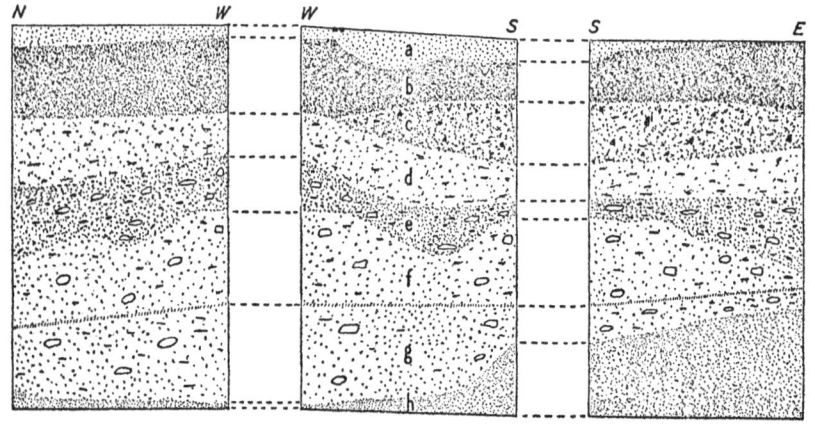

FIGURE 22.—Test pillar from fill in structure 10. N, W, S, and E, indicate north, west, south, and east corners.

side of the fill. The material apparently washed into the pits. The layer immediately below had been deposited with a pronounced downward slope toward the eastern edge, and c evened up the surface of the fill. It extended across from approximately the high point on d, the stratum below, to the east edge of the excavation. Stratum c contained some fragments of charcoal, some ash-bearing sand, and occasional nodules of adobe. In its general appearance it was somewhat darker than the stratum immediately above. From the point where it coincided with stratum d, layer c expanded to a depth of 10 inches (25.4 cm) at the south side of the pillar and narrowed to 6 inches (15.24 cm) at the east side. At the west side of the pillar strata b and d touched.

Stratum d was composed of light-colored sand containing occasional fragments of charcoal but no ashes. There were no indications of human handicrafts, such as worked bones, stones, or pottery fragments. As in the case of the two upper layers and the lens c, stratum d apparently was deposited at a time when there was little, if any, activity about the site. At the west side of the pillar this stratum measured 7 inches (17.78 cm) thick. Near the center it increased to 10 inches (25.4 cm) and at the east side narrowed to 5¾ inches (14.61 cm).

Stratum e was of particular interest because it consisted mainly of refuse material such as is deposited around an occupied site, and in addition had a long oval depression through its center somewhat similar to the drainage channel described for the first level. As a matter of fact, it would be more appropriate to say the top layer of stratum f contained the hollow and that the refuse material comprising stratum e had been deposited in the depression and over the general surface surrounding it. Stratum e consisted largely of ash-bearing sand with a heavy content of charcoal. In addition, bone fragments, potsherds, and stone chips and spalls were abundant. This material was unquestionably waste matter from a habitation. Stratum e was thickest at the east side where it measured 1 foot (30.48 cm) in depth, and was thinnest at the south corner where there was only 3 inches (7.62 cm) of material. The channel or ditch in the center gave that portion of the stratum a thickness of 8 inches (20.32 cm).

The next layer, stratum f, was composed chiefly of clean sand with sporadic fragments of charcoal and a few pieces of sandstone. There were no ashes, no bone, nor stone chips, such as resulted from the manufacture of stone implements, and potsherds. The layer as a whole gave the impression of a natural deposit that had accumulated from the action of wind and water. The layer had drifted from the southern end into the elongated depression caused by the pits and tapered off toward the north and east where the thinnest portion occurred. It was in the top of this layer that the hollow discussed in connection with stratum e occurred. Stratum f ranged in depth from 3 inches (7.62 cm) to 1 foot 2 inches (35.56 cm).

Stratum g was practically identical with f insofar as content was concerned. The distinction between the two was based on a thin layer of compact clay and sand that had formed the top surface of g prior to the deposition of f. The narrowest portion of g was at the east side of the pillar. Unlike f, there were no indications of a channel across the surface of g. No doubt this may be attributed to the fact that it was at a sufficient depth below the portion of the house pits to prevent a flow of water across its surface. Any water which ran into the pits at this period would of necessity have to remain there. The greatest depth in the stratum was found toward the south of the fill. Its surface sloped downward toward the north and upward toward the east. At the southwest corner of the pillar the deposit measured 1 foot 4 inches (40.64 cm). At the east side it was only 3 inches (7.62 cm) deep, and at the north 10 inches (25.4 cm).

The lowest layer in the fill, stratum h, consisted of clean sand that gave evidence of having been deposited by wind and water action. The sand was a distinct yellow in color. The line of demarcation between the top of h and the bottom of g was very distinct. Stratum h contained no traces of human presence, except at the very bottom which was the floor of the houses and where a few potsherds and some implements were found. The outstanding feature of the deposit was that it reached its greatest depth along the east side of the fill and was little more than perceptible at the west side. In addition, it sloped slightly upward toward the north. In other words, the first material that found its way into the pits where structures 9, 10, and 11 had been was banked up against the east and north walls of the series of three connected excavations. This would suggest that at the time of the deposition of this part of the fill the prevailing wind had been from the southwest, blowing the material against those two sides. Stratum h ranged in thickness from 1½ inches (3.81 cm) along the west wall to 1 foot 6 inches (45.72 cm) at the east.

From the data present in the fill of structures 9, 10, and 11, it is apparent that the pits were used as a dumping place for waste material from habitations at only one time during the interval in which the excavations were being filled to the ground level. This took place at about the middle period, as the refuse-bearing stratum was practically midway in the pillar. This evidence seems to warrant the conclusion that for some time after the combined structures were abandoned the area immediately adjacent to them was unoccupied, since no signs of human endeavor found their way into the pits. Then for a certain period people dwelt nearby and used the pits for a dumping place. When this ceased the depressions continued to fill in a natural manner with no assistance from human hands. The potsherd evidence obtained from stratum e indicates that the refuse material may be closely correlated with the remains of the small surface structure to the west of the group. This also demonstrates that the three pit structures preceded the surface house and probably represent an earlier stage in the development of the local cultural pattern.

The combination of three structures into one large dwelling shows an interesting development in the matter of house construction and thus far in the Southwest this group constitutes the only example of such a procedure. As previously mentioned, the early inhabitants of the district included in the Long H Ranch, some 42 miles (67.592 k) southwest from the Allantown site, grouped their pit houses in clusters of three but made no attempt to actually join them into one large structure.[42] Another example mentioned was that of Martin's houses in southern Colorado.[43] Significant features in the combination of structures 9, 10, and 11, as well as in 6 and 7, were that despite the fact that one long, narrow room was obtained, the units that went into its make-up were individually complete (pl. 11, b). This may be considered as an indication that the people were ready to combine their houses, but that they were not yet at the stage where they were willing to give up house characteristics that had long been present in the single dwellings.

Another factor of some importance is raised by this evidence of the joining together of three structures. In the early days of southwestern archeology a theory became fairly well established to the effect that the rectangular-roomed communal buildings of the Pueblo people developed out of the practice of combining a number of circular houses into one large structure and the subsequent discovery that a better building could be erected if the walls of the chambers were straight instead of curved.[44] Later work, particularly in the more northern parts of the area, contributed evidence which went against this theory and demonstrated that the rectangular house developed before the practice of combining many chambers into one large building.[45] If the present two groups comprising structures 6, 7, 9, 10, and 11 constitute a prototype for the communal building erected above ground in later cultural horizons it is evident that in this particular district the evolution of the house followed a different course from that observed for the more northern parts of the area. Furthermore, it would indicate that the old theory was not after all entirely wrong. However, the Allantown site contains one group of structures that seems to offer an example of a more logical step in house development. Because of this, the facts would suggest that the groups of combined pit structures, one containing two houses and the other three, were peculiar local developments that did not have a direct bearing on the subject of communal houses in general. They had a limited development, possibly the culmination of a purely local trend, that apparently had no influence whatever on subsequent Pueblo structures.

At first consideration it would seem that the problem of erecting a superstructure over three pits combined in the manner of Nos. 9, 10, and 11 would be a difficult undertaking. As a matter of fact,

---
[42] Roberts, 1931, fig. 1, pp. 25-40.
[43] Martin, 1930, pp. 29-33, pl. VII, fig. 2.
[44] Cushing, 1896.
[45] Roberts, 1929, p. 147; 1930, p. 62.

the construction probably was quite simple and would have been easier to accomplish had the builders not retained as far as possible all of the characteristics of individual and separate dwellings. The presence of four upright support posts in each chamber would materially strengthen the roof, but the covering could have been constructed with four less posts had the builders made two serve, instead of four, at each opening between the chambers. The rectangular frameworks placed on the upright posts in each chamber probably carried flat ceilings over the central portion and no doubt supported smaller poles whose upper ends rested against the main stringers and whose base ends rested upon the ground back of the edges of the pit (fig. 23). In this respect the superstructure would in general have been similar to those erected over single pits. The only place where a difference would have occurred was at the sides where the chambers opened into each other and here, as previously mentioned, there probably was an extension of the flat portion of each roof by means of timbers laid across the opening from chamber to chamber. Small poles bridged the space between these and the ground. While the postulated method of construction, as shown in figure 23, probably errs in minor details, it is thought that in general the reconstruction is fairly accurate and should give a good idea of the superstructure framework erected over the three pits.

SURFACE HOUSE B AND GRANARIES

Surface house B was located 23 feet 6 inches (7.162 m) west of the Nos. 9-11 group, and its south end was 4 feet (1.219 m) from the 6-8 structures (fig. 13). As in the case of surface house A, little remained of B. There were only a few courses of stone in position above the foundation and portions of the east and south walls were entirely missing. There was some question at the time of excavation as to whether or not the walls actually represented the remains of a house or indicated an enclosed court which had low walls and was without a roof. The absence of building stones in the debris suggested that the walls had not risen to any great height. On the other hand, it is possible, as was mentioned in the discussion of surface house A, that the building was stone-robbed at the time when the large Pueblo structures were erected, the builders making use of all available material in the vicinity. The stones used in laying these walls were only partially shaped for building purposes. The faces were not carefully dressed and the blocks were irregular in form.

If structure B was originally a house it consisted of a building containing only one long narrow room (fig. 24). There were no indications of walls or partitions. It is possible that the interior may have been separated into smaller chambers through the medium of wattle-

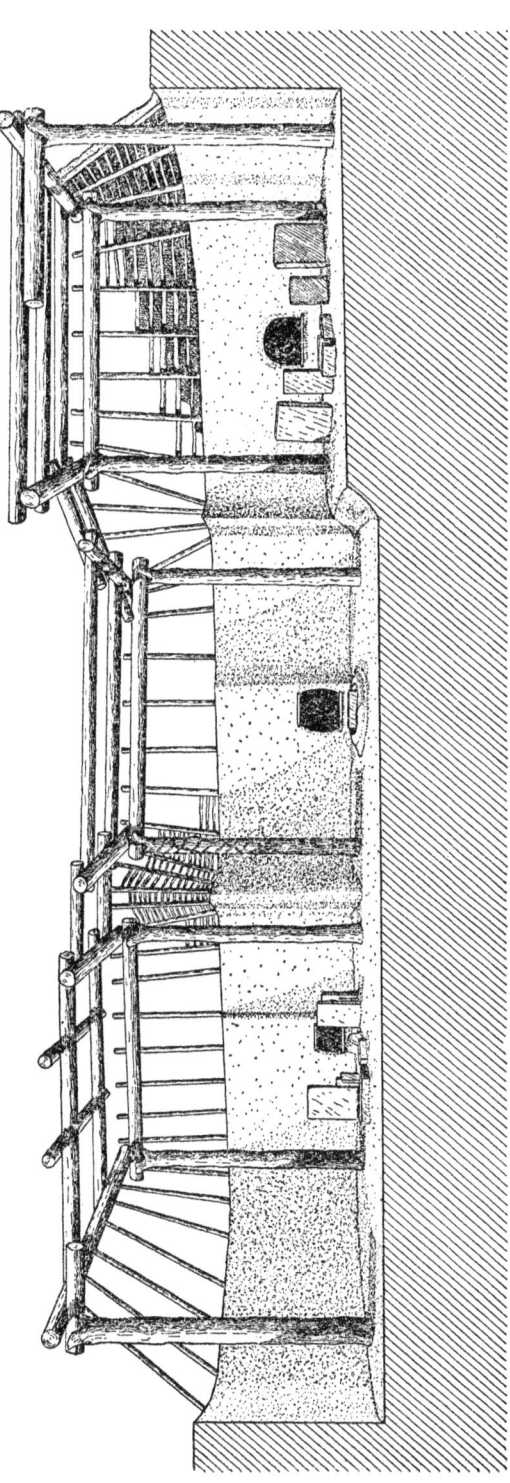

FIGURE 23.—Postulated reconstruction of timber arrangement in superstructure erected over pits 9, 10, and 11. Some of main support posts omitted at front of drawing to show construction more clearly.

and-daub walls, but if they were ever present no traces of them remained.

At the south end of the masonry walls were the remains of a storage cist (fig. 24, a). This cist was roughly rectangular in form, judging by what remained of it, and although the sides were fairly straight the corners were rounded. This place probably was a granary in which corn was stored. Just what type of superstructure was erected over it is not known. Possibly a framework of poles and brush was placed over it and the exterior surface was covered with plaster. The main timbers probably sloped from the ground level

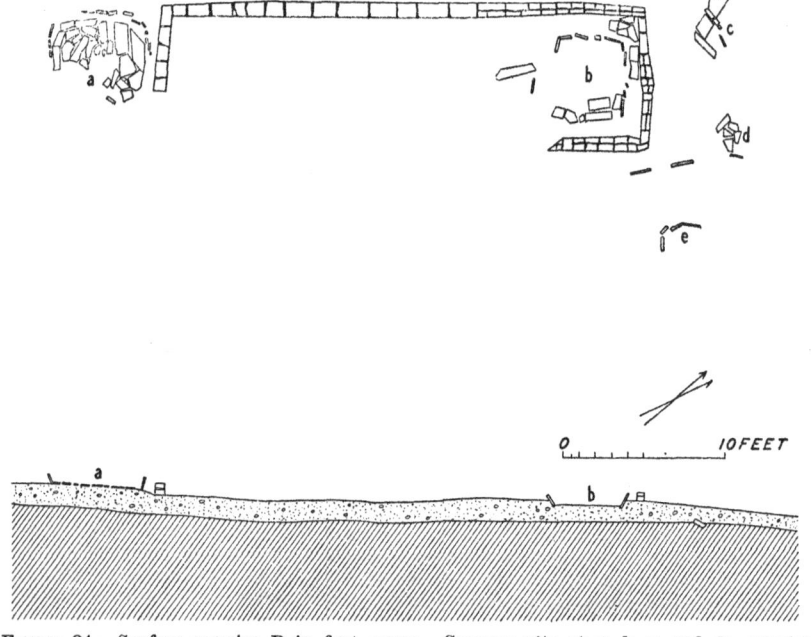

FIGURE 24.—Surface remains B in first group. Granary pits at a, b, c, and d; exterior fire pit at e.

to a point directly over the center of the cist where they joined. This would have formed a conical-shaped structure that in general appearance would have been not unlike the present-day sweat houses of the Navajos. Granaries of similar construction have been found in various portions of the Southwest, some of them practically intact.[46]

Because of this it seems logical to postulate that the method of construction in the present case was similar. The floor of the granary was paved with large slabs and around its periphery additional stones were set up on edge to make a low wall. A portion of the

---

[46] Morris, 1925, p. 270.

floor and bounding wall at the east side was missing but the major outline was present.

Within the inclosure formed by the rectangular wall were the remains of a similar cist (fig. 24, b). If the surface structure had been a house it is hard to explain why a granary had been built within it. On the other hand, it is possible that the feature in the north end of the structure does not represent such a granary but merely a slab-lined depression in the floor which served either for storage purposes or as a mealing bin.

Outside the inclosure at the north end was what remained of two additional cists (fig. 24, c, d). In addition, there was an exterior fire pit 5 feet (1.524 m) from the northeast corner of the masonry walls (fig. 24, e).

In general it may be said that the surface remains at this portion of the site corresponded in age to the group designated surface house A. They gave evidence of being later than the nearby pit structures 6, 7, 8, 9, 10, and 11. This was demonstrated by the fact that the foundations of the stone walls and the granaries were at a higher level than the surface of occupation at the time when the pit structures were inhabited. This is shown by the section through the building (fig. 24).

The masonry inclosure was 29 feet 10 inches (9.093 m) long and 8 feet 8 inches (2.641 m) wide, outside measurement. Inside the walls the length was 28 feet 8 inches (8.737 m) and the width 7 feet 3 inches (2.209 m). The average height of the remaining stones was 1 foot 6 inches (45.72 cm). The storage bin at the south end of the structure measured 6 feet (1.828 m) across. The upright slabs around the sides had an average height of 9 inches (22.86 cm). The north wall of the granary was 5 inches (12.7 cm) from the south wall of the masonry structure. The bin in the north end of the masonry inclosure measured 4 feet 2 inches (1.270 m) by 6 feet (1.828 m). Its floor was 6 inches (15.24 cm) lower than that of the inclosure. The slabs which bordered the pit had an average height of 1 foot (30.48 cm).

Located along the top of the ridge southwest from surface house B was a group of three granary pits (fig. 13). These pits were situated 21 feet 3 inches (6.477 m) from the surface remains and were 14 feet 6 inches (4.419 m) from pit structure No. 8. Two of the pits were roughly oval in form while the third was definitely rectangular. Two of the pits had slab facings on their walls while the third merely had a coating of plaster. All three had been destroyed by fire and there were large quantities of charred corn in them. Indications were that the upper portion of these structures had been of pole, brush, and plaster construction, such as that described for the granary *a*, in connection with surface house B. Great chunks of plaster burned to a bricklike consistency were found in the pits. These blocks of fired clay bore the imprints of the poles and brush upon which they had rested. A few potsherds found in the fill of the pits indicated that they had been contemporaneous with the semisubterranean structures rather than with the surface remains.

The two oval structures had diameters of 5 feet 11 inches and 5 feet 3 inches (1.803 and 1.600 m), and 3 feet 8 inches and 4 feet (1.117 and 1.219 m). The rectangular structure measured 5 feet feet 10 inches by 5 feet 9 inches (1.778 by 1.752 m). The depths varied. The northernmost pit in the group had an average depth of 8 inches (20.32 cm), the rectangular one had a depth of 1 foot (30.48 cm), and the southernmost of the group was 1 foot 6 inches (45.72 cm) in depth.

GROUP No. 2

STRUCTURE 12

Structure 12 was the first of the remains uncovered in the second group. It is located along the edge of the ridge north of the Great Pueblo ruins and at a considerable distance from the group discussed in preceding pages (fig. 25). A large portion of the east wall had been carried away by erosion, but the damage was not sufficient to destroy all the evidence essential to a reconstruction of the structure. The pit was much deeper than in many of the other examples and for that reason the major outline of the subterranean portion of the structure was still intact. Structure 12 was the largest of the entire group and differed from the others in that it had a bench encircling the upper borders of the pit. The pit was definitely D-shaped and more regular in outline than the majority of the excavations (fig. 26). The back of the bench was not as uniform as the main wall of the chamber but nevertheless conformed rather closely to its perimeter.

The superstructure erected over this pit was different from the types previously described. Because of the size of the pit additional timbers were needed to cover it. There had been four main support posts placed in the floor near the corners of the chamber. In addition there was a series of posts around the back of the bench. These also seemed to have functioned in a support capacity. Three of them were actually present and there were indications of a fourth where a portion of the bench had been carried away. Along the eastern and southern sides too much of the bench was missing to enable definite determination that such posts had been present. On the basis of the distances between those found it may be suggested that there were possibly two more—one near the east corner and one at the south. This would have made a total of six for the structure.

The timber portions of the roof had been destroyed by fire and as a consequence there were large sections of charred beams scattered about the floor. The positions of the various fragments were carefully

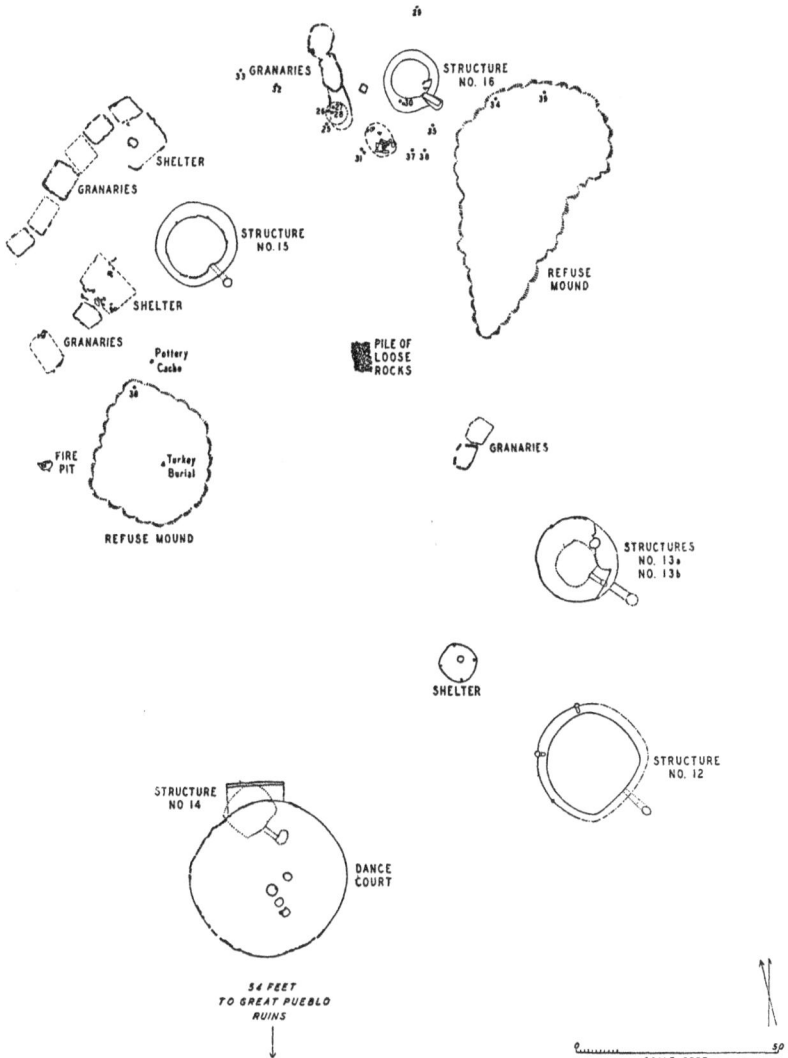

FIGURE 25.—Group 2 pit and surface remains. Numbered dots indicate location of burials.

plotted in the hope that they would indicate the type of roof employed. The results were not entirely satisfactory, although they do give some clue (fig. 27). One definite conclusion based on their evidence is that the roof was not cribbed. As a postulation the most plausible form of construction seems to be as follows: The four main posts set in the floor of the chamber carried a rectangular framework such as previously described for the smaller pit structures. In addition, the posts set in the back wall of the bench probably had stringers extending from the top of one to the top of another around the periphery. This is indicated by two factors. Two of the outer uprights were forked at their upper ends. This, together with a line of ashes and burned plaster extending along the top of the bench between two others, is considered evidence for the use of stringers. The outer framework was not as high as the central one; in fact it stood only a short distance above the surrounding ground level. Smaller poles were sloped upward from it to the central framework and downward to the ground level around the pit. These in turn supported light timbers placed crosswise, paralleling the outer framework. On top of them bark, brush, and a coating of plaster completed the covering. This superstructure would compare quite favorably with that of the large earth lodges of the Plains Indians.[47] The central portion probably had a flat ceiling, as in the case of the other structures, although it might have been partially cribbed with a flat portion near the center for the entrance and smoke-hole hatchway. The finished roof according to such construction possibly had an appearance closely approximating that shown in the postulated reconstruction (fig. 28).

The interior features for structure 12 were elaborate (pl. 12, a). Near the center of the chamber was a circular fire pit that had a bordering rim of adobe and a stone slab reinforcement at the ladder side (fig. 26, j). Near the fire pit was a second smaller depression in the position normally occupied by the ladder box (fig. 26, k), but in this case it unquestionably functioned as a depository for ashes. This smaller depression was also bordered by a rim of plaster and at the ventilator side had a large stone incorporated in the wall. This slab was the deflector. The ladder used in gaining access to the chamber was of the runged type and the base ends of the side poles were still embedded in the floor between the deflector and the ventilator opening when the room was cleared of its accumulated debris (fig. 26, m). The charred ends of the posts were set at an angle which showed that the smoke-hole hatchway must have been located directly above the fire pit.

There were numerous holes and depressions in the floor. In the space between the fire pit and the wall at the proper location for a sipapu there were two circular holes (fig. 26, i). Originally there had been two similar holes in about the same positions but these had been filled in and plastered over and two more provided. At one

---

[47] Bushnell, 1922, pl. 38, a; pl. 40, pp. 132, 133, and 135.

a. Pillar left from fill in pit for structure 10.

b. View across structures 9, 10, and 11.

BUREAU OF AMERICAN ETHNOLOGY   BULLETIN 121   PLATE 12

a. Floor in structure 12, showing ladder holes, deflector, ash and fire pits.

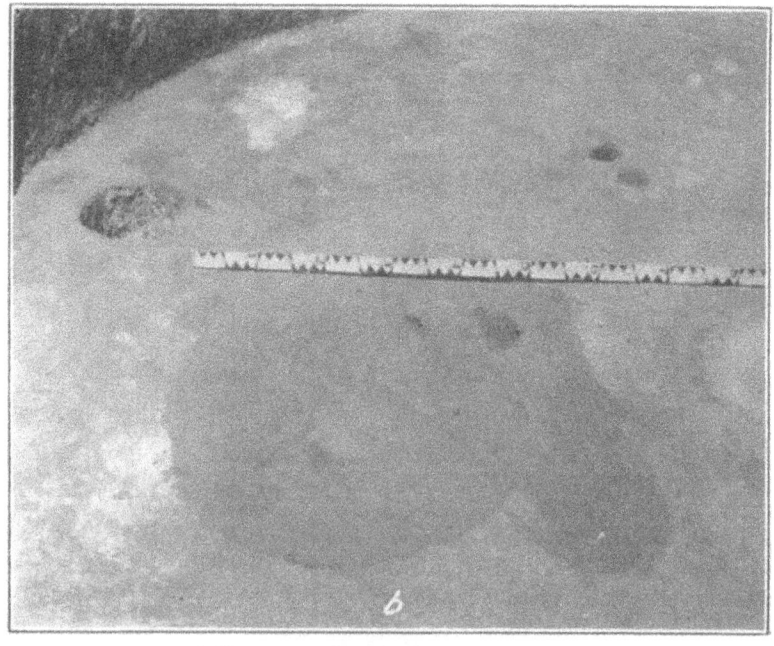

b. Plastered-over depression in floor of structure 12.

a. Pillar from fill, fire pit in fill, and logs on floor of structure 12.

b. Structure 13a.

a. Floor of structure 13b.

b. Portion of floor area, structure 13b.

a. Pillar from fill, fire pit in fill, and logs on floor of structure 12.

b. Structure 13a.

a. Floor of structure 13b.

b. Portion of floor area, structure 13b.

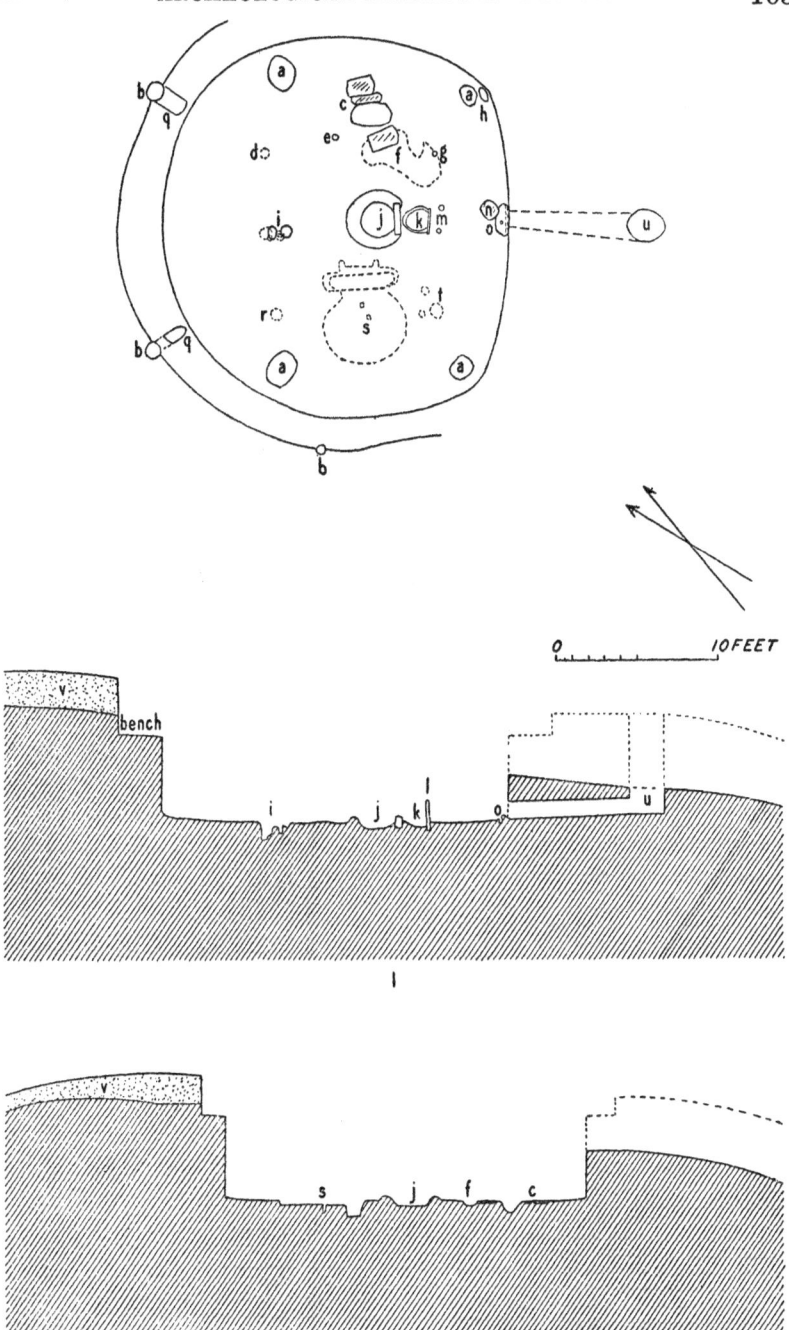

FIGURE 26.—Structure 12. *a*, holes for main support posts; *b*, secondary supports at back of bench; *c*, paving on floor; *d*, plastered-over hole in floor; *e*, storage hole; *f*, plastered-over basin; *g*, storage hole in floor; *h*, storage basin; *i*, sipapu holes; *j*, fire pit; *k*, ash pit; *l*, deflector; *m*, ends of ladder poles; *n*, cover stone for ventilator; *o*, shelf for cover stone and hole for small post to hold stone; *q*, plaster ridges on bench; *r*, plastered over hole; *s*, plastered over basin suggestive of subfloor kiva vault; *t*, plastered-over holes; *u*, ventilator shaft; *v*, sand accumulation.

time or another several holes had been treated in like manner. There was one series of three with a possible fourth which had formed a rectangle encompassing the central portion of the room (fig. 26, *d*, *r*, *t*). The fourth may have been in approximately the position occupied by the small hole (fig. 26, *g*), but a comparatively large area had been dug out of the floor at that place, refilled and plastered over (fig. 26, *f*). As a consequence all indications of a larger hole could have been obliterated. What these holes may have been for is not known, but the fact that they had once been present in so regular a grouping indicates something more than a casual placing of pockets for storage purposes. The thought occurred that possibly structure 12 may at one time have been considerably smaller and posts have been placed there to support a superstructure over a lesser pit. When the excavation was enlarged to the size of No. 12 it was found necessary to change the position of the uprights and to employ larger timbers. This is offered only as a suggestion, however, since there was no evidence to warrant the conclusion that alterations of so extensive a nature had been made. That such a conclusion would not be entirely unwarranted, however, is demonstrated in the case of structures 13a and 13b discussed in following pages.

At the east side of the chamber two stones were embedded in the floor, their tops flush with its upper surface. Along the fire-pit side of these stones was a shallow, oval-shaped depression in the floor. The purpose of this combination (fig 26, *c*) was not clear. The feature in general was similar to one found in structure 13b described in a following section of the report. It may be suggested that a metate or grinding stone rested on the slab, while the depression served as a container for corn to be ground or possibly as a catch basin for the meal as it dropped from the stone. The depression was bordered on the fire-pit side by a third stone laid in the floor (fig. 26, *f*). Between the east support posts and the wall was an oval-shaped depression (fig 26, *h*) that probably functioned as a storage place for small objects.

At the southwest side of the fire pit there originally was a curiously shaped depression which had been filled in and plastered over (fig. 26, *s*; pl. 12, *b*). How long this depression had been in use before it was abandoned and covered with flooring could not be determined. The pit itself consisted of two parts. The large circular portion at the southwest side was quite shallow, while the long oval segment next to the fire pit was comparatively deep. The nature of this combination is shown in section 2, *s*, figure 26. In the shallow circular part were two small holes that apparently had contained upright sticks. The latter were not of sufficient size to have had any connection with the superstructure and must have had some specific purpose apart from any association with the roof. What that may have been can be answered only by speculation. The important factor in connection with the presence of this floor feature lies in the fact that its general position and location corresponds in marked degree to the subfloor vaults found in kivas in ruins throughout this general district and also to the subfloor vaults generally present in great kivas or superceremonial chambers.[48] These vaults are generally rectangular in shape and of greater depth than the depression in structure 12. Their purpose

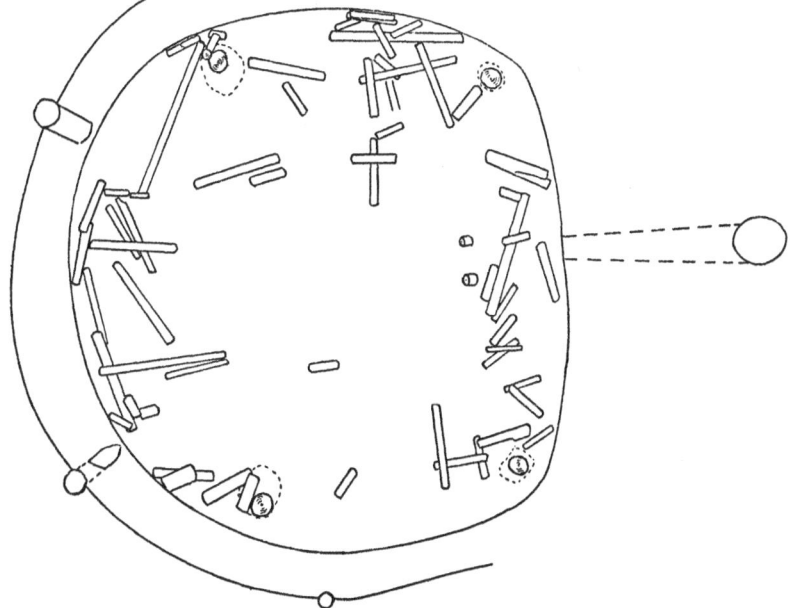

FIGURE 27.—Positions of burned timbers on floor of structure 12.

in kivas has never been determined and as a consequence they can throw little light on the present occurrence, but the analogy should be mentioned. The significant feature is that such a depression had been present in a position corresponding to that of the kiva vaults. Future investigations may in time furnish data that will definitely explain why they were placed in ceremonial chambers. It would be interesting to know what reason the occupants of structure 12 had for discarding the depression and filling it in. Unfortunately, that is one of many things that must remain unknown.

There were low ridges of adobe plaster at two places on the top of the bench. These are particularly worthy of comment because of

---

[48] Roberts, 1932, pp. 58–60, 69–70, 88–90.

the fact that they suggest a prototype for a feature commonly found in the kivas in the ruins in the Chaco Canyon,[49] at Aztec,[50] and at other sites belonging to the Chaco cultural pattern.[51] A series of low masonry boxes inclosing sections of logs are frequently noted in such ceremonial structures. These are located at intervals along the top of the bench. Generally there are four to six in the smaller kivas, the number increasing with the size of the structure. No timbers were incorporated in the plaster ridges in this structure, but in view of the fact that they extended out toward the face of the bench from the posts set in the wall at the back it may be suggested that there was a close correlation between them and the other forms. This tends rather definitely to indicate a relationship between them and the Chaco type. It is possible that the latter type was definitely derived from such an architectural feature, although in the Whitewater examples no definite function was indicated comparable to that of the Chaco forms serving as a base for the bottom tier of logs in a cribbed roof.

The ventilator in this structure had a low step of adobe plaster in front of the opening in the wall (fig. 26, o). The top of this ridge contained a groove in which to set a cover stone. The stone was even in position over the aperture when that portion of the room was uncovered. In addition to the groove there was a small hole where a piece of wood was placed in an upright position to aid further in keeping the cover in position. The aperture was carefully finished with adobe plaster. The passage was long and comparatively small. It had been constructed by the trench-and-cover method. The floor sloped slightly upward toward the shaft at the outer end and the width increased in the same direction. The shaft was oval in form. Only a small portion of it remained, however, because it was located at the side of the structure where erosion had been most active and a large portion of the earth was washed away.

Structure 12 in general suggested much more the kiva or ceremonial chamber than did any of the other pit remains, with the exception of structure 3. Furthermore, potsherds found in it were of a more developed type of ceramics than those secured from the others. The date of the structure obtained from the timbers, 918 ± 3,[52] shows a later horizon. As a matter of fact the timbers covered a span of 74 years, the dates being 844 to 918. Inasmuch as a little over one-third of the material gave the 844 date it is probable that those timbers were reused and may have come from a smaller structure located on the same spot, as was suggested by other features mentioned in preceding pages. Considering all of the evidence, the

---
[49] Judd, 1925, p. 88, figs. 99, 100. Pepper, 1920, pp. 104, 106.
[50] Morris, 1924, p. 243.
[51] Jeancon, 1922, p. 18.
[52] Miller, 1935, p. 31, listed as House A-1.

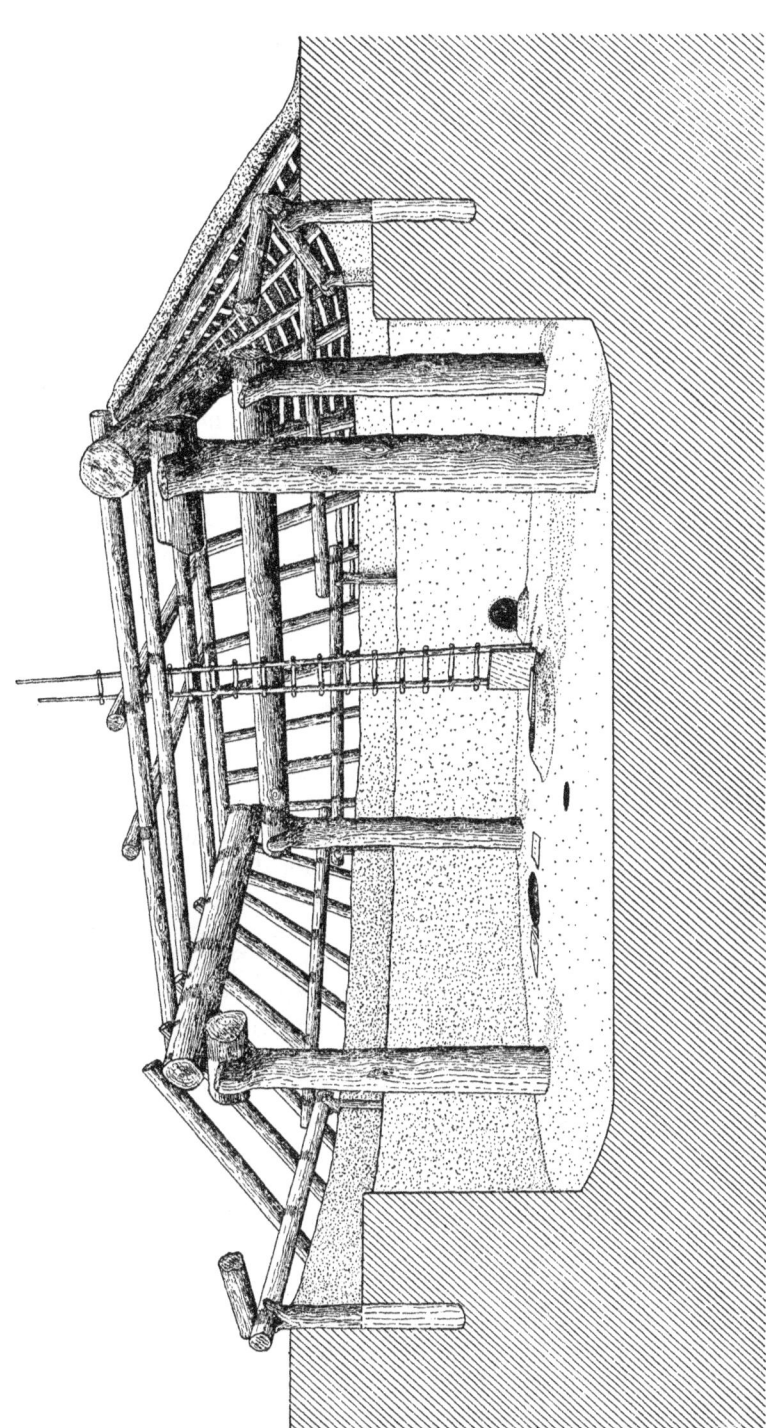

FIGURE 28.—Postulated reconstruction of superstructure erected over structure 12. Some of front timbers omitted from drawing so as not to complicate the diagram.

conclusion was reached that structure 12 was a ceremonial chamber, probably belonging to the late Developmental Pueblo horizon at the site. Remains of late Developmental structures are incorporated in the large ruins southwest from the pit of 12. It is possible, of course, that people lived in pit dwellings at this place until late Developmental Pueblo times, as dates from structure 15 overlap a number of those from the beams in No. 12, but such was not a common practice. In the Flagstaff, Ariz., area farther west, pit houses prevailed all through the Developmental period.[53]

The fill in the subterranean portion of this structure was somewhat different in character from that found in most of the pits. The first layer in the pillar (fig. 29, a) consisted of wind-blown sand. It contained some fragments of tabular sandstone, and potsherds were comparatively numerous. The stratum was uneven, probably due to the house being on the slope of the hillside. At the east corner of the pillar it measured 5 inches (15.27 cm), at the north corner 8½ inches (21.59 cm), at the south 9 inches (22.86 cm), and at the west was 1 foot 4½ inches (41.91 cm) thick.

The second level (fig. 29, b) was not a complete stratum, but part of a lens of material that did not extend entirely across the pit, on the southwest side. At the north corner of the pillar the top and bottom lines met; on the south face the lens extended only a few inches beyond the median line. The layer contained considerable charcoal, some adobe nodules, blow sand, and toward the bottom several streaks of water-deposited sand. Potsherds were not numerous and there was no stone or bone. The maximum thickness of the layer was at the east corner of the pillar where it measured 1 foot 2 inches (35.56 cm); at the south it was 6½ inches (16.51 cm).

Layer c was practically the same in content as b, except for the fact that it contained less charcoal. The main line of demarcation between the two was a distinct streak of water-deposited sand and clay. This line was on an old surface of occupation at about the level of the top of the bench. On this same surface, in another part of the room, was a fire pit that had been placed in the fill at a considerable height above the old floor (pl. 13, a). The material in stratum c was charcoal, adobe nodules, sand, and some clay. There were a few sandstone spalls and some bone fragments. Potsherds were present, but were not as numerous as in the layer above. Measurements for this stratum were: north corner 1 foot 4 inches (40.64 cm), east corner 10½ inches (26.67 cm), south corner 9½ inches (24.13 cm), and west corner 8½ inches (21.59 cm). Strata a and c came together at the west corner because of the lens nature of stratum b.

---

[53] Hargrave, 1930.

The next two strata, d and e, were clearly defined by streaks of charcoal. The material in the layers was the same as that for stratum c. The main differences were that there was a slight increase in the amount of stone fragments present in d, with a sharp drop in e. The number of potsherds present in d was the same as that for c, but a marked decline was noted in e. At the top of d, in the face of the pillar between the east and north corners (fig. 29), was a small pocket filled with water-deposited sand. This apparently was the remnant of a shallow puddle where water had collected in a depression when the top of d was the surface of the ground at that point. Stratum d measured: 6 inches (15.24 cm) at the north corner,

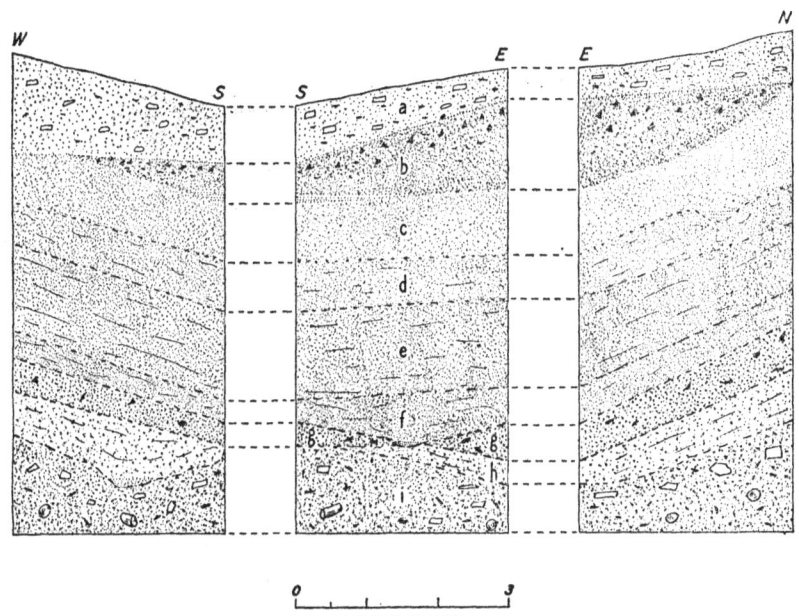

FIGURE 29.—Pillar left from fill in structure 12. E, W, N, and S. indicate east, west, north, and south corners.

7 inches (17.78 cm) at the east corner, 8 inches (20.32 cm) at the south corner, and 7 inches (17.78 cm) at the west corner. Stratum e had thicknesses of 10½ inches (26.67 cm) at the north corner, 1 foot 2½ inches (36.83 cm) at the east corner, 1 foot 2½ inches (36.83 cm) at the south corner, and 1 foot 2 inches (35.56 cm) at the west corner.

Stratum f was characterized by considerable quantities of burned sand, charcoal, lumps of clay, and a good showing of bone fragments. There was no stone and a total absence of potsherds. The layer was rather thin, except near the center of the east-south and west-north faces where a channel in the top of g increased the thickness. The stratum measured 5¼ inches (13.33 cm) at the north corner, 5¾ inches (14.60 cm) at the east corner, 4 inches (10.16 cm) at the south corner, and 4½ inches (11.43 cm) at the west corner. Along the course of the small channel the thickness was 9 inches (22.86 cm). This latter feature probably represented the remains of a natural drainage ditch, as there was water-deposited sand in its bottom.

Stratum g was separated from f by a layer of charcoal. The stratum contained numerous lumps of clay, adobe nodules, some burned sand, and wood ashes. The amount of bone was the same as that for the level above, but in addition there were fragments of stone and a few potsherds. Stratum g measured 8 inches (20.32 cm) at the north corner, 7 inches (17.78 cm) at the east corner, 4 inches (10.16 cm) at the south corner, and 5½ inches (13.97 cm) at the west. The small channel noted in the discussion of f completely cut through g and at that point strata f and h touched. The channel was 5 inches (12.7 cm) wide.

Stratum h was separated from g by a definite line of charcoal and ash. The layer had a larger content of sand than was the case in g and in addition some ashes, bits of charcoal, lumps of adobe, and balls of clay. There was a total absence of bone, stone, and potsherds. The layer measured: 8½ inches (21.59 cm) at the north corner, 3¾ inches (9.53 cm) at the east corner, was missing at the south corner, and 7½ inches (19.05 cm) at the west corner. About midway of the west-south face an old depression in the top of the layer below increased the thickness of h to 11 inches (27.94 cm). This pocket was 8 inches (20.32 cm) across and its bottom was filled with water-deposited sand.

Stratum i rested on the floor of the structure and consisted largely of burned plaster, charred beams, chunks of adobe, sand, and ashes. There were numerous fragments of sandstone, chips of chert and chalcedony, bits of bone, and a fairly good showing of potsherds. This layer was also irregular in thickness due to an uneven top surface with humps and pockets attributable in the main to the timbers and charred bits of roofing in the debris and to features on the floor. The layer measured: 1 foot 6 inches (45.72 cm) at the north corner, 8 inches (20.32 cm) at the east corner, 1 foot 2 inches (35.56 cm) at the south corner, and 1 foot 4 inches (40.64 cm) at the west corner.

The evidence in the content of the pillar points to two main factors. The first, that the fill accumulating in the pit after the structure was destroyed by fire and up to the level of the bench top, stratum c, was the result of a gradual and natural process. There was no intentional dumping of refuse and waste matter from occupied quarters in the pit during this interval. At no stage, however, was there complete absence of traces attributable to human activity and for this reason it may be concluded that the site in general was still occupied while the hole was being filled. The second feature is that the interval that followed the period marked by the surface of occupation on the level with the top of the bench, the top of stratum c, was characterized by deposits containing a large amount of refuse and debris, in this case definite dump material. This seems to correlate with the major period of expansion that included extensive construction work around the large stone buildings located southwest from structure 12. The potsherds from the upper levels of the pillar check with those from the Great Pueblo ruins and suggest a probable contemporaneity between the two.

Structure 12 measured 21 feet 6 inches (6.553 m) from wall to wall below the bench on the fire pit, ventilator line. Across in the opposite direction the measurement was 22 feet 8 inches (6.908 m). The bench varied in width from 1 foot 9 inches (53.34 cm) to 2 feet 10 inches (86.36 cm). At the ventilator side of the chamber the existing wall stood 2 feet 3 inches (68.58 cm). This, of course, does not represent the original height at that side of the room, since a portion of the structure had been carried away by erosion. At the opposite side from the ventilator the top of the bench was 4 feet 8 inches (1.422 m) above the floor. The back of the bench was 1 foot 3 inches (38.1 cm) high. There was an accumulation of sand above the original ground level which added 2 feet 2 inches (66.04 cm) to the latter measurement.

The base ends of the main support posts were still in the floor when the pit was uncovered, hence it is possible to give the actual measurements for the posts themselves. The north post had a diameter of 10 inches (25.4 cm); it was 1 foot (30.48 cm) from the wall. The timber was removed from the hole in order that the wood might be saved for study purposes. After this was done it was found that the hole had a depth of 2 feet 10 inches (86.36 cm). The east support post had a diameter of 10½ inches (26.67 cm) and was 8½ inches (21.59 cm) from the wall. The hole in which it was set was 1 foot 10 inches (55.88 cm) in depth. The south support post had a diameter of 10½ inches (26.67 cm), stood 9 inches (22.86 cm) from the wall, and was set at a depth of 1 foot 8 inches (50.8 cm). The post near the west corner was 11 inches (27.94 cm) in diameter, stood 1 foot (30.48 cm) from the wall, and was set at a depth of 2 feet 5 inches (73.66 cm).

The posts which were present in the bench were more variable in size than the central supports. That at the north side of the chamber had been placed in a hole 1 foot 2 inches (35.56 cm) in diameter. The post itself, however, measured only 10 inches (25.4 cm). The middle one of the three remaining posts stood in a hole 11½ inches (29.21 cm) in diameter from front to back and 1 foot (30.48 cm) from side to side. The post placed in it had a diameter of 8½ inches

(21.59 cm). The post near the south corner of the chamber was the smallest of the group; it was only 5 inches (12.7 cm) in diameter and was set in a hole which measured 7¾ inches (19.68 cm) across. Most of the larger timbers used in the superstructure had average diameters of 6 inches (15.24 cm). The smaller poles averaged 3 inches (7.62 cm) in diameter.

The fire pit (fig. 26, *j*) had a diameter of 2 feet 1 inch (63.5 cm) on the ventilator line and 2 feet (60.96 cm) at right angles to it. The bottom of the pit was only 4 inches (10.16 cm) below the floor level, but the depth was increased to 8 inches (20.32 cm) by the encircling rim of adobe. The rim ranged from 7 inches (17.78 cm) to 11 inches (27.94 cm) in width. Its average height was 4 inches (10.16 cm). The stone slab incorporated in one side was 1 foot 9½ inches (54.61 cm) long, 4 inches (10.16 cm) thick, and 9 inches (22.86 cm) high.

The ladder box or ash pit (fig. 26, *k*) had a depth of 3 inches (7.62 cm). The adobe rim which encircled it ranged from 1½ inches (3.81 cm) to 3 inches (7.62 cm) in width, and had an average height of 1½ inches (3.81 cm). The deflector slab which was placed at the ventilator side of this depression was 1 foot 5 inches (43.18 cm) long at the bottom and 1 foot 6 inches (45.72 cm) at the top. It had a thickness of 1⅝ inches (4.13 cm), and stood 1 foot 3 inches (38.1 cm) above the floor.

The ladder poles (fig. 26, *m*) were set in the floor 6 inches (15.24 cm) from the deflector. The holes were 1 foot 1 inch (33.02 cm) apart, indicating that the ladder was approximately 1 foot (30.48 cm) wide. The posts were 4½ inches (11.43 cm) and 4¾ inches (12.06 cm) in diameter. At the time when the debris was cleared from the floor the charred butts stood 8½ inches and 8¾ inches (21.59 and 22.23 cm) above the floor.

The sipapu holes (fig. 26, *i*) were 3 feet 5 inches (1.041 m) from the fire pit and 6 feet 6 inches (1.981 m) from the wall. The hole nearest the fire pit had a diameter of 8 inches (20.32 cm) and a depth of 5 inches (12.7 cm). The second was 3 inches (7.62 cm) from the first. It had diameters of 6 inches (15.24 cm) and 9 inches (22.86 cm) and a depth of 1 foot (30.48 cm).

The various holes scattered about in the floor had a considerable range in measurements. The hole *d*, figure 26, had a diameter of 6 inches (15.24 cm) and a depth of 6 inches (15.24 cm); *e* was 4 inches (10.16 cm) in diameter and 8¾ inches (22.22 cm) deep; *g* was 3½ inches (8.89 cm) in diameter and 1 foot 2 inches (35.56 cm) deep; *h* had diameters of 5 inches (12.7 cm) and 10 inches (25.4 cm), and a depth of 3 inches (7.62 cm); *r* had a 7-inch (17.78 cm) diameter and a depth of 9 inches (22.86 cm); *t* measured 9 inches (22.86 cm) and 10½ inches (26.67 cm) on two diameters, and had a depth of 11 inches (27.94 cm).

The large depression in the floor at the west side of the fire pit (fig. 26, *s*) which had been plastered over gave the following measurements: The oval portion had diameters of 4 feet 5 inches (1.346 m) and 5 feet 2½ inches (1.587 m). Its average depth was 2¼ inches (5.71 cm). The two small holes in this portion of the depression had diameters of 3½ inches (8.89 cm) and depths of 5½ inches (13.97 cm) and 9 inches (22.86 cm). The rectangular pit at the side of the circular depression had sloping sides so that the bottom was smaller than the top. Along the top it measured 4 feet 7 inches (1.397 m) long and from 1 foot (30.48 cm) to 1 foot 4 inches (40.64 cm) in width. At the bottom the length was 4 feet (1.219 m) and the width 10 inches (25.4 cm). The average depth was 11 inches (27.94 cm). The two small projections at the top of the east edge of this rectangular depression were 5 inches (12.7 cm) and 6 inches (15.24 cm) long. They were 4 inches (10.16 cm) wide. The depth averaged 2 inches (5.08 cm). The edge of the rectangular pit was 1 foot 2 inches (35.56 cm) from the fire-pit rim.

The oval depression at the east side of the chamber which had flat stones at either side (fig. 26, *c*) had a long diameter of 2 feet 6 inches (76.2 cm) and a short one of 1 foot 4 inches (40.64 cm). The depth was 8 inches (20.32 cm).

The plaster ridges on the bench in front of the back support posts (fig. 26, *q*) ranged from 1 foot 8 inches (50.8 cm) to 2 feet (60.96 cm) in length and from 9 inches (22.86 cm) to 1 foot (30.48 cm) in width. The height was 2 inches (5.08 cm).

The adobe step in front of the ventilator opening (fig. 26, *o*) was 1 foot 10½ inches (57.15 cm) long and 10 inches (25.4 cm) wide. It was 3½ inches (8.89 cm) high. The small hole in which a post for the ventilator cover was set had a diameter of 2½ inches (6.35 cm) and a depth of 5 inches (12.7 cm). The groove in which the cover stone was placed had a depth of 1 inch (2.54 cm) and a length of 1 foot 6 inches (45.72 cm). It was 1½ inches (3.81 cm) wide.

The ventilator opening was square and measured 11¼ inches (28.57 cm). The sill was at the same height as the bottom of the groove for the cover stone. It was 2½ inches (6.35 cm) above the floor level. The stone used to close the aperture measured 1 foot 3 inches (38.1 cm) long by 1 foot ¾ inch (32.38 cm) wide and 1¼ inches (3.17 cm) thick. The ventilator passage was 7 feet 6 inches (2.286 m) long. Where it entered the shaft it was 1 foot (30.48 cm) high and 1 foot 6 inches (45.72 cm) wide. The shaft had diameters of 2 feet 4 inches (71.12 cm) and 1 foot 11 inches (58.42 cm). The maximum depth was only 1 foot 6 inches (45.72 cm), but at the time of occupation this probably was about 6 feet (1.828 m).

STRUCTURES 13A AND 13B

Structures 13a and 13b were somewhat similar in nature to 5a and 5b in that 13a had been erected at the spot where they were located, then abandoned and filled in. Later the larger pit was dug at the same place and completely covered the older pit. In the process of investigation 13b was the first encountered. After it had been completely cleared a slight depression which encompassed most of the central part of the room was noted in the floor. A small section of the plaster was removed along the border of this depression and it was noted that there was a wall extending downward from that level. With this discovery the remaining material was dug out and a smaller pit uncovered. Inasmuch as the latter represented the older structure it will be discussed first.

The pit for 13a was smaller than the average for the site. It was roughly circular in form and in general corresponded to the majority of pits around the site (fig. 30; pl. 13, b). The house presumably had a superstructure similar to the others. Four posts had been set near the corners of the room to support the roof. Each one of these posts, judging from the holes which remained, stood almost against the wall. The interior features of the structure consisted of a fire pit, ladder box, sipapu, and five storage holes in the floor. In addition there was a wall pocket or cupboard near the west support post.

The fire pit in 13a was a simple basin that had been dug into the floor and lined with plaster (fig. 30, g). It was encircled by a rim of adobe plaster similar to those noted in some of the other houses. The adjacent ladder box (fig. 30, h) consisted of a shallow depression inclosed on three sides by an extension of the fire-pit rim. The fourth side, that toward the ventilator opening, was not inclosed. As a matter of fact a rim was not necessary along that part of the pit because the base ends of the ladder had been embedded in the floor. The sipapu (fig. 30, f) was located at the northwest side of the fire pit and consisted of a small circular hole. It differed from the many examples described in that it was jug-shaped. The walls and bottom were carefully plastered. Nearby were two other holes that could have served as additional sipapus (fig. 30, d, e) or for storage purposes. At the north side of the fire pit was such a hole (fig. 30, c). Near the east support post was a shallow, basinlike depression (fig. 30, b) that no doubt functioned in a similar capacity. The same was true for that marked i, figure 30.

Perhaps the most interesting feature in the pit was the storage pocket in the wall (fig. 30, j). This is one of the few examples at the site of such a provision for placing objects out of the way. The pocket was dug into the wall, its bottom slightly lower than the floor level. It was roughly oval in form and its sides, floor, and ceiling

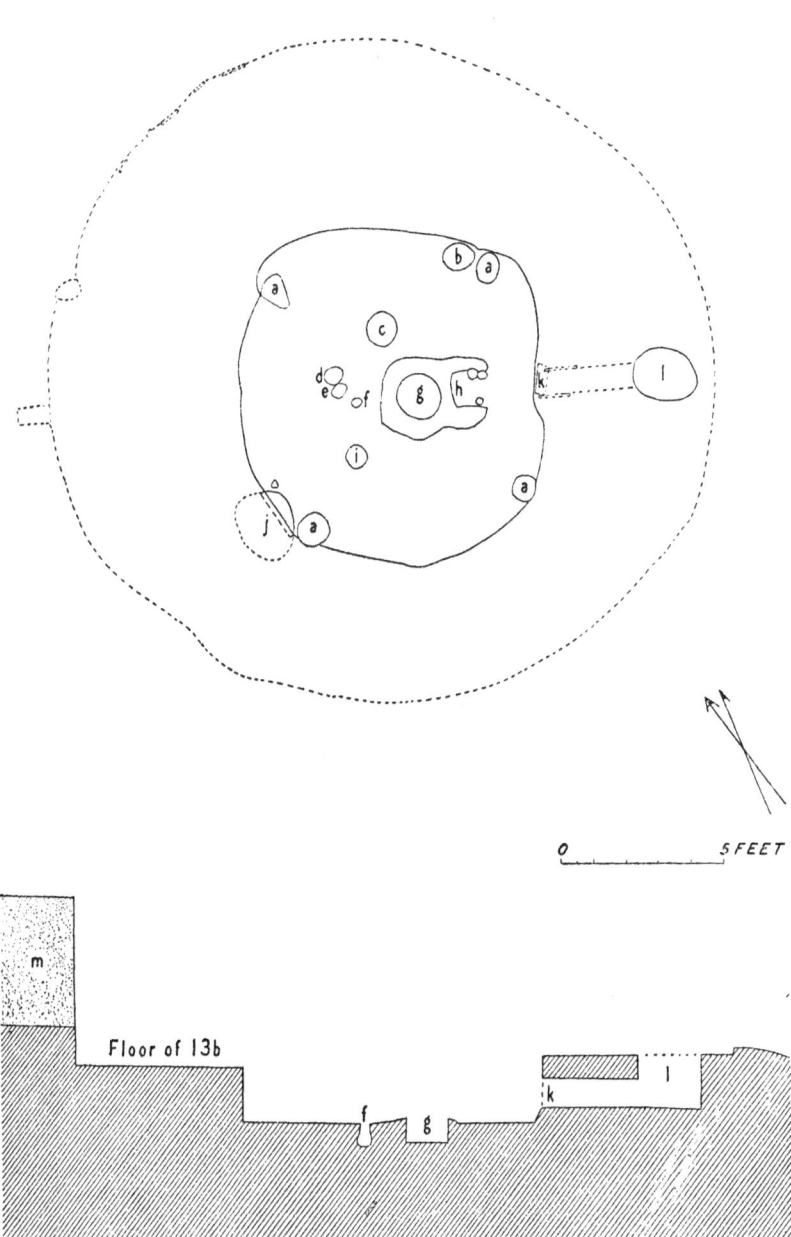

FIGURE 30.—Structure 13a. *a*, holes for superstructure support posts; *b, c, d,* and *e*, storage holes; *f*, sipapu; *g*, fire pit; *h*, ladder box; *i*, storage basin; *j*, storage pocket in wall; *k*, ventilator opening in chamber; *l*, ventilator shaft; *m*, accumulated sand. Dotted lines indicate position of 13b.

were carefully covered with plaster. A slab of stone was provided to close the opening. This was in position at the time when the pit was excavated. There was an almost imperceptible depression in the floor in front of the opening that may have been provided to facilitate the placing of the cover stone. Wall pockets of this type are not uncommon in some sections of the Southwest,[54] but for some reason were not made use of to any extent at this site. In some cases these recesses have bottoms slightly below the floor; in others they are slightly above the general level of the room. At the time when the cupboard was opened it contained nothing beyond a few potsherds and several cores from which stone chips, probably for use in the making of arrowheads, had been struck.

The ventilator was small and the passage was of the constructed type, that is a trench had been dug and then covered over with stones, plaster, and earth to form the horizontal portion of the ventilator. The opening at the room end was framed with stone. There was a stone lintel and stone sill and large slabs placed at either side extended back along the walls of the passage for some distance. The shaft was oval in form. In the photograph (pl. 13, b) the upper end is shown encircled by stones. The latter were not found in that position but were placed there to emphasize the presence of the opening.

The fill in house 13a indicated that the pit had not been used as a habitation for some time previous to the construction of 13b. On the floor was a thick layer of turkey droppings. Several broken eggs were found near the north post and the skeleton of one bird was lying near the center of the chamber. This indicates that the inclosure was used as a turkey pen. After it had been employed for that purpose the occupants of the site apparently decided to construct a second house on the same spot and accordingly filled the pit with refuse material and clean sand. Although it cannot be stated definitely that such was the case, it would seem that the fill was obtained through the process of enlarging the pit to make the second structure, 13b. When the remaining portion of 13a was completely filled an adobe plaster floor was laid across it. It was the settling of the material filling 13a and an attendant sinking of the floor that indicated the presence of the earlier structure when 13b was excavated.

The pit for 13a measured 6 feet 1 inch (1.854 m) on the sipapu, fire pit, ventilator line, and 9 feet 9½ inches (2.983 m) at right angles to it. At the ventilator side of the chamber the floor of 13a was 2

---

[54] Morris, 1919, p. 196. Guernsey and Kidder, 1921, p. 25. Roberts, 1929, p. 40; 1930, pp. 49–50.

feet (60.96 cm) below that of 13b. At the opposite side the bottom of pit 13a was only 1 foot 8 inches (50.8 cm) below that of 13b.

The holes for the support posts varied somewhat in size. That in the north corner was irregular in shape and measured 9½ inches (24.13 cm) by 1 foot 1 inch (33.02 cm). The hole had a depth of 1 foot 1 inch (33.02 cm). At one point on its periphery it touched the wall of the chamber. The hole at the east corner had diameters of 8 inches (20.32 cm) and 1 foot (30.48 cm). It had a depth of 7½ inches (19.05 cm). The edge of the hole did not touch the wall, although it was only ½ inch (1.27 cm) from it. The hole at the south corner of the room had diameters of 8½ inches (21.59 cm) and 9 inches (22.86 cm). The hole had a depth of 8 inches (20.32 cm) and touched the wall. The west hole had diameters of 1 foot (30.48 cm) and 1 foot ½ inch (31.75 cm). It had a depth of 1 foot 1 inch (33.02). This hole not only touched the wall but was partially incorporated in it.

The fire pit (fig. 30, *g*) had a diameter of 1 foot 4½ inches (41.91 cm) on the ventilator line and 1 foot 4 inches (40.64 cm) at right angles to it. The pit had a depth of 7 inches (17.78 cm) below the floor level. This was increased 2 inches (5.08 cm) by the encircling rim. The rim ranged from 5½ inches (13.97 cm) to 7½ inches (19.05 cm) in width. Its average height around the edges of the pit was 2 inches (5.08 cm); the outside borders merged with the floor.

The ladder pit, or rather the rectangular inclosure in which the base ends of the ladder were inclosed (fig. 30, *h*), measured 1 foot ½ inch (31.75 cm) by 1 foot 1½ inches (34.29 cm). The holes in which the ladder poles were placed had diameters of 3 inches (7.62 cm) and 3½ inches (8.89 cm). The holes had depths of 3½ and 4 inches (8.89 and 10.16 cm). A small hole adjacent to the one in which the east ladder pole had rested, and that probably was used for storage purposes, had a diameter of 3½ inches (8.89 cm) and a depth of 2½ inches (6.35 cm).

The sipapu (fig. 30, *f*) was 7 inches (17.78 cm) from the fire pit and 3 feet 4 inches (1.016 m) from the wall at the opposite side. The hole had a diameter of 4 inches (10.16 cm) on the floor level, but this was increased to 5½ inches (13.97 cm) below the floor because of the jug-like form in which it was made. The hole had a depth of 8 inches (20.32 cm). The storage holes located near the sipapu (fig. 30, *d, e*) had diameters of 6 inches (15.24 cm) and 7 inches (17.78 cm). Their depths were 5 and 6 inches (12.7 and 15.24 cm).

The large depression at the northeast side of the fire pit (fig. 30, *c*) was 6½ inches (16.51 cm) from the edge of the rim. It had diameters of 1 foot 1 inch (33.02 cm) and 1 foot (30.48 cm). It was 6 inches (15.24 cm) deep. The storage hole near the northwest corner of the pit (fig. 30, i) was 11 inches (27.94 cm) from the edge of the rim. It had diameters of 8 inches (20.32 cm) and 8½ inches (21.59 cm). Its depth was 5 inches (12.7 cm). The depression near the hole for the east post (fig. 30, b) had diameters of 1 foot (30.48 cm) and 10 inches (25.4 cm). Its depth was 3 inches (7.62 cm).

The storage recess in the wall near the west support post (fig. 30, j) measured 2 feet 2 inches (66.04 cm) by 1 foot 5 inches (43.18 cm). Its height was 1 foot 3 inches (38.1 cm).

The ventilator opening had a width of 9 inches (22.86 cm) and a height of 10½ inches (26.67 cm). The sill was 5½ inches (13.97 cm) above the floor level. The sill projected into the room 3½ inches (8.89 cm) from the edge of the opening. The passage had a length of 2 feet 9½ inches (85.09 cm). At the shaft end it had a width of 9 inches (22.86 cm) and a height of 10½ inches (26.67 cm). The shaft measured 2 feet (60.96 cm) in diameter on the passage line and 1 foot 7 inches (48.26 cm) at right angles to it. The bottom of the shaft was 1 foot 8 inches (50.8 cm) below the floor level of 13b.

Only a portion of the pit of structure 13b remained. It had been built on the edge of a sharp slope and weathering agents had washed away a large part of the surface in the interval between the time when it was abandoned and the remains were uncovered in the summer of 1931. Not only had surface water carried away a considerable portion of the slope but a large part of the walls along the eastern side of 13b had also disappeared. Enough remained, however, to give a general idea of the nature of the structure (pl. 14, a, b). On the whole it compared quite closely with the others described in preceding pages. The main difference between 13b and a majority of the others was that the pit was presumably much shallower. The old ground level was only 2 feet (60.96 cm) above the floor.

The shallowness of the excavation may in part account for the apparent ease with which the eastern walls were carried away. Despite the lack of depth to the pit there probably was not any marked difference in the type of structure erected over it. Evidence was that four upright posts had carried the main framework (fig. 31, a) for the roof and that this covering had a flat central portion and sloping sides. The main difference between the superstructure in this instance and the others of like type probably was in the length of the slanting side poles. When the pit was shallow these timbers would of necessity have been longer and more of the structure would have appeared above the ground level. Except for this there need not have been any marked difference. The longer poles would tend to create more pressure on the central framework than under ordinary circumstances and an additional brace seems to have been required.

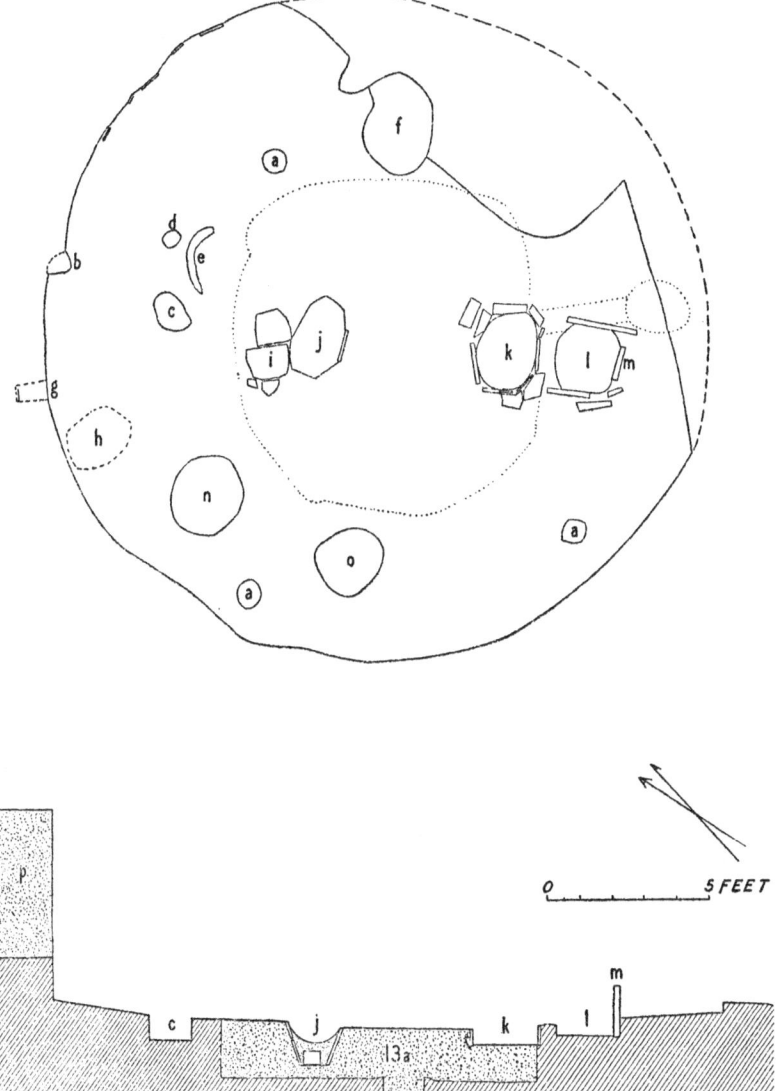

FIGURE 31.—Structure 13b. *a*, holes for main support posts; *b*, beam placement; *c* and *d*, storage holes; *e*, groove in floor; *f*, storage basin; *g*, wall pocket or Katcina niche; *h*, basin covered by floor plaster; *i*, stones embedded in floor; *j*, basin in floor; *k*, fire pit; *l*, ladder box; *m*, deflector stone; *n* and *o*, storage basins; *p*, drift sand. Dotted lines show position of 13a.

Evidence was that this was provided by a timber extending from the base of the wall at the north side of the chamber to the upper framework. The beam placement was present at *b*, figure 31. This corresponds to some extent with the situations described for structures 6, 7, and 9, where the use of braces was noted.

The pit of 13b more nearly approached the circular form than did many of those previously described. The interior features of the house comprised fire and ladder pits and a number of storage holes in the floor (fig. 31). There was a small niche or pocket in the west wall (fig. 31, *g*), suggestive of the Katcina Kihu in later-day ceremonial chambers. This was in contrast to the placements for roof braces noted in previous pits in that it unquestionably was for storage purposes. The size, shape, and finish indicated such a function and despite the fact that it was on the floor level it may have been a form of the Katcina niche,[55] a place where ceremonial objects were kept. Such wall pockets also occupied an analogous position to the niche for ceremonial articles in the wall opposite from the doorway in some of the Plain's earth lodges.[56]

Near the center of the chamber was a small section of paving on the floor that consisted of four stones (fig. 31, *i*), embedded in the plaster so that their upper surfaces were flush with the top of the floor. Between the flagging and the fire pit was a shallow basin (fig. 31, *j*), probably associated in purpose with the paving. A metate may have rested on the flagging and the concavity in the floor have served as a storage place for grain or a catch basin for the prepared meal dropping from the end of the grinding stone. This roughly oval-shaped depression was of particular interest from a constructional point of view. It was not a simple basin formed by plastering the interior of a shallow pit dug below the floor level. It had been made with a substantial foundation. The latter consisted of an octagonal cist formed by lining a hole in the fill in 13a with small stone slabs (fig. 31, *j*, section). The interior of the cist contained stones and mud plaster, tamped to form a solid, compact mass. All indications were that the latter was contemporaneous with the construction of the cist, not the result of later remodeling. The elaborateness of the feature shows that it had a definite purpose requiring a certain degree of durability.

The fire pit (fig. 31, *k*) was roughly rectangular in form and lined with stone slabs. The ladder pit (fig. 31, *l*) was also rectangular in shape and had stone borders on three sides. These stones were set in the floor so that they extended above it for several inches. The house had no sipapu and there were no remaining traces of a ventilator. The position which it would have occupied with respect to

---

[55] Mindeleff, 1891, p. 121.
[56] Bushnell, 1922, p. 158.

the rest of the structure was such, however, that it might easily have been carried away when the hillside was eroded. The fact that the end slab in the ladder pit was of sufficient height to have functioned as a deflector (fig. 31, *m*), suggests that there probably was a ventilator at that side of the chamber.

The storage holes (fig. 31, *c*, *d*, *f*, *n*, *o*) scattered about in the floor were larger than average and had carefully plastered sides and bottoms. One depression located near the west wall of the chamber had been filled in and plastered over (fig. 31, *h*). The crescent-shaped groove in the floor near the north support post (fig. 31, *e*) was an unusual feature. What purpose it may have had is not known. Nothing was found in it to suggest an explanation for its peculiar contour.

The fill in the pit consisted largely of drift sand containing some charcoal. Across the top was a thin layer of stone spalls suggestive of mason's debris from the nearby large stone buildings. At a number of places around the site the fragments of stone that were left after the building blocks were shaped were thrown out and the deposit here seems to have been of that nature. This would indicate that 13b antedated the large surface dwellings by an interval of some length. At one place in the fill a peculiar cache was found. This consisted of a large number of concretions, fossils, bones, some stone cylinders, and sandstone balls, suggestive of a medicine man's paraphernalia. The collection was just below the surface layer of broken stones and apparently belonged to the stone-house stage of occupation.

Complete measurements for 13b cannot be given because of the missing east wall. From north to south, however, the structure measured 20 feet 3 inches (6.172 m), which is a longer diameter than that found in a majority of the structures. The wall along the west side was only 2 feet (60.96 cm) high, measuring from the floor to the original ground level. The accumulation of drift sand and debris above the old ground level, however, increased the depth at the time of excavation to 5 feet 9 inches (1.752 m).

The north hole for a main support post had diameters of 9½ inches (24.13 cm) and 7½ inches (19.05 cm). The depth was 1 foot (30.48 cm). The hole for the east post had been carried away when that portion of the house was destroyed. The hole for the south post measured 9 inches (22.86 cm) and 10 inches (25.4 cm) in diameter. It had a depth of 1 foot 4 inches (40.64 cm). The south post stood 1 foot 1 inch (33.02 cm) from the wall. The hole for the west post had diameters of 8 inches (20.32 cm) and 9½ inches (24.13 cm) and a depth of 1 foot 2 inches (35.56 cm). It stood 10 inches (25.4 cm) from the wall. The placement for the roof brace (fig. 31, *b*) had diameters of 7 and 9 inches (17.78 and 22.86 cm). It was 10 inches (25.4 cm) deep.

The niche in the wall (fig. 31, *g*) measured 7 inches (17.78 cm) in width and 1 foot (30.48 cm) in height. It was 1 foot (30.48 cm) deep.

The fire pit (fig. 31, *k*) measured 1 foot 11 inches (58.42 cm) by 2 feet 3 inches (68.58 cm) and it had a depth of 6 inches (15.24 cm). The ladder pit (fig. 31, *l*) was 7 inches (17.78 cm) from the fire pit. The depression measured 1 foot 11 inches (58.42 cm) by 1 foot 11½ inches (59.69 cm). Its depth was 4 inches (10.16 cm). The slab forming the end of the box toward the side where the ventilator would normally have been located stood 1 foot (30.48 cm) above the floor level (fig. 31, *m*).

The oval depression adjoining the paving (fig. 31 *j*) had a long diameter of 2 feet 4 inches (71.12 cm) and a short one of 1 foot 6 inches (45.72 cm). At the center the pit had a depth of 8½ inches (21.59 cm). The crescent-shaped groove (fig. 31, *e*) in the floor had an average width of 2½ inches (6.35 cm). The groove was 3 inches (7.62 cm) deep.

The small circular hole adjacent to the groove (fig. 31, *d*) had diameters of 6 inches (15.24 cm) and 7 inches (17.78 cm). Its depth was 6 inches (15.24 cm). The larger, roughly oval-shaped hole near the south end of the crescent groove (fig. 31, *c*) had diameters of 1 foot 4 inches (40.64 cm) and 11 inches (27.94 cm). Its depth was 8 inches (20.32 cm).

The plastered-over basin (fig. 31, *h*) measured 2 feet (60.96 cm) by 1 foot 6 inches (45.72 cm). Its original depth was 6 inches (15.24 cm).

The large pit just north of the west support post (fig. 31, *n*) had diameters of 2 feet 6 inches (76.2 cm) and 2 feet 2 inches (66.04 cm). Its depth was 8 inches (20.32 cm). The pit southeast from the west support post (fig. 31, *o*) had a long diameter of 2 feet 1½ inches (64.77 cm) and a short diameter of 1 foot 10½ inches (57.15 cm). The depth was 1 foot (30.48 cm).

The large pit at the northeast corner of the room (fig. 31, *f*) was 2 feet 3 inches (68.58 cm) and 2 feet 2 inches (66.04 cm) in diameter. It had a depth of 2 feet (60.96 cm).

STRUCTURE 14 AND DANCE COURT

Structure No. 14 was located on top of the ridge some distance west of 12 and southwest from 13a and 13b (fig. 25). The significant factor about the remains of No. 14 was that they were partially covered by a rather unusual feature in the form of a dance court. The latter had been placed there after structure 14 had gone into ruin and its pit had become filled with debris. That this was not done immediately, however, was indicated by the presence in the fill of No. 14 of a small stone cist that was subsequent

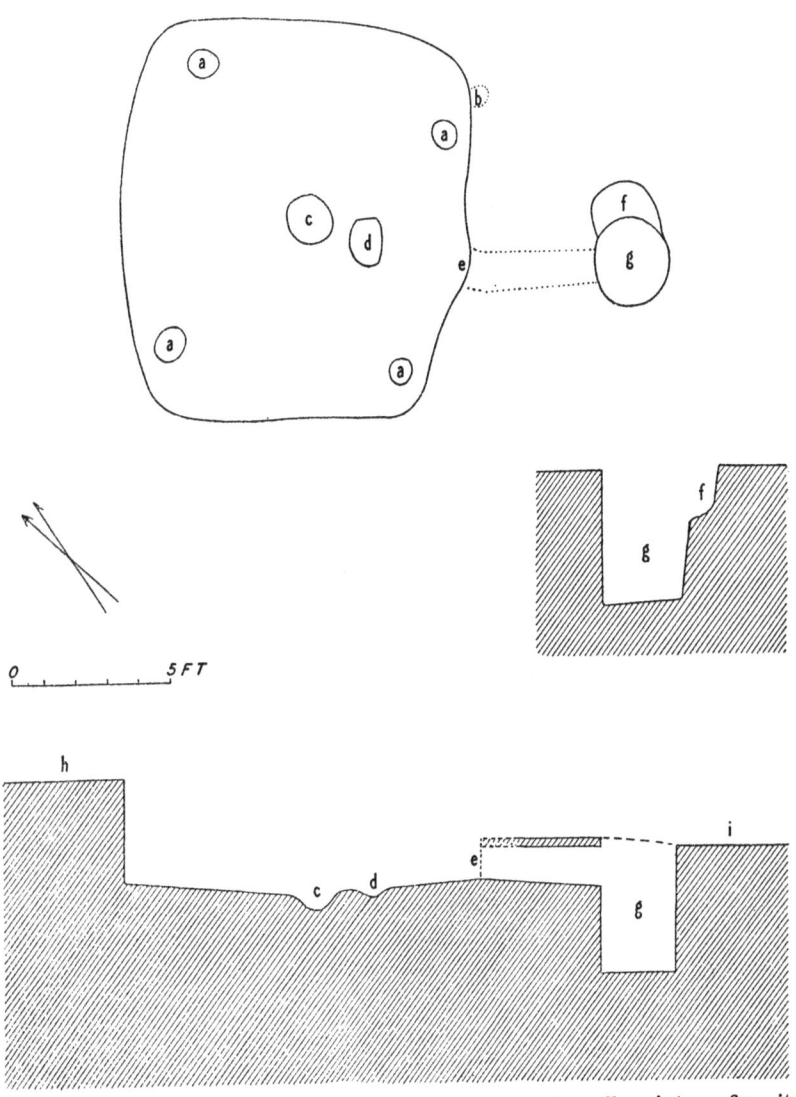

FIGURE 32.—Structure 14. *a*, holes for main support posts; *b*, wall pocket; *c*, fire pit; *d*, ladder box; *e*, ventilator opening; *f* and *g*, exterior opening to ventilator shaft; *h*, platform of dance court dais; *i*, floor of dance court.

to the abandonment of the structure but also antedated the court. The latter probably belonged to a phase associated with the early stages in the development of the large stone structure.

The pit for structure No. 14 was roughly rectangular in shape, although the corners were rounded and the side where the ventilator opened into the chamber was slightly irregular in the same manner as discussed for most of the other structures (fig. 32). The pit was rather shallow and in that respect corresponded to the lack of depth noted for structure 13b. The pit had been covered with a superstructure presumably similar to the flat-ceiling, sloping-sided type already described. There were four holes near the corners of the chamber where the main supports had been placed that indicate a roof of the usual form.

The interior features were simple indeed (pl. 15, a). There was a fire pit (fig. 32, c), near the center of the room and not far from it a ladder box (fig. 32, d). A small pocket in the wall near the east support post probably served for storage purposes (fig. 32, b). This feature was not as elaborate or extensive as the one in 13a and differed from it in that it was partially below the floor level. There were no storage holes in the floor of the chamber and there was no sipapu. Both the fire pit and the depression where the base ends of the ladder rested were simple basins cut in the floor and covered with plaster. No stones were used in their construction.

Perhaps the most interesting part of the construction of No. 14 was that of the ventilator. The passage leading from the chamber to the shaft was comparatively small and had been tunneled through the earth. The shaft at the outer end exhibited a characteristic which was unique in that it extended to a considerable depth below the bottom of the passage (fig. 32, section). As a matter of fact there was more shaft below than above the level (fig. 32, g). What the significance or purpose of such an arrangement was is not known. The only explanation that seems logical is that the builders intended to dig a deeper pit and prepared a ventilator shaft with that idea in mind. After the shaft had been excavated to the desired depth a change in plans was made and the pit for the structure was not carried to a similar depth. The shaft opening on the ground level suggested a figure 8 in contour (pl. 15, b). One segment of the "8" (fig. 32, f) extended only a short distance below the surface while the other furnished the main portion of the shaft (fig. 32, g). Here again, as in the case of the unusual depth below the passage, there is no explanation for the peculiarity of construction.

Potsherds found on the floor of the structure indicated that it belonged to the same general horizon as the other pit remains, namely, early Developmental Pueblo. The overlying dance court was late Developmental Pueblo in its horizon.

The dance court was so called because no other designation seemed more appropriate. Whether the place actually was used for such a purpose or not can not be stated. The court consisted of a well-laid adobe floor placed slightly below the surface of the ground (pl. 16, a). The floor was circular in contour and bordered by a series of small upright stone slabs (fig. 33). Near the center were three depressions placed in a row extending roughly on a north-south line. The northernmost of these pits (fig. 33, *g*), that was nearest the center of the paved circle, had been used as a place for fires. The middle one (fig. 33, *h*) was filled with wood ashes but gave no indication that fires

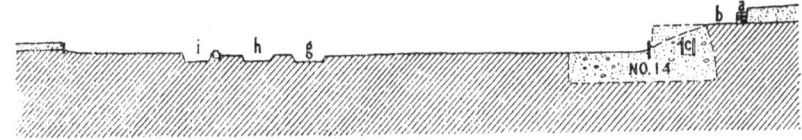

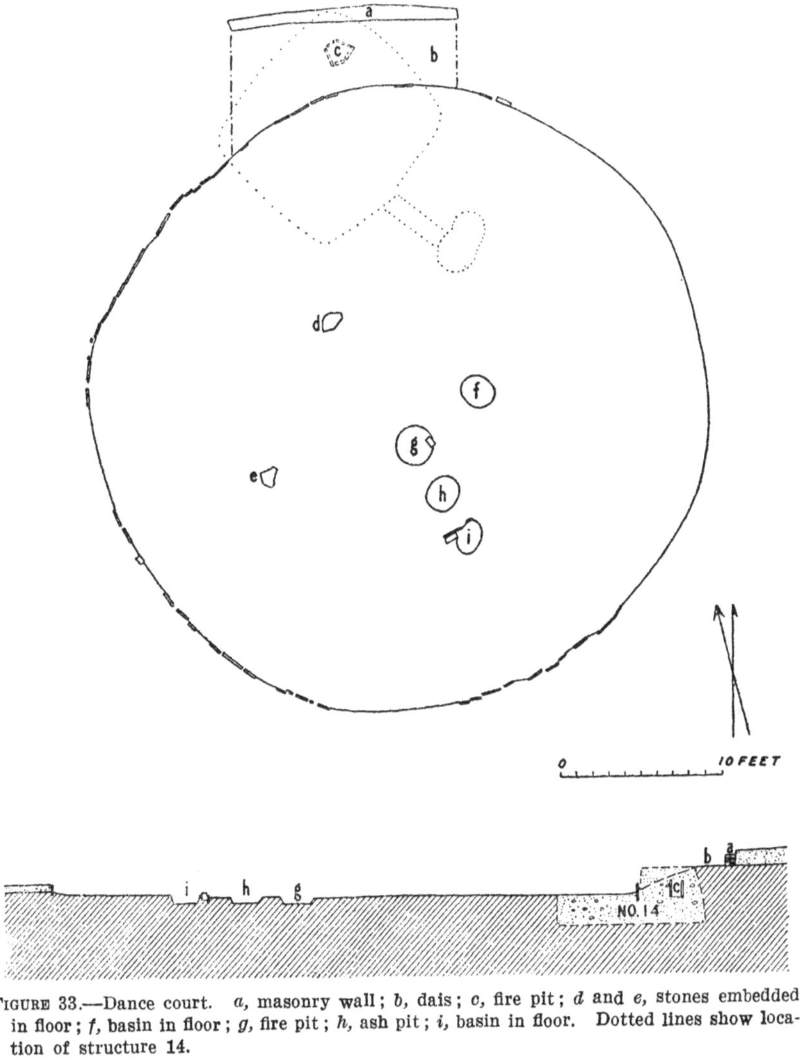

FIGURE 33.—Dance court. *a*, masonry wall; *b*, dais; *c*, fire pit; *d* and *e*, stones embedded in floor; *f*, basin in floor; *g*, fire pit; *h*, ash pit; *i*, basin in floor. Dotted lines show location of structure 14.

had been built in it. It presumably functioned as a depository for the ashes from the main fire pit. There was nothing whatever to indicate the purpose of the third depression (fig. 33, *i*). It was very shallow and although a few stones had been placed along one side it contained nothing but clean blow sand. A fourth basin was present at some distance east of the fire pit (fig. 33, *f*). The sides and bottom of this hole in the pavement were carefully plastered. Except for an accumulation of drift sand the pit was empty when the floor was cleaned. At two places stone slabs were embedded in the floor, their tops flush with the plaster paving (fig. 33, *d, e*). There was nothing to indicate why they should have been so placed and no evidence as to their function.

At the north side of the circle, at a slightly higher elevation, were the remains of a masonry wall that seemed to have formed part of an enclosure (fig. 33, *a;* pl. 16, *b*). The evidence was not as satisfactory as might be desired but all indications were that the masonry constituted the remnants of a three-sided structure that inclosed a form of dais along that portion of the circle. The side toward the court was open. This raised platform would have been a convenient place from which to watch dances or ceremonies being performed in the circle.

Neither the dais nor the circle itself gave indications of a superstructure. It is possible that the platform had been covered with a flat roof and all evidence of it had disappeared. It does not seem likely, however, that the circle could have been roofed over without leaving some indications of a superstructure. In view of these facts it seems logical to conclude that the court was not covered and that all ceremonies or dances held there must have been in the open. There is no direct evidence to warrant such a deduction but it is hard to ignore the suggestion of the basic plan of a great kiva or super-ceremonial chamber in these remains.[57] The size of the circle, together with the raised platform and inclosure at the north end, bears a striking similarity to the broad outlines of such structures. Many of the interior features of the latter are, of course, absent. As a postulation it may be suggested that during Developmental Pueblo times at this location such ceremonies and observances as later took place in the great kiva, one of which is present at the north end of the nearby Great Pueblo ruins, were held in the so-called dance court.

At only one other location in the Southwest has a comparable feature come to light. It was discovered during the same season, 1931, by Earl H. Morris in the course of his investigations in the Chuska Mountains along the Arizona-New Mexico border. Data concerning the latter are not available, as yet, and no comparisons can be drawn. From what Mr. Morris has said concerning the remains he discovered, it would seem that there was a close parallel between the courts at the two sites.

Structure 14 measured 10 feet 10½ inches (3.314 m) on the fire pit, ventilator line. Across the opposite direction it was 11 feet 9½ inches (3.593 m) from wall to wall. At the ventilator side of the chamber the

---

[57] Roberts, 1932, pp. 50, 51, 98; discusses the problem of great kivas in general.

a. Structure 14.

b. Ventilator shaft for structure 14.

a. Dance court as seen from end of Great Pueblo ruin.

b. Portion of structure 14 underlying dance court and dais.

a. Burned roof timbers in pit of structure 15.

b. Series of slanting side poles for roof of structure 15.

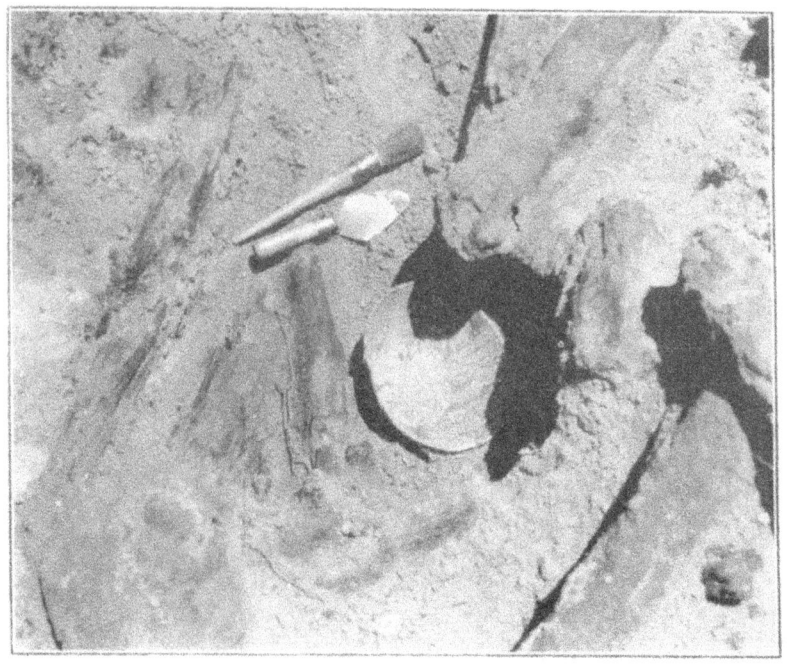

a. Bowl below roof timbers of structure 15.

b. Jar containing carbonized ears of corn lying on top of roof debris in pit of structure 15.

floor was 1 foot 3 inches (38.1 cm) below the level of the court and at the opposite side 3 feet 3 inches (99.06 cm) below the ground level.

The hole for the north post measured 1 foot ½ inch (31.75 cm) on its long diameter and 10½ inches (26.67 cm) on the short. The hole had a depth of 1 foot (30.48 cm) and was 10 inches (25.4 cm) from the wall. The hole for the east support post had diameters of 9 inches (22.86 cm) and 11 inches (27.94 cm). The depth was 1 foot 3 inches (38.1 cm) and the edge of the hole was 5½ inches (13.97 cm) from the wall. The hole at the south corner of the room had diameters of 9 inches (22.86 cm) and 8½ inches (21.59 cm). The hole was 6 inches (15.24 cm) from the wall and had a depth of 1 foot 1 inch (33.02 cm). The hole at the west corner was the largest of the group with a long diameter of 1 foot 1½ inches (34.29 cm) and 11½ inches (29.21 cm). The depth was 1 foot 4 inches (40.64 cm) and the hole was 6 inches (15.24 cm) from the wall.

The fire pit (fig. 32, c) had diameters of 1 foot 4½ inches (41.91 cm) and 1 foot 5½ inches (44.45 cm). Its greatest depth was 6 inches (15.24 cm). The ladder pit (fig. 32, d) was 7 inches (17.78 cm) from the fire pit and measured 1 foot 6 inches (45.72 cm) by 1 foot (30.48 cm). It had a depth of 3 inches (7.62 cm).

The pocket in the wall near the east corner (fig. 32, b) had a diameter of 8 inches (20.32 cm). The opening in the face of the wall was 6 inches (15.24 cm) wide. The bottom was 2 inches (5.08 cm) below the floor level and the top 6 inches (15.24 cm) above it. The back wall sloped from the bottom to the top so that at the top of the opening the pocket had no depth.

The ventilator opening (fig. 32, e) was 1 foot 3 inches (38.1 cm) wide and 1 foot 1 inch (33.02 cm) high. The passage was 3 feet 9 inches (1.143 m) long. Where it opened into the shaft the passage measured 1 foot (30.48 cm) in width and was 1 foot 2½ inches (36.83 cm) high. The shaft measured 2 feet 4 inches (71.12 cm) across the passage line. On the ground line it measured 3 feet 9 inches (1.143 m) from wall to wall. At a depth of 1 foot 6 inches (45.72 cm), however, the diameter at right angles to the passage line narrowed to 2 feet 9 inches (83.82 cm). The main part of the shaft had a depth of 4 feet 1 inch (1.244 m) below the level of the court at the passage side and 3 feet 11 inches (1.193 m) at the back wall.

The dance court had a diameter on the north-south line of 36 feet 8 inches (11.176 m) and on the east-west line measured 37 feet 6 inches (11.430 m). The floor of the court overlapped the house No. 14 pit, 2 feet 9 inches (83.82 cm) at the east corner of the older structure and 7 feet (2.133 m) along the southwest wall. The fire pit at the center of the floor (fig. 33, g) was 2 feet 4 inches (71.12 cm) in diameter and had a depth of 4½ inches (11.43 cm). Between it and the ash pit was a space of 7½ inches (19.05 cm). The ash pit (fig. 33, h) had diameters of 1 foot 9½ inches (54.61 cm) and 2 feet 3 inches (68.58 cm). Its depth was 4⅝ inches (11.75 cm). The third depression (fig. 33, i) was 1 foot 4 inches (40.64 cm) from the ash pit. It had diameters of 1 foot 5½ inches (44.45 cm) and 1 foot 11¾ inches (60.32 cm). The depth was 6 inches (15.24 cm). The fourth pit (fig. 33, f) was 3 feet (91.44 cm) from the central fire pit. It had diameters of 1 foot 10½ inches (57.15 cm) and 2 feet 2 inches (66.04 cm). Its depth was 11 inches (27.94 cm).

The remaining wall of the inclosure (fig. 33, a) at the north side of the circular floor was 14 feet (4.267 m) long and averaged 10 inches (25.4 cm) in width. It was only 1 foot (30.48 cm) in height. The east end of the wall was 4 feet (1.219 m) from the circle and the west end 7 feet 2 inches (2.184 m) from the pavement. The floor of the inclosure had been 1 foot 5 inches (43.18 cm) above that of the court.

SHELTER AND GRANARIES

The remains of a shelter 22 feet 6 inches (6.858 m) northwest from structure 12 and approximately midway between the dance court and structures 13a and 13b (fig. 25) were the best preserved of any found. The floor was roughly oval in outline (fig. 34) and although depressed below the surrounding ground level was not deep enough to be called a pit. The low earth walls sloped up from the floor level to the ground, giving the depression a saucerlike cross section. Indications were that the floor basin possibly resulted from continued sweeping of the area with an attendant removal of particles of earth on each occasion, rather than being intentionally dug. The floor was not plastered; the surface was merely hard-packed through use. Holes for posts to support a superstructure were present at four places near the periphery (fig. 34, a) and indicated a flat-roofed covering. The positions of these holes approximately coincided with the four major points of the compass. There were no traces of slanting side timbers, hence it is not known whether the place was merely an arbor or had walls of flimsy construction. Because the floor features here were more elaborate than in the other shelters previously described, the first thought was that the structure was a shallow-pit dwelling, but when no traces of pole, brush, and plaster walls could be found this idea was abandoned. The structure probably was an outdoor summer kitchen for one of the nearby domiciles.

Floor features consisted of a fire pit, storage holes, the mold left by a stone, and a niche in the wall that presumably was a seat for a roof brace. The fire pit consisted of a simple basin dug into the floor. It was practically circular in form and the sides were more vertical than usual, although the walls did slope in to some extent at the bottom. There was no rim around the edges of the pit on the floor level. When uncovered the basin contained wood ashes and small bits of charcoal. The sides and bottom were burned a deep red color. Close to the fire pit, on the northeast side, was a peculiarly

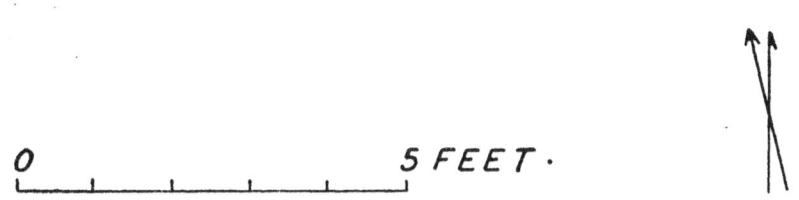

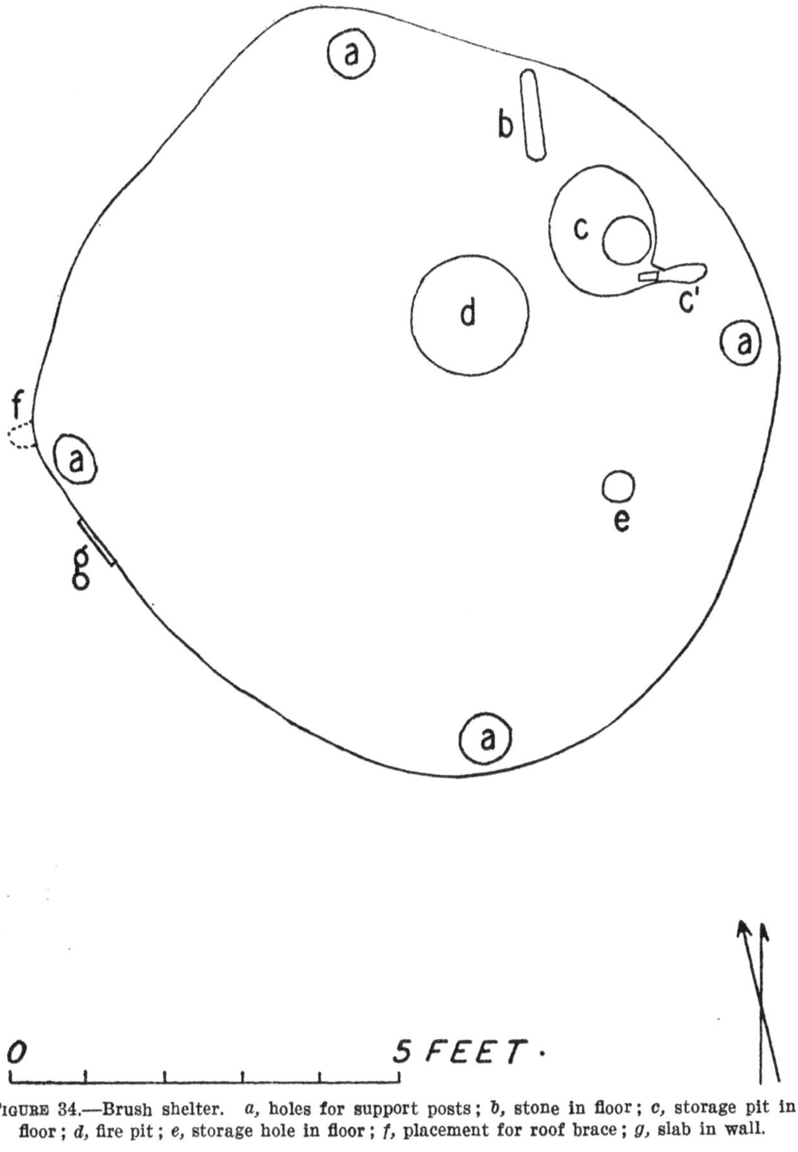

FIGURE 34.—Brush shelter. *a*, holes for support posts; *b*, stone in floor; *c*, storage pit in floor; *d*, fire pit; *e*, storage hole in floor; *f*, placement for roof brace; *g*, slab in wall.

shaped depression and hole (fig. 34, *c*) that possibly served for storage purposes or in connection with a mealing stone. There was nothing to indicate its exact function. The outer portion was shallow, the bottom curving down gradually to the edge of the inner hole in funnel-like fashion. The trough extending from one side (fig. 34, c') was blocked off from the main portion of the basin by a small stone set in the earth at that point. There is one suggestion in connection with the trough, namely, that it was a placement for a stone, corresponding to that at the opposite side (fig. 34, b). The latter gave clear evidence that the base end of a slab, subsequently removed, was embedded there. If a similar stone stood at the former spot the two would have formed a rough bin behind the funnel-shaped basin. The small circular hole in the floor at the southeast side (fig. 34, e) was unquestionably for the storage of small objects. The niche, suggestive of a placement for a roof brace, was located near the west support post. The bottom of the niche (fig. 34, f) was on the floor level. The sides were vertical, but the back sloped from top to bottom at an angle coincident with that which a slanting pole placed there would assume if its upper end joined the framework for the roof. A single slab of stone was set in the low wall near the west post (fig. 34, g). This was the only example of stone facing in the structure and at no place around the remainder of the periphery were there indications that similar slabs had been set but subsequently removed. There was nothing to indicate why the one was placed there.

On a line through the north and south support posts the diameter of the floor measured 9 feet 7 inches (2.921 m) and from wall to wall through the east-west posts was 9 feet 6 inches (2.895 m). The average depth of the floor below the old ground level, that of the period of occupation, was 8 inches (20.32 cm). The present surface is 3 feet 9 inches (1.143 m) above the floor level on the south side and 3 feet 2½ inches (97.79 cm) on the north.

The holes for the support posts did not vary greatly in size. In general they were smaller than those in most of the house structures. That at the north side had a diameter of 7½ inches (19.05 cm) and a depth of 1 foot 3 inches (38.1 cm). It was 2½ inches (6.35 cm) from the edge of the depression. The east hole was 6½ inches (16.51 cm) in diameter and 1 foot 5½ inches (44.45 cm) deep and stood 2½ inches (6.35 cm) from the wall. The hole at the south side had an 8-inch (20.32 cm) diameter, a depth of 1 foot 6½ inches (46.99 cm), and was 1½ inches (3.81 cm) from the edge of the pit. The hole for the west post was oval in form, the long diameter being parallel with the wall, and measured 6 inches by 7½ inches (15.24 by 19.05 cm). The depth was 1 foot 5 inches (43.18 cm) and the distance from the wall 1 inch (2.54 cm).

The fire-pit diameters were 1 foot 6 inches (45.72 cm) and 1 foot 6½ inches (46.99 cm) on the floor level. The sloping of the sides near the bottom reduced the diameter to 1 foot 2 inches (35.56 cm). The depth of the pit was 4⅝ inches (11.75 cm).

The funnel-shaped basin (fig. 34, *c*) had diameters of 1 foot 4½ inches (41.91 cm) and 1 foot 7 inches (48.26 cm). The greatest depth was around the edges of the central hole and measured 2⅜ inches (60.32 cm). The central hole had a diameter of 7½ inches (19.05 cm) and a depth of 5 inches (12.7 cm) below the bottom of the encircling basin. The groove (fig. 34 *c'*) was 7½ inches (19.05 cm) long by 3 inches (7.62 cm) wide and had a depth of 1¼ inches (3.17 cm). The stone at the basin end was 3 inches (7.62 cm) long, 1 inch (2.54 cm) thick at the west end and 1½ inches (3.81 cm) thick at the east end, and stood 3⅝ inches (9.21 cm) above the bottom of the basin.

The long oval-shaped groove (fig. 34, *b*) that had been the placement for a stone slab had a length of 1 foot 1 inch (33.02 cm), a width of 3 inches (7.62 cm), and ranged in depth from 2½ inches (6.35 cm) at the south end to 3 inches (7.62 cm) at the north. Near the center its depth was 3½ inches (8.89 cm).

The storage hole (fig. 34, *e*) was 5½ inches (13.97 cm) in diameter and had a depth of 5 inches (12.7 cm).

The roof-brace placement at the west side of the floor (fig. 34, *f*) was 4½ inches (11.43 cm) across the opening in the low wall and measured 4½ inches (11.43 cm) from front to back.

The mound of accumulated sand, stones, and other material above the remains of the shelter suggested a number of interesting items in the growth of the site. After the abandonment of the shelter the area was covered with a layer of sand deposited, for the most part, by wind action. The remains of the superstructure of the shelter may have formed enough of an obstruction to constitute a nucleus around which a low dune developed. The area was then used from time to time as a "workshop" where stones employed in construction work were shaped and dressed. Mason's debris was scattered all through the deposit and that in the lower levels seemingly correlated with the similar material, tabular bits of sandstone, noted in the top layer fill in structure No. 12, although the latter represented only the outer fringes of the accumulation. The main stone-dressing activity apparently centered to a large extent in the section overlying the shelter. After the mound had grown to a height of approximately 2 feet 3 inches (68.58 cm) above the old ground level, building operations increased and the top 1 foot 3 inches (38.1 cm) consisted almost entirely of such debris. This is shown in the section drawings (fig. 35, *2, 3*). Potsherds scattered through the layer of stones indicated that the deposit corresponded in time to the interval when considerable construction work was under way on the Great Pueblo dwellings.

One concentration of building stones, in the mound (fig. 35, e, e), presents a puzzling problem. The level where they occurred was only 6 inches (15.24 cm) above that of the old ground surface and they centered about the location of the shelter. When they were encountered in the excavation work it was thought that they had been used in walls for the structure, but the evidence was otherwise. The layer of wind-blown sand between them and the ground around

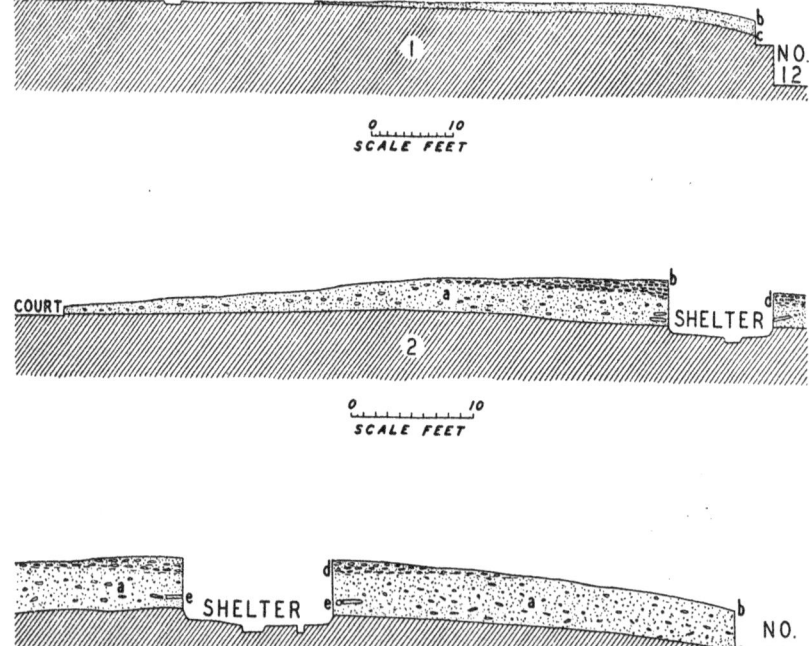

FIGURE 35.—Sections for structure 12, dance court and shelter.

the edges of the shelter floor demonstrated that there was a definite chronological break between the two features. To attribute the situation to coincidence does not seem an entirely satisfactory explanation, yet after careful consideration of all aspects of the case there can be no other conclusion.

Farther along the side north from the shelter were the remains of two granaries. They were located 24 feet (7.315 m) northwest from structure 13b. Fire had destroyed both of them and the pit portions were filled with carbonized corn and charcoal from the superstructures. In general they were quite similar to the granary pits discussed in preceding pages. Shallow excavations had been covered with a pole, brush, and plaster superstructure. One of the pits was lined with stone slabs, while the walls of the other were covered with mud plaster. The latter had slumped away from the walls, hence the exact dimensions of the pit could not be learned. There was nothing in either pit to link them with any particular structure. Judging from the normal location of granaries, with respect to other houses at the site, they would appear to belong with 13a or 13b.

The stone-lined pit was 5 feet 6 inches (1.676 m) long and 4 feet 6 inches (1.371 m) wide. At the south end it had a depth of 10 inches (25.4 cm) and at the north end 1 foot (30.48 cm). The second pit was slightly more pentagonal in outline and measured approximately 5 feet by 5 feet (1.524 by 1.524 m). Its depth was 2 feet (60.96 cm) at the south end and 2 feet 3½ inches (69.85 cm) at the north.

The pile of loose rocks located 27 feet (8.230 m) northwest from these granary pits (fig. 25) apparently consisted of material gathered for use in construction work. The stones were arranged in an orderly fashion, although simply piled there, and were not the remains of a fallen house. Perhaps they had been carried there from the sandstone ledges along the edge of the mesa and were waiting to be shaped and dressed for inclusion in a structure that was never built. There was nothing to show what stage in the history of the site was represented by this feature, although their location and the nature of the surrounding earth suggest that it was subsequent to the existence of the not far distant structure No. 15.

STRUCTURE 15 AND ASSOCIATED GRANARIES

The remains of structure 15 and the nearby granaries and shelters present an interesting example of a prototype for a unit or single-clan form of dwelling (fig. 25). The group as a whole is especially significant from the standpoint of the evolution of a characteristic late Developmental Pueblo type of house. Structure 15 was a typical pit dwelling of the form more commonly found in the regions north and east from the Allantown district, particularly the Chaco Canyon area. The pit was roughly circular in form and had an encircling bench (fig. 36). Both bench and inner pit were dug into the earth, although the bench was quite shallow. The back wall was just high enough to serve as a footing for the sloping side timbers of the superstructure. The top of the bench was covered with adobe plaster, but the back wall was not so treated and its face was merely the native earth. The wall of the main pit, however, had a facing

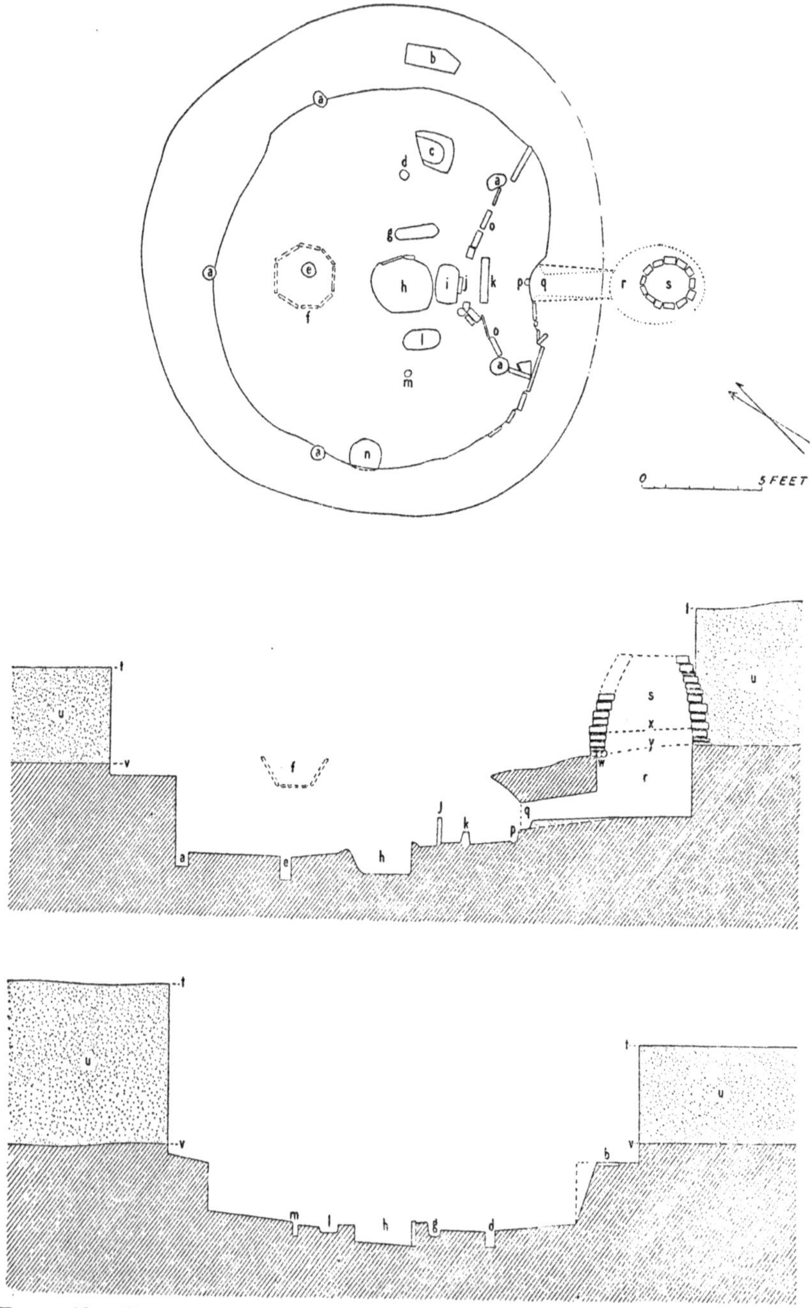

FIGURE 36.—Structure 15. *a*, holes for support posts; *b*, stone embedded in bench top; *c*, metate on floor; *d*, small storage hole; *e*, sipapu; *f*, fire pit; *g*, basin in floor; *h*, fire pit; *i*, ash pit; *j*, deflector; *k*, step and ladder brace; *l*, basin in floor; *m*, storage hole in floor; *n*, storage basin; *o*, compartment wall; *p*, hole for post to brace cover stone; *q*, ventilator opening; *r*, base of ventilator shaft; *s*, ventilator opening on ground; *t*, present surface; *u*, sand accumulation; *v*, original surface; *w*, wooden support for masonry; *x*, floor in granary; *y*, surface of accumulated material in shaft.

of stone slabs. These were covered with plaster. The latter had fallen away in some places, although it was still in position around most of the periphery.

The superstructure had been of the characteristic flat-center, sloping-sided type. It differed from most examples, though, in one feature. There were five main support posts instead of four. Three of these were set into the face of the bench, while the other two stood out from the wall but were incorporated in the low partition forming a compartment at the ventilator side of the room (fig. 36, a). The construction of the superstructure was easily determined here because the house had been destroyed by fire. Most of the timbers were only charred, the collapse of the roof smothering the flames before the wood was wholly consumed, and were lying in positions that clearly indicated their original locations (pl. 17, a). The five uprights carried a series of stringers that formed a pentagonal framework. Several large joists extended across the central portion from one side of this framework to the other and in turn supported smaller poles. The opening in the roof above the fire pit was rectangular in shape, the long measurement being on the fire pit, ventilator line. Stone slabs framed the opening and formed a protective border around its edges. The sloping ceiling consisted of a series of main beams slanting from the back of the bench to the heavy stringers on the uprights. Smaller poles were placed, running horizontally around the framework, on top of these (pl. 17, b). The plaster and earth outer covering was applied directly to the timbers to complete the roof.

When the structure was destroyed by fire two pottery vessels were sitting on the roof, one not far from the edge of the smoke-hole-hatchway, the other farther down the roof slope. They were found in the fill just above the burned timbers. One was a bowl (pl. 18, a) and the other a flat-topped jar filled with ears of corn (pl. 18, b). The corn was charred by the heat of the conflagration. Why the vessels were sitting on the roof can only be answered by postulation. The surfaces of the low-rounding superstructure mounds probably served as gathering places for the families living there and it would be natural that objects, for one reason or another, were occasionally left outside. Of course it is possible that an attempt was being made to salvage belongings from the fire and that these were carried as far as the roof and then abandoned. On the other hand, one of the women of the household may have been returning from the granary with her jar of corn and the bowl and seeing smoke pouring from the dwelling, rushed to determine the cause, setting the vessels down in the process.

The interior features of No. 15 were elaborate and more complex than in many of those previously discussed. The fire pit was dug into the earth and was roughly oval in contour (fig. 36, *h*). On one side two stones were set into the wall to reinforce it, but most of the periphery was covered with a heavy coating of mud plaster, burned a deep red in color. A low ridge of plaster encircled the pit on the floor level. When the chamber was excavated the pit was half filled with ashes and some small fragments of charcoal. On either side of the pit, in the floor, were two basins (fig. 36, *g*, *l*), of unknown purpose. They had rounded bottoms and were carefully plastered. They may have functioned as pot rests, vessels being placed there so that the heat from the fire would keep their contents from cooling too rapidly.

Next to the fire pit, in the position normally occupied by the ladder box, was a rectangular-shaped basin with rounded ends (fig. 36, *i*). A ridge of plaster separated it from the fire pit. At the side toward the ventilator the wall of the basin was reinforced by a stone slab that also served as a deflector (fig. 36, *j*). The basin apparently functioned as a depository for ashes, as it was a little more than half filled with such material when first uncovered. The ashes could not be attributed to the burning of the superstructure as they were fine and powdery and free from charcoal fragments. They were the kind produced by long and continuous burning of wood in a pit and unquestionably were intentionally placed in the basin. A similar feature was noted in some of the other houses or structures.

The ends of the ladder rested against a large stone set just inside the compartment (fig. 36, *k*). The poles were not embedded in the floor, but they had worn small, cuplike depressions in the surface of the plaster. The bracing stone was low and its top probably served as a step for anyone ascending or descending the ladder. Placed as it was, the ladder blocked the opening into the compartment and on entering or leaving the chamber it would have been necessary for one to step over the low partition. The position of the deflector stone (fig. 36, *j*) between the ladder and the fire pit was not common. A majority of the structures showed the reverse, the deflector being between the ladder base and the ventilator opening.

In the main part of the chamber there were two storage holes in the floor. They were on opposite sides of the fire pit and its adjacent basins (fig. 36, *d*, *m*). They were similar in form to those described for other houses. The sipapu was present in the customary position (fig. 36, *e*) and exhibited no unusual features. At the west side of the chamber, close to one of the main supports, was a large basin in the floor that slightly undercut the wall above it (fig. 36, *n*). The sides and bottom were carefully plastered and the top was encircled by a low ridge of plaster that raised the rim somewhat above the floor level. There was nothing in the basin at the time of excavation to show the purpose. It would have been a convenient place to keep a variety of things, however.

The metate or milling stone on the floor at the east side of the chamber (fig. 36, c; pl. 19, a) was in position when found. The heat from the burning roof timbers cracked the stone, but the pieces had not fallen apart. One hand stone (mano) was lying in the trough. Several additional manos were on the floor at one side of the metate. They varied from coarse, through medium, to fine in quality and no doubt were used for grinding meal of different grades. The metate stone was raised above the floor by a base consisting of three stones. This additional height would make it possible to set a shallow basket or tray under the open end of the trough and catch the meal as it dropped from the grinding stone. Metates frequently occupied such a position in houses of this period. It was not until the following or Great Pueblo era that the practice developed of placing several such stones in a bin.

The compartment at the southeast side of the chamber was formed by a series of stone slabs placed on end in the floor. Several were broken when the roof crashed in and others were cracked from the heat. They originally had been of approximately the same height, any discrepancy being compensated for by the heavy coating of plaster that covered the stones. There was a break or doorway to the low wall at the place where the ladder stood. There were no interior features in the compartment.

The ventilator was well made and had several features that differed from those previously described. In common with several, however, it had been reduced in size. The original opening into the chamber was considerably larger than that of the remodeled form. The first aperture had a framing of stone; the second and smaller one was entirely of plaster. In the final form there was a step or ledge that formed a rest for a stone cover for the opening. This ledge was on the level of the original floor of the passage. Just in front of the vent, in the compartment floor, was a hole in which a small post had been set to hold the cover stone in place (fig. 36, p). The front wall of the bench above the opening projected into the room to a degree not noted elsewhere (fig. 36, section). Whether this was intentional or had resulted from a sagging and displacement in the bench, with attendant repair work, is not known. The front edge was reinforced with a short log of wood (pl. 19, b), but it could not be determined whether it dated from the remodeling of the ventilator or had been placed there at some subsequent time. The wood was charred from burning and some of it fell away when the debris was being removed from the pit. The full length had carried it well across the opening and about midway of the upright stone slab that formed part of the original aperture (pl. 19, b), the stone at the right in the photograph.

The passage was short and also had been reduced in size. This was accomplished through use of large quantities of mud plaster. The width was narrowed and the floor raised to a higher level. It was not possible to determine the status of the original passage roof because the old one was removed and a new one installed. The original floor sloped upward to the bottom of the shaft at the outer end, while the later one was almost level. The passage was of the constructed type.

The shaft at the outer end had several features differing somewhat from others previously described. The lower and main part was oval in outline and much larger than many of those discussed in preceding pages. The walls from the old ground level to the bottom of the shaft were native earth covered with plaster. Several courses of stone were laid around the aperture on the surface, presumably to heighten the shaft. A similar condition, although in smaller degree, was mentioned in connection with structure No. 2. The presence of the masonry may indicate an attempt to prevent drifting sand from falling into the opening and blocking the shaft, or an effort to improve the ventilating functions. The extensive dome-like structure shown in the upper section of the drawing (fig. 36) does not belong to the dwelling proper. It is of later date. Subsequent to the destruction of the house by fire the ventilator shaft drifted full of sand to the height of the old ground level, as indicated by the dotted line in the shaft (fig. 36, y). The circle of rocks remained and was used as the foundation for a storage structure. The latter was built of stones laid in progressively contracting courses to produce the beehive-shaped structure uncovered in the digging. Before erecting the upper part, dump-heap material was placed in the bottom to level and raise the floor. The latter consisted of adobe plaster laid on top of the fill and smoothed to form an even surface (fig. 36, x). There was nothing to show the stage to which this structure belonged. Whether it was erected shortly after the destruction of the house or following an interval of some length is not known. That the upper courses were of later date was clearly shown by a difference in the color of the mud mortar used in the masonry. That in the original section was a dark yellow, discolored by smoke stains, while in the upper part it was red and not smudged. The entire dome was covered with plaster when completed. Most of it had fallen away, however, and only patches were clinging here and there when the remains were uncovered. The encircling courses of stone that were laid around the top of the shaft in the first place were an addition made after the completion of the ventilator in the original form. The stones in the arc on the house side of the shaft rested partially on the ground and partially on two timbers (fig. 36, *w*) that extended across that part of the excavation. The wood was in an advanced stage of decay when found and was only held in place by surrounding dirt. There were no traces of charring, indicating that the flames in the burning structure had not touched them. A significant factor in this connection is that the plaster on the walls of the original part of the shaft showed direct effects of fire, while the stones above did not. The latter were smoke stained, but they had not come into actual contact with flames. This suggests that the structure was damaged to some extent on an occasion prior to the addition of the stones to the shaft and later final destruction of the dwelling. The last conflagration probably produced the smoke stains on the stones. There were some indications in the dwelling proper of an earlier period fire to substantiate those in the ventilator shaft. Several places where the plaster had broken away from the face of the bench and from the bench top, the underlying material gave evidence of burning. These lead to the conclusion that there were two periods of occupation, each terminated by fire. After the first the structure was rebuilt and after the second it was abandoned.

The shaft in its original status was large enough to serve as an antechamber and with the unreduced passage could have been the entrance to the house. When the passage was made smaller it would not have been possible for a person to crawl through the aperture into the room. The conditions warrant the suggestion that in this house there is a record of the shift from antechamber, passage entrance to access by means of a ladder through the smoke-hole-hatchway in the superstructure. This shift, if such actually occurred, correlated with the first burning of the house and subsequent remodeling.

The fill in the main part of No. 15 consisted largely of charred timbers, burned plaster, and drift sand. At no time was the pit used as a dumping place for refuse. When the hole had filled to the old original ground level a definite surface of occupation developed and a fire pit was placed there (fig. 36, *f*). This pit was lined with stone slabs and had a large stone for its bottom. The slabs around the sides projected slightly above the ground level, with the result that the fire basin was deeper than the hole in which it was placed. This pit probably corresponded in time to the granary or bin erected above the old ventilator shaft. The accumulation of sand above the fire pit and the beehive-shaped structure apparently dates from a period subsequent to the abandonment of both.

The quantity of burned timber in the pit of No. 15 supplied ample material for dendrochronological studies and determining the age of the structure. The latest date obtained was 888, and the earliest 857, a spread of 31 years.[58] That the life span of the structure should be considered as of that duration is questionable. The logs of earlier date may have been taken from another structure. There is, of course, a possibility that they were part of the original superstructure and were employed in the rebuilding that took place when the ventilator was reduced in size and the encircling stones laid around the ground-level opening at the top of the shaft. To assume that such was the case is not warranted by the evidence, but it does suggest an interesting possibility. On the basis of the latest date it can be said definitely that the house was occupied, that is its final period of inhabitation, circa 888. This antedates by 30 years structure No. 12 and its 918. There was an overlapping in dates for certain logs in the two, however, as was mentioned in connection with the discussion of No. 12. How long both were occupied from the period of their latest dates until destroyed by fire is not known. That No. 15 was burned before No. 12 is indicated by the difference in potsherds found on the floors of each. Those from No. 12 definitely represent a later type.

Structure No. 15 had a diameter of 13 feet 1 inch (3.987 m) below the bench on the ventilator, fire pit, sipapu line, and 19 feet 1 inch (5.816 m) above the bench. At right angles to this line the inner diameter, below the bench, was 15 feet (4.572 m) and the outer, including the bench top, measured 20 feet 2 inches (6.146 m). On the ventilator side of the chamber the top of the bench was 2 feet 8½ inches (82.55 cm) above the floor. At the opposite side it was 3 feet 1 inch (93.98 cm). The back wall of the bench was 6 inches (15.24 cm) high. The floor at the ventilator side was 3 feet 9 inches (1.143 m) below the original ground level and 8 feet 7½ inches (2.628 m) below the present surface. At the opposite side of the room the floor was the same distance below the old ground level, 3 feet 9 inches (1.143 m), but was only 7 feet 9½ inches (2.374 m) below the recent level.

The holes for the support posts varied somewhat in size, but this was in part due to the edges being broken at the floor level. The timbers used for the main uprights apparently were about the same size. They seem to have approximated closely a 6½-inch (16.51-cm) diameter. The post at the north side of the chamber was set into the face of the bench for a little over half of the diameter. The plaster of the bench had touched the timber all along its surface and showed the log had a 6-inch (15.24-cm) diameter. The hole in the floor at the base of the bench was slightly oval in form with 6-inch (15.24-cm) and 7-inch (17.78-cm) diameters. The depth was

---

[58] Miller, 1934, p. 16, designated as House 4/32.

only 6 inches (15.24 cm). The enclosing bench wall furnished considerable support for the timber, hence greater depth was probably not essential. The hole for the support post in the east compartment wall measured 6 inches (15.24 cm) by 10 inches (25.4 cm). The depth was 1 foot 9 inches (53.34 cm), a much deeper placement than that in the bench. The post in the west compartment wall was set in a hole with diameters of 8½ inches (21.59 cm) and 9½ inches (24.13 cm) and a depth of 1 foot 10 inches (55.88 cm). The post at the southwest side, in the bench face, had a diameter of 6½ inches (16.51 cm). The charred butt was still in place and was not removed, so that the depth of the hole is not known. The timber in the western arc of the bench face also measured 6½ inches (16.51 cm) in diameter. The hole in the floor was 6 inches (15.24 cm) in depth.

The fire pit (fig. 36, h) measured 2 feet 6½ inches (77.47 cm) on the sipapu, ventilator line and 2 feet 1 inch (63.50 cm) across in the other direction. At the sipapu side it had a depth of 10 inches (25.4 cm) and at the ventilator side 1 foot 1 inch (33.02 cm). The plaster ridge separating it from the basin containing ashes was 1 inch (2.54 cm) thick at the narrowest point. The ash basin had a length of 1 foot 7 inches (48.26 cm) and a width of 11½ inches (29.21 cm). At the fire-pit side it had a depth of 1 inch (2.54 cm) and in front of the deflector stone it was 1½ inches (3.81 cm) deep. The deflector stone (fig. 36, j) measured 8 inches (20.32 cm) by 2 inches (5.08 cm) and stood 1 foot (30.48 cm) above the floor.

The sipapu (fig. 36, e) was 2 feet 3½ inches (69.85 cm) from the fire pit. It was slightly oval in form with diameters of 7 and 8 inches (17.78 and 20.32 cm). The depth was somewhat greater than in many of the examples and measured 9¾ inches (24.76 cm).

The hole in the floor (fig. 36, d) had a diameter of 5 inches (12.7 cm) and a depth of 2 inches (5.08 cm). The hole was practically midway between the fire pit and the wall, being 3 feet 2 inches (96.52 cm) from the latter and 3 feet (91.44 cm) from the former. It was only 9 inches (22.86 cm) from the end of the metate stone. The hole in a corresponding location at the opposite side of the room (fig. 36, m) had a diameter of 3 inches (7.62 cm) and a depth of 4 inches (10.16 cm). This hole was 2 feet 3 inches (68.58 cm) from the fire pit and 3 feet 3 inches (99.06 cm) from the wall.

The basins on either side of the fire pit (fig. 36, g, l) differed in size. The length for g was 1 foot 10 inches (55.88 cm), the width 5½ inches (13.97 cm) at the small end and 6½ inches (16.51 cm) at the large. The average depth was 5 inches (12.7 cm). This basin was 6½ inches (16.51 cm) from the fire pit. Basin l had a length of 1 foot 7 inches (48.26 cm), a width of 9½ inches (24.13 cm) at the broad end and 8½ inches (21.59 cm) at the narrow. The depth averaged 4 inches (10.16 cm), and the distance between the basin and the fire pit measured 8½ inches (21.59 cm).

The storage place at the base of the wall (fig. 36, *n*) had diameters of 1 foot 3 inches (38.1 cm) and 1 foot 4 inches (40.64 cm). It undercut the face of the bench 1½ inches (3.81 cm). The basin had a depth of 4 inches (10.16 cm). The plaster rim around the top averaged 3 inches (7.62 cm) in width and at the edge of the basin was 1 inch (2.54 cm) above the floor level.

The metate (fig. 36, *c*) had a maximum length of 1 foot 8½ inches (52.07 cm) and a maximum breadth of 1 foot 4½ inches (41.91 cm). The trough in the stone measured 1 foot 1 inch (33.02 cm) long on a median line and was 10 inches (25.4 cm) wide. The bulk of the stone was 5 inches (12.7 cm) thick and it was raised 3 inches (7.62 cm) above the floor level.

The stones forming the walls of the compartment varied in height, width, and thickness (fig. 36, *o*). Some of the stones had been broken when the roof fell, so that the measurements given are not in all cases their original height. At the southwest corner of the compartment the wall height was 2 feet 5 inches (73.66 cm) and at the northeast end was 1 foot 11 inches (58.42 cm). These measurements include the adobe plaster covering over the stones. Beginning at the northeast end of the compartment wall (fig. 36), the stones measured:

First, 1 foot 6 inches (45.72 cm) long, 2¾ inches (6.98 cm) thick, and 1 foot 9 inches (53.34 cm) high.

Second, 9 inches (22.86 cm) long, 1 inch (2.54 cm) thick, and 1 foot 8 inches (50.8 cm) high.

Third, 9 inches (22.86 cm) long, 2½ inches (6.35 cm) thick, and 8 inches (20.32 cm) high.

Fourth, 8½ inches (21.59 cm) long, 3½ inches (8.89 cm) thick, and 1 foot 2 inches (35.56 cm) high.

Fifth, 5 inches (12.7 cm) long, 3½ inches (8.89 cm) thick, and 1 foot (30.48 cm) high; the opening in the wall in front of the ventilator was 1 foot 9 inches (53.34 cm) wide.

The sixth stone was 3½ inches (8.89 cm) long, 2 inches (5.08 cm) thick, and 8 inches (20.32 cm) high.

The seventh measured 7½ inches (19.05 cm) long, 3½ inches (8.89 cm) thick, and 1 foot 4 inches (40.64 cm) high; the small bracing stone next to No. 7 was 5 inches (12.7 cm) long, 3 inches (7.62 cm) thick, and 3 inches (7.62 cm) high.

The eighth stone was 1 foot (30.48 cm) long, 1 inch (2.54 cm) thick, and 1 foot 10 inches (55.88 cm) high.

The ninth was 9½ inches (24.13 cm) long, 2½ inches (6.35 cm) thick, and 2 feet 1 inch (63.5 cm) high.

The tenth stone was 1 foot (30.48 cm) long, 2¼ inches (5.71 cm) thick, and 2 feet 3 inches (68.58 cm) high.

The ladder brace, just inside the compartment (fig. 36, k) was 1 foot 9½ inches (54.61 cm) long, 4 inches (10.16 cm) thick, and rose 6 inches (15.24 cm) above the floor.

The hole where a small pole had been set as a reinforcement for the end of the compartment wall at the southwest side of the doorway (fig. 36) was 3½ inches (8.89 cm) in diameter and had a depth of 3 inches (7.62 cm). There was nothing to indicate what the height of the pole had been. The hole in front of the ventilator opening, where a post to hold a cover stone in place over the vent had been set, measured 2 inches (5.08 cm) and 3 inches (7.62 cm) in diameter and had a depth of 2 inches (5.08 cm). The hole (fig. 36, p) was against the riser to the vent sill.

The ventilator aperture, in its final form, was 10 inches (25.4 cm) wide and 9 inches (22.86 cm) high. The sill was 5 inches (12.7 cm) above the compartment floor. The offset for the cover slab was 3½ inches (8.89 cm) deep at the sill. The original opening into the passage was 1 foot 6 inches (45.72 cm) wide. The height could not be determined. The passage was 3 feet 2 inches (96.52 cm) long. Where it entered the shaft it was 1 foot 2 inches (35.56 cm) wide and 1 foot 1 inch (33.02 cm) high. The original width was 1 foot 6 inches (45.72 cm). The shaft had a diameter of 3 feet 11 inches (1.193 m) on the passage line and 3 feet 2 inches (96.52 cm) at right angles to it. The bottom of the pit was 2 feet 11 inches (88.9 cm) below the original ground level and 8 feet 5 inches (2.565 m) below the present surface. The circle of stones first placed around the opening on the surface was 1 foot 2 inches (35.56 cm) high. The completed structure (fig. 36, s) rose 3 feet 6 inches (1.066 m) above the ground level. Inside the total height, from the adobe floor to the opening, was 2 feet 11 inches (88.9 cm). The opening at the top was approximately 2 feet (60.96 cm).

The fire pit built on top of the fill in the pit of No. 15, and dating from the same period as the stone structure above the vent shaft, was 2 feet 3 inches (68.58 cm) by 2 feet 5 inches (73.66 cm) and had a depth of 1 foot 2 inches (35.56 cm). The edges of the stone slabs lining the pit projected above the surface of the level of occupation 3 inches (7.62 cm). The bottom of the pit was 2 feet 9 inches (83.82 cm) above the floor of the dwelling. The top of the pit was 2 feet 2 inches (66.04 cm) below the present surface.

The group of granaries associated with structure No. 15 constituted one of the more significant features at the site. They were located 19 to 25 feet (5.791 m to 7.620 m) north and west from the dwelling and were built in an orderly row (fig. 37). The pit portions were rectangular and there was evidence to show that they had been covered with pole, brush, and plaster superstructures of the truncated pyramidal type. The walls in this type had only a slight slant and the roofs were flat. No internal supports were used. The corner posts were placed just at the edge of the pit and carried a

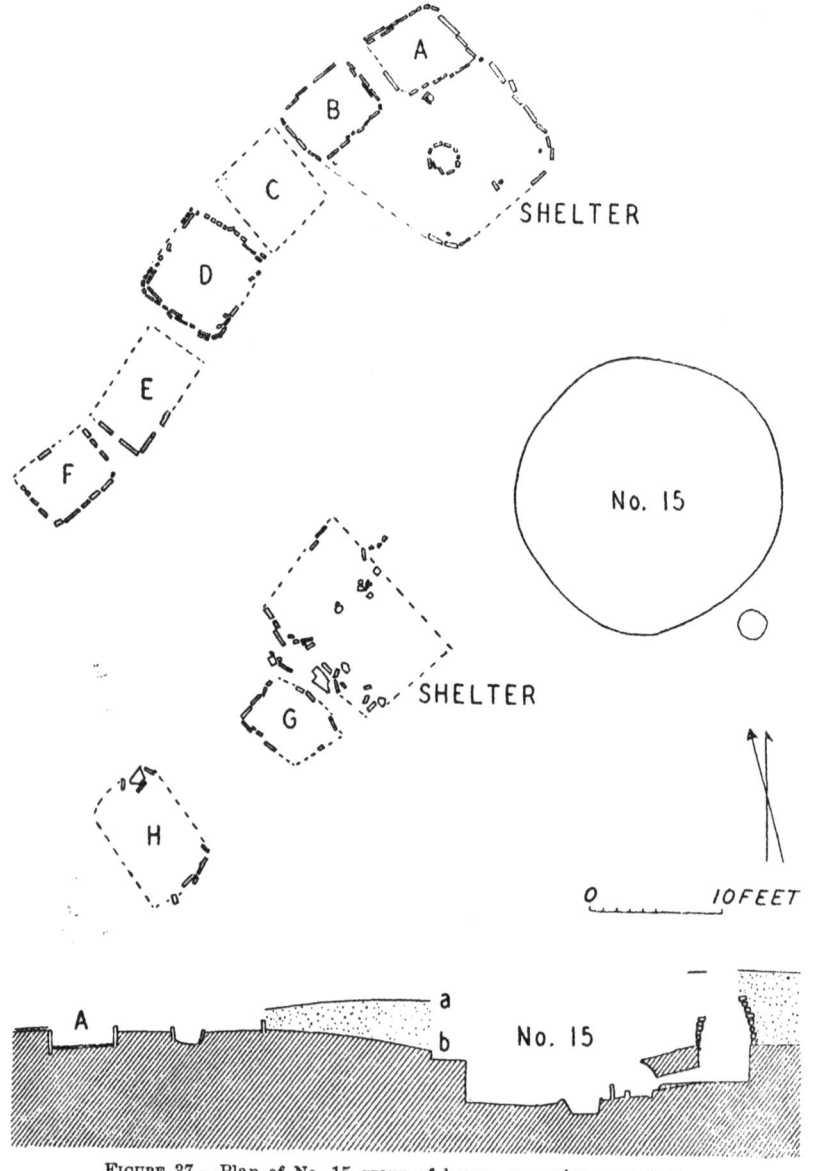

FIGURE 37.—Plan of No. 15 group of house, granaries, and shelters.

framework that supported both side poles and horizontal roofing timbers. The pits of all but one had been lined with stone slabs. The single exception may have had them at one time. Fire had destroyed the structure, however, and it is possible that the stone was removed for use elsewhere. The outlines of the pit were not sharp and clear as the earth walls had slumped in places and traces of the stones that might have been there were lost. This structure (fig. 37, C) was filled with corn when it burned and several inches of charred grain and cobs covered the floor. Granary E also burned and some of the stones were missing from its pit. There were signs on the walls, though, to show that stones were used there. In several of the examples a number of courses of horizontally laid stones were used to augment the height of the slabs and approximately half of one wall in another (fig. 37, B) consisted of this type of masonry. The floors of a number of the pits (A, D, and G) were completely paved with slabs, while in others scattered flagstones were embedded in the plaster. Two of the structures showed that small fires had been kindled on the floor near the center of the pit, although there was no actual fire basin present. This is an indication that on occasions, when they were not fulfilling their functions as storage places, the granaries were used as temporary habitations.

Two surface shelters were associated with the granaries. One of these was erected in front of the two at the north end of the row (fig. 37, A, B; pl. 20, a). An area on the surface was enclosed by a series of stone slabs set upright in the ground (fig. 38). In the center of this space was a stone-lined fire pit. Six upright posts, two placed midway along the front and back sides and four near the corners, had supported a rude arbor, probably a brush roof similar to those previously described. Except for the sides of the granaries, which would have served in that capacity at the back of the enclosure, there was nothing to indicate the former existence of any kind of walls. The rude structure thus formed would shelter the people from the sun and give some protection during light showers, but it would not have been very serviceable in times of severe storms. The remains of a similar shelter were present at the south end of the group. The latter was not as well preserved, although there were indications that the floor had been enclosed by slabs and that six posts were used to support the covering. The fire pit associated with this second structure was not in the enclosed space but just outside, between it and the dwelling. The important factor about this group of granaries is the manner in which they foreshadow the row of contiguous rooms and associated ceremonial chamber in the unit-type house of subsequent years. When the general plan and grouping of the No. 15 complex is compared with others discussed in following pages this becomes more apparent.

The granary pits varied somewhat in size and depth. A was 5 feet 10 inches (1.778 m) long and 5 feet (1.524 m) wide. At its north end it was 2 feet 6 inches (76.2 cm) deep and at the south end 2 feet 5 inches (73.66 cm). The distance between it and B was 1

148 BUREAU OF AMERICAN ETHNOLOGY [BULL. 121

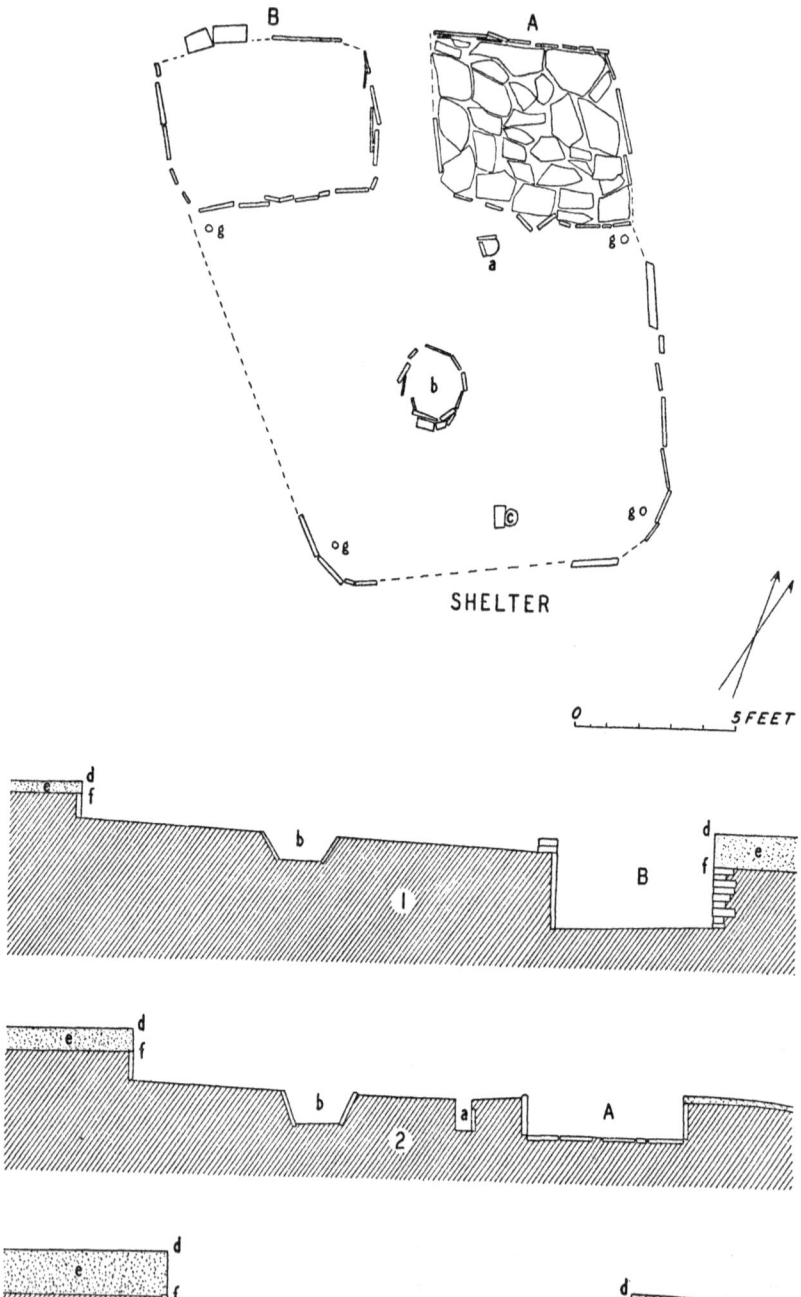

FIGURE 38.—Granaries A and B and shelter in No. 15 group. *a*, hole for support post; *b*, fire pit; *c*, hole for support post; *d*, present surface; *e*, sand fill; *f*, original surface; *g*, holes for corner supports for arbor.

foot 7 inches (48.26 cm). *B* was 6 feet 4 inches (1.930 m) long, 4 feet 9 inches (1.447 m) wide, and 1 foot 3 inches (38.1 cm) deep at both ends. *C* was approximately 6 feet (1.828 m) square, but exact measurements could not be determined. The depth at the ends of the pit was 2 feet 8 inches (81.28 cm). *D* was 7 feet 3 inches (2.209 m) long, 6 feet 4 inches (1.930 m) wide. The depth at the north end was 1 foot (30.48 cm) and at the south end 9 inches (22.86 cm). That was the shallowest pit in the group. *E* was 1 foot 6 inches (45.72 cm) from *D*, had a length of 7 feet 6 inches (2.286 m), a width of 4 feet 6 inches (1.371 m), and a depth of 2 feet (60.96 cm) at both ends. *F* was only 1 foot 3 inches (38.1 cm) from *E*. Its length was 6 feet (1.828 m), its width 4 feet 4 inches (1.320 m), the depth at the north end 2 feet 2 inches (66.04 cm) and at the south 2 feet 8 inches (81.28 cm). *G* was 19 feet (5.791 m) from *F*. The length of *G* was 5 feet 6 inches (1.676 m) and the width 4 feet 6 inches (1.371 m). The depth was 1 foot (30.48 cm) at both ends. *H* was 8 feet (2.438 m) from *G*. The stone had been removed from the sides of the pit but its outline was distinct. It had a length of 8 feet 2 inches (2.489 m) and a width of 5 feet 6 inches (1.676 m). Like *G*, the depth at each end of *H* was 1 foot (30.48 cm).

The shelter in front of granaries *A* and *B* covered an area 10 feet (3.048 m) by 12 feet (3.657 m). The enclosing slabs averaged 8 inches (20.32 cm) in height. The posts that supported the arbor averaged 6 inches (15.24 cm) in diameter. The fire pit near the center of the floor space had diameters of 1 foot 10 inches (55.88 cm) and 2 feet (60.96 cm) and was 10 inches (25.4 cm) deep. The shelter between granary *G* and the dwelling had a floor area 9 feet (2.743 m) by 12 feet (3.657 m). The posts used to support the arbor averaged 3 inches (7.62 cm) in diameter. This was about half the size of those noted for the other structure and the smallest noted for the entire site. The arbor that they supported could not have been as heavy as that for other similar structures at this location. The stones around the floor area, that is, those still in position, indicated that the wall height for the enclosure had averaged 1 foot (30.48 cm).

STRUCTURE 16 AND ASSOCIATED GRANARIES

The group consisting of No. 16 and its adjacent storage structures (fig. 39), represented an earlier stage in the sequence than the No. 15 group. Some of the features noted in the latter were present in the No. 16 assemblage in cruder and less developed form and clearly showed certain steps in the evolution of characteristic elements in the unit-type structure. The granaries were built in a row to the west and south of the house and differed to some extent

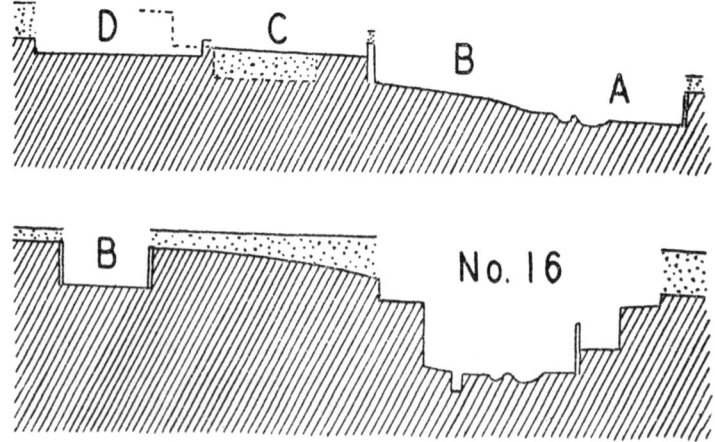

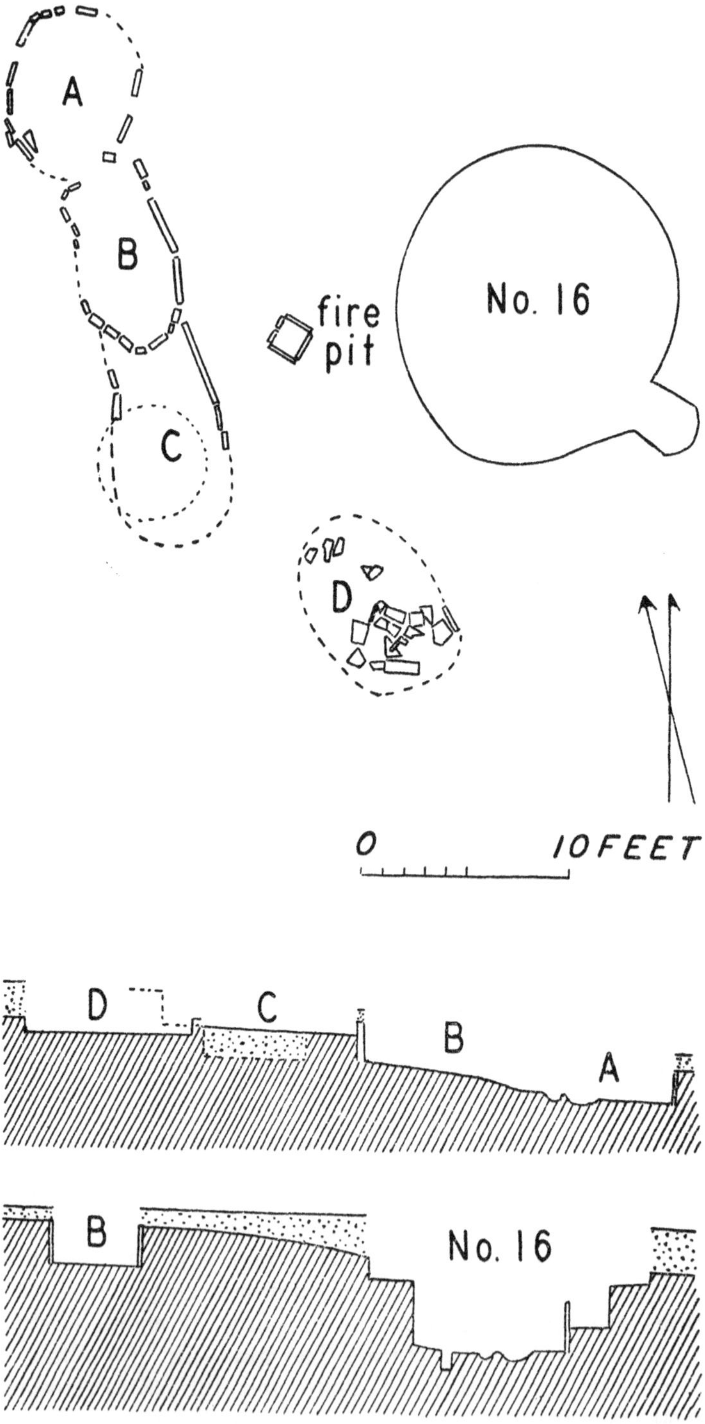

FIGURE 39.—Plan of No. 16 house and granary assemblage.

from those described for the preceding group. The main interest here, however, is in connection with the mode of entrance to the dwelling structure. This was not through the roof, as in most of those previously described, but through the opening at the southeast side that generally is considered as the ventilator.

Structure No. 16 was of the semisubterranean type with a roughly circular pit and bench (pl. 20, b). Both pit and bench were dug into the earth. As in the case of No. 15, the excavation for the bench was shallow and its back wall irregular, so much so, in fact, that the top of the bench was much wider in some places than in others. The walls of the main pit were not lined with slabs; they were simply covered with a thick coating of plaster. The superstructure was presumably of the truncated pyramidal type supported by a rectangular framework resting on uprights. There had been four main supports, but one had been reinforced by another smaller post. Two of the posts, one being that with a secondary brace, were set in the floor some distance from the wall of the main pit, while the other two, at the compartment side, practically touched the face of the bench. A few of the sloping side poles had their ends embedded in the earth at the back of the bench to hold them in position. Others merely rested in the angle formed by the back wall and the top of the bench. The portion of the periphery where the timbers were set in holes was that where the back wall of the bench was very low and the additional feature of the embedded ends may have been a necessary precaution against possible slipping when the superstructure was covered with earth and plaster. Only a few examples of the setting of sloping side poles in this manner were found at this site, although it was a common practice in other localities.

Interior finishings were not as complex as in some of the structures. The fire pit consisted of a simple circular basin (fig. 40, e) near the center of the floor space. No stones were used in its construction and the sloping sides and bottom were covered with plaster, a continuation of the layer that formed the floor. There was no ladder box, for reasons associated with the difference in the mode of entrance, and no basin for ashes. There was no separate deflector, the compartment wall functioning in that capacity. There were only a few holes in the floor. One of these (fig. 40, c) was the sipapu, one was for storage of small articles (fig. 40, b), and the third, more of a depression or small basin than an actual hole, was probably a pot rest (fig. 40, d). It was so placed that a round-bottomed vessel set there would not only maintain an upright position but it was close enough to the fire to keep its contents warm. The sides of the sipapu and the storage hole were vertical and both sides and bottom in each were carefully plastered. In the case of the storage hole this must have been difficult to accomplish as it was of small diameter and it would have required a small hand to work inside and properly apply the plaster.

There had been a compartment at the southeast side of the chamber, but most of the stones used in its wall had been removed. This possibly took place when the structure was abandoned. The molds where the stones stood were much in evidence, however, and the outline of the wall was easily traced on the floor (fig. 40, *g*). Six slabs had been used to form the wall and their surfaces and the spaces between were covered and filled with adobe plaster. At the west end of the wall a space large enough for an additional stone was entirely blocked in with the mud mortar. The wall had been continuous and since there was no break or opening near the center, between the fire pit and the aperture to the vent passage, a deflector stone was not needed. There was a small bin in the east end of the compartment. It was formed by cutting into the face of the bench and by blocking off the end of the compartment by the use of additional stone slabs (fig. 40, *f*). The floor in the bin was considerably higher than either that of the compartment or the main part of the chamber. The level was raised through the use of stones and mud mortar. The bottom of the bin was partially paved with small slabs set in the plaster. There was a shallow basin in the compartment floor directly in front of the vent-passage opening (fig. 40, *h*). In this instance it was not a post placement of the type described for some of the other structures, yet it could have served as a rest for a brace leaned against a stone slab blocking the aperture. It also might have functioned as a rest for a round-bottomed vessel, though its position would seem to be somewhat inconvenient for such use. What its actual purpose was is not known.

A stone was set in the floor in the opening into the vent passage (fig. 40, *i*). Whether this was a sill placed there to protect the edge of the passage floor, which was at a higher level than that of the compartment, or had risen some distance above the floor as a sort of secondary deflector could not be determined. The stone was broken and there was nothing to indicate its height at the time of occupancy, although the edge of the passage floor indicated that it had at least been flush with its surface if not somewhat higher. As previously mentioned, this passage had constituted the entrance to the dwelling. At its outer end it was wider than at the opening into the pit and its floor sloped upward from the room. Embedded in the floor at the outer end were the decayed butts of ladder poles (fig. 40, *k*) and for this reason it is concluded that the feature was an actual entrance rather than a ventilator. The side and end walls of the passage did not rise vertically. They sloped outward so that the passage was wider at the top than at the bottom. This would have facilitated

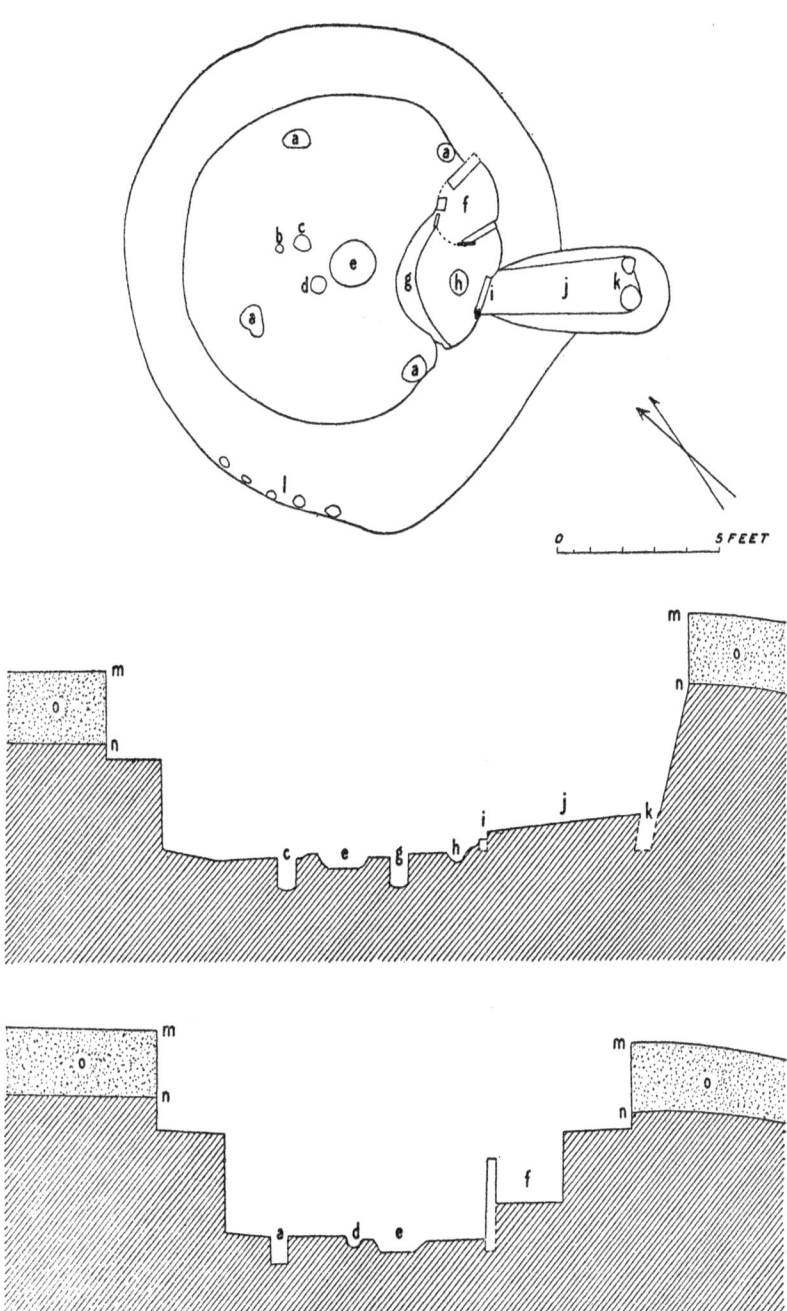

FIGURE 40.—Structure 16. *a*, holes for main roof supports; *b*, small storage hole; *c*, sipapu; *d*, pot rest; *e*, fire pit; *f*, storage bin; *g*, groove for compartment wall; *h*, basin in floor; *i*, sill in passage opening; *j*, passage; *k*, holes for ladder poles; *l*, placements for side poles; *m*, present surface; *n*, old surface; *o*, sand fill.

movement, as greater space would be provided for the body and shoulders of the person using it. The ladder had sufficient slant to make ascent and descent easy. The passage was of the trench type and had been covered with small poles along that part of its length where it cut through the bench, thus forming a short tunnel. The cross timbers were probably covered with adobe plaster, possibly a continuation of the surface extending along the bench top. The outer end was in the highest point of ground in the vicinity of the structure and surface water would have drained away from it on all sides. Everything considered, this construction undoubtedly made an efficient and convenient means of access to the house.

The fill in structure 16 had a number of significant features. From the floor to just above the bench top it was a natural accumulation consisting of wind-blown sand with a slight admixture of ashes and sporadic pieces of charcoal. There were no potsherds, stone chips, nor bone splinters in this portion of the deposit, showing that it was not refuse material. Just above the bench level were several streaks of water-washed sand and silt similar to those noted in the fill in some of the other pits. In this instance they were at a considerably higher level and if they were produced by the same phenomena as in the others would indicate a greater age for this structure. This was borne out by other factors suggesting that such was the case. Above the water-deposited layers was one of reddish-colored sand, wind-blown material. This in turn was overlain by sand mixed with ashes and charcoal. Numerous potsherds, stone chips, and bone fragments were scattered through this portion of the deposit. This was dump-heap material that had drifted down across the pit from the nearby refuse mound (fig. 25) subsequent to the abandonment of the house. The remains of a double burial, two children, were above the bench at the southwest side of the chamber (fig. 25, No. 30). The interment was made after the pit had filled to the bench level, as was shown by the fact that the bones were in the red sand above the layers of water-deposited material. Furthermore, it was prior to the drifting of the refuse material from the adjacent mound, as the latter extended across the burial pit in an unbroken line. The skeletons were poorly preserved and had no mortuary offerings with them, so it is not possible to place them in the general sequence for the site on the basis of associated objects. They may represent the stage of the No. 15 unit, but such cannot be established. When the grave was dug a portion of the back wall of the bench was removed, which accounts for the greater width of the feature at that part of its periphery.

There were no timbers in No. 16 of sufficient worth to give dendrochronological dates; the butts of the ladder poles were too decayed, and the actual age of the structure is not known. A few potsherds found on its floor (similar ones came from one of the nearby granaries) were of the type present in the lowest level in all test sections. Hence relatively the structure may be considered as early in the sequence, even though the definite years represented are not known.

Structure 16 had a diameter of 9 feet 7 inches (2.921 m) on the sipapu, fire-pit line below the bench. Above the bench it measured 14 feet 6 inches (4.419 m). Below the bench, at right angles to the first measurement, the diameter was 9 feet 9 inches (2.971 m), and on the same line above the bench 14 feet 5 inches (4.394 m). The top of the bench ranged from 1 foot 9 inches (53.34 cm) to 3 feet 5½ inches (1.054 m) in width. At the passage side of the room the bench top was 3 feet 10 inches (1.168 m) above the floor and the back wall of the bench was 4 inches (10.16 cm) high. The floor was 4 feet (1.219 m) below the old ground level and 6 feet 2 inches (1.879 m) beneath the present surface. At the opposite side the top of the bench was 3 feet 8 inches (1.117 m) above the floor and its back wall was 5 inches (12.7 cm) high. The floor of the chamber was 3 feet 4 inches (1.016 m) beneath the original ground level and 5 feet 4 inches (1.625 m) below the present. On the other diameter, at the west side of the room the bench top was 2 feet 9 inches (83.82 cm) above the floor and the back wall of the bench was 1 foot 4 inches (40.64 cm) high. The floor was 4 feet 1 inch (1.244 m) below the original surface and 7 feet 7 inches (2.311 m) beneath the present. At the east side the top of the bench was 2 feet 6 inches (76.2 cm) above the floor and the back wall was 4 inches (10.16 cm) high. The floor was 3 feet 2 inches (96.52 cm) below the old surface and 4 feet 9 inches (1.447 m) beneath the present. The holes at the back of the bench, for the slanting side poles, were from 3 to 4 inches (7.62 to 10.16 cm) in diameter.

The holes for the support posts were slightly irregular in outline and in the case of one the edges were broken at the floor line. The hole at the north side of the chamber had diameters of 6½ inches (16.51 cm) and 10 inches (25.4 cm) and a depth of 8½ inches (21.59 cm). The hole was 9 inches (22.86 cm) from the face of the bench. The hole at the east side of the chamber had diameters of 6 inches and 7 inches (15.24 and 17.78 cm) and a depth of 10¼ inches (26.04 cm). It was at the edge of the wall. The hole for the south post was also against the wall and had diameters of 7½ inches (19.05 cm) and 10 inches (25.4 cm). Its depth was 1 foot 1¼ inches (33.65 cm). The west hole, the double one, measured 8 inches (20.32 cm) by 11 inches (27.94 cm). It was 1 foot 4 inches (40.64 cm) from the wall.

The fire pit (fig. 40, e) had diameters of 1 foot 5 inches (43.18 cm) and 1 foot 3½ inches (39.37 cm). The depth of the pit was 5½ inches (13.97 cm). The sipapu (fig. 40, *c*) was 8½ inches (21.59 cm) from the fire pit. It had diameters of 6 inches (15.24 cm) and 7 inches (17.78 cm) and a depth of 10 inches (25.4 cm). The small storage hole (fig. 40, *b*) was 3 inches (7.62 cm) from the sipapu. The diameter was 3 inches (7.62 cm) and the depth 4 inches (10.16 cm). The pot rest (fig. 40, *d*) was 2½ inches (6.35 cm) from the fire pit. It was 6 inches (15.24 cm) in diameter and 3½ inches (8.89 cm) deep at the center.

The bin at one end of the compartment measured 2 feet 3 inches (68.58 cm) by 1 foot 5 inches (43.18 cm). The floor was 1 foot ½ inch (31.75 cm) higher than that of the room and the bin had a depth of 1 foot 4 inches (40.64 cm) on the room side. At the back, however, the top of the bench was 2 feet 1 inch (63.5 cm) above the bottom of the bin. The stones remaining in the bin, in order from top to bottom in the diagram (fig. 40), measured 1 foot 2½ inches (36.83 cm) long, 2 feet 2½ inches (67.31 cm) high, 4 inches (10.16 cm) thick; 4½ inches (11.43 cm) long, 2 feet 3 inches (68.58 cm) high, 3 inches (7.62 cm) thick; 5½ inches (13.97 cm) long, 1 foot (30.48 cm) high, 1 inch (2.54 cm) thick; 6 inches (15.24 cm) long, 10 inches (25.4 cm) high, ⅝ inch (1.58 cm) thick; 1 foot 1½ inches (34.29 cm) long, 2 feet 2 inches (66.04 cm) high, and 2¾ inches (6.98 cm) thick.

The basin in the floor of the compartment (fig. 40, *h*) had diameters of 6½ inches (16.51 cm) and 9 inches (22.86 cm) and a depth of 4 inches (10.16 cm). The basin was 8 inches (20.32 cm) from the opening into the entrance passage.

The entrance to the passage was 1 foot 3½ inches (39.37 cm) wide at the bottom and 1 foot 6½ inches (46.99 cm) wide at the top. The top part of the trench broadened to 2 feet (60.96 cm) a short distance back of the doorway. The top of the bench was 3 feet 6 inches (1.066 m) above the floor of the passage at the opening. The stone sill (fig. 40, *i*) was 1 foot 1½ inches (34.29 cm) long, 2 inches (5.08 cm) thick, and 2½ inches (6.35 cm) high. The floor of the passage was 4 inches (10.16 cm) higher than the floor of the compartment. The passage trench was 4 feet 8 inches (1.422 m) long at the bottom and 5 feet 8 inches (1.727 m) at the top. When in use, the tunnel portion was 3 feet (91.44 cm) long and the manhole was 2 feet 6 inches (76.2 cm) by 2 feet 8 inches (81.28 cm). The holes where the ladder ends rested (fig. 40, *k*) were against the end wall. One had diameters of 4 and 6 inches (10.16 and 15.24 cm) and the other 7 and 9 inches (17.78 and 22.86 cm). The bottom of the trench at the ladder placement was 3 feet 9 inches (1.143 m) below the old ground level and 5 feet 10 inches (1.778 m) below the present surface. The trench was 1 foot 8½ inches (52.07 cm) wide at the bottom of the ladder and 2 feet 7 inches (78.74 cm) at the top.

The row of granaries was 9 feet 6 inches (2.895 m) west of structure No. 16. Midway between the surface structures and the dwelling was a surface fire pit lined with stone slabs (fig. 39). There were no traces of a shelter or arbor like that in front of the No. 15 granaries, *A* and *B*. The fire was merely built in the open. The granaries differed from those in the group near structure 15 in that they were roughly oval or circular in form. They were of the same

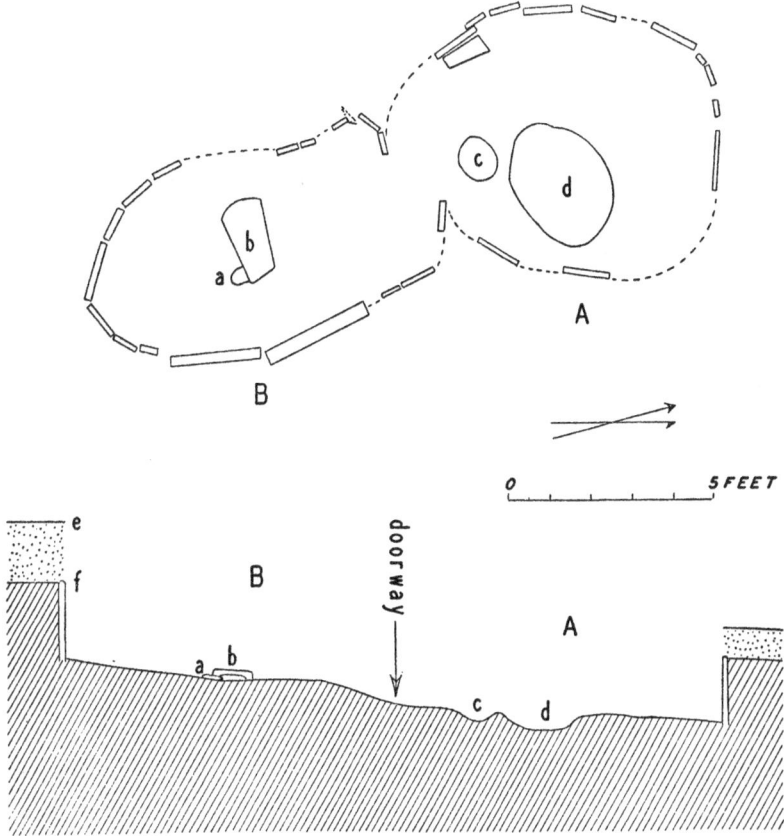

FIGURE 41.—Granaries A and B of the No. 16 group. *a*, mano or hand milling stone; *b*, metate stone; *c*, fire pit; *d*, storage basin; *e*, present surface; *f*, original ground level.

general construction, however, in that the walls of the pits were faced with stone slabs and there were a few examples of the use of horizontally laid stones above the vertical ones. Not all of the slabs lining the walls extended to the floor levels. Some of them were set into the wall so that their tops were flush with the ground, while the bottoms were several inches above the pit floor. The granaries had pole, brush, and plaster superstructures. The latter, in two examples, seem to have been pyramidal rather than flat-topped. The evidence for this was not as clear-cut as could be desired and it is possible that the other form was used. The other two (fig. 39, A, B) were of the truncated type, described in the discussion of the No. 15 group, as indicated by the timber molds at the edges of the pits.

Two of the granaries (fig. 39, A, B) were connected by a small doorway. This is unusual but is probably attributable to the fact that they were used, at least temporarily, as a dwelling. One of the pits (B) had a metate and mano lying on the floor at the center of the chamber and the other (A) had a small fire basin in the floor near the opening between the two pits (fig. 41). This basin was dug into the floor and had simple earth walls. It had sufficient use to burn the soil a deep red. Close to the fire pit and nearer the center of the pit was a depression in the floor that was almost filled with wood ashes. Whether the feature was originally intended for such use or had another purpose before serving as a depository for ashes could not be determined. It seems rather curious that so large a place should be provided for an ash receptacle in so small a structure unless the residue was definitely being retained for some specific purpose. Parts from two large storage jars were also in this room. Pieces from one of them were found on the floor in No. 16, a factor that is good evidence for the contemporaneity of the structure.

Granary C (fig. 39) had the same general shape and size as B. The floor had been paved with small, thin slabs of stone. The chief matter of interest in connection with the structure was in the fact that it overlay a circular pit containing a triple burial (fig. 25, Nos. 26, 27, 28). A young adult female and two children were interred there before the granary was created. There were no accompanying mortuary offerings to provide a clue to the stage to which they belonged. Only one of the skulls was in a condition to give any indications of its general characteristics and since it was undeformed, that fact suggests that the group was among the earlier settlers at the site. The burials were only 9 inches (22.86 cm) below the floor of the storage bin, but there was clear evidence that the pit for the bin was dug at some time subsequent to the placing of the bodies there.

An almost identical situation was discovered in connection with granary D. It also was above a burial, the only difference being that two instead of three individuals had been placed there. The skeletons were in a fairly good state of preservation and represented an aged female and an adolescent child (pl. 21, a). They had been placed side by side, in tightly flexed positions, in an oval pit. There were no mortuary articles in the grave and as in the case of the other burial there was nothing definite to show the phase of cultural development that they represented. Both were long-headed indi-

a. Pit and floor of structure 15.

b. Compartment wall and ventilator of structure 15.

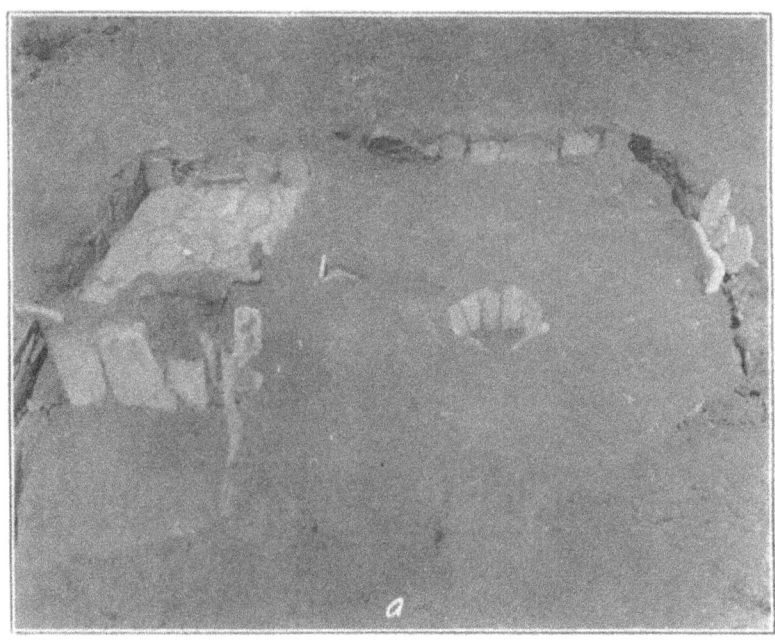

a. Granaries and shelter, structure 15 group.

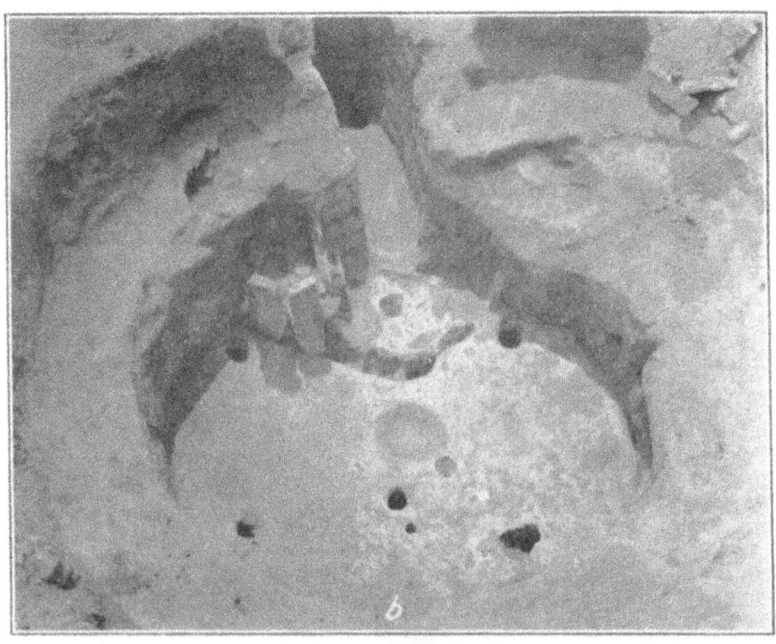

b. Pit and floor of structure 16.

a. Double burial beneath granary floor in structure 16 group.

b. View across Developmental Pueblo village.

a. Second unit in Developmental village.

b. Wall construction in second unit.

viduals, however, and in view of the fact that they had been buried before the construction of the granary it seems logical to conclude that they belonged to the oldest stage or the Modified Basket Makers. It is possible that in both this burial and that beneath the other granary baskets or woven materials were interred with the bodies as offerings and that all traces of them had disappeared through the course of subsequent centuries. The use of baskets and woven bags for such purposes was quite common in the Modified Basket Maker horizon, as has been demonstrated by burials found in caves and protected places where the complete dryness of the surrounding earth has preserved the materials. The bones of these individuals were 1 foot (30.48 cm) beneath the paved floor of the granary. They were in clean sand and unquestionably were buried before the construction of the granary. The latter was not in as good a state of preservation as the others in the group. Most of the flagstones for the floor were in position but a number of the wall slabs had fallen in and a few were missing. It was possible to trace the main outlines of the pit, however, and establish the fact that it was roughly oval in outline and approximately the same size as some of the others.

The main significance in this group of storage structures, as was the case for those associated with No. 15, is in their position with relation to the semisubterranean dwelling and the evidence that two of them had been used as living quarters. The complex again demonstrates the beginning of the unit type, but in slightly cruder form than in the No. 15 group.

The surface fire pit was approximately midway between granary C and structure No. 16. It was 3 feet 6 inches (1.066 m) from C and 4 feet (1.219 m) from the back of the bench of No. 16. The pit was a simple rectangular box lined with stone slabs. A single stone sufficed for each of three sides, but two were used for the fourth. The pit was 1 foot 10 inches (55.88 cm) by 1 foot 9 inches (53.34 cm) and 10 inches (25.4 cm) deep. The old ground level, the top of the slabs in the pit, was 1 foot 7 inches (48.26 cm) below the present surface.

Granary A was 8 feet (2.438 m) long, 6 feet (1.828 m) wide, 1 foot 6 inches (45.72 cm) deep at the north end and 2 feet (60.96 cm) deep at the south. The depression containing ashes was oval in outline with diameters of 3 feet 1 inch (93.98 cm) and 2 feet 3 inches (68.58 cm). The depth was $4\frac{1}{2}$ inches (11.43 cm). This basin was 6 inches (15.24 cm) from the east wall of the granary pit. The fire pit was only $3\frac{1}{2}$ inches (8.89 cm) from the ash basin. The pit was $10\frac{1}{2}$ inches (26.67 cm) by 1 foot $1\frac{1}{2}$ inches (34.29 cm) on its diameters and had a depth of 3 inches (7.62 cm). The pit was 1 foot 1 inch (33.02 cm) from the east wall, 1 foot 11 inches (58.42 cm) from the west, and 9 inches (22.86 cm) from the doorway. It was far enough to one side not to have interfered with use of the opening. The doorway was 1 foot 9 inches (53.34 cm) wide.

Granary B was also 8 feet (2.438 m) long. The width varied. At the north end it was 4 feet (1.219 m) and at the south, just before the walls began to curve to form the end, 4 feet 6 inches (1.371 m). The depth at the north end was 2 feet (60.96 cm) and at the south 1 foot 9½ inches (54.61 cm).

Granary C abutted B and was built subsequently to it. C had a length of 8 feet (2.438 m), was 3 feet 9½ inches (1.155 m) wide at the end near B and 5 feet 1½ inches (1.562 m) wide at the other. It was much shallower than either A or B. At the north end, next to B, it was 8 inches (20.32 cm) deep and at the south end 1 foot 1½ inches (34.29 cm).

Granary D was 4 feet 7 inches (1.397 m) from C. The wall slabs were either entirely missing or had fallen from their positions, so that the measurements are for the pit and for that reason are somewhat larger than they would have been with the stones in place. The pit had a length of 9 feet 3 inches (2.819 m) and a width of 6 feet 5 inches (1.955 m). The depth was shallow, being 7 inches (17.78 cm) at the north end and 8½ inches (21.59 cm) at the south.

Additional Pit Remains

Structure 17

Pit structure No. 17 was located on the floor of the valley below the main site. It was uncovered during the excavation of the small Developmental Pueblo village investigated in the 1933 season. The structure had been a typical pit dwelling, roughly circular in form with somewhat more irregular walls than noted in many of those described in preceding pages (fig. 42). The walls were of earth covered with a thick layer of adobe plaster. There was no encircling bench of the excavated type, but the sloping roof poles had been set far enough back from the top of the wall to supply the equivalent of such a feature. The superstructure appeared to be of the same type as that described for other pit structures. Four posts placed near the walls at approximately the cardinal points of the compass carried the main framework for the flat roof and slanting sides.

The interior features compared for the most part with those of other structures, except that there were more recessed subfloor wall pockets in this dwelling and a storage bin formed from stone slabs at one side of the chamber. There was no compartment in front of the ventilator opening. The usual combination of sipapu, fire pit, and ladder basin was present. The sipapu (fig 42, d) was farther from the fire pit than in most cases. The diameter was approximately the same as noted for a majority of the examples, although the hole was not deep. The sides and bottom were carefully plastered.

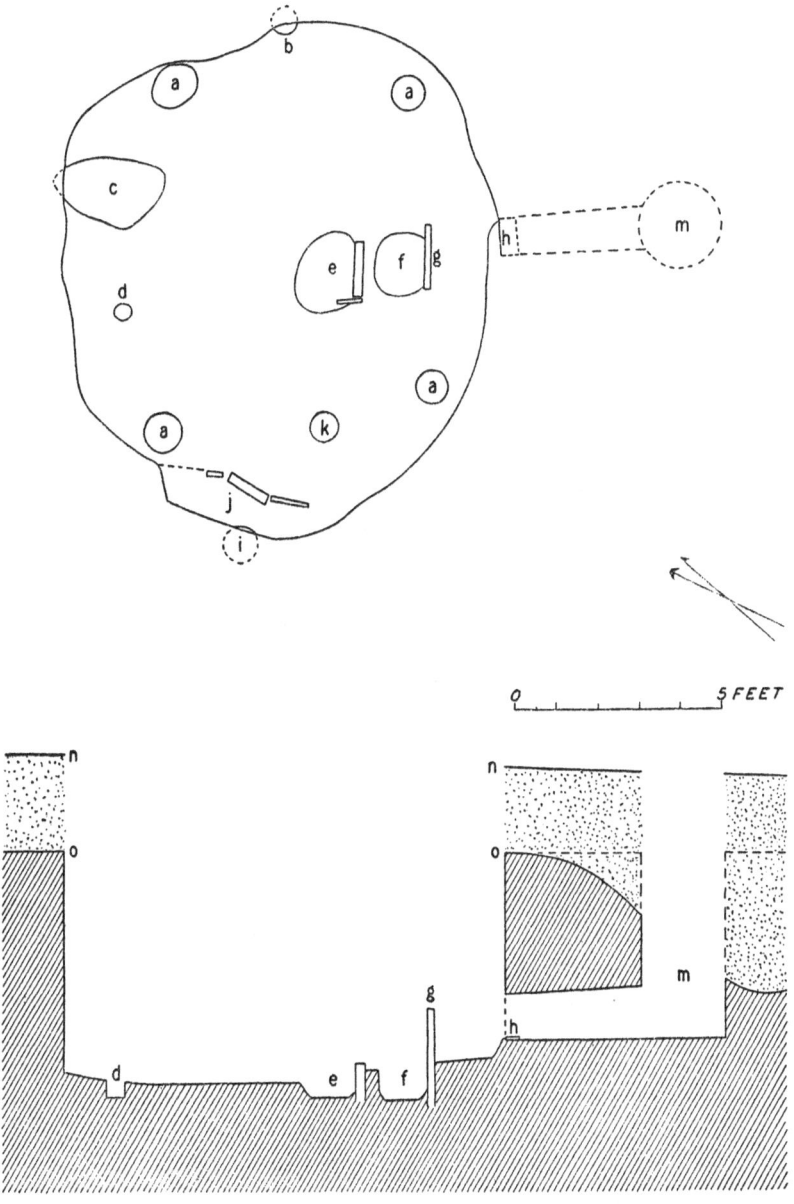

FIGURE 42.—Structure 17. *a*, holes for support posts; *b*, subwall pocket; *c*, storage pit; *d*, sipapu; *e*, fire pit; *f*, basin for ashes and ladder; *g*, deflector; *h*, sill in ventilator opening; *i*, subwall pocket; *j*, storage bin; *k*, pot rest; *m*, ventilator shaft; *n*, present ground level; *o*, original surface.

The fire pit was dug into the floor. It was D-shaped with the straight side toward the ladder pit. The face of the pit at that side was reinforced with a stone slab (fig. 42, *e*) and a small stone was set into the wall of the arc at the south corner. The remainder was of adobe plaster applied to the earth wall of the basin.

The ladder pit served a double purpose. The lower end of the ladder rested in it and it was used as a depository for ashes. This basin also was D-shaped (fig. 42, *f*). The straight side was toward the ventilator and was reinforced by the deflector stone (fig. 42, *g*). The latter was embedded in the floor and wall of the basin and rose above the floor of the chamber to a height sufficient to prevent air coming through the opening from blowing directly on the flames. The butts of the ladder poles rested in shallow depressions in the bottom of the basin at the ends of and against the stone. Whether these "cups" were intentional or merely the result of the abrasive action of the timbers could not be determined. Depositing ashes in the same basin with the ladder was not common. They must have been placed there when cold, otherwise they would have ignited the wood.

The two recessed subfloor wall pockets were at opposite sides of the room (fig. 42, *b*, *i*). When they were first noted, in the process of excavation, it was thought that they were placements for supplementary roof braces like those described for some of the houses in the first group. Careful inspection of the cleared holes, however, indicated that such was not the case, as their sides and bottoms were carefully plastered and bore no timber imprints. The recessed portions in the bench face sloped at approximately the angle that a roof brace would have followed, but the main part of the holes in the floor had vertical sides. Slightly more than half of one pocket (*b*) was beneath the wall, while practically all of the other (*i*) occupied that position. These features certainly provided convenient places for the storage of small objects.

One end of the roughly oval-shaped basin in the floor near the north corner of the chamber (fig 42, *c*) also extended beneath the wall. It was recessed in much the same way as the two smaller holes. The sides of this depression were vertical, the bottom was level, and both sides and bottom had been plastered. There was no bordering rim on the floor as in the case of some of the basins in other structures. The purpose of this feature in structure 17 was not learned, as there was nothing in it when the room was excavated. It could have served as a repository for corn, baskets, jars, or other articles used by the people.

The bin at the southeast side of the chamber (fig. 42, *j*) was constructed of three upright stone slabs augmented by large quantities of adobe plaster. One end was joined to the wall of the pit, while the other stopped short of a juncture and a space was left open to form a small doorway. The offset in the wall of the pit at the point where the partition forming the bin joined it produced a larger area inside that feature than would have been the case had the wall followed its normal arc along that section of the periphery. This might be considered as indicating that the builders had the bin in mind when the main pit was dug and provided the concavity for that purpose, although it is possible that the jog in the wall suggested the construction of the bin and it was a subsequent addition to the structure. There was no evidence to show which was the case. One of the subfloor storage pockets (i) was in the back of this bin.

The only additional interior feature was a pot rest (fig. 42, k) at the southeast side of the chamber. This shallow depression in the floor was circular in contour and its sides curved downward to the center of the hole. The diameter and curve of the basin were of the proper proportions to accommodate one of the large culinary or storage jars typical of the stage represented by this type of structure.

The ventilator opening was too small to have functioned in any capacity except that of an inlet for air. The aperture was several inches above the floor level and had a stone sill (fig. 42, h). The sides and top of the opening, which was arched, were covered with plaster. The passage was of the tunneled form with a circular shaft at the outer end. The latter had been damaged by flood waters at some time after the abandonment of the house and it was difficult to determine its original size.

Structure No. 17 was filled with refuse and dump material that was deposited there soon after the abandonment of the dwelling. Indications were that this accumulation came from the unit in the village that was north of the pit structure and that the latter was built during the occupancy of the semisubterranean structure. It is possible that the group using No. 17 had joined in the construction of the nearby unit and that they had moved into it when it was completed. The absence of all artifacts and the fact that the refuse material was lying on the floor, without any intervening layer of sterile material, suggests that the occupants deliberately moved out and took their belongings with them, while the remainder of the site continued to be inhabited. The position and stratigraphy of the fill was such that the deposition of material in an open pit was indicated and this leads to the conclusion that the superstructure was removed at the time of the abandonment. Perhaps the timbers were needed in new construction work and were salvaged from the old structure. There was no decayed wood in the holes for the main supports nor were there any traces of timbers throughout the fill. The holes where the uprights stood were broken around the edges, particularly the one at the north, as though the timbers had been pulled out.

At least two granaries had been associated with No. 17. They were located several feet west of the structure in a position approximating that noted for some of the other dwellings. One was largely obliterated as the result of subsequent activities, but the other was intact. Both were of the rectangular form with slab-lined pits. The one that remained was found beneath the occupation level of the second unit in the village. One end of the pit extended under the foundations and part of the floor of one room in the surface dwelling. The main factor of interest in this connection is the additional evidence that the above-ground structures were of later date than the pit-granary form. This particular granary had a central basin in the floor similar to those described for some of the others. Whether it was originally intended for use as a fire pit or had some other purpose could not be determined, but there was evidence that small fires had been lighted at one end of the depression. Traces of the timber placements for the superstructure were meager, although a few scattered holes along the walls indicated that the covering over the pit was of the type described for the rectangular granaries associated with structure No. 15. The location and relationship between this granary and the later unit dwelling is shown in the plan of the Developmental village (fig. 44) in a subsequent section of this report.

Structure 17 had a diameter of 10 feet 7 inches (3.226 m) on the ventilator, fire pit, sipapu line. At right angles to this measurement the diameter was 11 feet 11 inches (3.632 m). At the ventilator side of the room the floor was 4 feet 10 inches (1.473 m) below the level of the old surface of occupation and 6 feet 10 inches (2.082 m) below the present top of the ground. At the opposite side of the chamber the depth was 5 feet 2½ inches (1.587 m) below the old surface and 7 feet 5½ inches (2.272 m) below the present.

The holes for the main support posts were somewhat larger than those in a number of the structures. That at the north side of the chamber had diameters of 1 foot (30.48 cm) and 11 inches (27.94 cm) and a depth of 2 feet (60.96 cm). The back edge of the hole touched the wall. The hole for the east post had a diameter of 10 inches (25.4 cm) and a depth of 1 foot 4½ inches (41.91 cm). It was 3 inches (7.62 cm) from the wall. The south hole was 9 inches (22.86 cm) in diameter and 1 foot 6 inches (45.72 cm) deep. It was 6 inches (15.24 cm) from the wall. The hole for the upright at the west side of the room was 11 inches (27.94 cm) in diameter and 1 foot (30.48 cm) deep. It was located near the end of a low partition forming the storage bin and was 4 inches (10.16 cm) from the wall.

The fire pit (fig. 42, *e*) was 1 foot 7 inches (48.26 cm) long, 1 foot 4 inches (40.64 cm) wide, and 11 inches (27.94 cm) deep at the center. In front of the stone facing at the ventilator side of the pit the depth was only 7 inches (17.78 cm). The large stone in the pit lining was 11 inches (27.94 cm) long and 2 inches (5.08 cm) thick. The smaller stone was 5 inches (12.7 cm) long and 1 inch (2.54 cm) thick. The ladder box (fig. 42, *f*) was 5 inches (12.7 cm) from the fire pit. It measured 1 foot 3 inches (38.1 cm) by 1 foot 5 inches (43.18 cm). It had a depth of 9 inches (22.86 cm). The deflector slab (fig. 42, *g*) formed the face of the ladder basin at the ventilator side. This stone was 1 foot 4¼ inches (41.27 cm) high, above the floor level; was 1 foot 3½ inches (39.37 cm) wide at the base, 10 inches (25.4 cm) wide at the top, and 1¼ inches (3.17 cm) thick.

The sipapu (fig. 42, *d*) was 4 feet 1 inch (1.244 m) from the fire pit. The hole had a diameter of 5 inches (12.7 cm) and a depth of 4 inches (10.16 cm). It was closer to the wall than in most cases, being but 1 foot (30.48 cm) removed from it.

The irregular-shaped depression in the floor (fig. 42, *c*) had a maximum length of 2 feet 4 inches (71.12 cm) and a width of 1 foot 9 inches (53.34 cm). It projected 5 inches (12.7 cm) under the wall of the room. The average depth of the basin was 10 inches (25.4 cm).

The subfloor wall pocket at the north side of the chamber (fig. 42, *b*) was 5½ inches (13.97 cm) wide, extended under the wall for 6 inches (15.24 cm), and was 5 inches (12.7 cm) deep. The recessed upper portion in the face of the wall began 5 inches (12.7 cm) above the floor level. The second recessed pocket (fig. 42, *i*) was larger. It extended under the wall for a distance of 9 inches (22.86 cm) and was 11 inches (27.94 cm) wide at the opening. The lower portion, the subfloor pocket, was 11 inches (27.94 cm) in diameter and 4 inches (10.16 cm) deep. The recessed portion in the face of the wall started 1 foot (30.48 cm) above the floor level.

The bin at the southwest side of the room (fig. 42, *j*) was 3 feet 6 inches (1.066 m) long and 1 foot (30.48 cm) wide. The opening at one end was 10 inches (25.4 cm) wide. The three stones used in the wall varied in size. The first, that at the north end of the partition, was 8½ inches (21.59 cm) wide, 9 inches (22.86 cm) high, and 1 inch (2.54 cm) thick. The top of the stone indicated that it had been broken off, so the original height was probably greater than the measurement given. The second stone was 1 foot (30.48 cm) wide, 1 foot 7 inches (48.26 cm) high, and 3 inches (7.62 cm) thick. The third had a width of 1 foot (30.48 cm), a height of 1 foot 4 inches (40.64 cm), and a thickness of 1 inch (2.54 cm).

The pot rest (fig. 42, *k*) was 8 inches (20.32 cm) in diameter and 2 inches (5.08 cm) deep at the center. The sides curved downward to the center from the edges of the basin.

The ventilator opening was 1 foot (30.48 cm) high and 1 foot 1 inch (33.02 cm) wide. The sill was 4½ inches (11.43 cm) above the floor level. The stone forming the sill was 11½ inches (29.21 cm) long, 5 inches (12.7 cm) wide, and 1 inch (2.54 cm) thick. The floor of the tunnel was 1 inch (2.54 cm) below the top of the sill. The tunnel was 3 feet 5½ inches (1.054 m) long. Where it entered the shaft it was 1 foot 2 inches (35.56 cm) wide and 1 foot 3 inches (38.1 cm) high. The exact dimensions of the shaft could not be determined, but it closely approximated a diameter of 2 feet (60.96 cm). The bottom of the shaft was 4 feet 5 inches (1.346 m) below the old ground level and 6 feet 3 inches (1.905 m) below the present surface.

The single intact granary had a length of 5 feet 3 inches (1.600 m) and a width of 4 feet 3 inches (1.295 m). At one end it was 2 feet (60.96 cm) deep and at the other 1 foot 10 inches (55.88 cm). The floor was 3 feet 6 inches (1.066 m) below the present ground level. The basin in the center of the floor measured 2 feet 8 inches (81.28 cm) long, 1 foot 9 inches (53.34 cm) wide, and 4½ inches (11.43 cm) deep. The granary was 5 feet 9 inches (1.752 m) from the structure.

STRUCTURE 18

The second of the pit structures not located on top of the ridge at the main site was associated with the unit-type ruins 1 mile (1.609 k) up Whitewater Valley from the village where No. 17 was situated. No. 18 was a fully developed structure of the same general type as those described in preceding pages. The pit more nearly approximated the circular form than many of the others, but in the main it differed little from them. There were no indications of a definite bench. The sloping side poles of the superstructure were set back from the edge of the wall, however, so that there actually was a shelf around the pit between the top edge and the roof timbers. The superstructure was supported on four uprights set close to the wall of the chamber. This arrangement placed the rectangular framework of stringers close to the periphery of the pit and as a result the sloping portion of the ceiling was at a sharper angle than in some examples; the side walls more nearly approximated the vertical.

Interior features were few. Near the center of the floor space was a circular fire pit (fig. 43, *f*) that was merely a basin dug into the earth. No stones reinforced the walls; they were simply covered with plaster. There was no ladder box and no deflector. The plastered floor midway between the fire pit and the ventilator opening was slightly depressed and the surface was abraded in such a way as to suggest that the lower end of a ladder rested there. There was nothing to indicate whether it had been of the pole-and-rung type or of the notched-log variety. Because there was good evidence for the former in so many of the structures it is probable that the same kind was used here.

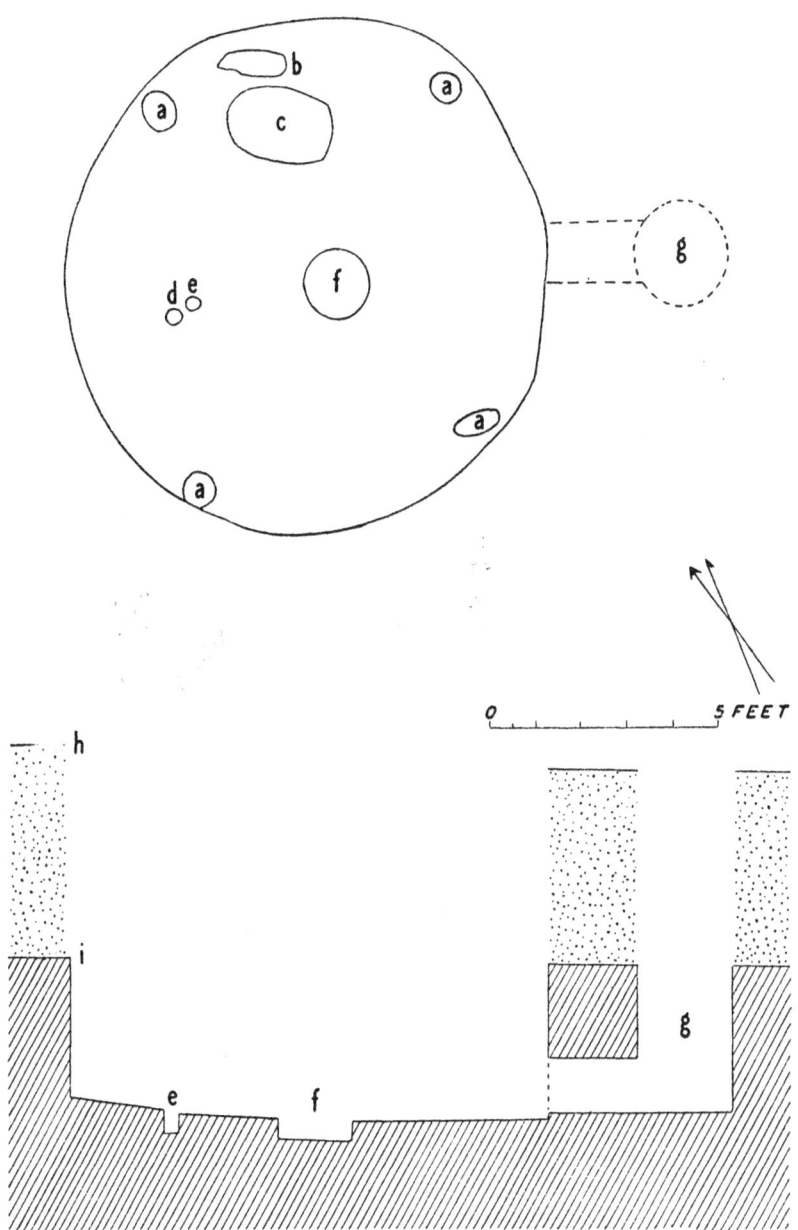

FIGURE 43.—Structure 18. *a*, holes for roof supports; *b*, storage pit in floor; *c*, storage basin; *d* and *e*, sipapus; *f*, fire pit; *g*, ventilator shaft; *h*, present surface; *i*, old ground level.

At the north side of the chamber was an oval basin in the floor (fig. 43, c) comparable to others noted in various structures. The sides of the basin were vertical and the bottom was approximately level. Around the edges the floor level had an almost imperceptible raise suggestive of a rim, but it was not actually such a feature. This basin was rather shallow. It probably was similar in function to those noted in other structures, although its real purpose was not learned. Between this basin and the wall was an oval trough (fig. 43, b) with curved sides and rounded bottom. The feature may have served as a rest for a series of round-bottomed vessels, or it may have had some special function in connection with the larger bin.

The only other holes in the floor were those in the position of the sipapu (fig. 43, d, e). Here, as in other examples previously cited, either hole could have been the sipapu or both may have served in that capacity. There is a possibility that they were not contemporaneous; that one was used, then filled in for some reason or other and the second one provided. If that was the case, any evidence of such was missed in the digging. The holes were approximately the same size, the same depth, their sides were vertical, and both sides and bottoms were covered with plaster.

The ventilator opening was trapezoidal in shape. The sill and lintel were stone slabs but the sides were plaster. The sill was raised above the general floor level. A plaster offset, encircling the aperture at the back, probably served as a rest for a cover stone. The passage was tunneled, the floor sloping upward toward the shaft. The latter was roughly oval in form.

Structure 18 had been abandoned and the roof timbers were either removed or had completely decayed, because there were no indications of them in the pit. The lack of timber prevented any dendrochronological dating of the structure. Potsherds found on the floor were of the same types as the material from the houses on the main site and the structure unquestionably belongs to the early part of the Developmental period. The pit was filled with wind-blown material from the top of the wall to the floor. It had not been used as a dumping place for refuse. The accumulation was wholly a natural one.

The main feature of interest in No. 18 is in the fact that it gives independent evidence for the greater antiquity of the semisubterranean type of dwelling as compared to the surface type of building. The proof is in the stratification at the site. The pit remains did not underlie any part of the later unit. Their earlier existence, however, was clearly demonstrated in another way by conditions as convincing as an actual superposition. After the pit structure was abandoned, its roof decayed and fallen in, and the pit filled with drift material, a layer of reddish clay was washed down from the talus slope above and swept across the site. The foundations of the nearby unit house rested on top of the clay stratum, while the filled pit was beneath it. As a matter of fact the latter was only accidentally discovered when a workman, following the top of the red layer, broke through into the older structure. When the hole for the kiva of the unit dwelling was dug it passed through the clay layer, which also demonstrates the later horizon for the unit. There probably were granaries accompanying No. 18, but they were not definitely located. A few upright slabs were found in scattered positions beneath the floors in two of the rooms in the nearby unit house. These probably were remnants of granaries, although activities associated with the erection of the surface building had so modified the area that their actual outlines could not be traced. They were in proper location with respect to the pit structure and they extended below the red clay, so that they seem to date from the same period as that house.

Structure 18 had a diameter of 10 feet 7 inches (3.225 m) on the ventilator, fire pit, sipapu line. The measurement at right angles to this line was 10 feet 9 inches (3.276 m). At the ventilator side of the chamber the floor was 3 feet 3 inches (99.06 cm) below the old ground level and 7 feet 5 inches (2.260 m) below the present surface. At the opposite side of the room the floor was 2 feet 10 inches (86.36 cm) below the former surface and 7 feet 4 inches (2.235 m) below the recent ground level. The floor at the north side of the room was 3 feet 1 inch (93.98 cm) below the old surface and 6 feet 8 inches (2.032 m) below the present. The measurements at the south wall were slightly greater, with the depth below the old surface 3 feet 2 inches (96.52 cm) and below the recent ground level 7 feet 10 inches (2.387 m).

The holes for the support posts showed that the timbers used had approximately the same diameters, as the differences were not great. The hole at the north side of the room had diameters of 9 inches (22.86 cm) and 10½ inches (26.67 cm) and was 1 foot 3 inches (38.1 cm) deep. The hole was 1½ inches (3.81 cm) from the wall. The east hole had diameters of 8 inches (20.32 cm) and 8½ inches (21.59 cm) and a depth of 1 foot 4 inches (40.64 cm). It was 3 inches (7.62 cm) from the wall. The south hole was oval in shape on the floor level but tapered to a circular form near the bottom. At the floor the diameters were 1 foot (30.48 cm) and 6 inches (15.24 cm). From midway of the depth to the bottom the diameter was 6 inches (15.24 cm). The hole was 1 foot 1 inch (33.02 cm) deep and was 2 inches (5.08 cm) from the wall at its east end and 7 inches (17.78 cm) away at the west. The hole at the west side of the chamber was 9 inches (22.86 cm) in diameter and 1 foot (30.48 cm) deep. It touched the wall.

The fire pit (fig. 43, *f*) was 1 foot 6 inches (45.72 cm) in diameter at the floor level and 1 foot 4 inches (40.64 cm) at the bottom of the basin where the sloping sides reduced the measurement. The pit had a depth of 5 inches (12.7 cm).

The two holes at the location of the sipapu (fig. 43, *d*, *e*) were 1 foot 3 inches (38.1 cm) and 1 foot 9 inches (53.34 cm) from the fire pit and 2 feet ½ inch (62.23 cm) and 2 feet 6 inches (76.2 cm) from the wall. Hole *d* was 4 inches (10.16 cm) in diameter and 6 inches (15.24 cm) deep. Hole *e* was 1½ inches (3.81 cm) from *d* and had a diameter of 3 inches (7.62 cm) and a depth of 6 inches (15.24 cm).

The large oval-shaped basin (fig. 43, *c*) had diameters of 2 feet 4½ inches (72.39 cm) and 1 foot 7 inches (48.26 cm). The average depth was 5 inches (12.7 cm). The adjacent elongated depression (fig. 43, *b*) was 2½ inches (6.35 cm) from *o*. It had a length of 1 foot 6 inches (45.72 cm). For 5 inches (12.7 cm) of its length it had a width of 4½ inches (11.43 cm), while for the remainder it was 6 inches (15.24 cm). The depth was 4½ inches (11.43 cm). The sides and ends curved downward to form the rounded bottom. The ends of the trough were 5 inches (12.7 cm) and 8 inches (20.32 cm) from the wall of the room.

The ventilator aperture was 1 foot 5½ inches (44.45 cm) wide at the bottom, 1 foot 2 inches (35.56 cm) wide at the top, and 1 foot 2½ inches (36.83 cm) high. The sill was 2 inches (5.08 cm) above the floor of the chamber. The slab of stone used in the sill measured 1 foot 4 inches (40.64 cm) in length, 6 inches (15.24 cm) in width, and 1½ inches (3.81 cm) in thickness. The lintel was 1 foot 3 inches (38.1 cm) long, 6 inches (15.24 cm) wide, and 1 inch (2.54 cm) thick. The plaster offset, for a cover stone around the opening, was set back 3¾ inches (9.52 cm) from the edge. The ridge was 2 inches (5.08 cm) wide and 1½ inches (3.81 cm) high.

The ventilator passage was 2 feet 1½ inches (64.77 cm) long. The opening into the shaft was 1 foot 6 inches (45.72 cm) wide and 1 foot 7 inches (48.26 cm) high. The diameter of the shaft was 3 feet (91.44 cm) on the north-south axis and 2 feet 6 inches (76.2 cm) on the east-west. The bottom was 2 feet 6 inches (76.2 cm) below the old surface and 6 feet 10 inches (2.082 m) below the present.

Unit-Type Structures

The remains of three definite unit-type structures were investigated. Two of these comprised the early Developmental Pueblo village at the foot of the talus below the main site and the third, a late Developmental form, was one mile (1.609 k) up the Whitewater on the south side of the valley. These units are interesting from several standpoints. They represent three stages in the growth of the type and show the general trend of development. In addition, they demonstrate clearly certain changes taking place in specific features during the progress from one form to another. Each unit consisted of a number of above-ground enclosures and a semisubterranean or subterranean chamber. The general plan was much the same for all three. The surface buildings were located northwest from the underground structures and the surface area between the two forms showed extensive use for general occupation purposes. All three units were situated on sloping ground, so that there was drainage away from the structures on at least three sides. This was an essential consideration for below-ground chambers and also had decided advantages as far as the surface buildings were concerned. This was particularly true of the two units in the one village because the floors of the rooms in both of the surface houses were depressed below the general ground level. Even in the case of the dwelling in the third unit, where the floors were on the surface level, it prevented standing water from seeping into the mud mortar and softening the foundations.

The village containing the two units (fig. 44; pl. 21, b) was of particular significance because it recorded a shift in function in the subterranean structures and a definite change in the status of the surface rooms. The culmination of this transition and the subsequent perfection of the features involved were exemplified in the third unit. The latter, in many respects, evidenced so marked an improvement in some constructional phases that it seems as though there must have been additional stages between it and the second in the series. The elapsed time from the date of the first to that of the third, as well as the character of some of the lesser objects of the material culture, also suggests that there may have been intervening steps. The differences, however, are in the nature of refinements rather than major changes, and for that reason do not have any marked effect on the main outline of the growth of the unit type.

There are additional small house ruins in the valley located between the two groups herein described, and it is quite likely that some of them may contain evidence of the evolutionary processes. Surface indications, the potsherds particularly, are that at least two of these sites represent a time intermediate between the second and third units.

UNIT NO. 1

The first unit in the series was located at the northeast end of the Developmental village (fig. 44). It consisted of a surface structure containing three rooms, a portico, and a small court; several outside fire pits, the remains of brush shelters, and a semisubterranean chamber, marked Kiva A on the plan. There is some question about the correctness of this designation, as there is no doubt but what the structure did serve as a dwelling during a part of the unit's history. Some of its features, however, were indicative of a ceremonial chamber, and for that reason it was so named. As a matter of fact the structure represents the evolutionary stage when the shift from secular to ceremonial functions was taking place and because of that it is difficult to assign it to either category.

The refuse mound for the unit was situated across an old watercourse some distance east of the buildings. This channel, indicated by the dotted lines in the diagram (fig. 44) carried the run-off of surface water from the higher slopes following heavy rains. Some time after the first unit was built the channel was blocked and the water diverted to the valley bottom south and east from the dwellings, possibly for use in flood-water irrigation of the fields, and the old bed gradually filled with an accumulation of blow sand and rubbish from the settlement. At a much later period, after the abandonment of the entire village, one or two large floods swept across the southeastern half of the site and a new channel was cut through a portion of the refuse mound belonging to the second unit. The latter has no bearing on the site so far as any archeological features are concerned.

The surface structure was approximately rectangular in plan, although its walls were not straight and the rooms were somewhat irregular in form. The three definite rooms (1, 3, and 5, fig. 44) were built in a single row. In front of them were the portico and the small court. The rooms were about the same size and their original floors were 6 inches (15.24 cm) below the level of the surrounding ground. None of the three contained fire pits and there is some question as to whether they should be regarded as living quarters or storage places. In view of their size, which was considerably greater than that of the usual granary, it seems as though they must have served, on occasions at least, as domiciles. Many of the rooms in later Pueblo buildings do not have fire pits, hence their presence or absence is not necessarily a requirement for a secular chamber. Because of the several fire pits in the portico and court, as well as those associated with shelters, it may be that all of the culinary tasks were performed there and that no provision was made for such activity in the actual rooms. Under these conditions there would be no need for fire in the rooms, except in winter weather when the people may have retired to the nearby semisubterranean structure. The latter possibility will be considered in greater detail in the discussion of the kiva.

There was little fallen material in the fill in the rooms and not much in the accumulation of earth around the outside walls. There are two possible explanations for this condition. One is that the upper walls were mainly of adobe mud that had melted down and washed away, hence there was little indication of their former existence. The other is that the house was stone-robbed to supply material needed in the building of the second unit. The latter seems more logical. Even when mud walls are entirely eroded away sufficient material usually collects on the floors and around the foundations to suggest their former presence. Since there was almost no slumped plaster in the rooms the walls probably consisted for the most part of masonry and the upper courses of stone were removed after the structure was abandoned. Enough of the walls remained, however, to show the type of foundation and the nature of the construction directly above. The shallow rectangular pit forming the base of the rooms was lined with upright stone slabs placed around the periphery in the same manner as those used in the granary and some of the house pits. Large quantities of adobe plaster were employed in conjunction with the slabs. Above these were several courses of horizontally laid stones. The outside portion of the masonry rested on the surface of the ground, while the inside was supported by the tops of the lining slabs. Where the latter projected above the ground level they were incorporated in the bottom courses of the masonry. Little attempt was made to dress or shape the blocks of stone employed in the walls and there was a minimum of chinking. There was no definite nor consistent breaking of joints and such bonding as occurred between the two rows of stones forming the thickness of the wall was purely accidental. The builders apparently relied on generous applications of mud plaster to strengthen the construction.

Only one of the rooms, No. 5, had the remains of a doorway. It was near one corner and opened to the court at the southeast side of the building. The other two rooms probably had openings in their walls at the portico side. There was not sufficient construction left to demonstrate this fact, but their existence was indicated by upright stones placed close to the wall in positions suggesting steps. The latter were present in the second unit under conditions clearly showing that they undoubtedly were to aid people stepping into or out of the chambers and a similar purpose is postulated for those in this series of rooms. There were no evidences of windows because of the meager height of the wall remnants, but an item that raises an intriguing line of thought was found in room 3. A slab of translucent selenite measuring 8 inches (20.32 cm) long, 3 inches (7.62 cm) wide, and ¾ inch (1.90 cm) thick was picked up from the floor midway of the outer wall. In Pueblo structures of late periods small windows were glazed with pieces of this material and the question arises as to whether or not the builders of this structure used the example found there in some comparable way. Thus far no evidence has come to light indicating that the practice was known in pre-Spanish times and until a slab of selenite is actually found in place over an opening in an early wall it probably is assuming too much to suggest that such was the case in this instance. The possibility is merely mentioned to call attention to the fact that some architectural features in fully developed Pueblo buildings may have had a comparatively early origin.

There was nothing to indicate what type of roof covered the rooms. In view of the fact that there were no post molds and no signs of embedded poles around the walls it seems logical to suppose that the roof timbers were supported by the walls and that the covering was flat. From the standpoint of construction that type of roof would not have caused the builders any great structural difficulties. Large beams placed across the short way of the rooms would have supported smaller poles, brush, and a plaster upper surface that would be satisfactory.

The floor of room 1 was paved with stone slabs and room 3 originally had a similar feature, but a second floor was placed in the latter chamber at some subsequent date and the level raised several inches. The later floor was smoothed plaster supported by a foundation of stones resting on the old floor. These stones were large, unworked blocks fitted together as closely as their uneven surfaces would permit. Small stones were placed in the interstices as chinking. The plaster above the stones was 2 inches (5.08 cm) thick. The floor in room 5 was hard-packed mud plaster applied to the native earth of the bottom of the shallow pit.

There was a slight offset in one wall of room 3 that had no apparent purpose. From the southwest corner of the chamber for a distance of approximately 3 feet (91.44 cm) the wall was much thicker than for the remainder of its length. It is possible that the builders decided a thinner wall would suffice, or that the structure was erected from the ends toward the center, and some of the builders were more generous in their use of material than others. On the other hand, there may have been a certain amount of reconstruction and remodeling in the house that produced the feature and this not be apparent in the remaining ruins of the structure. Whatever the cause, there does not seem to be any definite function for the jog.

The portico (fig. 44, *2*) was suggestive of the arbor associated with two of the granaries in the No. 5 pit-structure group. The floor space was enclosed by a low wall that formed a rectangular enclosure, although a wide opening was left at the southeast corner toward the semisubterranean structure. A roof or shade of some kind was erected over this space. Three upright posts set near the front or outside wall of the enclosure supported this covering. The other ends of the main beams probably rested on the walls of rooms 1 and

3, as there were no indications of support posts along the wall. One post was placed some distance from the wall in the south half of the arbor as an additional brace. Five fire pits are shown in the drawing (fig. 44). All were not contemporaneous, however. As in the case of room 3, the portico had two different floors. Four of the pits belonged to the original level and one to the later. There was no evidence to show it, but the upper level may correspond to the second one in room 3 and have been laid at the same time. Four of the pits were slab lined, but the fifth was a simple plaster-covered basin. The fill between the two floors was earth containing some refuse material, except for a small area underlying the later fire pit where a foundation of stone was provided to furnish support for the stone sides of the pit and also to serve as a paved bottom. The mud-plaster surface of the upper floor was applied directly to the top of the fill. There were two storage bins in the southwest corner of the portico. One was built in the corner and the other was along the wall adjacent to it. The corner example had a slab-covered exterior surface, a thick wall of adobe, and a smoothly plastered interior. Its bottom was below the floor level of the room. Three slabs that were part of the original wall formed the back of the bin. The other consisted of upright slabs covered with plaster. The enclosure in the corner would have been an excellent place for storing grain, while the other would have satisfied a number of needs.

The court (fig. 44, *4*) was somewhat comparable to the portico, only not as elaborate. It was entirely open on the side toward the semisubterranean structure and may not have been covered. There were no indications of upright posts to support a roof, although timbers extending over the space could have rested on the walls at the ends if the latter were high enough to function in that capacity. There was no evidence to show that either the north or south walls had risen to the required height, but they were not as low as the north and east walls of the portico. The north wall of the court was erected at the same time as the walls for rooms 3 and 5. This was demonstrated by the fact that it was tied into them in the sense that it was all part of the same construction. The wall at the south end of the court was built after room 5 was completed and abutted the corner of the building. The same type of construction was used in it, although the floor was not depressed. The bottoms of the upright foundation slabs were sunk in the earth for several inches and the horizontal stones laid around them, so as to suggest an all-masonry wall.

There were two fire pits in the court, one near the front at the northern end and the other near the back corner at the south end. Both were on the same level and appeared to have been used contemporaneously. Stone slabs served as lining in both pits, but some were missing from one wall in the pit near the corner. The only additional feature was an upright stone slab near the doorway to room 5. This stone was not properly placed to form a deflector or screen for the doorway, and in addition to that was too low to have served in that capacity. No step was needed at that place and since there was nothing to indicate its purpose no explanation can be given for its presence.

Just outside the portico was a surface fire pit that gave the appearance of being a double pit. Investigation showed that a slightly smaller and somewhat older pit had been replaced by a larger one. The later example partially cut into the side of the older one and some of the stones were removed from it, possibly for use in the new pit. Charcoal and ashes filled the bottom half of the new pit. On top of this deposit were a number of charred fragments of deer bones and a lower jaw from a dog. The latter bore no traces of fire and must have fallen or been thrown into the pit after the embers were cold. Furthermore, no fires were lighted there subsequent to its deposition. The deer bones no doubt represent scraps from a meal. Whether or not the dog jaw has a similar connotation is open to question. The Pueblos probably ate dogs at times of great need, but the practice does not seem to have been as common with them as with some other Indian groups. It certainly was not a general custom in this district because numerous articulated dog skeletons were discovered under conditions showing that they were intentionally buried. Stray bones were so rare that they constitute a practically negligible percentage in the kitchen-midden material. In no case were examples found that had been split for the marrow, a consistent characteristic of the bones from other kinds of animals. The chances are that the jaw in question had been picked up from the refuse mound where it had either washed out or been uncovered by digging, perhaps for a burial, and was tossed into the pit. The sides of this pit were faced with stone slabs and the bottom was paved.

The few slabs at the south end of the building just outside of the wall of the court, *4*, gave little indication of their purpose. They probably were the remnants of a granary or storage enclosure. Not enough was left of the construction, however, to be certain just what they represent. There was some alteration of the surface attendant on the erection of the building and the short wall forming the enclosure. This activity probably was responsible for the lack of evidence relating to the significance of these particular stones.

Along the ridge southwest from the surface building and the semisubterranean structure were the remains of several shelters. They are shown on the plan of the village (fig. 44) in the area between the two units designated Court. Every indication was that the group of fire pits and holes for arbor posts nearest to Kiva A and the buried watercourse were contemporaneous with the first unit. There is some question about those just below the legend, Court, and it is possible that they date from the period of the pit structure, No. 17, although they may have bridged the transition from that to the first unit. Accumulations of wind-blown sand and some refuse material on the surface of occupation indicated that they did not correlate with the second unit group, as potsherds identical with those from the latter occurred above the thin deposits. These shelters seem to have been much like those previously described. There were holes for upright posts to support a shade or covering and fire pits for cooking. There were no evidences of side walls. Two of the shelters were separated by a row of upright slabs extending north from enclosure No. 6, and the two on the edge of the watercourse were partially delimited in like manner. Further evidence for use of such places as general outdoor foci of domestic activity is noted in the metate located adjacent to one of the fire pits. This grinding stone was not in the position noted as a result of fortuitous events. It was definitely placed there and rested on a base of stones similar to the metate placement described for structure 15. All of the fire pits associated with these remains were lined with stone. Some of the pits were round, others rectangular. A number of the holes where support posts stood were reinforced by small stone slabs.

The structural remains marked *6* in the plan of the site (fig. 44) present a problem that cannot be solved satisfactorily from the meager evidence obtained from the excavations. There was nothing to show definitely its relationship to other elements in the village and there is some question about its function. In many respects it seems as though there should be a correlation between it and the nearby pit structure, No. 17, yet there were slight indications that it could be regarded as more closely associated with the first unit. The only definite factor is that it antedated the second unit and seemingly was abandoned and covered over by accumulated debris and rubbish before the second unit was built. In the fill in the structure there were no potsherds of a type that was characteristic of the second unit, despite the fact that it was very near that unit. Since potsherds of that particular form were exceedingly abundant about the site their absence from enclosure 6 is a good indication of its antecedent status.

There were two stages or two phases in the occupation of 6. Originally it had had a fairly large shallow pit. Later the size was reduced by the erection of an inner wall of stone slabs surmounted by rough masonry. The space between the old and new walls was filled in with debris and refuse. Both the large and small forms had been covered with some sort of superstructure supported on three uprights. This feature was unique for that district. Whether the uprights merely supported a flat shade or arbor such as suggested for the brush shelters or a three-sided truncated roof comparable to the four-sided type described for the pit structures could not be determined. There were no traces of slanting side poles, although they could have been used without leaving marks around the edges of the pit.

Near the center of the floor space was a fire pit of the generalized D-shape. The edge of the basin was reinforced at one side by a stone slab, but the remainder of the periphery was native earth surfaced with a coating of plaster. The most interesting interior feature, however, was a subfloor cache pit at the west side of the enclosure. The circular opening into this storage place was against the wall. The cache pit proper was jug-shaped, although the opening was decidedly off center, and extended under the floor and beyond the wall of the enclosure. The location and size in relation to the main part of No. 6 are shown by the dotted lines in the drawings (figs. 44 and 49). At one side of the storage pit, just below the opening, was an upright slab of stone so placed that it formed a step to aid in getting down into it. Some such provision was necessary because it was not possible to reach the farther limits from the top of the opening. To place corn or other materials around the wall, or to remove objects located there, would require a person's being in the pit and a step of this type was practically essential because the small size of the opening and the depth of the pit made access without some form of footrest a difficult process. The pit was carved out of the earth. The upper walls sloped down and away from the opening and met the vertical lower walls 1 foot 6 inches (45.72 cm) above the floor. Except for the step, no stone was used in its construction. The walls and bottom were covered with plaster. A cover of some kind was probably provided for the opening. None was found, but it does not seem likely that the pit was used without one. Stone slabs were frequently employed in that capacity, particularly when openings were in the floor of an enclosure. Absence of such a feature is not conclusive evidence that nothing of the kind was used. A cover stone might have been removed to serve some purpose in another structure when No. 6 was abandoned.

The cache pit in No. 6 was the only example found inside a structure in this district. A somewhat similar pit was present at the site of the third unit, but it was removed some distance from the buildings. Comparable granary or storage pits occur at various places in the Southwest. In one of the units of a Developmental village in southern Colorado there was a large storage pit in the floor of a lean-to or shed that offers an analogous combination of structure and granary.[59] In most cases, though, they are outside and do not con-

---

[59] Roberts, 1930, p. 9, fig. 5.

stitute a part of any structure. An interesting factor in connection with these storage pits is that they appear to occur in the earlier horizons in different areas in the Southwest rather than in the well-established phases. Just why this should be, or what its significance is, has not yet been determined. It is possible that need for them was removed in the later type of structures with their various lower back rooms available for storage purposes. Not enough work has been done in sites representing Developmental stages to warrant attempts at definite conclusions on the storage-pit feature or its importance in the cultural complex.

The cache pit in No. 6 was filled with some refuse and considerable wind-blown sand. There were no potsherds in the material. This is rather curious when their occurrence on the floor and in the fill of the associated enclosure is considered. Their absence may be either wholly accidental or due to the fact that the lower pit had become completely filled before any waste matter found its way into the upper structure. No great importance can be attached to the circumstance because there is no question but that the cache pit and No. 6 were contemporaneous.

The problem of what No. 6 represents is a puzzling one. Whether it should be regarded as a variant form of pit dwelling, a brush shelter, or an enlarged granary is a difficult question to answer. Particularly since there is so little satisfactory evidence. The general features are more suggestive of the brush-shelter type of construction, yet the depressed floor level and slab facing on the walls of the pit are more like those of the granaries or dwellings. The pit is larger than the general run of granaries and not quite as large as the majority of those for domiciles. The presence of a true fire pit bespeaks a dwelling place but the shallow pit, the lack of any form of ventilator, and the peculiar triangular frame for a superstructure set it apart from the usual form for such structures. When all of the various phases of the problem and the numerous ramifications of each are considered it seems that the most logical conclusion is that the enclosure was an adjunct to the nearby pit structure. It was a more elaborate development of the shelter than customary, possibly was used over longer periods of the year, and for that reason exhibited more of the characteristics of a true house. The shallow depth for the pit was not altogether unusual; it will be recalled that both 13a and 14 were characterized by a similar condition, but the absence of a ventilator in such a house is rare and for that reason the shelter idea is given preference. Shallow pits of approximately the same size and depth were present at the Long H Ranch, but the houses did have ventilators.[60] There is no good proof for the foregoing conclusion, however, and it is presented solely in the form of a questionable

---

[60] Roberts, 1931, pp. 43-48, houses A and B.

explanation. The granary function of No. 6 was served by the subfloor cache pit.

Kiva A was similar in some respects to the semisubterranean structures discussed in preceding pages, but in others it was quite distinct. The pit did not approximate a circular form as closely as most of those in this area, as it tended to the rectangular with rounded corners. The upper portion of the pit was encircled by a narrow bench. Both pit and bench were dug into the earth. The entire periphery of the chamber at the floor level was encircled by upright slabs. Horizontally laid masonry rested on top of the vertical stones, which were not uniform in height, and carried the wall to a higher level. The stones used in the courses above the slabs were of different sizes and shapes. Some were large, others small, some tabular in form, and others cubical. They exhibited very little dressing or shaping and apparently were laid in the wall just as they came from the quarry. On the whole they were larger and more variable than usual for kiva construction. A few small pieces of stone were employed as chinking, but the latter was not extensive. The top of the masonry at the bench level was covered with a good coating of plaster. The top of the earthen part of this feature was not so treated, however, and was quite irregular in comparison to the narrow ring of the wall. The main part of the wall, from the bench to the floor level, was originally well plastered. At the time of excavation, though, large patches had fallen off.

The superstructure that covered the pit was of the truncated pyramidal type supported by four upright posts placed near the corners of the room, but set out from the wall. There was a series of small holes around the back of the bench where the butt ends of the slanting poles rested. The post pockets at the corners were larger than the others, indicating, presumably, that heavier timbers were used in those positions. One of these corner placements, that at the southeast, was reinforced by a stone slab set in the front side of the hole. The structure had one unusual feature in the presence of a few irregular pockets in the back wall on the bench level between the sloping poles. These served for the storage of small objects, as was shown by the presence in them of some bone awls and punches and two small pottery ladles.

The fire pit near the center of the room (fig. 45, *g*) was D-shaped. A stone slab was set in the side toward the ash box and ventilator. The remainder of the basin was surfaced with mud plaster. The pit was encircled by a plaster ridge or rim that was a continuation and a part of a ridge that extended from wall to wall and separated the floor space into two approximately equal parts (fig. 45, *f*). Similar plaster ridges are frequently found extending from the fire pit to the bottoms of the main support posts at the ventilator side of the chamber,[61] but the occurrence of such a feature passing straight across the approximate center of the room is rare. The nearest comparable

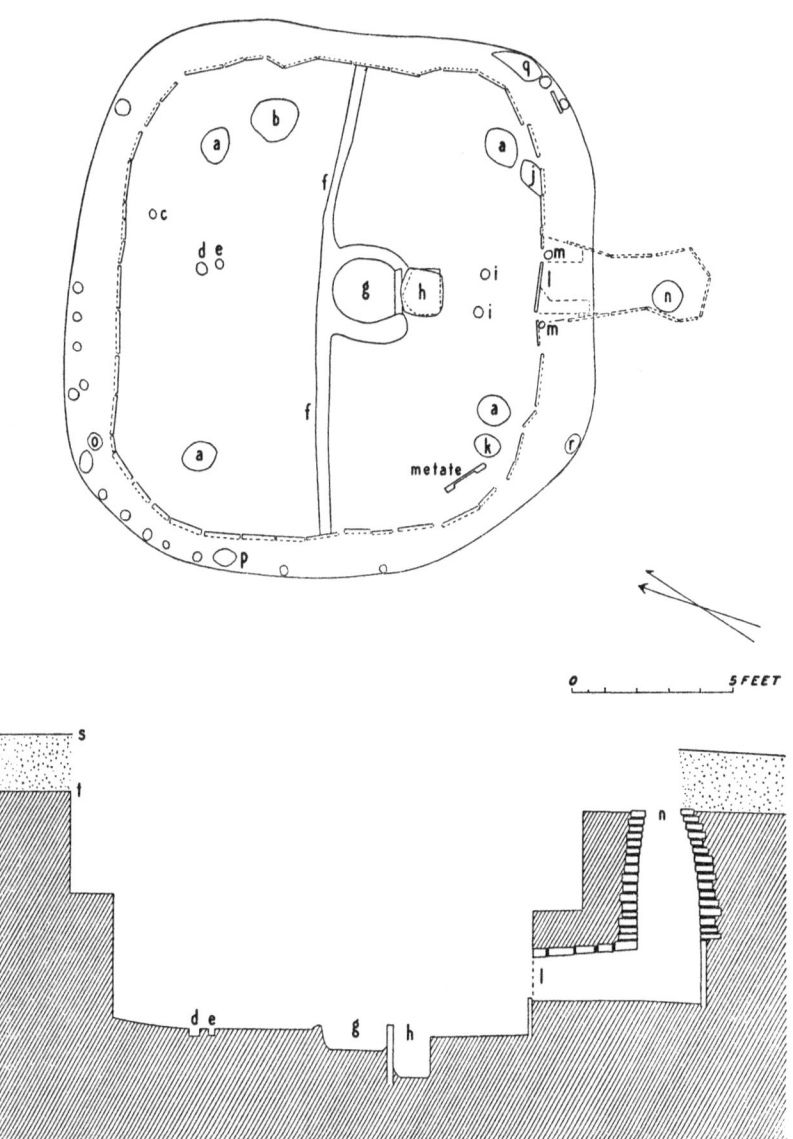

FIGURE 45.—Kiva A. *a*, holes for roof supports; *b*, storage pit; *c*, storage hole; *d* and *e*, sipapus; *f*, plaster ridge on floor; *g*, fire pit, *h*, old ladder pit; *i*, ladder pole depressions; *j*, storage pocket; *k*, pot rest or storage pocket; *l*, ventilator aperture; *m*, poles reinforcing ventilator opening; *n*, ventilator shaft; *o*, slanting timber placements; *p, q, r,* storage pockets on bench top; *s*, present surface; *t*, old ground level.

[61] Judd, 1926, p. 113; Roberts, 1929, pp. 25, 29–50, 54, 57–58; 1931, pp. 26–29.

example was in a small house belonging to the Modified Basket Maker stage located in the Chaco Canyon.[62] The function or significance of such ridges is not known. In the Modified Basket Maker houses they appear to be derived from the placement for the slabs that formed the compartment on the ventilator side of the chamber and seemingly represented that feature in delimiting a certain portion of the floor area. In some cases logs were buried in the floor to form a foundation for these radiating ridges. Undoubtedly there was a good reason for their inclusion in houses, but what it was has not been learned. The ridge in Kiva A was the only example found in the Allantown district. No wood was used in its construction; it consisted wholly of plaster.

Adjoining the fire pit in the position usually occupied by the ladder box was a pentagonal pit that could have served such a purpose, although it apparently did not (fig. 45, h). The pit was covered with a stone slab. When the room was excavated there was a layer of fine wood ashes on top of the stone, yet only a small amount in the pit. The latter seemingly had sifted through the cracks between the stone and the edges of the pit. The bottom and sides of the latter were not stained in the manner common to those where ashes have remained for any length of time, hence it did not serve as a depository for them. The ladder stood on the floor of the chamber between this pit and the ventilator opening, as shown by two small basins worn in the plaster where the butts of the poles rested (fig. 45, i). The pit originally may have functioned as a ladder rest, as a slight abrading of the bottom at the ventilator end indicated. Then for some reason the position of the ladder was changed and the pit covered with the stone. Why it was not used as an ash depository as in some other houses is not known. It might have served as a storage place on occasions, particularly for small objects, but that is purely conjectural, as none were found in it. There was no deflector and no signs that one had been present during the occupancy of the structure.

There were several holes at various places in the floor of the chamber. At the location of the sipapu there were two, d and e, either one of which could have represented that symbolic feature. Both were shallower than usual and somewhat smaller in diameter. Their sides and bottoms were carefully plastered. Close to the wall north of them was another small hole, c, that evidently was for the storage of minor objects. Its sides and bottom were also plastered. Near the base of the support post at the northeast corner of the room was an irregularly shaped basin, b. It was deeper than many of those occupying similar positions in other structures. The walls

---

[62] Roberts, 1929, pp. 57–58.

were vertical and the bottom comparatively level. The walls and bottom did not form a sharp angle, rather a curved one. Both walls and bottom were covered with plaster. The basin near the post at the southeast corner, *j*, was at the base of the wall. One side of the depression was bordered by part of the slab forming the wall at that point on the periphery. The basin was oval in contour and quite shallow. The sides curved downward from the edge on the floor level to the maximum depth near the center. Perhaps this was a pot rest. The shallow basin, *k*, near the support post at the southwest corner also seems to have been for a pot rest. The diameter and depth suggest that it was the placement for a large culinary or storage jar. When the room was excavated a thin-slab metate of the open-end form was leaning against the wall near the basin and the support post.

The ventilator passage and shaft were dug as a trench and then covered over. No tunneling was used in its construction. The end of the trench where it penetrated the wall of the room widened to a marked degree, but it was reduced in size by the erection of a crude masonry framework for the opening. This stonework cut off more of the trench at the west side than at the east, as may be seen from the dotted lines in the drawing (fig. 45). The aperture proper was framed by plaster reinforced by poles. Two small poles were set in the wall at either side of the opening and a short timber was laid across their tops on a level with the top of the bench. The crosspiece was above the lintel of the opening, which was a stone slab. The construction was covered with plaster so that at the time the chamber was occupied the timber was not exposed to view. The sill of the opening was above the floor level and was paved with a stone slab. The walls of the passage were lined with upright slabs; the ceiling consisted of slabs and the floor was paved with them. The walls and floor were covered with plaster for about half the length of the passage. The bottom of the ventilator shaft was lined with upright slabs surmounted by horizontally laid stones. The latter were drawn in course by course as the masonry extended upward until the opening on the ground level was quite small. The work was not as good as it might have been and the small hole at the top was somewhat off center. The floor of the passage sloped slightly downward from the aperture in the chamber to the bottom of the shaft. This was not the case in many of the structures, although such a slope would have merit, in that rain or surface water falling into the shaft would collect at the outer end and not run into the room. There was little danger of the latter, however, as the ground sloped sharply away from the top of the shaft toward the old watercourse.

There were several interesting features in the fill in Kiva A. When the pit was excavated a pillar 3 feet (91.44 cm) square was left at the center, like those described for some of the other structures, and a careful check made of various phenomena recorded there. Through the central portion of the pillar the layers were thinner than those at the top or bottom and contained more refuse material, particularly stone chips, charcoal, bone fragments, and potsherds. Indications were that an interval of some length passed between the abandonment of the structure and the use of the pit as a dumping place. After the refuse had filled it to a level approximately midway between the top of the bench and the old ground level it was no longer used for that purpose and subsequent layers resulted from natural agencies. Indications were that the presence of the old pit had been marked by a depression for a considerable length of time and that water had gathered and stood there at intervals. Subsequent to the abandonment of the village all traces were obliterated by wind-blown sand and drift from the higher levels.

On two occasions during the period when the pit was functioning as a depository for refuse some structure in the village was damaged by fire. This was shown by the layers of sand mixed with charcoal, bits of burned stone, and fragments of burned plaster, debris resulting from reconstruction activities. The levels at which this material occurred were sufficiently separated to suggest that a number of years elapsed between the conflagrations. One of the last layers laid down prior to the discontinuance of dumping waste matter in the pit consisted almost entirely of stone spalls, broken building stones, and pieces of mud plaster. This debris probably came from the nearby surface building and may indicate the period when it was dismantled for the material used in its construction. If such is the case it suggests that the second unit was occupied for some time before the first was robbed of its stone and timbers. The fact that it also occurred just above the last layer of debris from a burned structure carries the implication that the abandoned first unit supplied the material needed to replace the portion of the second unit damaged by the flames. That such actually took place is not known, of course, but in view of the evidence the conclusion that it did does not seem to be unwarranted.

One strange find in the fill was not included in the stratigraphic pillar. It consisted of a human skeleton lying along the bench at the west side of the chamber. A portion of the skull rested on the bench. The remaining bones were just below that level and somewhat scattered, but not sufficiently disarticulated to indicate the burial of an already decomposed body. There were no leg or foot bones, however. The pelvic bones were present and in good state of preservation. They were normal in every respect. The acetabula, the cup-shaped articular cavities in the hip bones where the ends of the thigh bones rest, were undamaged and showed that the individual originally had legs. All of the remaining fill was carefully sifted but not one additional bone was recovered. There are several intriguing questions concerning the remains that cannot be answered in a satisfactory manner. Was the skeleton buried where found, or did it tumble into place after the pit was partially filled? If the latter, where did it fall from and what happened to the legs? The bones were not in a definite grave dug into the fill. They were on a former surface and overspread with refuse. Indications were that the legless body was deposited there and covered with material scraped from the surrounding area. Why it had no legs is not definitely known, but what became of them can be answered in part by finds in the second unit and therein lies a possible explanation for their absence.

A left femur or thigh bone of proper size for this individual was uncovered in the corner at the outside of the building where the walls of Nos. 7 and 9, figure 44, meet. One end of the bone was gnawed. The teeth marks were too large to be those of a rodent and possibly were made by a dog. At the back of the recess between Nos. 9 and 11, in the northwest corner formed by the walls 9 and 10, a complete left foot, including the ankle bones, was uncovered. The foot had been sealed in the corner, after being covered with earth from the refuse mound, by a thick coating of plaster. The bones, except for two in the ankle, were articulated and showed that the member had been interred while held together by flesh and ligaments. These two occurrences open an interesting field for speculation. The teeth marks on the femur suggest that the body in the pit of Kiva A had not been covered as thoroughly as the situation demanded and that some of the village dogs may have dug into the grave and pulled out the legs and torn them apart. Then some of the grisly fragments were gathered up by the inhabitants of the village and reburied in the spots close to the building instead of in the refuse mound or old house pit. Perhaps they thought that by so disposing of them they would be protected from further violation. This is, of course, pure conjecture and may not be an even approximate reconstruction of what happened. The leg bone and the foot may have belonged to entirely different individuals. The burial of parts of the body occurred sporadically throughout the Southwest and it is possible that these represent some such happening rather than that they are missing members from the legless skeleton. Since they are the proper size for that individual, however, and the leg bone shows markings from animal teeth, the conclusion that they belong together is not unreasonable. Unfortunately the condyle on the femur that would rest in the socket in the pelvic bone was the end that had been gnawed off. As a consequence it is not possible to obtain the evidence that would settle the question, that of fitting the one into the other.

An almost identical situation was encountered at the opposite side of the chamber just above the floor level where a partial dog skeleton came to light. Both hind legs and one front leg were missing from these remains. The skull and other bones were present and articulated. The same questions raised by the human remains apply to those of the animal, but even less convincing explanations can be offered in answering them. No stray bones that could be attributed to the dog were found elsewhere. It is possible that after the creature's demise and the disposal of the body in the old house pit rodents made away with the legs. There was nothing to show that, however. In view of the number of dog burials about the site it does not seem likely that the remains were just tossed into the pit. The nature of the earth around the bones was such that a gradual accumulation was indicated. Hence intentional burial probably was not practiced in this instance. One plausible explanation is that the dog fell into the pit, possibly while the superstructure or portions of it were still in place, died there and before drifting sand had covered the remains they were mutilated by other animals. The problem is not an important one and has no definite bearing on the cultural status of the community, but it is an example of one of the interesting incidentals occasionally noted in an archeological site. The complete skeleton of a dog was found on the floor of a pit structure in the Chaco Canyon under conditions suggesting that the animal was trapped and perished in an abandoned dwelling.[63] The somewhat analogous occurrence at this site is an additional indication that the prowling proclivities of the Indian dogs were likely to lead them into a combination of circumstances that were fatal.

The status of Kiva A, whether dwelling or ceremonial chamber, is difficult to establish. If it was associated with a cluster of simple granary remains, like those near structures 15 and 16, it unquestionably would be called a domicile. On the other hand, if found with a well-developed surface house there would be no hesitancy in considering it a ceremonial structure, although one in which certain features were not as highly specialized as in most examples. The significance in this seeming paradox is the evidence that it gives for a transition in function in the semisubterranean structure. Also that at the present stage of knowledge of the Southwest it is not possible to tell from the internal nature of a structure, dating from this period in the growth of the cultural pattern, whether it was house or kiva. Conclusions must be aided and governed by the associated

---

[63] Roberts, 1929, p. 66.

remains. The fact that the nearby surface building had features that qualified it for use as a dwelling tends to argue for a ceremonial function for the underground chamber. The latter, however, was so similar to pit structures on the site that definitely were dwellings that it is difficult to disregard that aspect of the problem. The truncated pyramidal superstructure was characteristic of the form found on dwellings, but the horizontally laid wall masonry is a feature more commonly present in kivas. The floor depth below the top of the bench and original ground level was somewhat greater than customary for houses, although the chamber was not as deep as the average kiva. Considered from all points of view the structure is intermediate in type between a dwelling and a ceremonial chamber. There is no definite proof to show that such was the case, but it seems probable that the pit structure was built first and used as a habitation, then the surface rooms were constructed and there was a gradual shift from one to the other. The few scattered evidences that regular slab-pit granaries occupied the site of the surface building prior to its erection suggest that possibility. Even after the surface rooms were occupied the people may have reverted to the old underground house during the winter season. As was pointed out in the discussion of the surface building, there was no provision for fires in the rooms and it is doubtful that those blazing in the pits in the floor of the portico or the court would have given off enough heat to warm the house in cold weather.

Charcoal suitable for dendrochronological studies was scarce in the fill in the kiva. Sections from two of the slanting roof poles were salvaged from holes at the back of the bench. One of these could not be correlated with the ring chart and a number of outside rings were missing from the other. The closest approximation to a date is 845. Due to the range in the timbers for other houses it is evident that too much stress cannot be placed on the 845. There is no way of knowing whether it is at the earlier or later end of a series covering a long span of years, such as 31 in No. 15 or 74 in No. 12, or falls midway in some comparable sequence. There is also the possibility that the particular pole was salvaged from the nearby abandoned pit structure, No. 17, and hence older than the kiva. It will be recalled that the former structure gave evidence of having been dismantled. On the basis of evidence from some types of potsherds the kiva appears to be roughly contemporaneous with the final stage in No. 15, yet other types indicate that the correlation should be with the first stage described for that structure. If synchronous with the final stage the date for the kiva would be some 40 years later.

Several interesting questions are raised by the 845 date and it is tantalizing not to know what interpretation to place on the structure. If 845 is correct for the year when the house was built it suggests that the people in this unit were more advanced in architectural development than those in No. 15. The implications are that they not only had adopted a surface structure with contiguous rooms at a time when the others were still building the old style granaries and only occasionally using them as habitations, but that they preceded them in this advance by two generations. Considering the proximity of the two structures this does not seem reasonable. Of course, as pointed out in the discussion of the kiva, it is fairly evident that the surface building was erected subsequent to the semisubterranean chamber and allowing for a lapse of a number of years between their construction the discrepancy would not be as great, although still of marked character. On the other hand, when compared with the 867 of No. 3, the 845 does not seem as far out of line. Especially when it is recalled that some of the timbers there showed cutting dates of 842 and 852 and that No. 3 apparently was a kiva for a surface structure quite comparable to that in this unit. Here again is the indication that No. 15 was a laggard unit. This has further significance in the fact that the dominant type of potsherds in the 15 assemblage was a form centering to the north and west from the Allantown district, the western type of Developmental pottery generally called Kana-a black on white. From this it seems that 15 may represent an addition to the community of a group that was not as progressive in house building and was somewhat conservative in the adoption of new forms. Other evidence about the site showed that the form of pottery in question was later in its appearance in this district than other Developmental forms.

The 845 date, if considered as being indicative of No. 17 rather than the kiva, correlates quite well with other aspects of the remains in the district in that the pit structure compares favorably with others closely approximating the same age. Considered from the broad point of view, the import of the whole matter probably is that the 45-year interval represented by these structures covers the period when the transition in house types and other cultural traits was at its maximum. The combination of circumstances and implications raised by this particular piece of charcoal emphasizes the fact that too much importance must not be placed on a house date based on a single specimen of wood. As an indication of the approximate period represented it is helpful, but it is not to be considered conclusive.

The surface building in this unit had a maximum length of 32 feet (9.754 m) and a width of 18 feet 6 inches (5.638 m). Inside measurements for room 1 were: length 8 feet 6 inches (2.591 m), width 6 feet 6 inches (1.981 m). Room 2 (the portico), length 18 feet 10 inches (5.740 m), width 8 feet 9 inches (2.667 m). The opening at the southeast corner was 4 feet (1.219 m) wide. Room 3 was 11 feet (3.352 m) long and 7 feet (2.133 m) wide. The offset at the southwest corner was 3 feet (91.44 cm) long and 9 inches (22.86 cm) wide. Room 4 (the court) was 10 feet 3 inches (3.124 m) long. The wall at the north end measured 5 feet 9 inches (1.752 m) in length and that at the south end 4 feet 9 inches (1.447 m). The doorway between 4 and 5 was 1 foot 6 inches (45.72 cm) wide. Room 5 had a length of 9 feet 6 inches (2.895 m) and a width of 6 feet 3 inches (1.905 m).

The fire pits in room 2 in order from north to south measured as follows: The first, diameters 2 feet (60.96 cm) by 1 foot 9 inches (53.34 cm), and depth 6 inches (15.24 cm); the bottom was 5½ inches (13.97 cm) above the old floor. The second diameters 1 foot 4 inches (40.64 cm) by 1 foot 3 inches (38.1 cm) and depth 5½ inches (13.97 cm). The third, diameters 1 foot 4 inches (40.64 cm) by 1 foot 6 inches (45.72 cm) and depth 6 inches (15.24 cm). The fourth, diameters 1 foot 8 inches (50.8 cm) by 1 foot 6 inches (45.72 cm) and depth 7 inches (17.78 cm). The fifth, the plaster pit, diameters 2 feet 3 inches (68.58 cm) by 1 foot 7 inches (48.26 cm) and depth 5½ inches (13.97 cm).

The holes for the support posts for the arbor over the portico did not show a marked range in size; that at the northeast corner had a diameter of 6 inches (15.24 cm) and a depth of 8½ inches (21.59 cm); the post stood 1 foot (30.48 cm) from both walls. The hole midway along the front wall had a diameter of 6 inches (15.24 cm) and a depth of 10 inches (25.4 cm). It was 1 foot 6 inches (45.72 cm) from the wall. The two holes near the fire pit at the southeast opening had diameters of 7 inches (17.78 cm) and 6 inches (15.24 cm) and depths of 9½ inches (24.13 cm) and 4 inches (10.16 cm). The larger hole was 11 inches (27.94 cm) from the wall and 9 inches (22.86 cm) from the fire pit; the smaller hole was 4 inches (10.16 cm) from the larger and 3 inches (7.62 cm) from the fire basin. The hole for the post near the back of the south end of the room had a diameter of 10½ inches (26.67 cm) and a depth of 6¾ inches (17.14 cm). It was 1 foot 10 inches (55.88 cm) from the back wall.

The rectangular-slab bin along the wall near the southwest corner measured 2 feet 6 inches (76.2 cm) by 1 foot (30.48 cm). The slabs were 1 foot 4 inches (40.64 cm) and 1 foot 9 inches (53.34 cm) high. The granary in the corner of the portico had inside measurements of 1 foot 4 inches (40.64 cm) by 1 foot 9 inches (53.34 cm), with a depth of 2 feet 2 inches (66.04 cm). The plaster rim or wall had an average thickness of 6½ inches (16.51 cm).

The fire pits in the court (No. 4, fig. 44) were approximately the size of those in the portico. That at the north near the front of the space had diameters of 2 feet 2 inches (66.04 cm) and 1 foot 10½ inches (57.15 cm) at the top, and 1 foot 3 inches (38.1 cm) and 1 foot 8 inches (50.8 cm) at the bottom. The depth was 5 inches (12.7 cm). The pit was 9 inches (22.86 cm) from the north wall. The pit at the southwest corner had diameters of 1 foot 9 inches (53.34 cm) and 1 foot 10 inches (55.88 cm) at the top and 1 foot (30.48 cm) and 1 foot 4 inches (40.64 cm) at the bottom. The depth was 7 inches (17.78 cm). The pit was only 3 inches (7.62 cm) from the west wall and 1 foot 2 inches (35.56 cm) from the south. The stone slab set in the floor of the court was 1 foot 3 inches (38.1 cm) long, 6½ inches (16.51 cm) high, and 3½ inches (8.89 cm) thick. It stood 9 inches (22.86 cm) from the wall. The old pit beneath the floor close to the stone had diameters of 1 foot 3 inches (38.1 cm) and 1 foot 8 inches (50.8 cm), with a depth of 1 foot 2 inches (35.56 cm).

The fire pit in front of the building, just outside of the portico, measured 1 foot 8 inches (50.8 cm) by 2 feet (60.96 cm) and had a depth of 10 inches (25.4 cm). The older pit, which it replaced, measured 1 foot 6 inches (45.72 cm) by 1 foot 9 inches (53.34 cm) and was 1 foot (30.48 cm) deep. The old pit was 9 inches (22.86 cm) from the portico wall and the later one was 2 feet (60.96 cm) away.

The remains of the brush shelter with the two fire pits and the metate, located on the edge of the old watercourse, were 12 feet (3.657 m) from the corner of the surface building. The rectangular pit measured 1 foot 9 inches (53.34 cm) by 1 foot 7 inches (48.26 cm) and was 3½ inches (8.89 cm) deep. The metate was 1 foot (30.48 cm) from the fire pit. The metate was 1 foot 11½ inches (59.69 cm) long, 1 foot 4 inches (40.64 cm) wide at the open end and 1 foot (30.48 cm) wide at the closed end. The trough was 1 foot 2 inches (35.56 cm) long, 10 inches (25.4 cm) wide, and 4 inches (10.16 cm) deep. The stone was 4½ inches (11.43 cm) thick. The second fire pit measured 1 foot 7 inches (48.26 cm) by 1 foot 9 inches (53.34 cm) and had an average depth of 7½ inches (19.05 cm). The standing stones that partially separated the floor area around the two pits had a combined length of 1 foot 10½ inches (57.15 cm) and stood 11½ inches (29.21 cm) above the floor. The holes for the support posts for the arbor erected over the pits ranged between 6 and 7 inches (15.24 and 17.78 cm) in diameter. Their depths were 1 foot (30.48 cm).

The fire pit south of the above group measured 1 foot 2 inches (35.56 cm) by 1 foot 3 inches (38.1 cm) and was 1 foot (30.48 cm) deep. The wall of upright slabs to the west of this pit, separating the general area of occupation marked "Court" on the diagram (fig. 44), had a length of 12 feet (3.657 cm). The fire pit on the west side of this wall measured 1 foot 2 inches (35.56 cm) by 1 foot 3 inches (38.1 cm) and was 8 inches (20.32 cm) deep. The surrounding holes for posts ranged from 7½ inches (19.05 cm) to 9 inches (22.86 cm) in diameter and from 10 inches (25.4 cm) to 1 foot 6 inches (45.72 cm) in depth.

The original enclosure at No. 6 had diameters of 9 feet (2.743 m) and 10 feet 6 inches (3.200 m). The smaller room was 6 feet (1.828 m) by 9 feet 3 inches (2.819 m). The floor of the original room was 2 feet 1 inch (63.5 cm) below the old ground level at the south side. The stone wall for the reduced enclosure rose 2 feet 10¼ inches (86.99 cm) above the floor at the south side, 2 feet 9 inches (83.82 cm) at the east, 3 feet 5¼ inches (1.047 m) at the north, and 2 feet 5 inches (73.66 cm) at the west. The single hole for a support post in the corner of the old room was 8 inches (20.32 cm) in diameter and 1 foot 7½ inches (49.53 cm) deep. The hole at the south corner in the smaller room was 5½ inches (13.97 cm) and 6½ inches (16.51 cm) in diameter and 6 inches (15.24 cm) deep. The hole near the east corner was 4 inches (10.16 cm) and 5 inches (12.7 cm) in diameter and 4¾ inches (12.06 cm) deep. The hole at the north corner was 5 inches (12.7 cm) in diameter and 6½ inches (16.51 cm) deep. The fire pit measured 1 foot 3 inches (38.1 cm) by 1 foot 7 inches (48.26 cm) and was 7 inches (17.78 cm) deep. The stone that faced one side was 1 foot 1 inch (33.02 cm) long, 3 inches (7.62 cm) thick, and projected 2 inches (5.08 cm) above the floor.

The opening into the cache pit or granary beneath the floor of No. 6 was 1 foot 9 inches (53.34 cm) in diameter. The bottom of the pit was 3 feet 8 inches (1.117 m) below the floor of No. 6. The bottom of the cache pit was oval in contour with diameters of 4 feet (1.219 m) and 4 feet 10 inches (1.473 m). The wall was approximately vertical for a distance of 1 foot 6 inches (45.72 cm) above the floor, then curved inward to the circular opening in the upper floor. The stone slab set in the pit floor just below the opening was 1 foot 6 inches (45.72 cm) high, 8½ inches (21.59 cm) wide, and 3½ inches (8.89 cm) thick.

Kiva A had a diameter of 15 feet 10 inches (4.826 m) on the sipapu, fire pit, ventilator line above the bench and 13 feet 5 inches (4.089 m) below it. Along the direction of the plaster ridge on the floor the diameter was 16 feet (4.876 m) above the bench and 13 feet 9 inches (4.191 m) below it. On the ventilator side of the chamber the floor was 8 feet 7½ inches (2.628 m) below the present ground level and 7 feet 7½ inches (2.323 m) below the old surface. At the northeast end of the plaster ridge the floor was 7 feet 7½ inches (2.323 m) below the present surface and 6 feet 7 inches (2.006 m) below the old ground level. At the southwest end of the ridge the depth was 7 feet 2½ inches (2.196 m) from the present ground level and 6 feet 2½ inches (1.891 m) from the old surface.

The holes for the support posts were larger in this structure than in many of the others. That near the north corner had diameters of 10 inches (25.4 cm) and 1 foot 2 inches (35.56 cm) and a depth of 2 feet ¾ inch (62.86 cm). It was 1 foot 8½ inches (52.07 cm) from the wall. The hole for the east post was 1 foot (30.48 cm) and 1 foot 4 inches (40.64 cm) in diameter and 2 feet ¼ inch (61.59 cm) in depth. The hole was 6 inches (15.24 cm) from the wall. The hole for the support at the south corner was 8 inches (20.32 cm) and 9 inches (22.86 cm) in diameter and 1 foot 8 inches (50.8 cm) deep. It was 6 inches (15.24 cm) from the wall. The western post was set in a hole with diameters of 9½ inches (24.13 cm) and 1 foot 2 inches (35.56 cm). The hole was 1 foot 6 inches (45.72 cm) from the wall.

The fire pit in the floor of the kiva (fig. 45, *g*), had diameters of 1 foot 10½ inches (57.15 cm) and 1 foot 11½ inches (59.69 cm). The bottom of the pit was 8¾ inches (22.22 cm) below the floor level. The surrounding rim of plaster increased the depth, however, to 10½ inches (26.67 cm). The stone in the edge of the pit was 1 foot 4 inches (40.64 cm) long, 3½ inches (8.89 cm) thick, and its top projected 1 inch (2.54 cm) above the plaster rim. The rim ranged from 4 inches (10.16 cm) to 7 inches (17.78 cm) in width and had an average height of 1½ inches (3.81 cm) above the floor. The ladder box or pit covered with the stone slab (fig. 45, *h*) was separated from the fire pit by the stone slab. This pit measured 1 foot 2½ inches (36.83 cm) by 1 foot 4 inches (40.64 cm) and had a depth of 1 foot 2½ inches (36.83 cm). The cover slab was 1 foot 4½ inches (41.91 cm) by 1 foot 5 inches (43.18 cm) and 1 inch (2.54 cm) thick.

At one side of the room the plaster ridge (fig. 45, *f*) was quite regular in width and did not vary greatly from the 4½-inch (11.43 cm) average. The continuation at the opposite side, however, ranged between 2½ inches (6.35 cm) and 4 inches (10.16 cm). The height was quite consistent along the whole length and deviated only slightly from the 1½-inch (3.81-cm) average.

The cache or storage pit in the floor near the north support post (fig. 45, *b*) had diameters of 1 foot 3 inches (38.1 cm) and 1 foot 6 inches (45.72 cm). The depth was 1 foot 2 inches (35.56 cm). The hole was 9 inches (22.86 cm) from the hole for the support post and 1 foot (30.48 cm) from the wall. The small pocket (fig. 45, *c*) had diameters of 2½ inches (6.35 cm) and 3½ inches (8.89 cm) and a depth of 2½ inches (6.35 cm). It was 8½ inches (21.59 cm) from the wall. The two holes occupying the position of the sipapu were of slightly different size. The larger (fig. 45, *d*), was 4 inches (10.16 cm) and 4½ inches (11.43 cm) in diameter and 2⅜ inches (6.03 cm) in depth. The hole was 2 feet 5 inches (73.66 cm) from the wall. The smaller hole (fig. 45, *e*), had diameters of 3 inches

(7.62 cm) and 3½ inches (8.89 cm). The depth was 2 inches (5.08 cm). Hole e was 3 inches (7.62 cm) from d and 3 feet 5 inches (1.041 m) from the fire pit.

The two cuplike depressions in the floor where the ends of the ladder poles rested (fig. 45, i) were 1 foot 1 inch (33.02 cm) and 1 foot 3 inches (38.1 cm) from the end of the slab-covered pit in the position of the ladder box. The depressions were 1 foot 1 inch (33.02 cm) apart. They had diameters of 3½ inches (8.89 cm), suggesting that 3-inch (7.62-cm) poles were used in the ladder. The depressions were 1 foot 6 inches (45.72 cm) from the base of the ventilator opening, giving ample foot space for a person using the ladder.

The oval-shaped basin (fig. 45, j) at the base of the wall near the east support post had diameters of 1 foot 3 inches (38.1 cm) and 7 inches (17.78 cm). The sides sloped downward from the rim of the basin to a depth of 2½ inches (6.35 cm) near its center. The basin touched the wall along one side. It was only 3 inches (7.62 cm) from the edge of the hole for the post. The similar floor feature (fig. 45, k) near the south support post had diameters of 8 inches (20.32 cm) and 10½ inches (26.67 cm). Its depth was greater, being 4½ inches (11.43 cm). The hole was 3½ inches (8.89 cm) from the edge of the hole for the post and 6 inches (15.24 cm) from the wall.

The ventilator opening (fig. 45, l) was 9½ inches (24.13 cm) wide and 1 foot 4 inches (40.64 cm) high. The sill was 1 foot (30.48 cm) above the floor of the chamber. The original trench where it cut through the wall of the room was 2 feet 7 inches (78.74 cm) wide. The stonework reducing this size and forming a frame for the aperture was 1 foot (30.48 cm) wide at the west side of the opening and 9 inches (22.86 cm) at the east side. On the west side the construction extended back into the tunnel 1 foot 8 inches (50.8 cm), where there was a 5-inch (12.7-cm) jog. On the east side the masonry extended only 1 foot 2½ inches (36.83 cm) along the tunnel wall. The jog was the same size as that on the opposite side, 5 inches (12.7 cm). The poles employed to reinforce the framework filling in the trench opening (fig. 45, m) had diameters of 2½ inches (6.35 cm) and 3 inches (7.62 cm). The stone slab used as a riser from the floor of the chamber to the sill of the aperture was 1 foot ½ inch (31.75 cm) high. The slight projection of its top above the sill was compensated for when the structure was occupied by the adobe plaster that covered the sill. The passage, from the aperture to the place where it entered the bottom of the shaft, was 3 feet 4 inches (1.016 m) long. The width at the outer end was 1 foot 5 inches (43.18 cm). The height of the opening was 1 foot 7 inches (48.26 cm). The bottom of the shaft measured 1 foot 9 inches (53.34 cm) by 2 feet 1½ inches

(64.77 cm). The bottom of the shaft was 7 feet 9 inches (2.362 m) below the present ground level and 5 feet 11 inches (1.803 m) below the old surface. The opening on the ground level (fig. 45, n) had diameters of 1 foot 1 inch (33.02 cm) and 1 foot 1½ inches (34.29 cm).

The bank of the buried watercourse was only 1 foot 6 inches (45.72 cm) from the outside edge of the ventilator opening. The side of the old channel dipped sharply to the bottom, which was 4 feet (1.219 m) below the present ground level and 2 feet 2 inches (66.04 cm) below the former surface of occupation.

The pockets on the bench between the base ends of the slanting roof poles were of different sizes. The circular one (fig. 45, o) at the west corner was 5½ inches (13.97 cm) in diameter and 3 inches (7.62 cm) deep. The back edge of the pocket was against the back wall of the bench. Pocket p, figure 45, undercut the back wall of the bench to some extent. About half the pocket was beyond the line of the wall. The pocket was 9 inches (22.86 cm) long, 6⅜ inches (16.19 cm) wide, and 4 inches (10.16 cm) deep. It cut into the wall a distance of 3½ inches (8.89 cm). The largest pocket of the group was q, figure 45, which was entirely in the wall at the back of the bench. It had a length of 1 foot 9½ inches (54.61 cm) and a width of 8½ inches (21.59 cm). The bottom of the pocket was 2 inches (5.08 cm) below the top of the bench. The opening into the pocket was 1 foot 2 inches (35.56 cm) long and 4 inches (10.16 cm) high. The pocket near the south corner (fig. 45, r) was smaller. It also was entirely subwall in its form. The total length was 8 inches (20.32 cm) and the width 4½ inches (11.43 cm). The opening was 5 inches (12.7 cm) long and 3 inches (7.62 cm) high. The bottom of the pocket was only 1 inch (2.54 cm) below the level of the bench top. The diameters for the holes for the butts of the roof timbers were consistently in the range of from 3 inches (7.62 cm) to 4½ inches (11.43 cm). The majority varied only slightly from a 3½-inch (8.89-cm) diameter.

UNIT NO. 2

The second unit, also a part of the Developmental village, was larger and more complex than the first one (pl. 22, a). It consisted of a surface structure containing six rooms, the remains of several shelters, and a subterranean chamber designated Kiva B on the plan of the village (fig. 44). There is little question in this case but that the circular structure had a ceremonial function, particularly in the final phase of its occupation. The refuse mound was east of the house remains. A portion of it was beyond the watercourse. Originally all of it had been separated from the house site by the channel, but as it grew in size some of it contributed to the fill in the old stream bed and ultimately spread across it. The mound was much larger than that for the first unit. It covered a larger area and also was deeper. The north end probably consisted in part of material deposited by people using the shelters of the first unit and of that deposited by the one-time inhabitants of the pit structure. Slightly more than the southern half unquestionably was the accumulation of refuse from the second unit. This part of the mound was by far the deepest and, even making allowances for an increase in the size of the group living there, indicates a longer period of occupation.

One noticeable feature in connection with the second unit is that of the outside fire pits. They not only were around the house, between it and the kiva, but were scattered over the surface of the refuse mound. In one or two cases there were indications that some sort of shade had been erected nearby. Most of them, however, were used without any such accompanying construction. Whether they were used for cooking fires or were simply places where people gathered, in the manner of modern Indians, for warmth and light in periods of relaxation and sociability could not be learned. As a matter of fact they probably served both purposes, although it is likely that most of the culinary activity centered around those where the walls of the surface building served as a windbreak or the users were protected by an arbor.

The buried watercourse passed much closer to the second unit than to the first. Part of the kiva was even constructed in and below the channel. The blocking of the stream some distance above the unit and diversion of the run-off from the higher slopes, as previously mentioned, made possible the placing of the kiva in that location. Otherwise the structure would have been exposed to danger of damage from flood waters and a seepage of moisture into its pit. The slope of the bank and the bed of the channel no doubt reduced the amount of digging necessary for the kiva pit, but also required some provision for compensation for the lack of depth at that side. The location was satisfactory from the standpoint of the surface water drainage because the slope was sufficient to carry away the accumulations from falling rain and melting snow. As long as the diversion wall above the village held there was little likelihood of inundation from the old channel. After the abandonment of the site the wall fell into disrepair and water began flowing toward the kiva along the former course. The accumulations of refuse and other debris were such, however, that the flow was shifted to the right and a new channel cut. On one or two occasions, probably following cloudbursts, enough water came down to overflow the banks and sweep sand and gravel across the ventilator portion of the kiva.

The surface structure in this unit approximated a rectangular block in plan, although there was a small wing at one end and a niche or recess at one side. The rooms were in a double tier with four in one row and two and the niche in the other. The rooms were not uniform in size. They fall roughly into three groups, however, with Nos. 7, 10, and 12 corresponding quite closely in general measurements, 9 and 11 being approximately the same, and 8 standing alone. Three of the rooms were definitely equipped for dwelling purposes in that they contained fire pits and some form of storage bins. The other three had no such features. They were the smaller chambers and it is quite possible that they were storage places rather than actual living quarters. Granting such to be the case it is interesting to note the proportion of one dwelling room to one store room. On the basis of comparison with practices among some of the modern village dwellers in the area the division in this structure suggests that the group here may have consisted of three units or families, a family consisting of husband, wife, and children. The relationship in general possibly was that of mother and father with unmarried children in one apartment and a married daughter with her husband and children in each of the other two. The likelihood of some such status is indicated by the evidence that two of the dwelling rooms, 9 and 11, as well as two of the storage rooms, 7 and 12, were subsequent additions to the original nucleus of 8 and 10. While it cannot be proved definitely that such was the order, foundation and floor levels, in relation to the old surface, indicate that 12 was added first, then 11, followed by 7, and finally by 9. Whether a part of the remodeling process when 9 was built or the result of some other occurrence could not be learned, but there was considerable reconstruction in the wall separating 8 and 9.

Construction methods and wall types were much the same in the second unit as those in the first. There was more horizontally laid masonry in the second. The floors in the rooms were below the general ground level and the foundations were laid along the walls of the shallow room pits. The central portion of the structure, particularly rooms 8 and 10, was characterized by the use of large, unworked blocks of stone (pl. 22, b). This was true for both the slab foundation and the horizontally laid walls. In the later additions smaller stones were employed, the proportion of mud mortar to building blocks was greater, and small spalls were inserted as chinking. There was abundant use of mortar and small stones in a sort of rubble finish on the exterior of many of the walls. This was particularly noticeable on those with the upright slab foundations. The probabilities are that the necessity of compensating for the uneven tops of the slabs and providing a comparatively level base led to the development of that style finish. Added to this was the uneven nature of a wall made up of heterogeneous shapes and sizes of stones and the tendency to lay them so that the inside face was smooth. Alining them along one side would make the irregularities more pronounced on the other and the use of mud and small fragments of stone would furnish a satisfactory means of obtaining a more regular surface. The practice of chinking with small tabular bits of stone may have developed out of this constructional feature. There does not appear to be any marked significance in the difference in wall types. The fact that there was a blending and mixture of all three variations in the same wall and that the steps leading from one form to another were obvious in the house suggests a local development rather than an influence from the outside or a change resulting from alien increments to the village.

Room 7 was a simple enclosure with a flagstone floor. The only interior feature was an upright stone set in the floor midway of the length of the wall on the side toward the kiva side of the building. This is one of the stones that is thought to represent a step. This function was suggested not only by the position and height of the stone, but by the worn surface on the top as well. The ridges and rough spots were smoothed in a manner quite indicative of the tread of feet. All other surfaces on the stone were rough. Occurring midway of the wall it suggests that the opening or doorway into the chamber was at that point and that the center of the wall was the customary place for a doorway. No evidence of that feature remained in the wall itself, although it seems likely that the sill could not have been much above the level of the remaining wall. One end of room 7 partially overlay the pit of one of the granaries that is thought to be correlated with the remains of pit structure No. 17. The floor of room 7 cut into the fill in the granary to some extent, but its floor was 1 foot 3 inches (38.1 cm) above the floor of the granary. The original ground level dropped away rather abruptly at this end of the building and the north wall of the granary projected above the old surface to a greater degree than usual for such structures. Three of the walls in room 7 were of the slab foundation and horizontal masonry type. The fourth was wholly of horizontal masonry. It was the end of the original building, the outside of room 8. The two side walls of No. 7 abutted it.

Room 8 was one of the dwelling chambers. The enclosure was long and narrow. There was sufficient fallen material in the fill to show that the walls had risen to the height of a single story, approximately 6 feet 6 inches (1.981 m) above the old ground level. This added to the depth of the floor would give ample head room for the inhabitants. The upper part of the fill was mainly hard-packed sand and adobe mixed with wall stones. The adobe probably was slumped plaster from the wall and roof and the sand wind-deposited material. From the floor to approximately 1 foot (30.48 cm) above the fill was sand with some admixture of ashes. The nature of this layer suggested that the room was unoccupied for some time before the walls fell in, the sand being blown in through the doorway. On the floor were numerous potsherds and stone implements. The walls of the room were built of large, unshaped blocks of stone laid in courses. There was little chinking in three of them but the fourth, that separating 8 and 9, did have small spalls in addition to the larger blocks. So many of these were used in places that they became courses of small stones rather than chinking. This wall, as previously mentioned, appeared to be of later construction than the others in this room and probably correlated with the remainder of room 9 rather than with 8. This wall rested in part on the base of the original wall for room 8, but the faces of the two did not coincide, and as a result there was a narrow offset along that side of the room just above the top of the stone step (pl. 23, a).

The step in room 8 was similar to those in the other chambers. It was a rectangular block, unworked, set in the floor approximately midway of the eastern wall. The top was slightly worn and smoothed from use. The fire pit for the room was nearby. From the position of the step, it would appear that the fire pit had been almost in front of the doorway. The pit was partially lined with stones and partially faced with plaster. A bin or storage box once stood in the northwest corner. The slab walls for this enclosure were missing, but the stone paving for the floor was still intact. Traces of the wall slabs were noted in the floor along the edges of the paving stones. Rectangular, corner bins of this type, made by using upright slabs, were common in Zuñi in comparatively recent times and occasionally one is built even now. They served for the storage of beans, corn, and the like.[64] There was a small stone at the end of the room that had no apparent purpose. Its top was flush with the floor. It was not a part of the bin. There was nothing beneath it. The stone had simply been set in the floor at that place for some purpose not indicated by the remains. There were no other features in the enclosure.

Room 9 was one of the later additions to the house. It was the largest enclosure in the building and had more internal features than the others. There were a number of interesting items in its construction. Three of the walls consisted, for the most part, of large, horizontally laid blocks of stone alternating with small, thin stones like the construction shown in the upper part of the wall in the photograph (pl. 23, a). The south end of the room presents a problem in

---

[64] Mindeleff, 1891, p. 210.

BUREAU OF AMERICAN ETHNOLOGY BULLETIN 121 PLATE 23

a. Stone step and wall construction in room 8.

b. Corner bin in room 11.

a. Corner of building outside room 11 and bin.

b. Original floor in Kiva B

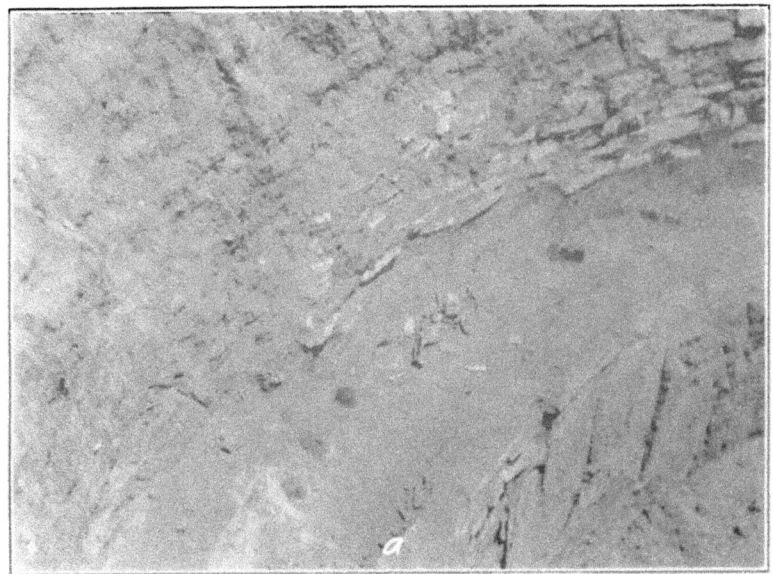

a. Holes for slanting side poles at back of original bench top in Kiva B.

b. Katcina niche in wall of Kiva B.

a. Subwall storage bin in Kiva B.

b. Ventilator openings in Kiva B.

that there is a question as to whether or not it actually had a complete wall. The enclosure was finished at that end by a row of upright stone slabs. What form of construction had risen above the tops of these slabs, if any, is a matter of some doubt. From the amount of debris composed of small stones and chunks of mud mortar found along the bases of the slabs on both sides of the row, it would seem that a rubble wall of the type previously described once stood there. Yet the tops and sides of the slabs were so completely devoid of any adhering material of this nature that there was no actual evidence to show that it once rested on and around them. For that reason a statement that there was a wall of such construction is not wholly warranted. On the other hand, it is questionable that the end of the room was left open, except for the low barrier of standing stones, and as a consequence the best conclusion seems to be that there was a rubble wall. It is possible, of course, that the enclosure was a shed rather than a room.

Support posts for the roof were set at three places in the room. One was incorporated in the outside wall not quite midway of its length and the other two were along the inside wall at approximately one-third its length from each end. These uprights may have been placed there to carry the main weight of the roof at the time the room was built or they may have been installed later as braces for a sagging ceiling. The fact that the one on the outside was built into the wall is good evidence that it was a part of the original construction, or at least was set there early in the occupancy of the room. Several possibilities are suggested by the combination of factors here indicated. There was a slight variation in the type of masonry in the outer wall on each side of the post. That extending to the northeast corner and thence to the corners of rooms 7 and 8 was all of one form, while that between the post and the end of the upright slab wall was noticeably different, although conforming to the same general style. This suggests that the original room may have terminated at the post and then subsequently was enlarged by the erection of the shorter length of wall and the slab construction at the end. Certain irregularities in the floor and below it, on a line between the outer post and the one opposite near the inner wall, may have resulted from the razing of an end wall, which would substantiate the above postulation.

The reinforcing of corners by the use of timbers was not a common practice in this district and it is curious that two examples should be found in this room. One explanation for the occurrence is that in the beginning room 9 was a portico like No. 2 in the first unit and that it was later built into a room, the support posts for the roof being included in the rising walls. In its final stage it unquestionably was a room, because the fallen wall material was too extensive for a court. Another possibility is that a bit of misfortune was responsible for the condition found, including the new wall between rooms 8 and 9. Because of the additional roof weight that would be directly correlated with the larger size of room 9, the original wall for room 8 may have buckled. The attendant reconstruction would account for the type of masonry in the wall between 8 and 9, also its thickness and the use of uprights to aid in supporting the roof, the enlarging process taking place at the same time. There is no definite evidence that any of these explanations are correct. They are postulations offered merely to call attention to certain possibilities in the history of the room.

There were two fire pits in room 9. The larger was in the approximate center and the smaller at one side. Both were partially lined with stones and partially faced with mud plaster. At the time when the debris was cleared from the floor the smaller pit was filled to the brim with fine wood ashes. Practically no charcoal was present in the ash. The larger pit was only half filled with ashes and charcoal. The situation suggests that the smaller pit was functioning in the capacity of an ash depository, while the large one was actually serving as a place where fires burned. Just why there was the definitely intentional saving of ashes as noted in so many instances in this district is not known. There were several uses for them, however. The adobe plaster occasionally was mixed with ashes, which gave it a harder, more cohesive quality. They also may have been needed in other pursuits for which there is no evidence. The modern Zuñi, in preparing hominy, mix a quantity of wood-ash paste in a pot of cold water and then put corn, removed from the cob, in it. The pot is set over a fire and after the corn has come to a boil it is stirred with a stick.[65] The stirring and boiling remove the hulls. Wood-ash lye was also used in the preparation of the well-known Pueblo wafer bread. Similar culinary practices may have prevailed in earlier times and some of the ashes have been preserved for such purposes in this village.

The storage bin or granary in the southwest corner of the room was built of stone slabs set on end. They were placed in a curved row that cut off the corner. Five stones were used in the construction. They no doubt were covered with plaster at the time of occupancy of the house. The bottom of the bin was below the floor level, as in the case of that in No. 2 in the first unit. The shape of the feature, when considered in the light of the jog in the wall at that end of the room, suggests that it might have been in existence prior to the completion of the chamber and then incorporated in it during the remodeling. There was no evidence either for or against this possibility, but the general form is indicative of it. When the

---

[65] Stevenson, 1904, p. 367.

slabs in the recess along the wall of room 11 are included it looks very much as though there had been a large circular granary in front of rooms 8 and 10 and that it was partially dismantled when room 9 was erected. In fact, the end wall of 9 may have cut across the granary instead of the smaller bin being incorporated in it.

To provide a level floor in room 9, because of the natural slope of the ground which dropped away rather abruptly from in front of the original structure, it was necessary for the builders to fill in along the outside wall. Approximately one-third of the floor space was treated in this way. Refuse-mound material and broken stones were employed for that purpose. The mud-plaster flooring was laid on top of this fill (fig. 49). The outer wall was close to the wall of the pit for the subterranean structure, but with the roof in place and covered with earth the latter would have had no effect on the surface house. As a matter of fact the area was probably leveled off so that the roof of the kiva formed a dooryard in front of the dwelling.

Room 9 did not have one of the stone steps like those in the other rooms. For that reason there is no indication of the location of the doorway. The most suitable place for an opening would have been at the south end of the room next to the corner storage bin. If it was placed there a step would not have been needed, as the building up of the floor level at that side of the room brought it to about the ground level and a person entering the chamber would not be required to step down into it as on the others. That may explain the absence of the step.

Room 10 was a simple chamber of the storage type. Its walls were similar in construction to those of room 8, except for the one at the south where a slab foundation type was used. This wall appeared to be a part of the original structure, although it is possible that it was rebuilt when room 12 was added. Digging the pit for the floor of the latter enclosure could have produced some settling in the masonry, with the result that a new piece of construction was deemed advisable. The only additional feature of interest in the masonry was in the northwest corner of the room, where the normal juncture of the walls was modified by a short, diagonal series of courses that gave the floor plan a pentagonal instead of a quadrangular form. There was nothing to indicate whether this thickening of the walls was intentional or accidental. Midway of the wall on the side toward room 11, in the position occupied by the stone step in other rooms, a small post had been set in the floor. Its original height is not known. Because of its location it is possible that it was also a step, although one of wood rather than stone. On the other hand, it may have been a brace to hold a covering in place over the doorway. Since it stood some distance from the wall the step interpretation seems more logical. The floor in this room was mainly smoothed plaster, but there were two slabs embedded in the surface at the north end of the enclosure.

When the interior of room 10 was being cleared of its accumulated debris an unusual mass of beads was found on the floor. They were all in one group, as though they had been in a pouch or container of some perishable substance that had disintegrated after being covered with earth. There was no apparent reason for their presence in the room. Probabilities are that they either were dropped and not recovered or that the bag was hidden there and then for some reason or other was not retrieved. The beads are all made from shell, some pink, some white, some red, and a few a slight orange shade. There was a variety of sizes from the standpoint of diameter, but none were very large. Most of them were a simple disc in form. A few were shaped like a figure 8 with the perforation for stringing through the smaller end. There was a marked consistency in thickness and they averaged 20 beads to the inch. There was no way of telling whether they had been strung or what kind of necklace, if strung, they formed. When threaded on a single strand they made a string 37 feet 4 inches (11.379 m) long. There were approximately 9,000 beads in the group. In addition to the beads, a number of pieces of azurite and malachite and a few fragments of turquoise were present in the assemblage. They, too, seemed to have been in the same container as the beads.

The recess or niche between rooms 9 and 11 gave no evidence that it had ever been roofed. It would have been a simple matter, however, to lay timbers across from the end of one room to the end of the other and thus provide a covering for the space. Under the circumstances no traces of such a roof would remain and it is impossible to say what the nature of the enclosure was when the building was occupied. It may have been open to the heavens or it could have been topped with timbers and brush. With a roof it would have made a serviceable adjunct to the house. Various objects could have been kept there out of the weather. The indication of a bin at the back of the recess has been mentioned already in connection with room 9. If the upright slabs placed here were not a part of a former granary they at least partially enclosed the southwest corner at the rear of the recess and contributed to its qualifications as a place for keeping things. It was in the corner in this enclosure that the human foot, mentioned in the discussion of the skeleton in Kiva A, was found sealed behind adobe plaster.

Room 11 was similar to room 9 in its general size and shape. It did not have any support posts, however, and the wall construction was mainly of the slab foundation rather than the horizontal block type, although there was some of the latter in two places. A little more than half of the north wall was built in that fashion and a section near the southeast corner also consisted of large blocks laid horizontally from the ground up. The slab-founded walls in this enclosure had a larger percentage of rubble exterior finish than any other part of the structure. This was particularly true of the one at the south end. The fire pit in the room was merely a small circular basin in the floor. It was not as deep nor as large in diameter as those in rooms 8 and 9 and it had no stone facing. Close to the fire pit, in almost the center of the room, was a metate or milling stone. Midway of the outside wall was a hole in the floor where a post had been placed. It occupied a position similar to that of the post in room 10 and may also have been a wooden rather than a stone step. On the opposite side of the wall, outside of the room, a stone similar to the steps in several of the rooms was set in the ground close to the base of the wall. It unquestionably was a step and indicates that the doorway to the chamber was in that portion of the outer wall. A person could easily have stepped from the stone through the opening and onto the short wooden post inside. The southwest corner of the room was approximately bisected by a large stone slab. It appeared to be all that remained of a bin or storage place comparable to those in the corners of 2 and 9. The rest of the enclosing wall probably was of rubble construction. There was sufficient debris, composed of small irregularly shaped rocks and chunks of mud plaster, on the floor in that vicinity to suggest that such had been the case. The actual limits of the bin could not be determined. The mud and rock part of the wall apparently fell before the remainder of the room had collapsed and the floor was so damaged that traces of the wall's footing were not discernible.

The most interesting feature in room 11 was the granary or storage place incorporated in the wall near the southwest corner. While in a broad sense it was comparable to those in rooms 2 and 9, it actually was unique for the district. Although smaller, its general form was much like that of the regular detached granaries. A shallow pit was lined with slabs placed upright around its edges. The slabs projected some distance above the ground level and were topped with courses of horizontally laid masonry. The actual wall was thicker than the slabs and from the ground level to the beginnings of the horizontal courses the additional "body" was supplied by rubble construction. There were a few scattered places where two or three stones were laid in a semblance of horizontal masonry; but the bulk of the wall around the slabs was of the rubble type. A doorway connected the granary with the room (pl. 23, b). The sill of the opening consisted of a stone slab set on edge. The jambs at each side were single upright slabs to a height of 1 foot 6 inches

(45.72 cm) and 2 feet (60.96 cm) above the floor. Above these the sides of the opening had been the horizontal block masonry. The floor of the closet was 9 inches (22.86 cm) below the floor of the room and was paved with thin slabs of stone. The fallen wall material in the granary and along its outside walls indicated that it had risen to approximately the same height as the room. Corner closets or granaries of this type are not common. A good example of one was found in a Great Pueblo ruin on the Zuñi Reservation.[66] The latter is probably a century or more later in date and it is curious that so advantageous a feature in house form was not more widely used, particularly since it was known for so long a period. Constructional complications and the tendency to a weakening of the walls may have overbalanced the convenience of such a storage place to the extent that it did not attain to popular use.

Room 12, like 7 and 10, had no interior features of note. The walls were of the slab-foundation type and that on the side toward room 11 was very irregular. There was no apparent reason for the uneven surface or the unusual thickness of the construction. The wall at the end of the building rested upon and incorporated in its foundations a few slabs from an older granary. It is possible that a similar condition prevailed along part of the wall between rooms 11 and 12 and that the variability of both surface and thickness were due to the inclusion of parts of an older structure. This was not apparent on the exterior surfaces of the wall, however, and the construction was not disturbed.

There was no step in room 12. Whether there ever had been one, or one was present and subsequently removed, could not be determined because the enclosure had been used as a burial place and the interment had caused some disturbance of its original status. The surface of the floor was broken in several places along the base of the wall in the approximate location for a step, judging from the positions of those in other chambers, and any traces of its placement that might have survived were obliterated. The burial was that of an adult, probably a male, and was peculiar in that the body had been placed front down with the face turned to one side. The legs were tightly flexed. The left arm extended along the side and the right was crossed over the back. The positions of the arm bones suggested that the person had been bound, his hands tied behind his back. The individual appeared to have been dumped on the floor and then covered with refuse, stones, and mud plaster. The latter was poured around and over the stones but not smoothed. It set and held the covering firmly in place over the remains. Why the person was buried in this manner would make an interesting story. The

---

[66] Roberts, 1932, p. 31, fig. 1.

fact that there were no accompanying mortuary offerings and that the individual apparently was tied suggests a captive or prisoner of war. Being disposed of in a room rather than interred in the refuse mound, as was the case with most of the burials, indicates some exceptional circumstances, possibly a desire to conceal the fact that the person had been disposed of or had succumbed. There was nothing to show how long before the abandonment of the house the interment took place. The people may have lived there for some time subsequent to that event or it is possible that it was a contributing factor in the group's moving. One other skeleton exhibiting a similar position, sprawled face down with the arms crossed over the back and the left foot drawn up as though tied to the lashings that held the wrists, was uncovered in a shallow pit beyond the limits of the refuse mound (fig. 44, No. 4). This burial also lacked funerary offerings and the implication is that it was the final resting place of an unwelcome alien or a vanquished foe.

At the southwest corner of the building, adjacent to room 11 and its granary, was a partially enclosed area containing a fire pit. This sheltered spot, in the lee of the house, probably served as an outdoor kitchen. A masonry wall extended from the granary several feet toward the southeast, forming a protection on that side. At the corner formed by the juncture of the slab-founded and horizontal masonry walls in room 11 a single large stone slab was set on end to aid in delimiting the area. First impressions were that this had been an additional room, but no evidence was found for the other two walls or that the construction had ever been more extensive. A stone placed near the horizontal masonry wall was analogous in position and shape to the steps in the various rooms. It does not seem to have had this purpose, however. It would have been serviceable as a seat or a place to set objects used in cooking. The fire pit was roughly circular in form and faced with stones (pl. 24, *a*).

Close to the fire pit, on the north side, was a long stone slab, embedded in the floor of occupation. The top of the stone was flush with the level of the surrounding area. Underneath the stone were the remains of a young child. The body had been placed in a shallow pit. The arms were folded across the chest and the knees drawn up close to the body; it was a tightly flexed burial. Small poles were laid across the top of the pit and the slab placed on them. The stone was large enough to extend beyond the rim of the pit and it is likely that the grave was sealed by the use of mud plaster around the edges of the stone. Children were often buried close to a hearth in the Southwest and there undoubtedly was some significance in the custom. The actual reasons for the practice are not known, but by analogy from a similar custom among the modern Indians in the area several suggestions can be offered. One explanation is that when buried near the center of domestic activity the little one will be less lonesome. Another is that it is an effort to keep the family circle unbroken, a custom that has been world-wide in its distribution among peoples of less developed cultures. Or it might be that the mother wanted the remains kept as near to her as possible as the result of some purely maternal reaction to the loss of a cherished offspring. Another youngster was interred in the area on the opposite side of the wall, not as close to a fire pit as the former, but well within the boundaries of all household activities. Both of these burials belonged to the final stages of occupancy of this unit because the mortuary offerings of pottery consisted of vessels of the type correlating with the final phase of the Developmental village.

The area bounded by room 11, the granary, the extension wall from the granary, and the kiva was also a center of domestic activity. There was a slab-lined fire pit in the approximate center of the space and the old surface was packed and stained from the tramp of many feet. There were several standing stones near the fire pit. Their purpose was not apparent, but they undoubtedly had some connection with the pit. Possibly they were merely provided as places on which to put pots or baskets so that they would be off the ground. There were no traces of support posts and the area probably had no shade or covering erected over it. There was a similar center for outdoor cooking in the corner formed by rooms 7 and 9. The slab-lined fire pit located there was more than half filled with ashes and small fragments of charcoal. Numerous splinters of burned bone occurred in the pit and on the surface around its rim. An arrowhead and a bone scraper were found at the base of the wall of room 9 near the corner.

Southeast from the surface structure, across the old channel and at the edge of the present watercourse, were the remains of a brush shelter. This example was more elaborate than many and quite reminiscent of the one located at the main site on top of the ridge close to structures 12 and 13. This shelter was suggestive of a small pit dwelling in some respects but it was not deep enough, although the floor was below the surrounding ground level, and had no form of ventilator. The shade or arbor erected over the shallow pit was supported by four upright posts set near the corners of the depression. There were no indications that side walls were provided. Slanting poles may have been used to form a windbreak on two or more sides, but there were no traces on the ground around the edges of the floor pit that could be regarded as an indication of the presence of such timbers. The fire pit was at one side of the floor space close to the north support post. The pit was D-shaped. The flat side was faced with a stone slab and the curved face was covered with plaster. A plaster rim encircled the pit on the floor level. Two stones were placed near the west corner of the pit. One was set in the floor 6 inches (15.24 cm) from the wall in a position suggesting that it might have been a step. The other was lying on the old ground level and its location in relation to the first was such as to indicate that it may have been a tread to protect the edges of the pit from damage when people stepped up or down. There were two storage places along the southwest wall. One was a circular pit in the floor (fig. 46, d) and the other a subwall recess (fig. 46, e). The storage pit was merely a hole in the floor with vertical sides and approximately level bottom. Both the sides and the bottom were covered with plaster. The pocket in the wall was close to the circular pit. It was cut in the native earth, the back wall sloping down to form a curved back. The bottom was a continuation of the general floor level of the main part of the shelter. The pocket was not deep nor high but would have been a convenient place to keep various objects.

One question in connection with this shelter and that on the ridge above concerns the possibility that they actually were the basal portions of houses rather than mere shelters. The depressed floors and the definite provision of storage places suggests something more permanent than an ordinary summer kitchen. As pointed out in the discussion of both places, there were no evidences of slanting side poles from the framework at the top of the main posts to the ground back of the edges of the floor pits. The character of the ground is such, however, that any traces left by the butts of timbers placed in that way could be obliterated without much difficulty. Hence the possibility that faint indications of poles were missed in the digging. Both structures could have had flimsy jacal walls and all traces of them have vanished. If such was the case the more elaborate floor features would not be out of place. Jacal construction was not unknown in the region, as evidences of houses made in that way were found at the Long H Ranch in a horizon approximately contemporary with that in this village.[67] As a consequence, some form of it could have been used here, although there was nothing to show that such had been the case. The most logical conclusion to draw from the evidence is that the places were brush shelters, but the possibility of their being remnants of another form of house should be borne in mind.

Kiva B contained a number of interesting features and is the first of the underground structures thus far considered to exhibit most of the characteristics of a ceremonial chamber. The structure had two distinct phases with a marked difference in certain

---

[67] Roberts, 1931, pp. 86–88.

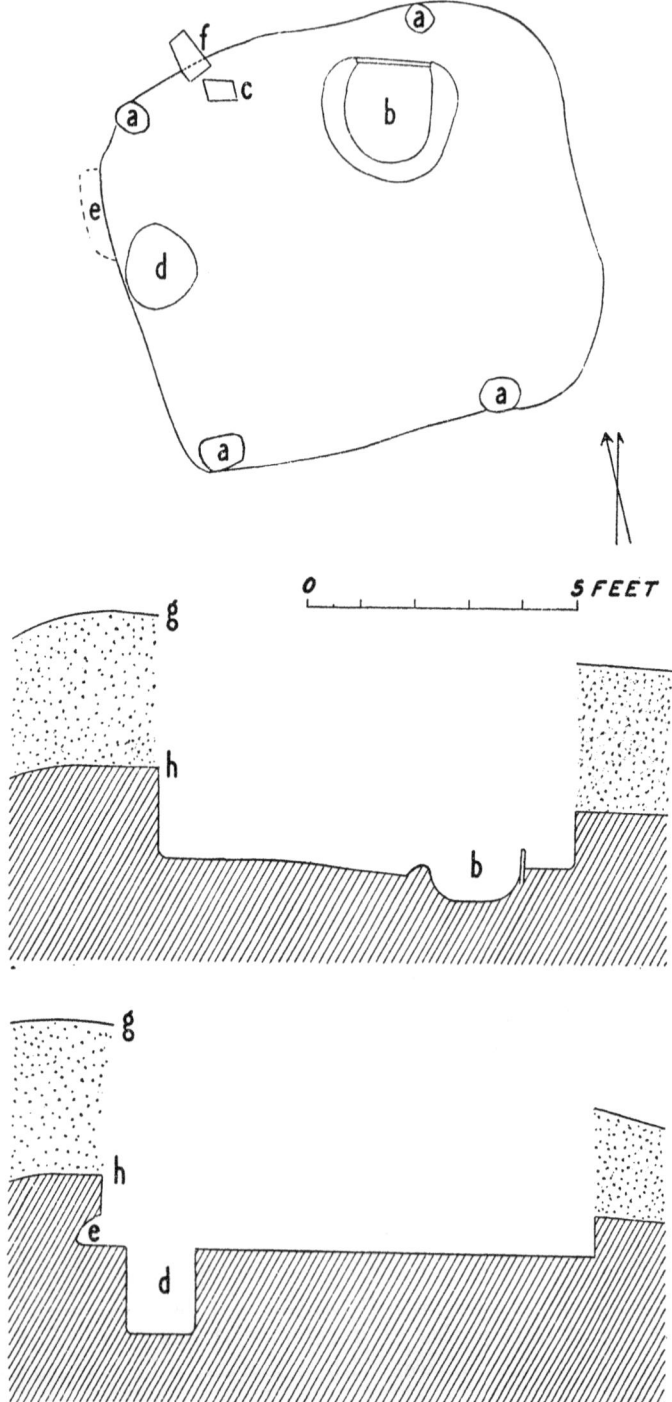

FIGURE 46.—Brush shelter. *a*, holes for roof supports; *b*, fire pit; *c*, stone step; *d*, storage pit in floor; *e*, subwall pocket; *f*, stone tread; *g*, present surface; *h*, old ground level.

constructional elements in each. As far as this locality is concerned, Kiva B probably marks the transition stage in which there was a definite shift from the older pit-type dwelling to the strictly ceremonial chamber. This was evidenced by a change in the type of roof construction and a modification of some other features to the extent that they produced a complex comparable in all respects to the circular ceremonial rooms of later horizons.

The pit for Kiva B was roughly circular in form and was inclosed by a definite bench (fig. 47). The bench was partially dug and partially built up. At several places around the periphery the excavation for the lower portion of the pit had cut back too far into the bench and it was necessary to fill in with refuse and rubble behind the masonry wall that formed the face of the bench. On a little more than half the circumference of the upper and back wall of the bench masonry construction was used to compensate for the lack of depth resulting from the slope of the ground toward the old watercourse. This stonework was not a part of the original structure. It was put there during the remodeling process when the character of the chamber was changed. During the first stage the addition to the back wall was not needed, as the low earth face was sufficient. When the alterations were made, however, the bench level was raised and the builders had to add to the wall height. The face of the bench or wall of the main part of the chamber was of stone construction. On about three-fourths of the periphery the wall consisted of horizontally laid stones resting on the tops of upright slabs (pl. 24, *b*); the remainder was horizontal masonry from top to bottom. Some of the slabs used in the facing were so tall they extended almost to the bench top and had only one or two courses of stones above them; others were very short and were topped by many layers. The horizontal masonry in this structure was better than that in Kiva A. Smaller stones were used for the most part and there were some indications of attempts at shaping and dressing a number of the blocks.

The covering over the pit in its final stage of use consisted of a cribbed roof, the form of superstructure characteristic of later-day ceremonial rooms. None of the timbers were present when the remains were uncovered, but the top of the bench clearly showed the imprint of logs lying along it in the positions that the bottom row of timbers would occupy in a cribbed roof. Furthermore, there were no holes for upright support posts in the floor that correlated with this phase. The original roof, however, was of the truncated pyramidal type with sloping side poles and flat center supported on four uprights. The holes for the uprights were found in the old floor below the plaster of the upper floor and when the addition to the top of the bench was removed to the old bench level some of the placements for the slanting side poles were uncovered (pl. 25, a). These occurred sporadically around the bench. In some cases the

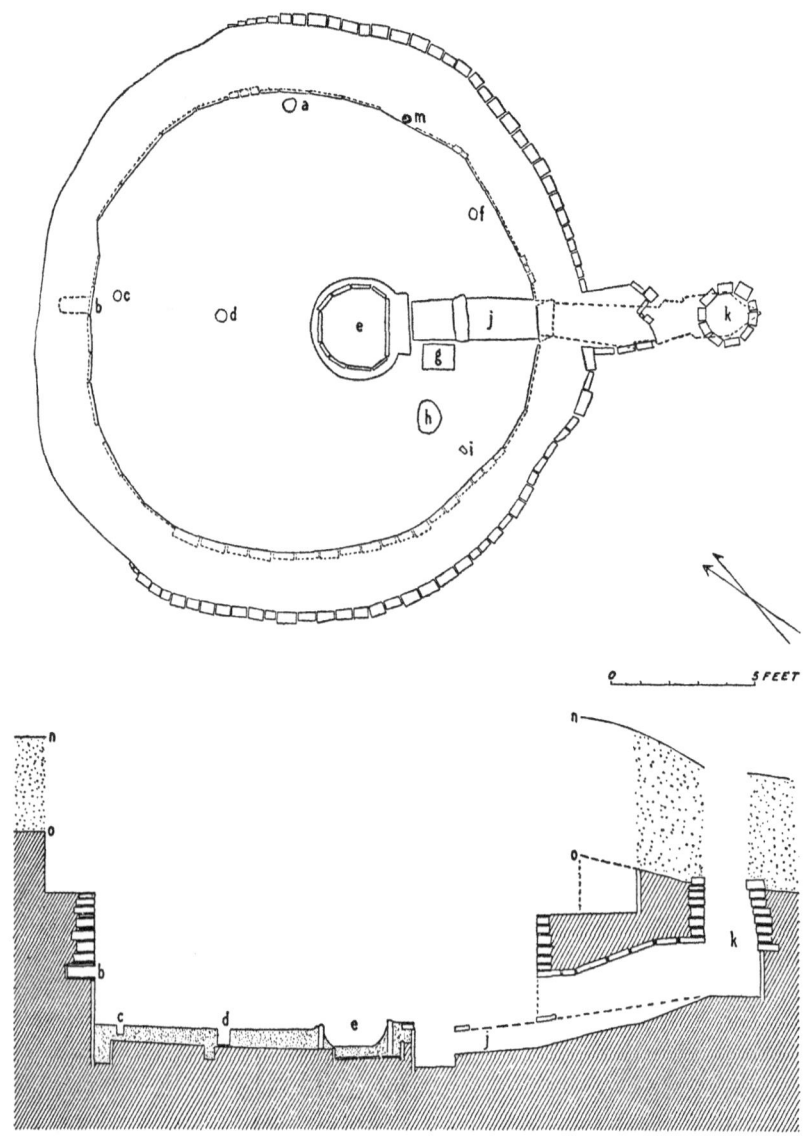

FIGURE 47.—Kiva B, upper floor level. a, storage hole in floor; b, Katcina niche; c, storage hole in floor; d, sipapu; e, fire pit; f, storage hole; g, ash pit; h, stone in floor; i, stone in floor; j, subfloor ventilator trench; k, ventilator shaft; m, post incorporated in bench; n, present ground level; o, original surface.

butts rested in the angle formed by the back wall and the top of the bench; in others they were set in the shallow holes.

When the old style superstructure was in place there was little need for a high back wall to the bench. As long as there was enough of a face to hold the side poles in position, nothing more was required. The brush, earth, and plaster covering would be carried to the ground level and a low bench wall would be an advantage in that all necessary provision for drainage would be supplied without the use of too much fill material. Due to the domelike nature of a cribbed roof and the practice of filling in with larger quantities of dirt until the surface surrounding the hatchway was comparatively level, a much higher back wall was needed to hold the earth covering the logs. This reason, coupled with the fact that the original back wall was decreased in height by the construction of a new top on the bench, made it essential to build up the back wall on the ventilator side and explains the courses of horizontally laid masonry found there. On the side toward the house the pit was deep enough to answer all requirements. When the fill over the cribbed roof was put in place, however, the workmen did not stop at the old ground surface but carried the level higher, so that a comparatively flat area was formed in front of the surface building. In all probability the dooryard, from the walls of rooms 9 and 11 to the kiva entrance, was approximately level during the final period of occupancy in the unit.

Interior features varied somewhat in the two stages of occupancy. Those belonging to the later period, that of the cribbed roof, consisted of the fire pit, sipapu, a Katcina niche, several small holes in the floor for storing minor articles, two stones embedded in the floor, and a ventilator. The fire pit (fig. 47, e) was D-shaped and lined throughout with small stone slabs. The stones projected above the floor and were incorporated in an encircling rim of adobe plaster. This pit was built over and around the pit belonging to the older floor level. In comparison with those in many of the houses it was shallow. The stones and plaster rim were colored from the fires that burned there and the lower part of the pit was filled with ashes and small fragments of charcoal. None of the latter were of sufficient size to furnish material for dendrochronological studies. The position normally occupied by the ladder box or ash pit, in the pit houses, was taken over by the end of the subfloor ventilator. At one side of this feature, however, was a small rectangular pit (fig. 47, g) that contained some ashes. The pit was shifted to one side, but it had approximately the same relative position with respect to the fire pit as in structures where there was no ventilator opening of the type found here.

The sipapu (fig. 47, d) was a simple circular hole with vertical sides. The sides and bottom were carefully plastered. The holes a, c, and f were mere plain, plastered storage places of the kind described for the other structures. One of them, f, was in the location of one of the support posts for the superstructure of the original chamber. It was not as large in diameter as the hole for the post and its bottom penetrated only a short distance into the fill. The flat stone embedded in the floor at one side of the fire and ash pits (fig. 47, h) was in approximately the same position and about the same size as others noted in the discussion of various structures. As previously suggested, these stones may have been rests for a drum or basket serving as a drum, like those in some of the kivas in modern pueblos. This function would be in keeping with the indication of ceremonial character for the chamber. Of course, it may have had some use entirely distinct from religious observances. The second stone (i) stood several inches above the floor. Its lower end passed entirely through the upper floor and was embedded in the hole for the support post that formerly stood there. There was nothing to suggest the purpose of this stone.

The Katcina niche was located in the wall at the side of the room opposite from the ventilator (fig. 47, b). It was placed high up in the masonry, just above the top of one of the upright facing slabs (pl. 25, b). The niche was a rectangular box lined with small stone slabs. Similar niches are frequently found in the walls of later-date kivas at the same side of the chamber. They are also present in the kivas of today in the Hopi country and at Acoma. The name is taken from the Hopi term for them. They may or may not have had a comparable designation in olden times. The full Hopi name is Katcina Kihu, the house of the Katcinas, the Katcinas being impersonations of the gods. During the progress of a ceremony, the masks worn by certain dancers are placed in the niche when not in actual use. The significance among the Acoma is slightly different; it is considered as the "doorway" through which the spirits of the gods enter and leave the kiva. Also, when prayers are offered up to the deities of the Sun and the Moon, and of the northern, eastern, and western mountains, they are made into that opening. Occasionally in ruins, pipes, pieces of turquoise, and fetishes are found in the niches. There was no way of telling whether or not the niche in this structure was present in both stages of occupancy. It may have been provided when the alterations were made or it could have been a part of the original chamber. They are rare in the older pit dwellings, however, and it is more likely that it was a later addition.

The ventilator in this structure is interesting because it is the only example of the subfloor type found in the excavations. In addition to the usual form with an aperture in the wall, there was a trench extending across the floor from the side wall to the fire pit. This trench started below the normal vent opening in the wall. It was the same width as the tunnel portion of the main ventilator and was lined with thin stone slabs. When the chamber was in use it had been covered with a series of stone slabs that were plastered over to conform with the general floor surface. Near the fire pit was a rectangular opening that provided passage for the air coming in

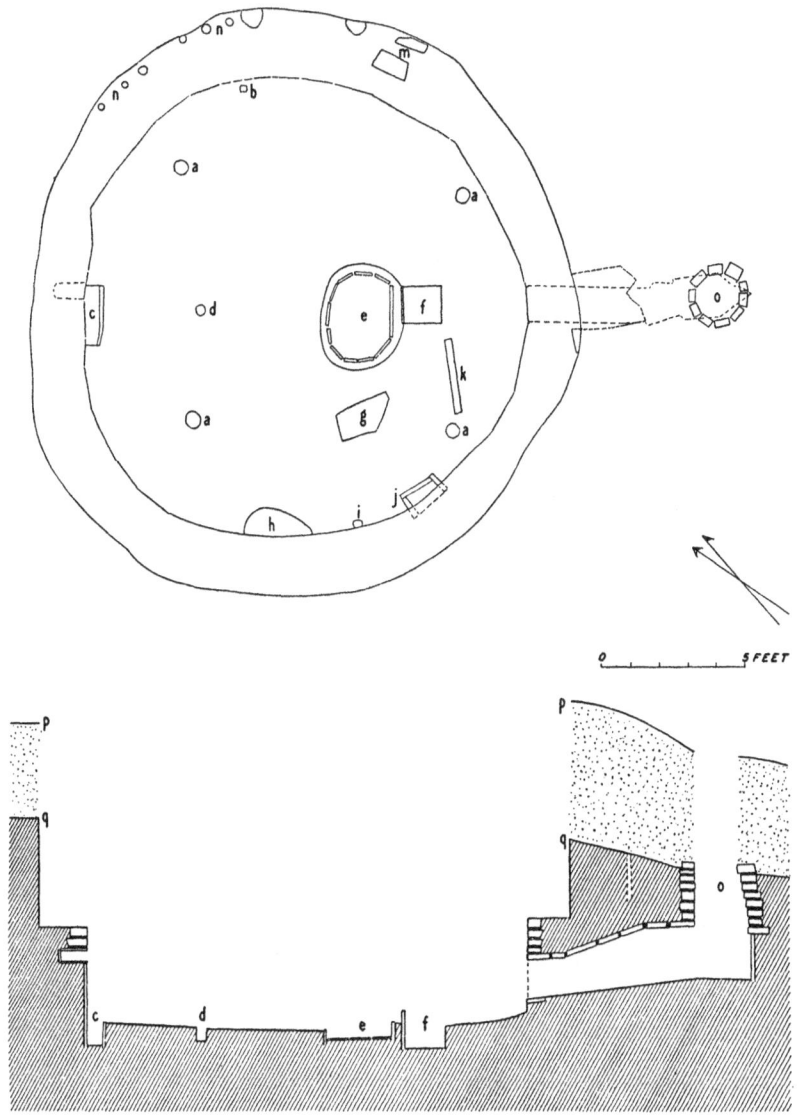

FIGURE 48.—Kiva B, original floor level. *a*, holes for main roof posts; *b*, stone in floor; *c*, storage box; *d*, sipapu; *e*, fire pit; *f*, ladder box; *g*, stone embedded in floor; *h*, storage pit; *i*, storage hole; *j*, subwall storage box; *k*, stone in floor; *m*, stones embedded on bench top; *n*, holes for slanting side poles; *o*, ventilator shaft; *p*, present ground level; *q*, original surface.

through the tunnel beneath the floor. This subfloor feature was not part of the original house. It was installed when the changes were made at the time of putting in a new floor and adding to the bench height. This was shown by the fact that the wall slabs of the trench cut through the old floor and the plaster rim around the old fire pit was broken out to make room for the end stone. There was some reconstruction work around the base of the vertical aperture in the wall and the floor of the passage was dug out to the extent that it was below the ends of some of the slabs lining the walls just back of the old opening. Subfloor ventilators of this type are not uncommon in kivas of later stages in Pueblo development. They rarely occur in the earlier phases, however, and the present example is one of the oldest to come to light thus far. The type is not unusual for this general region. Two kivas excavated by Hodge near Hawikuh,[68] and two at another site on the Zuñi Reservation [69] exhibited the feature. One of the latter was quite comparable to the present in that it exhibited the same double nature with a horizontal vent in the floor and a vertical opening in the wall. There probably is some significance to the subfloor type of ventilator, but what that may be has not yet been determined. Thus far there have been no indications of causes or reasons for its development nor definite evidence of its particular group affiliations.

The passage through the wall of the structure and the shaft at the outer end were essentially the same for both ventilators. The original tunnel was built up. A trench was dug, lined with stone slabs, roofed with a series of slabs, and then covered with a dirt fill to the level of the bench top. The original floor had sloped upward from the sill of the vertical opening to the bottom of the shaft. The later floor sloped gradually upward from the edge of the rectangular pit just below the vent in the floor to a point near the outer end of the old passage and then turned sharply up to meet the bottom of the shaft. The shaft was more irregular in contour at the bottom than in most of those in this district. Instead of having an oval or circular form it was practically pentagonal. The lower portion was lined with upright slabs. The remainder of the shaft had horizontally laid masonry resting on the tops of these standing stones. The space where the passage entered the shaft was bridged with a heavy lintel of stone which supported the wall of the shaft on that side.

The presence of two ventilators raises the question as to whether or not both were used at the same time. It is possible that one or the other openings was stopped; in fact there is a suggestion that there was a cover slab for the vertical opening. When the debris was removed from the room during the process of excavation a number of stones were found on the floor in front of the vent aperture. Some

---

[68] Hodge, 1923.
[69] Roberts, 1932, pp. 54–55, 67–69.

were part of the wall above the opening, that had fallen in, and others were pieces from a larger slab that had been broken. The latter in its original form would have answered the purpose of a covering for the hole. That it actually did so is a matter of uncertainty.

There were no indications of a deflector and it is probable that none was present in the chamber. As a matter of fact such an arrangement would not be necessary with a subfloor ventilator, as air coming into the room through the horizontal opening in the floor would not strike the fire but pass upward over it. Some kivas in later ruins where that type of ventilator is present also have a deflector, while others do not. The ruin on the Zuñi Reservation, previously cited, where two kivas contained the subfloor ventilator, had an example of each, one with and one without the deflector feature.[70]

The placement of the ladder in this structure may have proved somewhat of a problem. Because of the opening in the floor next the fire pit, it would need to rest farther away from the pit unless its base actually stood in the vent opening. The latter position would not be entirely out of the question and may be the explanation for the boxlike pit in the end of the subfloor passage immediately below the rectangular opening in the floor. The ladder poles would not interfere to any great extent with the incoming air and the wall of the pit would prevent their slipping and damaging the stone covering the passage and framing the opening at that side. The cover stone was thick enough to have supported a person using the ladder; in fact from the standpoint of ordinary activity in the chamber, there would be no difference between the ordinary floor and the present example after plaster had been applied over the stones roofing the ventilator trench. Hence there may have been a combination ladder box and vent opening. The only alternative would have been to set the ladder on the floor beyond the opening and beyond the ash pit (fig. 47, *g*). There were no traces of pole abrasions in the plaster on either side of the trench to indicate such a placement. Of course the ladder could have rested on top of the covering over the trench and all signs of its presence have been lost by the collapse of the roofing. This situation, however, would not be wholly satisfactory because there probably was a ridge in the floor above the vent passage due to the failure to set the cover slabs entirely below its level, and some likelihood of the ladder slipping to one side or the other. Without definite evidence in the matter, the better conclusion seems to be that the lower ends of the latter poles did rest in the box below the opening in the floor.

---

[70] Roberts, 1932, pl. 12.

The original floor in the chamber had a number of features not present in the later level of occupation. Before discussing them it is necessary to mention one item of note concerning the distinction between the two horizons. That is, there was a definite line of demarcation between them in the form of a layer of purple-colored clay. The latter was ordinary earth with a heavy admixture of purple hematite. A layer of refuse-mound material was first spread over the old floor, filling all holes and depressions, and then the hematite mixture was laid down. After this was evenly distributed over the surface the plaster of the upper floor was applied. What significance the use of hematite in this fashion may have had is not known. Occasionally a kiva or pit house is found where it was employed in a similar way to that in this structure. Consequently it was more than a restricted local development.

Features on the old floor level consisted of a fire pit, sipapu, holes for the support posts for the superstructure, storage pits, a subwall storage cist, and stones embedded in the floor. The fire pit (fig. 48, e) was of the same general style and shape as that on the later level. It was somewhat smaller, however, and did not have as large an encircling rim. The entire pit had been faced with small stone slabs and the bottom had stone paving. Installation of the subfloor ventilator obliterated all traces of a ladder box, if there was one. There is a possibility that the ventilator opening may have incorporated the former ladder box and the rectangular pit at the end of the subfloor trench be the remains of such a box. There was nothing in the construction to show that that had been the case, but the contingency should be mentioned. The question of the former presence of a deflector is another that cannot be answered. Any evidence relative to that feature was destroyed by the remodeling activities when the new ventilator was installed. The sipapu was not in the same location as the later one, although it had similar general characteristics. It was merely a circular hole with vertical walls and sides and bottom covered with plaster. The diameter and the depth were not quite as large as the one on the first level.

The stone set on the floor near the base of the wall (fig. 48, b) at the north side of the chamber was similar in nature to the one located at the south side in the upper floor. It was of squarish shape with a flat top and projected several inches above the floor. The base was firmly embedded in the plaster. There was no indication of the purpose of the stone. At one side of the fire pit a large slab was embedded flat in the floor, its top flush with the plaster, in approximately the same position as the one described for the later level (fig. 48, g). This stone was larger than the first one, but in all probability it was placed there for the same purpose. Another stone was set in the floor on edge in a position suggesting that there originally was a compartment on the ventilator side of the room (fig. 48, *k*). The stone as found did not represent the former total height, because the top showed that it had been broken off. There were no traces of additional stones on the opposite side of the vent trench, but the floor in that area had been sufficiently damaged to remove any indications of that nature. Hence it is possible that the structure did have a compartment during its early stage. On the other hand, it may well be that there was only a storage bin at one side and that the remaining stone is all that had been placed there.

The storage places for this stage of occupancy were interesting because they were more carefully constructed than most of those previously described. At the base of a wall on the side opposite the ventilator, just below the Katcina niche, was a rectangular pit (fig. 48, *c*) with vertical sides and an approximately level bottom. The outside wall was faced with a large stone slab. The inner or back wall was formed by the slabs in the main facing of the wall of the chamber. The two ends were of earth covered with a thick coating of plaster. This is the only example of such a bin in the entire group of excavated structures. A smaller and better storage place, somewhat comparable to the one just described, was situated at the base of the wall not far from the south support post (fig. 48, *j*; pl. 26, *a*). This box was dug into the floor and extended below the bench so that approximately half of it was under the wall. The pit was rectangular in shape and faced on all four sides with stone slabs. The edges of the stones projected slightly above the floor level, forming a rim around the opening. A box of this type would have been very convenient for keeping articles safe from accidental damage and out of the way of the occupants in the chamber. Both of those boxes or bins had been filled with refuse before the second floor was laid.

The basin or depression in the floor midway along the wall between the two bins just described was similar to many noted in other structures. The front edge was curved and the back was formed by the base of the wall of the room (fig. 48, *h*). The sides sloped downward from the edge on the floor level to the bottom. The interior was plastered. Nearby was a small, circular hole (*i*) that probably was a pocket for small articles, such as awls, punches, and other implements.

One interesting feature that occurred above the bench level was the niche in the back wall above the ventilator (pl. 26, *b*). Whether it was present in simpler form in the original construction or was introduced at the time of the remodeling was not apparent. From a general point of view the most logical supposition is that it was one of the elements added when the style of roof was changed. The significant factor in its occurrence is that it apparently was an adumbrant form of the recess in the kivas of later horizons. Several examples of the feature were found in the ceremonial rooms in the large ruin at the Long H Ranch southwest from this site;[71] it was present in most of the kivas in the village of the Great Kivas on the Zuñi Reservation southeast from the Allantown district;[72] and is quite common in the regions to the north. It occurs at Mesa Verde,[73] in the ruin at Aztec,[74] N. Mex., in the Chaco Canyon,[75] and in northeastern Arizona.[76] The feature is particularly prominent in the unithouse ruins investigated by Prudden along the San Juan River,[77] and seems to be a northern characteristic. The purpose of the recess is not known. They may be analogous to the spectator's bench in the Hopi kivas,[78] the platform where members of the group not participating in ceremonies gather to watch the performance of the rites. The present example was too small for any such use, but it has the same general shape and location and can be considered as the forerunner of the larger forms.

One aspect of the niche raises a question that is difficult to answer. With a cribbed type of roof starting from the bench, provision of a means of access to the niche would not be a simple matter. In the later forms of kivas the roof timbers generally were supported by pilasters and raised high enough above the bench to leave a good-sized opening to the recess. That was not possible when the roof started from the bench. Hence the question concerning the opening. A small aperture could be provided by starting the lower ring of logs at each side of the break in the wall and the additional timbers could be placed in such a way that it would not be necessary for a beam to cross in front of the niche until the third or fourth tier was reached. This may have been done. There is the possibility that no opening was provided and that as far as the interior of the chamber was concerned there was no recess. That such was the case does not seem reasonable, though, in view of the careful way in which the niche was built. Some sort of doorway undoubtedly was left there. The niche here is the earliest example thus far reported and indicates that the feature developed rather soon after the beginning of definite ceremonial chambers. Why it was present in some kivas and not in others is a problem still to be solved.

The fill in Kiva B had several features that threw some light on conditions subsequent to the abandonment of the structure. On the upper floor, the last one used, were several thin layers of water-deposited clay mixed with bits of charcoal. These indicate that

---

[71] Roberts, 1931, pp. 93, 97, 100, 107.
[72] Roberts, 1932, pp. 67–69, 72–73, 81, 83–84.
[73] Fewkes, 1909, pl. 1; 1911, b, pl. 8.
[74] Morris, 1924, map of ruin.
[75] Judd, 1930, ground plan of Pueblo Bonito.
[76] Kidder, 1924, fig. 12, p. 69.
[77] Prudden, 1914.
[78] Fewkes, 1911, p. 24.

flood waters found their way into the pit while the superstructure was still in place. Above these layers was a thick deposit of wind-blown sand containing some ash and sporadic pieces of charcoal. This stratum probably represents an appreciable interval, as it was rather evenly spread throughout the pit and of greater depth than average for this kind of material in the district. Above this was a thick stratum of coarse clay streaked with lines of decayed wood. The level unquestionably represents the stage when the roof col-

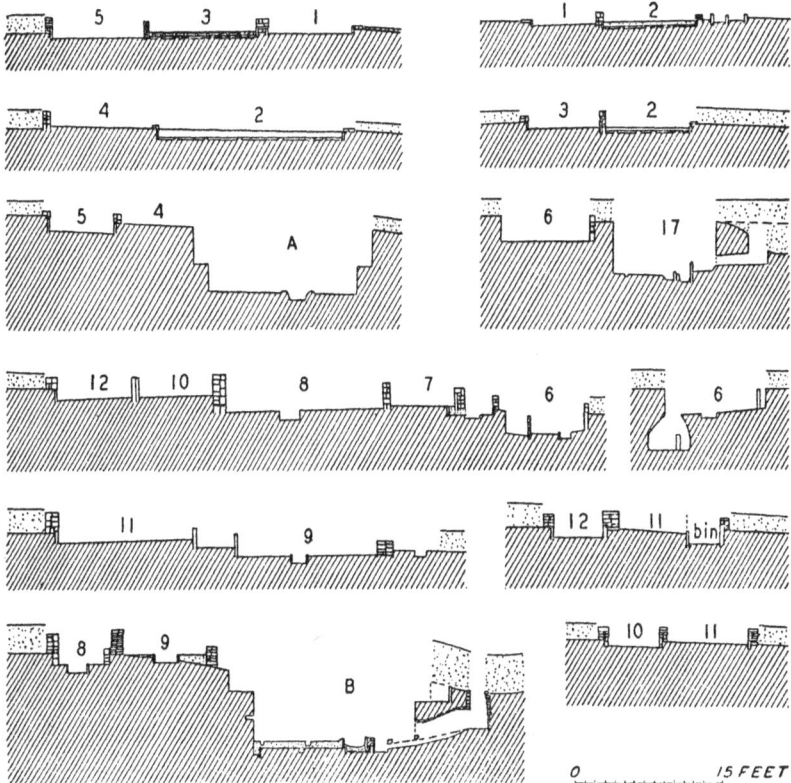

FIGURE 49.—Sections in first and second units.

lapsed and fell into the partially filled pit. The clay was the melted-down plaster and roof material. On top of this layer were half a dozen thinner strata composed of water-washed sand and clay containing some small fragments of charcoal and occasional traces of ashes, and two thicker layers of sand, clay, and charcoal. These unquestionably were carried into the depression by an intermittent series of small floods sweeping down across the site. When the latter had been deposited the pit was filled to the top of the masonry wall at the back of the bench. Then several layers of clean sand and gravel were left there and these in turn were covered by wind-blown material. In fact a small dune was formed over the remains of the structure and part of the fallen walls at the southeast side of the surface building. The water action responsible for the layers above the bench level in the pit also damaged the upper part of the construction in the ventilator shaft and washed out a portion of the back wall in the niche above the ventilator tunnel. The chief significance of the fill is in the evidence it gives that the site was abandoned at the same time as the kiva and that neither was reoccupied. There was no dump material in the fill. The traces of charcoal and ashes, and the sporadic potsherds present were carried into the pit from the surrounding surface and were not thrown in as refuse from a habitation. Had people continued to live in the surface house there would undoubtedly have been some trash on the kiva floor or in the layers between the floor and the stratum formed by the decay and collapse of the superstructure. Also, if the site had been occupied again at a later date there would have been some signs of it in the higher strata in the pit.

Room 7 was 7 feet 6 inches (2.286 m) long and 5 feet 4 inches (1.625 m) wide. Three of the outside walls, those that were slab-founded, averaged 1 foot (30.48 cm) in thickness. The fourth, which was the end of the original building, averaged 7 inches (17.78 cm). The stone step was 1 foot 3 inches (38.1 cm) high, 6½ inches (16.51 cm) wide, and 2¼ inches (5.71 cm) thick. It stood 2 inches (5.08 cm) from the wall.

Room 8 was 16 feet (4.876 m) long and 4 feet 10 inches (1.473 m) wide. The north wall was 7 inches (17.78 cm) thick; the east, above the offset where it rested on the original wall, averaged 1 foot 5 inches (43.18 cm); the south averaged 1 foot 4 inches (40.64 cm), and the west 1 foot 4 inches (40.64 cm). The step was 1 foot 4 inches (40.64 cm) high at the front edge and 1 foot 3 inches (38.1 cm) high at the side next the wall. The stone was 5 inches (12.7 cm) wide and 4 inches (10.16 cm) thick. It stood 1 inch (2.54 cm) from the wall. The fire pit measured 2 feet 3 inches (68.58 cm) by 1 foot 10 inches (55.88 cm) and was 7 inches (17.78 cm) deep. The storage bin at the corner of the room had a length of 4 feet (1.219 m) and a width of 1 foot 3 inches (38.1 cm). The height of the wall was probably 2 feet 6 inches (76.2 cm) but this could not be determined for certain. The offset along the east wall varied in width. Along a greater part of the length it averaged 4 inches (10.16 cm) but at one point toward the north end of the room reached a maximum of 1 foot (30.48 cm).

Room 9 was 14 feet 9 inches (4.495 m) long and ranged from 8 feet (2.438 m) to 8 feet 9 inches (2.667 m) in width. The wall at the north end averaged 1 foot 5 inches (43.18 cm) in thickness. The east wall varied from 1 foot 4 inches (40.64 cm) at the northeast corner to 8 inches (20.32 cm) at the southeast. The south wall was entirely slabs and their thickness averaged 3½ inches (8.89 cm). The west wall, that between rooms 8 and 9, averaged 1 foot 5 inches (43.18 cm) thick. The fire pit measured 2 feet 4 inches (71.12 cm) by 1 foot 9 inches (53.34 cm) and had a depth of 7 inches (17.78 cm). The ash basin measured 1 foot 6 inches (45.72 cm) by 1 foot 3 inches (38.1 cm) and was 6 inches (15.24 cm) deep. The bin in the southwest corner was 4 feet 3 inches (1.295 m) long and 2 feet 5 inches (73.66 cm) wide. The posts set at various places in the floor averaged 6 inches (15.24 cm) in diameter.

Room 10 was 7 feet 9 inches (2.362 m) long and 5 feet 4 inches (1.625 m) wide. The north wall averaged 1 foot 5 inches (43.18 cm) in thickness, except at the northwest corner where it attained a maximum of 2 feet 9 inches (83.82 cm). The east wall ranged from 8 inches (20.32 cm) to 1 foot (30.48 cm). The south averaged 6 inches (15.24 cm) and the west varied from 11 inches (27.94 cm) to 1 foot 5 inches (43.18 cm) in thickness. The butt end of the post that has been considered as representing a wooden form of the step had a diameter of 5 inches (12.7 cm). The post stood 2 inches (5.08 cm) from the wall.

Room 11 had a length of 13 feet 6 inches (4.114 m), was 8 feet 1 inch (2.463 m) wide at the north end, 7 feet 6 inches (2.286 m) wide at the location of the doorway into the granary, and 5 feet 6 inches (1.676 m) wide at the south end. The north wall averaged 7 inches (17.78 cm) in thickness. The east measured 8 inches (20.32 cm) and the masonry section near the granary 2 feet 2 inches (66.04 cm). The south wall was 1 foot 6 inches (45.72 cm) thick at the southeast corner and tapered to 1 foot 3 inches (38.1 cm) at the southwest corner. The west wall was somewhat irregular, measuring 2 feet (60.96 cm) at the southwest corner, 2 feet 3 inches (68.58 cm) at the approximal center, and 1 foot 3 inches (38.1 cm) at the northwest corner. The fire basin had diameters of 1 foot 6 inches (45.72 cm), 1 foot 2 inches (35.56 cm), and a depth of 4 inches (10.16 cm). The slab at the southwest corner, that had formed a part of a storage bin, was 2 feet 5 inches (73.66 cm) long, 3½ inches (8.89 cm) thick, and 2 feet (60.96 cm) high. The metate lying on the floor had a length of 2 feet (60.96 cm), a width of 1 foot 6 inches (45.72 cm), and a total thickness of 4 inches (10.16 cm). The trough was 1 foot 9 inches (53.34 cm) long, 10 inches (25.4 cm) wide, and 2¼ inches (5.71 cm) deep. The step at the east side, that is the wooden post, had been placed 2 inches (5.08 cm) from the wall and had a diameter of 5¼ inches (13.33 cm). The stone step on the outside was 8 inches (20.32 cm) wide, 5 inches (12.7 cm) thick, and 1 foot 4 inches (40.64 cm) high.

The granary opening off room 11 had an inside measurement of 2 feet 11 inches (88.9 cm) by 1 foot 9 inches (53.34 cm). The doorway was 1 foot 3 inches (38.1 cm) wide. The top of the stone sill was 3 inches (7.62 cm) above the floor of room 11 and 1 foot 3 inches (38.1 cm) above the floor of the bin. The granary floor was 1 foot (30.48 cm) below the floor of the room. The wall averaged 9 inches (22.86 cm) in thickness.

Room 12 was 7 feet 9 inches (2.362 m) long, 5 feet 4 inches (1.625 m) wide at the north end, narrowed to 4 feet 3 inches (1.295 m) near the center, and measured 4 feet 4 inches (1.320 m) at the south end. The west wall was 9 inches (22.86 cm) thick and the south 10 inches (25.4 cm). The north was the same as the south for room 10 and the east corresponded to the west wall of room 11.

The wall extending toward the southeast from the outside of the granary had a length of 6 feet 3 inches (1.905 m) on the north side and 6 feet 9 inches (2.057 m) on the south. It had an average thickness of 1 foot 2 inches (35.56 cm), stood 2 feet 1½ inches (64.77 cm) high at the west end and 1 foot ½ inch (31.75 cm) at the east end. The stone slab extending from the corner of room 11 to delimit the other side of the area was 1 foot 10 inches (55.88 cm) long, 1 foot 1 inch (33.02 cm) high, and 2½ inches (6.35 cm) thick. The fire pit in this corner area measured 1 foot 10 inches (55.88 cm) by 1 foot 8 inches (50.8 cm) and was 8 inches (20.32 cm) deep. The large stone nearby that covered the child burial was 3 feet 4 inches (1.016 m) long, 1 foot (30.48 cm) and 1 foot 7 inches (48.26 cm) wide, and 2½ inches (6.35 cm) thick. The stone near the masonry wall was 10 inches (25.4 cm) high, 7 inches (17.78 cm) wide, and 4 inches (10.16 cm) thick. It stood 8 inches (20.32 cm) from the wall.

The fire pit in the area on the opposite side of the wall was 1 foot (30.48 cm) long, 9 inches (22.86 cm) wide, and 9 inches (22.86 cm) deep. The stone in the floor close to it measured 3½ inches (8.89 cm) by 4 inches (10.16 cm) and stood ½ inch (1.27 cm) above the occupation level. The second stone, a little farther removed from the fire pit, was 4 inches (10.16 cm) long, 1 inch (2.54 cm) wide, and 1½ inches (3.81 cm) high. The fire pit in the corner formed by the walls of rooms 7 and 9 measured 1 foot 4 inches (40.64 cm) by 1 foot 7 inches (48.26 cm) and was 7 inches (17.78 cm) deep. It was 3 feet 4 inches (1.016 m) from the wall of room 7 and 2 feet 1 inch (63.5 cm) from the wall of room 9.

The brush shelter at the southeast corner of the site was 15 feet 6 inches (4.724 m) from the end of the masonry wall outside the granary of room 11 and 15 feet 4 inches (4.673 m) from the kiva. The floor depression of the shelter was 8 feet 6 inches (2.590 m) by 7 feet 4½ inches (2.247 m). At the north side the floor was 11½ inches (29.21 cm) below the old ground level and at the south side 1 foot 8½ inches (52.07 cm) below it. The holes for the supports for the arbor varied in diameter. That near the northeast corner was 6 inches (15.24 cm). The depth was 1 foot 1 inch (33.02 cm). The southeast hole had diameters of 7 inches (17.78 cm) and 9½ inches (24.13 cm) and a depth of 1 foot 2 inches (35.56 cm). The southwest hole was 7½ inches (19.05 cm) by 10 inches (25.4 cm) on its two diameters and 11 inches (27.94 cm) deep. The northwest hole was 6 inches (15.24 cm) by 7 inches (17.78 cm) with a 1 foot 1 inch (33.02 cm) depth. All four holes touched the side walls. The fire pit had diameters of 1 foot 7 inches (48.26 cm) and 1 foot 8 inches (50.8 cm). The bottom was only 5½ inches (13.97 cm) below the floor level of the room but the encircling rim of plaster increased the depth to 8 inches (20.32 cm). The rim averaged 5 inches (12.7 cm) in width, except for a length of 6 inches (15.24 cm) near the stone where it measured 4 inches (10.16 cm). The rim had an average height of 2½ inches (6.35 cm). The standing stone near the northwest corner (fig. 46, c) was 6½ inches (16.51 cm) wide, 4 inches (10.16 cm) thick, and 8½ inches (21.59 cm) high. It stood 1 foot (30.48 cm) from the wall. The storage pit (fig. 46, d) had diameters of 1 foot 4 inches (40.64 cm) and 1 foot 6 inches (45.72 cm) and a depth of 1 foot 6 inches (45.72 cm). At one point on the periphery it touched the wall. The subwall niche (fig. 46, e) was 1 foot 7 inches (48.26 cm) long at the opening in the wall, 1 foot 3 inches (38.1 cm) long at the back, and had an average depth of 5 inches (12.7 cm). The opening in the wall was 6 inches (15.24 cm) high.

The fire pits scattered over the surface of the refuse mound did not vary greatly in size, although there was a considerable range in depths. There were four with diameters ranging from 2 feet 3 inches (68.58 cm) to 2 feet 6 inches (76.2 cm) and depths from 7½ inches (19.05 cm) to 2 feet (60.96 cm). The two smaller pits, both of which were rectangular, measured 1 foot 2 inches (35.56 cm) by 1 foot (30.48 cm), with 6 inches (15.24 cm) depth, and 1 foot 7 inches (48.26 cm) and 2 feet (60.96 cm), and 1 foot 10 inches (55.88 cm) deep.

Kiva B had diameters of 18 feet 9 inches (5.715 m) above the bench and 15 feet 4 inches (4.673 m), below the bench, on the sipapu, fire pit, ventilator line. Across the chamber in the opposite direction the diameter above the bench was 19 feet 6 inches (5.943 m) and below it 14 feet 10½ inches (4.533 m). At the ventilator side of the room the upper or last floor was 10 feet 1 inch (3.073 m) below the present ground level and 4 feet 11 inches (1.498 m) below the surface at the time of occupation. The old floor was 3 inches (7.62 cm) below the later one at this point. The top of the bench was 3 feet 10 inches (1.168 m) above the upper floor. In its original form the bench top was just 3 feet (91.44 cm) above the old floor level. At the opposite side of the chamber, in front of the Katcina niche, the last floor level was 9 feet 7 inches (2.921 m) below the present ground and 6 feet 3 inches (1.905 m) below the old surface. The original floor was 6 inches (15.24 cm) below the second one at this point. The bench top was 4 feet 5 inches (1.346 m) above the second floor level and for the original construction the old top was 3 feet 1 inch (93.98 cm) above the old floor. At the east side of the chamber the floor was 8 feet 2 inches (2.489 m) below the present surface and 5 feet 3 inches (1.600 m) from the old level. The later floor was 3 inches (7.62 cm) above the original one. The top of the last bench level was 3 feet 8 inches (1.117 m) above the later floor. The original bench top was 3 feet 1 inch (93.98 cm) above the old floor. At the west side of the room the last floor was 9 feet 9 inches (2.971 m) below the present surface and 5 feet 6 inches (1.676 m) below the old level. The old floor was 4 inches (10.16 cm) below the later one. The last bench top was 3 feet 9 inches (1.143 m) above the last floor and the original floor was 3 feet 3 inches (99.06 cm) below the top of the original bench.

The holes for the support posts for the original superstructure were less variable in size than in many of the structures previously described. That for the north support had a diameter of 6½ inches (16.51 cm) and a depth of 1 foot (30.48 cm). The hole was 1 foot 6 inches (45.72 cm) from the wall. The hole at the east side of the room had diameters of 6 inches (15.24 cm) and 7 inches (17.78 cm) and a depth of 1 foot 3 inches (38.1 cm). The hole was 5½ inches (13.97 cm) from the wall. The hole for the south support post had diameters of 5½ inches (13.97 cm) and 6 inches (15.24 cm) and a depth of 1 foot 2 inches (35.56 cm). It was 8½ inches (21.59 cm) from the wall. The hole at the west side of the room had diameters of 6 inches (15.24 cm) and 7 inches (17.78 cm). The hole was 2 feet 10 inches (86.36 cm) from the wall and had a depth of 1 foot 3 inches (38.1 cm). The holes at the back of the original bench top, where the lower ends of the slanting roof poles rested, ranged from 2½ to 3¾ inches (6.35 to 9.52 cm) in diameter. They were quite shallow, the depths varying from 2 inches (5.08 cm) to 3 inches (7.62 cm). The two pockets at the back of the bench measured 8½ inches (21.59 cm) by 5 inches (12.7 cm), with a 4-inch (10.16-cm) depth; and 9½ inches (24.13 cm) by 6½ inches (16.51 cm) with an 8-inch (20.32-cm) depth.

The Katcina niche was 4 inches (10.16 cm) high, 6½ inches (16.51 cm) wide, and 11 inches (27.94 cm) deep. It was 1 foot 9 inches (53.34 cm) above the final floor and 2 feet 7 inches (78.74 cm) below the last bench top. It was 2 feet 1 inch (63.5 cm) above the original floor and 8 inches (20.32 cm) below the old bench top.

The fire pit for the room in its final form had inside diameters of 2 feet 2½ inches (67.31 cm) and 2 feet 7 inches (78.74 cm). The depth at the center was 6 inches (15.24 cm). The plaster ridge encircling the pit ranged from 4 inches (10.16 cm) to 6 inches (15.24 cm) in width. On the sipapu side it had a height of 1 inch (2.54 cm) and on the side toward the ventilator was 4 inches (10.16 cm) high. The other, underlying fire pit had diameters of 2 feet 2½ inches (67.31 cm) and 2 feet 9 inches (83.82 cm) and a depth of 4 inches (10.16 cm).

The sipapu for the last or upper floor was 2 feet 9½ inches (85.09 cm) from the fire pit. The hole had a diameter of 5 inches (12.7 cm) and a depth of 6 inches (15.24 cm). The sipapu for the original floor was 4 feet (1.219 m) from the fire pit. This hole had diameters of 3 inches (7.62 cm) and 4 inches (10.16 cm) and a depth of 5 inches (12.7 cm). The small storage hole (fig. 47, c) near the base of the wall on a line with the sipapu of the upper floor level had diameters of 3½ inches (8.89 cm) and 4 inches (10.16 cm). It was 8 inches (20.32 cm) from the wall and had a depth of 3½ inches (8.89 cm). The storage hole placed inside the hole for the east support post of the old level (fig. 47, f) had a diameter of 4 inches (10.16 cm) and a depth of 5 inches (12.7 cm). The ash pit or box-like pit in the floor near the end of the ventilator tunnel (fig. 47, g) measured 1 foot (30.48 cm) on the length paralleling the vent passage and 10 inches (25.4 cm) on the opposite direction. The pit was 4 inches (10.16 cm) deep.

The stone embedded in the floor (fig. 47, h) was 1 foot 2 inches (35.56 cm) long, 9½ inches (24.13 cm) wide, and 2 inches (5.08 cm) thick. The stone on the old floor, in approximately the same position, was somewhat larger (fig. 48, g). It had a length of 1 foot 11½ inches (59.69 cm) and a width of 1 foot 1 inch (33.02 cm). The thickness was 2¼ inches (5.71 cm). The upper floor stone that was placed in the hole for the south support post (fig. 47, i) measured 2 inches (5.08 cm) by 3 inches (7.62 cm) and was 3 inches (7.62 cm) high. The similar stone located at the opposite side on the original floor level (fig. 48, b) measured 2½ inches (6.35 cm) by 3 inches (7.62 cm) and was 2½ inches (6.35 cm) high. It was 1½ inches (3.81 cm) from the wall. The stone slab that suggested part of a compartment on the floor of the original chamber (fig. 48, k) was 2 feet 5½ inches (74.93 cm) long, 3 inches (7.62 cm) thick, and stood 2 inches (5.08 cm) above the floor. That was not its original height, however, as the top of the stone had been broken off.

The subfloor bin at the base of the wall below the Katcina niche (fig. 48, c) was 5 inches (12.7 cm) wide, 2 feet (60.96 cm) long, 10 inches (25.4 cm) deep. The stone forming the face of the outside wall of the pit was 2 feet (60.96 cm) long and 1½ inches (3.81 cm) thick.

The top projected 1 inch (2.54 cm) above the old floor level. The subfloor, subwall storage box at the south side of the room measured 1 foot 1 inch (33.02 cm) in length, 9 inches (22.86 cm) wide at one end, 8 inches (20.32 cm) wide at the other end, and 8 inches (20.32 cm) deep. The box extended 4 inches (10.16 cm) under the wall.

The large storage basin at the base of the wall in the old floor at the southwest side of the chamber (fig. 48, h) had a total length of 2 feet 5 inches (73.66 cm) and a total width of 11½ inches (29.21 cm) and a depth of 5 inches (12.7 cm). The small hole between this basin and the subwall box (fig. 48, i) had diameters of 2½ inches (6.35 cm) and 4 inches (10.16 cm). The depth was 3 inches (7.62 cm).

The horizontal ventilator opening in the floor near the fire pit of the upper level measured 1 foot 5½ inches (44.45 cm) on the passage line and 1 foot 4 inches (40.64 cm) in the opposite direction. The rectangular pit directly below this opening was 1 foot 3½ inches (39.37 cm) long and 1 foot 3 inches (38.1 cm) wide. The bottom was 1 foot 5 inches (43.18 cm) below the upper floor level and 5 inches (12.7 cm) below the sloping bottom of the subfloor trench. The subfloor trench was 4 feet 4 inches (1.320 m) long, from the end near the fire pit to the point where it penetrated the wall of the chamber. Its depth at the edge of the opening in the floor was 1 foot (30.48 cm) and where it passed under the wall was 10 inches (25.4 cm). The width ranged from 1 foot 2½ inches (36.83 cm) to 1 foot 3 inches (38.1 cm). The point where it joined the old passage floor at the edge of the shaft at the outer end was 5 feet 4 inches (1.625 m) from the edge of the wall.

The vertical opening in the wall of the room, the aperture to the original ventilator, was 1 foot 1 inch (33.02 cm) wide and 1 foot (30.48 cm) high. The sill was 6 inches (15.24 cm) above the floor level of the latest occupancy and 9 inches (22.86 cm) above that of the original room. The sill stone was 1 foot 3 inches (38.1 cm) long, 6½ inches (16.51 cm) wide, and 1½ inches (3.81 cm) thick. The original passage was 5 feet 4 inches (1.625 m) long. Where it entered the shaft it was 1 foot 1½ inches (34.29 cm) wide and 2 feet 2 inches (66.04 cm) high.

The base of the shaft, that portion lined with upright slabs, was 2 feet 7 inches (78.74 cm) long and 1 foot 5 inches (43.18 cm) wide. The bottom of the shaft was 3 feet 10 inches (1.168 m) below the old ground level and 7 feet 6 inches (2.286 m) below the present surface. The opening on the old ground level measured 1 foot 6 inches (45.72 cm) by 1 foot 5 inches (43.18 cm).

UNIT NO. 3

The third unit, located 1 mile (1.609 k) up the valley from the first and second, was a typical single-clan or unit type of the late Developmental Pueblo period, the stage usually referred to as Pueblo II. A surface structure with six rooms and a court, an exterior storage pit, one outside fire pit, and a subterranean chamber or kiva completed the group. The above-ground dwelling was located on a slight knoll, just beyond the foot of the talus of the ridge lying to the south, so that it had been sufficiently elevated above the surrounding terrain to assure proper drainage on all sides. An intermittent watercourse that carried the run-off from the higher ground passed the site on its western side, not far from the southwest corner of the dwelling. This stream bed was probably present at the time of occupation, the ensuing years serving to broaden and deepen the channel but not to change its location. At two places some distance above the ruins were traces of masonry walls on the banks of the channel. Their position and nature indicated that small check dams had been placed there, probably to hold back some of the water flowing along the course after rains, and to form small reservoirs for the community. The refuse mound for the unit was situated to the east of the structure. It was fairly deep, as the middens for such units go, and had served as a cemetery. The antecedent pit structure, No. 18, previously described, was between the northeast end of the surface building and the refuse mound.

The surface structure was built on an approximation of the block plan with a double tier of rooms, 2 in one row and 4 in the other (fig. 50). The structure was not erected as a complete building on a preconceived ground plan, but, as in the case of the second unit, grew as the result of additions to an original nucleus. The first construction was that of rooms 2 and 4. This was followed by the erection of rooms 3 and 5, and subsequently by 1 and 6. There was nothing to show the relation between 1 and 6. Whether one or the other was added first or both represent a single stage of activity was not evident in the remains. The general status, however, indicated that there was no great interval of time represented by the various additions. It is quite possible that 3 and 5 were started soon after the completion of 2 and 4 and that 1 and 6 were not long in following. The construction work was much better in this building than in either the first or second units. The walls were of horizontally laid masonry. One course of large blocks served for the foundations. Above these the stones were smaller, more tabular in shape, and formed a solid, compact wall. Many of the blocks were shaped and dressed. There was a greater percentage of stone to mud mortar in this structure than in the preceding ones and more use of small

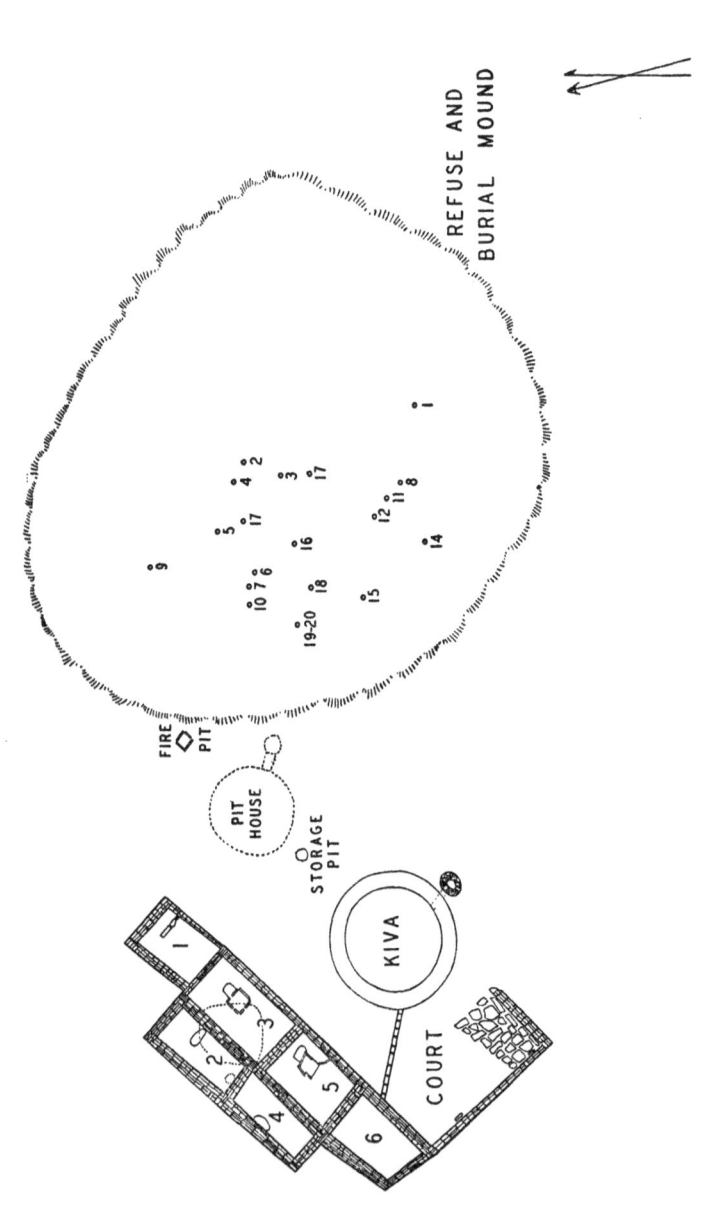

FIGURE 50.—Plan of unit No. 3. Dotted lines indicate location of pit structure 18. Numbered dots show positions of burials.

chinking stones. The walls stood only from 1 foot (30.48 cm) to 1 foot 6 inches (45.72 cm) in height at the time of excavation, but there was sufficient fallen material to show that they formerly were of single story height. The debris indicated that the masonry had been consistent throughout. The general appearance of the remaining walls was comparable to that of the late construction in the surface building of the second unit, room 9 particularly, although in this instance the work was better done and exhibited an improved technique (pl. 27, a).

The floors were approximately on the old ground level. They were not depressed like those in the first units. There was not enough wall construction remaining to show the number or nature of the openings provided in them. There undoubtedly had been doorways between 2 and 3, and 4 and 5, but they were high enough in the wall to have disappeared with the collapse of the upper courses. This also holds true for exterior openings for the chambers comprising the front row. In accord with the general custom of this stage the sills probably were from 1 foot 6 inches (45.72 cm) to 2 feet (60.96 cm) above the floor level, hence would have been a course or two higher in the wall than the tops of the remaining portions. Two of the rooms had fire pits, three contained storage bins or basins, and the remaining chamber had no interior features. The combination suggested a structure for two families. Rooms 1 and 6 were unquestionably for storage purposes, while 3 and 4 may have combined the functions of dwelling and storage places. This indicates a higher percentage of space per family than that suggested for the second unit. Such a relation, however, would be in keeping with later trends where three rooms, occasionally more, to a family unit was a common situation.

Room 1 had little in the way of interior features. It seems to have been for storage purposes. There was a small bin near one corner. A low wall of horizontally laid stones formed the enclosure. The floor of the room was of hard-packed adobe plaster.

Room 2 was larger than the first chamber, although it was as lacking in interior features. It was part of the original building and also seems to have served for storage purposes. The size was such, though, that it could well have augmented the actual living quarters as well as being used as a place in which to keep surplus food supplies and other objects. Close to the wall, separating it from room 3, was an oval-shaped basin in the floor. There was nothing in it to indicate its purpose. It had been dug into the ground and was lined with plaster at the time when the floor was laid. The latter continued unbroken down the sides and across the bottom of the basin.

Room 3 was one of the dwelling chambers. It was of particular interest because it had two floor levels. The upper one contained a rectangular fire pit lined with slabs of stone, while the lower one had a simple plaster-lined circular basin for that purpose. The upper floor also had a small ash pit adjacent to the fire pit. When the room was excavated this pit was filled with fine wood ashes. Completely underlying both floors and the foundations of room 3, as well as a portion of room 2, were the remains of a shelter that seemingly was similar to those previously described. It was not possible to trace its entire outline, but the holes for the four posts that had supported the shade or arbor were found, as well as a small storage pit, a shallow depression in the floor, and a small fire pit. All of these were below the layer of red clay that the house foundations rested on and that was discussed in connection with the pit structure, No. 18. This occurrence suggests that the shelter was associated with the old pit dwelling. At all events it definitely antedated the surface building of which room 3 was a part (fig. 52).

Room 4 was another of the chambers without a fire pit. Presumably it also was for storage purposes; possibly was a combination living and storage chamber. Approximately midway of the room along the outside, western wall, was an oval-shaped basin in the floor. The wall of the room formed a part of one side of the basin. Here, as in room 2, the lining of the sides and bottom was of plaster, a continuation of the layer that formed the floor of the chamber. When the room was being cleared of the debris from fallen wall material the skeleton of a turkey was found on the floor. The bird either had been confined and died there or its body tossed into the chamber after death. The bones were articulated, showing that the remains were those of a complete fowl and not kitchen scraps. The bird had not been kept there long because there were no indications of droppings on the floor. Traces of a short occupancy could well be missed, but one of any duration would have been quite evident. The turkey may have been left there when the house was abandoned and succumbed from lack of food and water. Or its demise merely may have coincided with the period of departure and the body placed there as a final act on the part of one of the inhabitants. The number of definite turkey burials in this district was such as to indicate that any haphazard disposal of dead fowl was not common procedure. Hence it is quite possible that lack of time to bury it properly led to the body's being deposited in the room when the group was moving from the site. Certainly it would not have been left there in a decomposing condition if the house had continued to be occupied.

Room 5 apparently was the other definite living chamber. It contained a rectangular, slab-lined fire pit near the center of the floor area, an adjoining rectangular plaster-lined ash pit, and the remains of a storage bin that had been placed between the fire pit and the outside wall of the room. The combination of fire and ash pits is interesting because the position, nature, and general status is the same as that found in room 3. The complex seems to have been a structural feature and not a fortuitous association. This no doubt represents provision for saving ashes that had the same purpose behind the practice as was suggested in the discussion of similar features in the other units. The bin between the fire pit and the eastern wall was roughly crescentic in form. The low partition that formed the enclosure was constructed of upright stone slabs and adobe plaster. Four of the stones were still in position, and although the others had fallen, the outline of the bin was clearly apparent on the floor. One of the slabs used in its wall also served as part of the lining in the fire pit. The stone was embedded in the bottom and eastern face of the fire pit and rose to sufficient height to fill in that portion of the bin wall. The edge of the ash pit at its southeast corner was at the base of the bin. This feature probably functioned in the same general way as other storage places. A variety of things could have been placed there. The floor in room 5, like those in the other chambers, was of hard-packed, well-smoothed adobe plaster.

Room 6 was a simple rectangular enclosure with no interior features. It undoubtedly served as a storage room. The remaining walls did not exhibit quite as good constructional work as most of those in the structure, but they were of the same general type. The floor was adobe plaster.

The court at the southeast corner of the dwelling (fig. 50) was enclosed by a low masonry wall that was erected at the same time as those forming room 6. Judging from the amount of fallen material and the remaining portions of the wall, the total height had never been more than approximately 3 feet (91.44 cm). Due to the slope of the original surface at this point, it was necessary for the builders to do some terracing. The southeastern third of the enclosure was built up with dirt and rocks and the upper surface paved with stone slabs. The wall at this end originally extended to the kiva and both it and the paving seem to have been carried across the kiva roof to the hatchway. This was indicated by the presence of wall material and large slabs well up in the deposits in the pit for that structure. A low wall, connecting room 6 and the kiva, also served to terrace that side of the court and hold back the earth placed there to level that part of the area. There was nothing to suggest that the wall had ever risen above the floor level along that side. The entire enclosed surface, including the paved section, was covered with hard-packed adobe flooring. There were no indications that fires had been lighted anywhere in the court. Not far from the southwest corner a stone slab was set on end close to the enclosing wall. In all respects this stone was similar to the steps described for the other units and may have been placed there to aid people in stepping over the wall and to obviate the necessity for a person going all the way around the court to reach the outside. A similar stone was found on the ground outside the wall opposite this one. It may represent a similar step at that point. As it was not in position and there were no clear traces of its placement, such a function can only be suggested. This court in its broader aspects of location and general features is analogous to the area lying between room 11, the wall extending from the granary, and the kiva in the second unit. There is also a similarity between it and the shelter associated with pit structure 15 and its adjacent granaries. The present example probably illustrates the developed form of the feature adumbrated by the others.

The storage pit in the area between the kiva and the old pit structure unquestionably belonged to the unit house. It was dug through layers that accumulated subsequent to the abandonment of the pit structure and passed through the stratum of red earth previously described. The shape of the pit was not unlike that of a large pottery jug. The opening was small, and there was a short, necklike shaft with vertical sides. From the bottom of these the walls sloped outward to the point of maximum diameter and then curved in toward the bottom. The latter had a somewhat shorter diameter than the area of greatest circumference (fig. 52, bottom section). The inside of the pit was plastered when it was in use. Only scattered patches remained on the walls when the debris was cleaned from the interior, but these were sufficient to show that the entire surface was originally so treated.

The outdoor fire pit (fig. 50) was a rectangular box lined with stone slabs. There were no traces of any shelter or arbor near it. It probably was like those scattered over the refuse mound for the second unit, merely a place where fires could be kindled when no shade or protection was needed. Some cooking was done there, however, because the ashes and charcoal that filled the pit had some splinters and fragments of charcoal and bone scattered through them.

The kiva, located in the angle formed by the surface building and the court (pl. 27, *b*), more nearly approximated the circular form than any of the semisubterranean structures hitherto described. Both the back wall of the bench and the main wall of the chamber were more regular. The bench was partially dug and partially built up. When the pit for the main part of the chamber was dug, a narrow encircling shelf was left at the level for the bench top. Then when the walls of the pit were lined with stone the masonry was carried to that point and the width increased in proportion to the thickness of the wall. The stonework was very good; in fact it was the best wall

a. Surface structure in third unit.

b. Clearing debris from kiva for third unit.

a. Wall construction in bench of third unit kiva.

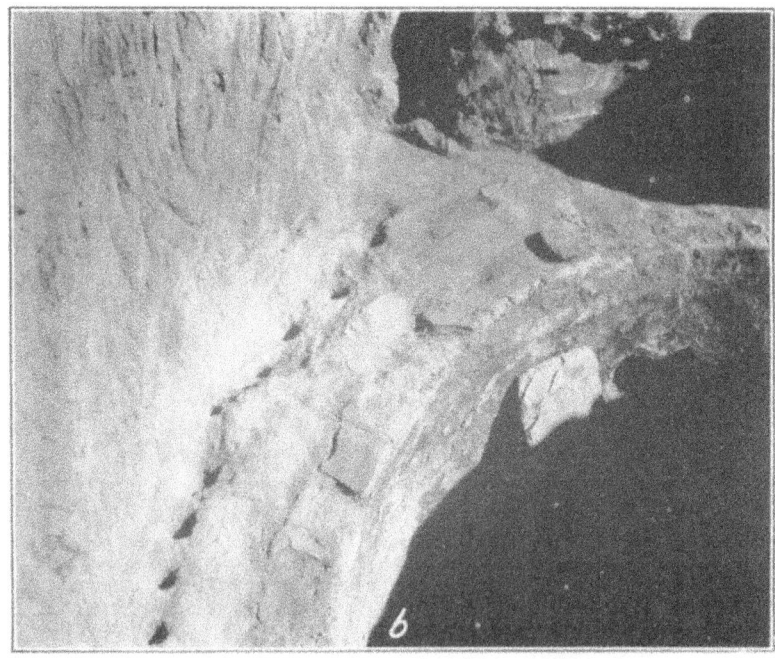

b. Holes for wainscoting poles at back of kiva bench.

a. Floor in kiva for the third unit.

b. Mound covering large building in Great Pueblo group.

a. Portion of Great Pueblo ruins, corner of building below and to left of standing figure.

b. Arroyo cut through refuse mound.

construction found in the course of the excavations. Medium-sized tabular blocks were used for the main courses, except for a few larger stones that occurred near the top of the wall, and many small fragments were employed as chinking (pl. 28, *a*). A thick coating of adobe plaster gave a smooth-finished surface to the wall.

One interesting structural feature in the kiva wall consisted of four timbers incorporated in the masonry at approximately the positions that support posts for the truncated pyramidal type of superstructure occupied in some of the pit dwellings (fig. 51, *a*). The ends of these timbers were flush with the bench top. When the latter was covered with plaster they did not show. They may have been placed there solely to reinforce the wall. On the other hand they may have had a certain ceremonial significance. It will be recalled that in house 15 three of the support posts were incorporated in the face of the bench. In some sections the use of actual posts for supporting kiva roofs continued into later horizons, as shown by reports of early Spanish explorers [79] and by archeological work in various ruins.[80] A possible variant of the survival factor is that of the inclusion of short beams or posts in the masonry boxes that formed the pilasters in the kivas in the Chaco Canyon ruins, a feature discussed in connection with the plaster ridges on the bench in structure 12 at this site. Had the builders intended the posts incorporated in the bench in this kiva to serve wholly as reinforcements for the stonework, it is odd that they restricted the number to four and that they were placed in the positions that actual supports would occupy. The wall proper did not have a vertical face. The diameter on the floor level was slightly greater than that at the bench level, so that the wall curved inward to a degree. This curve started a short distance above the floor. That it was intentional may be questioned, because similar construction in kivas is extremely rare. In this particular case it seems more likely that it was fortuitous.

The upper wall at the back of the bench had been finished with a wainscoting of poles and plaster. Nothing remained of the construction except the butts of the poles, the holes where they were set (pl. 28, *b*), and some traces of the plaster along the bench top. This was sufficient, however, to show that there had been such a feature. The poles averaged 2 inches (5.08 cm) in diameter and were set vertically at more or less regular intervals around the periphery. They may have been placed there to serve as a support for the walls of the excavation. The nature of the earth at that location is such that it will hold a firm face and for that reason it does not seem that any reinforcement would be necessary, particularly when the fill of dirt over the roof timbers would cover that portion of the excavation.

---

[79] Winship, 1896, p. 520.
[80] Cummings, 1915, p. 275. Jeancon, 1929, pp. 15–16.

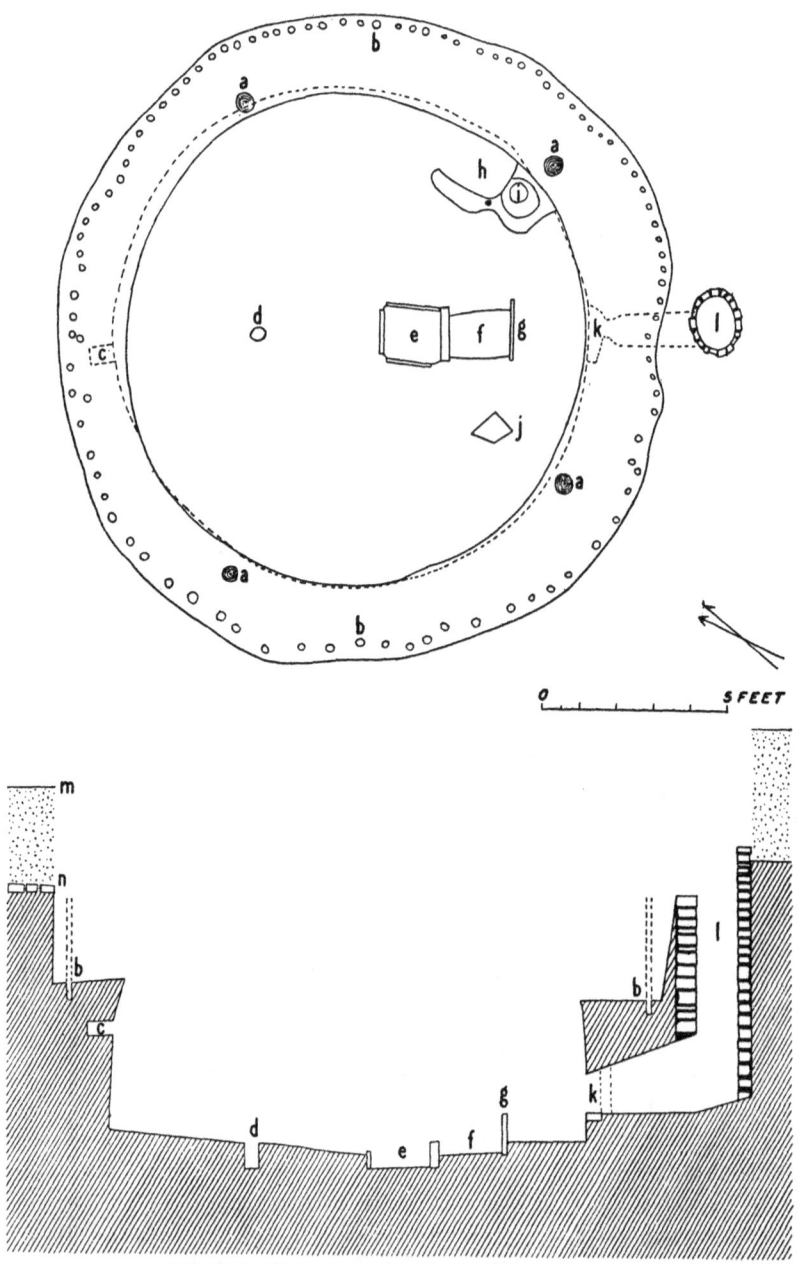

FIGURE 51.—Kiva for unit No. 3. *a*, posts incorporated in bench to reinforce wall; *b*, holes for poles forming wainscoting; *c*, Katcina niche; *d*, sipapu; *e*, fire pit; *f*, ash pit and ladder box; *g*, deflector; *h*, shallow basin in floor; *i*, small circular basin with stone bottom; *j*, stone embedded in floor; *k*, ventilator opening; *l*, ventilator shaft; *m*, present surface; *n*, old ground level.

Hence they may have been put there with some other purpose in view. The wall of the excavation may not have been as regular as the builders deemed necessary, and in order to obtain a smoother contour they erected the jacal facing. On the other hand, a wainscoting of this form possibly had some function other than a purely utilitarian one. Some of the kivas of the Great Pueblo period in other districts were characterized by a similar structural feature and in them there could be no question of a need for reinforcing the back walls because they were built of stones and mortar and in no way likely to crumble or slump. This led to the suggestion that since the kivas were the outgrowth of the old semisubterranean pit dwellings and many features from the latter survived in the ceremonial chambers, the wainscoting may have represented the sloping side timbers of the original type of roof. On the other hand, they could be a direct continuance of a pithouse practice of lining the upper wall for purely utilitarian purposes, although occurrences of the latter have not been noted with sufficient regularity to indicate that it was of any great significance in the evolution of the house type. Future work and more information on both house and kiva forms may solve this problem. All that can be done at present is to suggest possible explanations for the feature.

The roof over the kiva was of the cribbed type, starting from the top of the bench. The bottom tier of logs rested directly on the bench in the manner described for the kiva of the second unit. There was direct evidence of this in the charred remains of the timbers lying along the bench. The superstructure was destroyed by fire, but enough of the charred wood remained to give an excellent idea of the roof type. The charcoal fragments also supplied a good series of specimens for dendrochronological studies.

Interior features consisted of a Katcina niche, a sipapu, fire pit, ash and ladder box, a deflector, a shallow bin formed by a plaster ridge on the floor, and a slab of stone embedded in the floor at one side of the chamber (pl. 29, *a*). The Katcina niche (fig. 51, *c*) was in the wall directly opposite from the ventilator. It was a rectangular stone box incorporated in the masonry and quite comparable to the one in the kiva of the second unit. The sipapu was an oval-shaped hole (fig. 51, *d*) with vertical sides and a flat bottom. The inside was well finished with a carefully smoothed coating of adobe plaster. The fire pit was rectangular in form (fig. 51, *e*) and the four sides were faced with stone slabs, one to each side. The stones did not meet at three of the corners and the interstices were filled with mud plaster that produced slightly rounded corners. The ash pit-ladder box was a shallow basin faced with plaster (fig. 51, *f*). The only stone in it was the deflector which formed one end. The ends of the ladder rested against the deflector stone and the ashes were placed at the opposite end near the fire pit. The deflector slab (fig. 51, *g*) was either broken when the roof collapsed or cracked by the heat from the burning timbers and the top knocked off by falling debris. The lower end was still embedded in the plaster when the pit was cleared, but the fragments from the upper portion were scattered over the floor in its vicinity. These showed that the original height of the stone was half again as great as the standing remnant. In its intact form it would have functioned properly in preventing the draft coming through the vent opening from blowing directly on the fire. The flat stone in the floor (fig. 51, *j*) occupied a position similar to those described for the two floor levels in the kiva of the second unit. In the present case, however, the top was not flush with the floor but projected above it. The top of the stone was smoothed from rubbing. There was nothing to indicate whether this had been done before it was placed there or resulted from the use to which it was put after installation.

The plaster-rimmed enclosure (fig. 51, *h*) at the eastern side of the chamber was the only one of this type noted in the Allantown district. From a broad aspect it was somewhat comparable to the storage basins described for some of the pit structures, but in its more specific details it was unique. As the photograph of the floor of the chamber (pl. 29, *a*) and the plan of the floor (fig. 51) show, the feature was along the base of the wall and open at one end. The main part of the enclosure was rectangular in shape, while the closed end was characterized by a circular basin (fig. 51, *i*). The floor of this part of the enclosure was slightly lower than that in the rectangular portion and was paved with a stone slab. The outside of the adobe ridge curved down to the floor of the room and the inside along the straight portion and part of the curved end was practically vertical. The remaining section curved concavely to the bottom, forming the basin at the end. Near the juncture of the straight and curved ridges a small pole was set, rising vertically above the plaster. The upper part of this stick burned when the house succumbed to the flames and its original height could not be learned. The charred end, still in position, showed that it had extended above the rim. The purpose of this stick is not known and the junction of the enclosure proper can only be postulated. A metate was present on the floor near the open end and it is possible that it was a form of bin for use in grinding meal for ceremonial purposes. The circular portion at the end would have made a good rest for either a basket or large pottery jar to contain the meal. Firewood could have been stacked there and a water jar, rather than one for other purposes, could have stood in the basin. Or the feature may have had some connection with or functioned as part of the equipment needed in a ceremony. In this connection attention may be called to the fact that a large slab of stone, dressed around the edges, was lying on the floor between the circular basin and the ventilator. The size and shape of this slab were such that it would have neatly covered the enclosure and ridge if placed there. This stone is shown leaning against the wall in the photograph (pl. 29, a). Whether it served that purpose or was provided as a movable cover for the ventilator opening is not known. It would have answered either purpose, yet may not have been so employed. Instead it may have been a cover for the hatchway and have fallen into the position found at the time of the destruction of the roof.

The ventilator for the structure was of the tunneled type. The passage apparently was cut through from the bottom of the shaft. The interior was lined with stone. From the sill of the opening to the bottom of the shaft the passage floor was practically level. The bottom of the shaft sloped sharply upward from the passage. The ceiling of the latter had a pronounced upward slant and the opening into the shaft was much higher than the aperture in the wall of the chamber. The opening into the room had a stone sill and stone lintel. The sides were part of the masonry of the main wall construction. Some of the latter had fallen from one lower corner of the aperture, giving it a slightly irregular shape, as shown by the picture. Originally that side was vertical like the one opposite. The heat of the conflagration cracked the lintel across the middle and it had dropped out of position. Only a few of the stones in the wall above were dislodged by the occurrence; the remainder were still solidly in place. Sometime after the completion of the ventilator the opening was reduced by putting narrow plaster walls at each side. They were set back several inches from the edge of the original opening. The aperture which they formed was roughly oval rather than rectangular in form and only about half as large as the former one. The ventilator in all probability functioned too well when first built and as a consequence the occupants found it necessary to reduce the size. When the chamber was cleared of its accumulated debris a stone covered with green paint and a small paint mortar stained with red pigment were found on the shelf formed by the vent sill and the inset plaster walls.

The ventilator shaft was oval in contour and its sides approximately vertical. The bottom sloped sharply from the outside edge to the opening into the passage. The shaft was lined with horizontally laid masonry from top to bottom. There were no upright slabs in the foundation as noted in the other structures. The opening into the passage was topped by a thick stone lintel that supported the construction on that side of the shaft. The stonework was not as well done as that in the main part of the structure. Larger blocks of stone were used and there was not as much chinking. Because of the small space in which to work, the builders must have experienced some difficulty in laying the wall. It served the purpose, however, as well as one with more finished construction.

The fill in the kiva indicated that it had been occupied up to the time that it was destroyed by fire. The charred timbers of the superstructure were lying directly on the floor and the other roof material was on top of them. On the southwestern side of the chamber the roofing material was surmounted by large slabs and

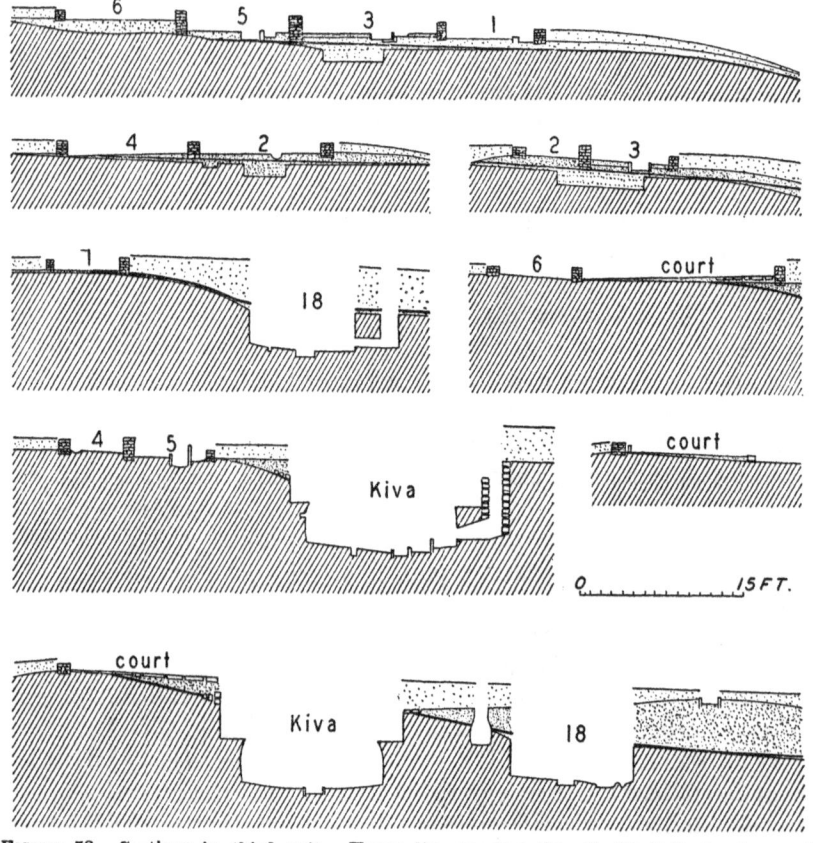

FIGURE 52.—Sections in third unit. Heavy line passing through fill indicates layer of red earth separating occupation level of pit structure and that of subsequent unit.

building stones, debris from the paved and terraced end of the court. The remaining portion of the pit contained a mixture of sand, ashes, charcoal, and lumps of plaster—all drift material that was deposited in the pit by natural forces. The top 2 feet 2 inches (66.04 cm) above the kiva was clean, wind-blown sand. The character of the fill clearly indicated that the site was abandoned after the burning of the kiva. That catastrophe probably was an integral factor in the movement. It could have been the cause of the departure or may have been burned intentionally as the people were leaving in order to prevent others from making use of it.

Charcoal from the site gives an interesting series of dendrochronological dates. Those from the house range between 994 and 1004. A number of rings apparently are missing from the outside of each and with the estimated bark date taken into consideration the maximum in the range would give 1005 to 1014, a spread of nine years. The kiva timbers give 1000 to 1011 and with the correction for estimated missing rings would be 1007 to 1013.[81] On the basis of either set of figures there is good evidence that the house was erected first, or at least a part of it, and then the kiva was built. The spread of years in this unit is much less than that in some of the other dated structures and indicates less reused timbers and possibly a shorter period of occupation. The latter can be estimated in this instance, however, on the basis of group size and total burials. The evidence from the latter is not as clear-cut as could be desired but with certain allowances for two factors, the older pit structure and some previous digging in the refuse mound, is probably fairly accurate.

A total of 20 burials was found in and below the refuse mound. Of this number, four were definitely of the pit-house phase. This was shown by their location in clean sand below the mound and the nature of the accompanying mortuary offerings. The previous digging in the mound had uncovered four, probably five, burials that were in the upper levels and unquestionably were late, as their pits had not penetrated to the bottom of the deposits. The bones had been left in place but the funerary furniture removed. The question concerning the exact number was raised by the possibility that one had been a double burial, that of an adult and an infant. The latter had reached such an advanced stage of disintegration that only a few fragments of bone were present and in the disturbed state of the material might be questioned as acceptable evidence. Omitting the 4 pit-house burials and the doubtful later one from consideration and granting a removal of 4 from the subsequent interments, leaves the number at 20. Of this total 8 were adults and 12 were children. On the basis of 6 to a family and 2 families to the unit, the average population would be 12. Using the death rate figures suggested by Dr. Hooton in his studies of the Pecos skeletal material [82] of approximately 3 per 100 each year, the rate here would be one death about every 28 years. With a total of 20 burials, the span would be 56 years. This seems longer than is warranted by the general aspects of the site and it may be the figures are too low.

---

[81] Miller, 1934, p. 16.
[82] Hooton, 1930, p. 333.

It is possible the average population was greater and the death rate higher, and that a number of burials were missed, although the latter would tend to increase the number of years. Probably elements of all three were involved. The inhabitants of the unit may well have numbered 15 over most of the period of occupancy and the death rate have been on the basis of from 4 to 5 per 100 or one death in the present group approximately every year and a half. On this basis the life span of the unit would be about 30 years, which would correlate fairly well with other aspects. The answer nearest to the correct one is probably two generations.

Room 1 was 8 feet 2 inches (2.489 m) long and 5 feet 8 inches (1.727 m) wide. The bin at the northeast corner of the enclosure measured 3 feet 2 inches (96.52 cm) by 1 foot 6 inches (45.72 cm) and was 4½ inches (11.43 cm) high. The western wall was 1 foot 1 inch (33.02 cm) thick, the northern 1 foot 2 inches (35.56 cm), the eastern varied from 6 inches (15.24 cm) at the southern end to 8 inches (20.32 cm) at the northern; and the southern wall was 7 and 8 inches (17.78 and 20.32 cm) thick at the western and eastern ends.

Room 2 was 10 feet 10 inches (3.302 m) and 10 feet 6 inches (3.200 m) long on the west and east walls, respectively. The width was 4 feet 10 inches (1.473 m) at the northern end and 4 feet 4 inches (1.320 m) at the southern end. The wall at the northern end averaged 1 foot 2 inches (35.56 cm) in thickness, the eastern 1 foot 4 inches (40.64 cm), the southern ranged from 10 inches (25.4 cm) to 1 foot 2 inches (35.56 cm), and the western from 1 foot 2 inches (35.56 cm) to 1 foot 4 inches (40.64 cm). The oval storage pit in the floor of the room was 2 feet (60.96 cm) long and had a maximum width of 1 foot 1 inch (33.02 cm). It was 6 inches (15.24 cm) deep. The eastern end was only 1 inch (2.54 cm) from the base of the wall.

Room 3 was 12 feet (3.657 m) long on the eastern wall and 11 feet 10 inches (3.606 m) on the western one. At the northern end it was 6 feet 6 inches (1.981 m) wide and at the southern 6 feet 10 inches (2.082 m). The northern wall was 7 inches (17.78 cm) thick at the western end, 10 inches (25.4 cm) at the eastern. The wall at the east side of the room was 1 foot (30.48 cm) thick at the northeastern corner and 10 inches (25.4 cm) at the southeastern. The wall at the southern end of the room did not vary more than a fraction from 1 foot 2 inches (35.56 cm) throughout its length. The wall at the west side was in common with room 2, and was 1 foot 4 inches (40.64 cm) average thickness. The slab-lined fire pit measured 2 feet (60.96 cm) by 1 foot 11 inches (58.42 cm). Its depth was 6 inches (15.24 cm). The small ash pit adjoining it on the north side measured 1 foot 5 inches (43.18 cm) by 1 foot 2 inches (35.56 cm) and had a depth of 4 inches (10.16 cm). The original floor was 3 inches (7.62 cm) below the later one. The fire pit for the original floor was in practically the same location as the later example and the latter partially cut into it. As far as could be determined the first pit measured 1 foot (30.48 cm) by 1 foot 2 inches (35.56 cm) and was 4 inches (10.16 cm) deep. The remains of the shelter were 2 feet (60.96 cm) below the floor of room 3 and were approximately 7 feet 9 inches (2.362 m) long by 5 feet 6 inches (1.676 m) wide.

Room 4 was 10 feet 2 inches (3.098 m) long on the west side and 10 feet 11 inches (3.327 m) on the east. The width at the north was 4 feet 4 inches (1.320 m) and at the southern end 3 feet 10 inches (1.168 m). The northern wall was 1 foot 2 inches (35.56 cm) wide at the northwest corner and 10 inches (25.4 cm) at the northeast. The wall at the east side was 1 foot 2 inches (35.56 cm) thick at the northeast corner and 1 foot 5 inches (43.18 cm) at the southeast. The southern wall was 1 foot 2 inches (35.56 cm) thick at both the southeast and southwest corners. The wall along the west side of the room ranged from 1 foot 2 inches (35.56 cm) in thickness at the southwest corner to 1 foot 6 inches (45.72 cm) at the northwest. The oval-shaped depression in the floor along the base of the west wall was 2 feet 5 inches (73.66 cm) long. Its greatest width was 1 foot (30.48 cm). The depth was only 2 inches (5.08 cm).

Room 5 was 10 feet 4 inches (3.149 m) long on the west side and 10 feet 9 inches (3.276 m) long on the east. The width at the north end of the room was 6 feet 9 inches (2.057 m) and at the south 6 feet 5 inches (1.955 m). The wall at the west side was 1 foot 2 inches (35.56 cm) wide at the northwest corner and 1 foot 5 inches (43.18 cm) at the southwest. The north wall was very regular; the wall was the same as that for the southern end of room 3, and was 1 foot 2 inches (35.56 cm) thick at both the northwest and northeast corners. The wall at the east side of the room was 9 inches (22.86 cm) thick at the northeast corner and 1 foot (30.48 cm) at the southeast. The southern wall was 1 foot 4 inches (40.64 cm) thick at the southeast corner and 1 foot 2 inches (35.56 cm) thick at the southwest corner. The fire pit measured 2 feet 1 inch (63.50 cm) by 1 foot 11 inches (58.42 cm) and had an average depth of 8 inches (20.32 cm). The ash pit at the north side was 1 foot 10 inches (55.88 cm) long, 1 foot 2 inches (35.56 cm) wide, and 4 inches (10.16 cm) deep. The storage bin along the wall had a maximum length of 4 feet 6 inches (1.371 m) and a maximum breadth of 1 foot 6 inches (45.72 cm). Indications were that the wall had had an average height of 1 foot 7 inches (48.26 cm) when the stone slabs were topped by the adobe plaster that supplemented the stones.

Room 6 measured 10 feet 5 inches (3.175 m) along its east wall and 8 feet 11 inches (2.717 m) along the west. The north end of the room was 6 feet 2 inches (1.879 m) wide and the south 5 feet 10 inches (1.778 m). The north wall was 1 foot 2 inches (35.56 cm) thick at the northwest corner and 1 foot 3 inches (38.1 cm) thick at the northeast corner. The wall at the east side of the room measured 1 foot 3 inches (38.1 cm) at the northeast corner and 1 foot 2 inches (35.56 cm) at the southeast. The wall at the south was 1 foot (30.48 cm) thick at the southeast corner and 10 inches (25.4 cm) thick at the southwest. The west wall was 1 foot 1 inch (33.02 cm) thick at the southwest corner and 1 foot 8 inches (50.8 cm) at the northwest corner.

The court had an inside measurement of 17 feet 4 inches (5.283 m) along the southern wall. The remaining portion of the wall at the east side was 9 feet 4 inches (2.844 m) long. The wall at the south side was 11 inches (27.94 cm) thick at the west end and 6 inches (15.24 cm) thick at the east end. The east wall measured 1 foot (30.48 cm) at its southern end and 11 inches (27.94 cm) at the north. The paved area was 4 feet 6 inches (1.371 m) wide at its southern end and 6 feet 5 inches (1.955 m) at the north side. Its length was the same as that of the court wall, 9 feet 4 inches (2.844 m). The wall joining room 6 and the kiva and forming a terrace at that side of the court was 10 feet 10 inches (3.302 m) long. At the end abutting room 6 it was 6 inches (15.24 cm) thick and at the kiva was 5 inches (12.7 cm) thick. The upright stone, possibly a step, at the base of the wall on the southern side of the court was 1 foot 1 inch (33.02 cm) long, 6 inches (15.24 cm) high, and ¾ inch (1.90 cm) thick. It stood 2 inches (5.08 cm) from the wall.

The storage pit was 13 feet 10 inches (4.216 m) from the wall of the surface dwelling and 6 feet 3 inches (1.905 m) from the kiva. The opening at the top was 1 foot 6 inches (45.72 cm) in diameter. The bottom was 2 feet (60.96 cm) in diameter and at a point 1 foot 4 inches (40.64 cm) above the bottom had a diameter of 2 feet 4 inches (71.12 cm). The bottom of the pit was 5 feet 4 inches (1.625 m) below the present surface and 3 feet 2 inches (96.52 cm) below the old ground level.

The outdoor fire pit was 18 feet 2 inches (5.537 m) from the northeast corner of the house and 26 feet 6 inches (8.077 m) from the kiva. It was 18 feet 6 inches (5.638 m) from the storage pit. The rectilinear fire box was 1 foot 5 inches (43.18 cm) by 1 foot 6 inches (45.72 cm) and 6 inches (15.24 cm) deep.

The kiva had a diameter of 16 feet 6 inches (5.029 m) above the bench on the sipapu, fire pit, ventilator line. On this same level from bench edge to bench edge the diameter was 12 feet 3 inches (3.733 m). On the floor level it was 12 feet 9 inches (3.886 m). At right angles to this line the diameter above the bench was 16 feet 6 inches (5.029 m), and from bench edge to bench edge was 12 feet 7 inches (3.835 m). On the floor level it was 12 feet 10 inches (3.911 m). At the ventilator side of the room the floor was 10 feet 8½ inches (3.263 m) below the present surface and 7 feet 7 inches (2.311 m) below the old ground level. The bench was 3 feet 7 inches (1.092 m) high at this point. At the opposite side of the chamber the floor was 8 feet 9 inches (2.667 m) below the present surface and 6 feet 1 inch (1.854 m) below the old level. The bench was 3 feet 10 inches (1.168 m) high. At the southwest side of the room the floor was 10 feet 8 inches (3.251 m) below the present surface, 8 feet 11 inches (2.717 m) below the floor of the court, and 6 feet 6 inches (1.981 m) below the original ground level, that underlying the fill for the terrace. The bench was 3 feet 9 inches (1.143 m) high at this point. At the opposite side of the room the floor was 8 feet 11 inches (2.717 m) below the present surface and 5 feet 1 inch (1.549 m) below the original ground level. The bench was 3 feet 8 inches (1.117 m) high.

The timbers incorporated in the bench wall in the approximal position of the old roof supports had diameters of 3½ inches (8.89 cm), 5½ inches (13.97 cm), 6 inches (15.24 cm), and 6 inches (15.24 cm). The posts that formed the wainscoting around the back of the bench had diameters ranging from 2 to 3 inches (5.08 to 7.62 cm).

The Katcina niche (fig. 51, c) was 2 feet 5 inches (73.66 cm) above the floor and 1 foot 1 inch (33.02 cm) below the top of the bench. The niche was 7½ inches (19.05 cm) long at the bottom and 8¼ inches (20.95 cm) long at the top. The opening in the wall measured 5½ inches (13.97 cm) across the lintel and 6 inches (15.24 cm) across the sill. The north side was 4½ inches (11.43 cm) high and the south side 4 inches (10.16 cm).

The sipapu was 3 feet 7½ inches (1.104 m) from the wall. The hole had diameters of 4 inches (10.16 cm) and 5½ inches (13.97 cm) and was 9 inches (22.86 cm) deep. From the edge of the sipapu to the edge of the fire pit was 3 feet 1 inch (93.98 cm). The fire pit (fig. 51, e) measured 1 foot 6 inches (45.72 cm) by 1 foot 4 inches (40.64 cm). The depth varied from 4 inches (10.16 cm) below the floor level at the sipapu side to 7 inches (17.78 cm) at the ventilator end. The slab at the shallow end projected 1½ inches (3.81 cm) above the floor, making the actual depth 5½ inches (13.97 cm). The ash pit was 1 foot 7½ inches (49.53 cm) long, 11½ inches (29.21 cm) wide at the end next the fire pit, and 1 foot 2½ inches (36.83 cm) wide at the base of the deflector stone. The depth was 4 inches (10.16 cm). The deflector stone (fig. 51, g) was 1 foot 7 inches (48.26 cm) long, 1 inch (2.54 cm) thick, and in its broken condition stood 1 foot (30.48 cm) above the floor. Originally it had a height of 1 foot 6 inches (45.72 cm). The stone embedded in the floor (fig. 51, j) measured 8 inches (20.32 cm), 9 inches (22.86 cm), 7 inches (17.78 cm), and 7½ inches (19.05 cm) on its four sides. The top of the stone was 1½ inches (3.81 cm) above the floor. The stone was 1 foot 4 inches (40.64 cm) from the ash pit.

The enclosure formed by the adobe ridge (fig. 51, *h*) was 1 foot 10 inches (55.88 cm) long and 1 foot 3 inches (38.1 cm) wide in its rectangular portion. The circular part at one end had diameters of 11½ inches (29.21 cm) and 11 inches (27.94 cm). The stone in the floor measured 6 inches (15.24 cm) by 5½ inches (13.97 cm). The adobe ridge ranged from 5 inches (12.7 cm) to 6 inches (15.24 cm) in width along the straight portion. Where the small pole was erected it was only 3 inches (7.62 cm) wide and the curved end did not vary greatly from a 3-inch (7.62-cm) average. The height varied only a fraction at different points along the ridge from a 2¾-inch (6.98-cm) average. The pole set in the ridge at the juncture of the curved and straight portions had a diameter of 1 inch (2.54 cm). Its original height could not be determined. The large stone slab found on the floor at one end of this enclosure was 1 foot 3½ inches (39.37 cm) wide at one end and 1 foot 1¾ inches (34.92 cm) wide at the other. One side was 2 feet 5 inches (73.66 cm) in length, while the other was 2 feet 6½ inches (77.47 cm) long. The stone averaged 2¾ inches (6.98 cm) in thickness.

The original ventilator opening was 1 foot 2 inches (35.56 cm) wide at the sill and 1 foot (30.48 cm) wide at the lintel. The east side was 1 foot 1½ inches (34.29 cm) high and the west 1 foot ½ inch (31.75 cm) high. The sill was 8 inches (20.32 cm) above the floor of the room. After the two plaster walls were placed in the original aperture the size of the opening was reduced to 4½ inches (11.43 cm) at the bottom, 7½ inches (19.05 cm) across the center, and 4½ inches (11.43 cm) at the top. The passage was 3 feet (91.44 cm) long. Where it entered the shaft it was 1 foot (30.48 cm) wide and 2 feet (60.96 cm) high. The roof sloped upward from the aperture in the wall of the chamber to the point where it entered the shaft. The inside of the shaft had diameters of 1 foot (30.48 cm) and 1 foot 5 inches (43.18 cm). The bottom of the shaft was 9 feet 6½ inches (2.907 m) below the present ground level and 3 feet 1½ inches (95.25 cm) below the original surface.

Great Pueblo Ruins

Outstanding among the house remains in the Whitewater district are those of two structures belonging to the Great Pueblo period. They are located in the central portion of the main site on top of the ridge south of Allantown (pl. 29, *b*). The largest concentration of people in one community in this district probably occurred in these buildings. No excavations were attempted in these ruins, hence it is not possible to give any extended description of them. A slight amount of debris was moved to locate the walls at several corners and at a few places along the outside walls, but beyond this no digging was done (pl. 30, *a*). By locating the ends of walls and such corners as were visible, a plan was drawn showing the general outlines of the structures and those features apparent on the surface (fig. 53). The larger of the two main buildings conformed to a rectangular-block plan. The smaller was made up of two units joining so as to form an obtuse angle and provide a court in which a large kiva or ceremonial chamber was located. Near one end of the smaller structure was a great kiva that was connected to it by a wall extending from the corner to the curved wall of the circular chamber. This wall served to accentuate, or perhaps better to complete, the court feature. Some distance from the two large mounds were the remains of two small rectangular structures. They stood in front of the main buildings and seem to have been either single-roomed houses or the lower parts of towers. This could not be determined without excavation. Their location and relation to the other remains is somewhat unusual. The ground plan of the group as a whole has a regularity and symmetry that suggests the builders were following some preconceived idea and not just erecting houses. The refuse mounds for the community were located to the east of the buildings. One of them had been cut by drainage water from the area surrounding the ruins and as a result was traversed by two sizable arroyos. These exposed the stratification and showed the depth of the accumulation (pl. 30, *b*).

The smaller of the two buildings, that at the northern end, was interesting because it gave indications of more than one stage of growth. The original portion was a large rectangular block presumably consisting of a double tier of rooms. As far as could be determined from surface evidence the rooms in this structure were all rectangular and numbered 9 or 10 to the row. The second row at the back of the building, the side away from the kiva, was at least two stories in height. Parts of the second-floor walls were still standing. If the second floor had a similar number of rooms the original unit probably contained 29 to 30, possibly even more, secular chambers. The presence of a small kiva in the block of the building or a variation in room sizes would alter the number, but from all appearances it seems that 30 would be a fair estimate. After the completion of this structure a smaller one, pentagonal in plan, was added at the southwestern end. The new wing contained a kiva and at least five rooms. There were other enclosures indicated. They were formed by the spaces between the curved walls of the kiva and the surrounding straight ones. Judging by the nature of these odd-shaped cells, as shown by excavations elsewhere, it is not likely that they were of any significance here. This part of the building apparently was only one story in height.

The original kiva probably was the one located in front of the building. It was rather large compared with the general average

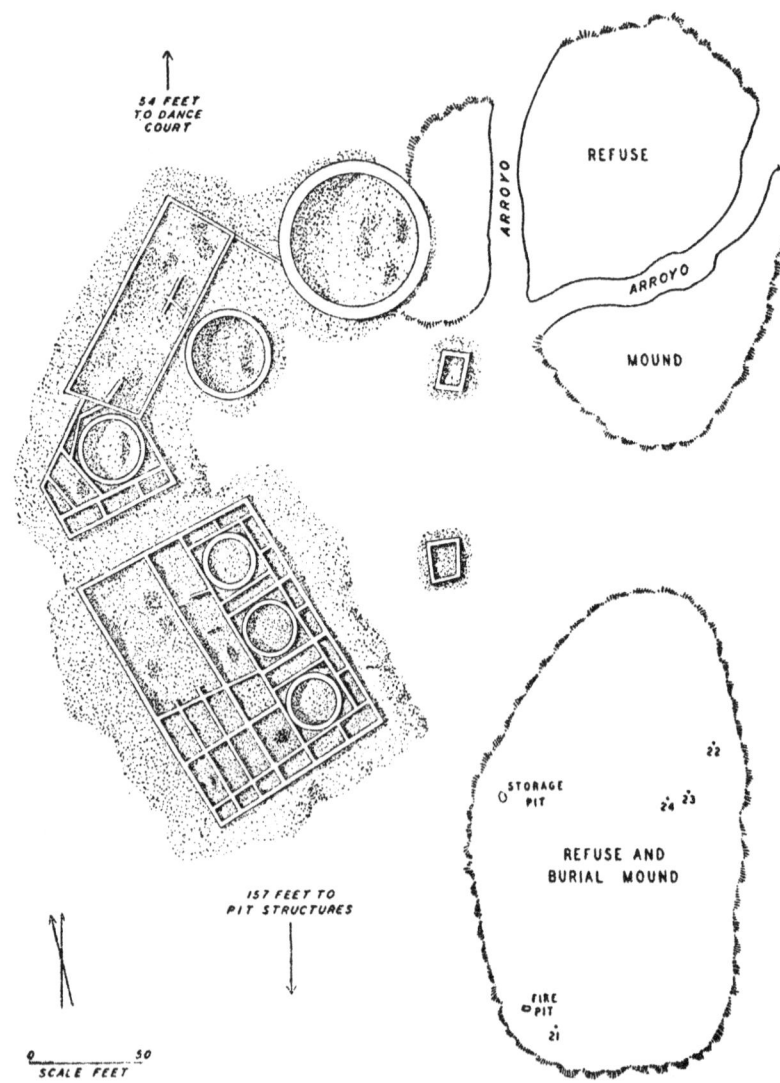

FIGURE 53.—Plan of large ruins of Great Pueblo period.

for such structures. There is a possibility that it is a smaller example of the great kiva type, but it is not too large to fall within the range of the ordinary ceremonial chamber. Of course, excavations might reveal various internal features usually associated with great kivas and then there would be no question. The diameter inside the upper wall, above the bench, was 38 feet 6 inches (11.734 m) and inside the bench 33 feet 6 inches (10.210 m). The kiva in the south wing had an upper diameter of 29 feet (8.839 m) and a lower one of 25 feet (7.620 m). The main part of the rectangular structure was 95 feet (28.956 m) long and 34 feet 6 inches (10.515 m) wide. The wing measured 41 feet 6 inches (12.649 m) along the northwest wall, 26 feet 6 inches (8.077 m) along the southwest wall, 54 feet 6 inches (16.611 m) on the southeast wall, and 32 feet (9.754 m) on the northeast wall.

There was nothing to indicate the exact relationship between the great kiva at the northwestern corner of the structure and the building proper. The wall connecting the two was erected after the completion of both structures. The circular chamber was of impressive size even for great kivas. The diameter between the walls above the bench was 62 feet 10 inches (19.152 m), while inside the bench it was 57 feet (17.374 m). The structure compares favorably with the great kiva in Pueblo Bonito with its 60-foot (18.288-m) diameter and with the so-called Great Bowl in Chettro Kettle, also in the Chaco Canyon, which has a reported diameter of 62 feet 6 inches (19.050 m).[83] It is not as large as the great kiva in Casa Rinconada in the Chaco Canyon, located across the canyon from Chettro Kettle and Bonito, with its 72 feet (21.946 m), nor the one at the Village of the Great Kivas on the Zuñi Reservation that measured 78 feet (23.744 m).[84] On the other hand, it surpasses the second example at the same location that has a diameter of 51 feet (15.545 m) above the bench and 47 feet 6 inches (14.478 m) below it.[85] Also one in the Aztec Ruin in northern New Mexico measuring 48 feet 3½ inches (14.719 m),[86] and that at the Lowry Ruin in southwestern Colorado with a 47-foot (14.326-m) diameter.[87] How it compared with these remains in the matter of interior features can be determined only by excavation. There were slight suggestions, however, of the presence of subfloor vaults in the central portion of the floor where there was only a small amount of fallen wall material and other debris.

The purpose of these superceremonial chambers is still to be learned. They unquestionably are a heritage from Modified Basket Maker times. An example was found in a village belonging to that period in the Chaco Canyon,[88] and the La Plata district farther north in southern Colorado has several dating from that horizon. In the discussion of the one in the Chaco Canyon it was suggested that the large communal rituals, those in which the whole village was con-

---

[83] Hewett, 1922, p. 122.
[84] Roberts, 1932, p. 96.
[85] Roberts, 1932, p. 95.
[86] Morris, 1921, p. 115.
[87] Martin, 1936, p. 46.
[88] Roberts, 1929, pp. 73–81.

cerned, were performed in these great kivas while ordinary ceremonies restricted to special groups took place in the smaller circular chambers. Morris in discussing the structures in his report on the example at Aztec postulated that they were sanctuaries for the entire pueblo where the most sacred rites known to the people of that period were performed by members of the various priesthoods.[89] On the other hand, it is possible that dances of the kind now held in enclosed courts or patios in the modern villages were originally restricted to the great kivas. The significance in the presence of one of these structures at this site lies in the fact that they generally occur in association with some form of the Chaco cultural pattern, as well as at places where the latter had a definite influence on developments. At the present time there is a question concerning the origin and growth of the superkiva. Some think that its elaboration took place in the Chaco center and that it spread outward from there. Others believe that it attained its greatest development in the southern Colorado region and spread from there to the Chaco and thence on toward the south and the west. Present evidence tends to support the Chaco adherents, although it is too early to attempt definite conclusions. There is no question, however, but what it is a northern feature and that it is one of the traits usually found in the Chaco pattern complex. As suggested in the discussion of the dance court in earlier pages in this report, there likely was some similarity in purpose between it and the great kivas. It is possible that the dance court here was merely a temporary arrangement to answer ceremonial needs while the great kiva was under construction.

The second building, the larger of the two, consisting of a rectangular block with a series of kivas along the front, although incorporated in the structure, gave outward indications of having been built from a definite plan. That it was erected as a unit could not be established without excavation and while all exterior walls traced along the surface appeared to be continuous it seems more likely that it actually was constructed in several sections along preconceived lines. The group of rooms forming a rectangular block comprising three rows at the back of the building is like the original block in the smaller building to the north and may represent the nucleus of this structure. To this was added the row of wider rooms and then the kiva group. The series of small chambers along the south end of the building probably represents the last of the construction work. However, it is not wise to be too emphatic in the matter, as excavations frequently reveal curious and unexpected features in large buildings. The last two rows of rooms, those farthest removed from the kivas, at one time were at least three stories in height and it is

---

[89] Morris, 1921, p. 135.

not improbable that the outside row was four. There was sufficient fallen material along the outside wall to have formed a fourth floor. Portions of the bases of third-story walls were still standing in the second row from the back. The third row gave indications of only two stories and the next, one. It is doubtful that the kivas and the rooms adjacent to them stood a full story above ground, judging from the debris. At all events the building had been a characteristic terraced dwelling of Great Pueblo type.

The series of rooms along the south end and the east side, the front of the building, possibly were for storage purposes. Their size and shape suggest that function rather than dwelling chambers, although some of them could have served in the latter capacity. The larger rooms in the main block back of the kivas unquestionably were the main domiciliary enclosures. It is doubtful that all were used as living quarters. The lower and back chambers in buildings of this type generally were dark and poorly ventilated, particularly those on the ground level where no openings were left in the walls, and were used as storage places. The roofs of the kivas and the rooms surrounding them probably served as a dooryard for the first row of rooms, the roofs of the latter bearing the same relation to the second-floor chambers of the next row and so on to the top and final row. Under such an arrangement, approximately 40 rooms would open to the outside light and air, and these no doubt were the main living quarters. On the basis of conditions in more recent villages this would indicate a probable maximum occupation of 40 families. It is not likely that there ever was a complete contemporaneous use of all these rooms, so that an estimate of 30 families is more in keeping with the conditions indicated in most communities of this type. On this basis the population may be postulated as ranging between 150 and 200. The three kivas suggest three clans with a possible 8 to 10 men for each ceremonial chamber. These figures are, of course, purely speculative, but the general indications augmented by knowledge of conditions elsewhere warrant the opinion that they are not far from a reasonable approximation of the possible size of the group. This building had a length of 121 feet 6 inches (37.033 m) and a width of 87 feet (26.518 m). The kivas were approximately 20 feet (6.096 m) in diameter.

Whether the second structure was built by the people living in the first and smaller one, that appeared to have been constructed first, or by groups withdrawing from various outlying unit villages and joining the community at the old site is not known. The first building may have continued in occupation after the completion of the second or possibly was partially abandoned in favor of new accommodations in the larger structure. The smaller one may have been deserted gradually until only portions of it were inhabited at the time when the entire community withdrew from the district. The maximum population for the original dwelling was probably between 50 and 60 people. A group of this size would not require a structure as large as the second and there is little question but what they were joined by others from the immediate neighborhood. If both were completely filled at the same time the village would have approximated a population of from 200 to 250 people. Judging from potsherds scattered about the ruins of the buildings and in the refuse mounds, the site was abandoned before the peak of the Great Pueblo period was reached. Reasons for the withdrawal were not indicated by any of the surface features.

The walls in both structures, where visible, were built of carefully selected stones shaped for the purpose and dressed along the edges. They formed the outside surfaces while the inner portion, the core of the wall, consisted of earth and small stones—a rubble fill. Very little mortar was used between the courses. There was some chinking in the form of small stones and a sporadic course of thinner blocks appearing here and there in the walls suggested some of the banding so characteristic of Chaco Canyon masonry. It was not as pronounced nor as extensive here, nevertheless it was reminiscent of that construction. The masonry was also suggestive of that in the ruin on the Zuñi Reservation that was accompanied by two of the superkivas,[90] and had some similarities to walls in the surface ruin at the Long H Ranch.[91] Both of these sites exhibited definite affinities to the general Chaco cultural pattern, and they, as well as the present ruins, probably represent some of the more important centers in the southern periphery of the Chaco range.

The two small rectangular structures in front of the main house mounds are somewhat puzzling because their purpose is not clear. It is not common to find remains of this type in association with larger ruins in this part of the Anasazi province. Whether they were single-roomed domiciles, granaries, or the bases of towers is not known. There was sufficient fallen material around them to have carried the walls to a height of approximately a story and a half. It was this factor that suggested the possibility of their having been towers, although low examples of that form of structure. The San Juan region in the north, particularly the southern Colorado area on the north side of that river, has many structures of that type in association with regular communal dwellings.[92] If the ruins here are the remains of that form of building they indicate a considerable spread for the feature. The function of towers has not been determined as yet. Some have suggested that they were for lookout

---

[90] Roberts, 1932.
[91] Roberts, 1931.
[92] Fewkes, 1919.

purposes, others that they were for defense, or were observatories and aided in the astronomical studies by which ceremonial performances were governed. They have been considered in the light of places where special rites connected with the worship of astral phenomena were held, or simply as granaries. At the present site they would not have been particularly advantageous lookout positions because people on the housetops could have seen farther. The main buildings undoubtedly had ample storage space in the lower, back rooms, so the granary function hardly seems logical. They could have served as defensive towers, in that men on their roofs would have been in advantageous positions to harass the rear or flanks of an attacking party that had reached the front walls of the dwellings, but this indicates a better understanding of military tactics and strategy than is generally accorded the peoples of that group and period. They certainly would have had little defensive value beyond that of the large buildings from the standpoint of enemies approaching the site from the front and sides. Hence that explanation does not seem very plausible. There were conditions under which they could have been of value in making observations of the position of the rising sun to aid the priests in setting the time for winter or summer solstice ceremonies or for those pertaining to the spring and autumnal equinoxes. There is no way of establishing such functions and they can only be postulated. Perhaps they should not be thought of as anything but the remains of small secular structures. Their location, both with respect to each other and to the main buildings, seems too exact and definite to be mere coincidence and for that reason the various suggested explanations have been presented. The structure at the south end measured 18 feet (5.486 m) and 17 feet 3 inches (5.257 m) on the sides and 15 feet 9 inches (4.800 m) and 14 feet 10 inches (4.521 m) on the ends. The remains were 48 feet 6 inches (14.782 m) from the larger dwelling. The second small structure was 63 feet (19.202 m) north of the first. It was 17 feet 6 inches (5.334 m) and 17 feet (5.181 m) on the sides and 13 feet 10 inches (4.216 m) and 14 feet (4.267 m) on the ends. It was 27 feet 6 inches (8.382 m) from the great kiva and 105 feet (32.004 m) from the smaller of the two dwellings.

The two arroyos that had cut their ways through the northern refuse mound exposed most of the layers in the deposits. This made it evident that the waste material from the village had been thrown on the slope of the ridge dropping away from the village toward the edge of the low bluffs to the east of the site. The refuse attained a maximum depth of 7 feet (2.133 m) just below the upper edge of the slope and fanned out gradually down the hillside. Portions of it had been washed some distance from the original termini of the dump. The main factor of importance revealed by the banks of the arroyos was the total absence of all human bones. Generally when a mound of such size is disturbed to the extent this one was, a number of burials are exposed or washed out. It is not possible to reach conclusions on the problem without complete investigation of the mound, but it appears that very few of the inhabitants could have been interred there and in this respect there is another similarity to Chaco remains. Burials are only rarely found in the refuse heaps associated with the large house ruins of that cultural pattern. They are often present in the dumps of small-house remains but not the large ones. The reason for this has not yet been determined.

The mound at the south was thoroughly trenched because it was thought that it might cover some pit dwellings. That work revealed four burials, three of which were below the bottom of the mound and were accompanied by late Developmental style pottery and hence could not be attributed to the dwellers in the large structures. The fourth did have mortuary offerings characteristic of the Great Pueblo period, but that does not vitiate the comparison to Chaco traits because a sporadic example is sometimes found even in the main centers of that pattern. This second mound was large in extent but rather shallow. Its maximum depth was 3 feet (91.44 cm). The mound cut by the arroyos was the first, judging from potsherd material, and probably represents, for the most part, the sweepings and waste matter from the original structure. The northwestern side, in the vicinity of the great kiva, incorporated most of a refuse mound that contained Developmental type potsherds. As a matter of fact, part of the great kiva pit had been dug into the old dump. This material may have come from structures 12 and 14 but it is more likely that part of the original large dwelling was erected over the remains of some pit structures. The second refuse mound undoubtedly correlates with the larger structure.

The potsherds and other material scattered through and over the surfaces of these two mounds indicate that community was roughly contemporaneous with the Great Pueblo village on the Zuñi Reservation, where the two examples of great kivas, previously mentioned, are located. In some respects the indications suggest a slightly earlier beginning for the structures near Allantown and an earlier termination of occupancy. This may be relative rather than actual, however, and the result of a cultural lag. Dendrochronological dates for the Village of the Great Kivas place its beginning at 1015 to 1030. That date would agree rather well with the indications here, because there is a definite overlap in the nature of the potsherds from the north mound and those from the third unit in the valley bottom where the dates were 1005 to 1014 for the house and 1007 to 1014 for the kiva. On the basis of this evidence, meager to be sure, when it is considered that there has been no excavation in the large ruins, it may be suggested that the first section of the Great Pueblo center was built at about the same time as the third unit and that the abandonment of the latter possibly correlates with the beginning of the second and larger dwelling. There is no question but what the large ruins fall within the eleventh century, because there were no traces of pottery types prevalent in this general area that have been dated to the early twelfth century and the beginning of the village must be placed after 1000 A. D. Complete excavation and careful study of these structures would no doubt throw interesting light on a number of problems connected with the diffusion of cultural traits from various districts and relationships between different patterns. These ruins are on the very periphery of the westward expansion of the Chaco pattern and at the eastern edge of influence from Little Colorado centers located farther west. As a matter of fact, it is necessary to go only a few miles west until, in the vicinity of Houck, differences in the pattern become quite apparent. This is true for the earlier horizons as well as those of the more highly developed stages.

SUMMARY AND DISCUSSION

In the Whitewater district in the vicinity of Allantown, in eastern Arizona, are numerous remains belonging to several stages in the growth of the Anasazi cultural pattern. Three season's work in the ruins concentrated in one small section of the region produced considerable information on various elements in the complex and threw interesting light on some phases in the growth of characteristic features. Although there are traces of Modified Basket Maker and some large ruins representing the Great Pueblo period, most of the digging was done in Developmental Pueblo remains. This resulted from the fact that the area under excavation produced only scattering indications of Modified Basket Maker, more were expected when the project was started, and from the necessity of bringing the investigations to a close before the digging planned for the Great Pueblo structures could be begun. Such Modified Basket Maker features as had been present on the site were so disturbed and mixed by the activities of the subsequent occupants that little could be learned about them beyond the fact that they had been there. A fairly complete picture of the nature and trends of the Developmental Pueblo period is presented by the information obtained from 20 pit structures and their accompanying granaries and surface shelters, and from three unit-type ruins with associated ceremonial chambers. The remains clearly show the growth from small single-roomed pit dwellings with brush and plaster covered truncated-pyramidal superstructures supported by four upright posts set in the floor of the chamber, to above-ground houses with several contiguous rooms, masonry walls, and flat roofs. Correlated with this is the shift in function of the semisubterranean domicile from secular to ceremonial purposes. These changes were accompanied by comparable ones in other features, particularly in the lesser objects of the material culture, such as pottery, stone and bone implements, that are considered in a second part of this report to be published at a later date.

The pit structures on the whole are comparable to those in other sections of the Anasazi province. There are various individual and local differences of a minor nature that probably have no significance as far as the structural type is concerned. They no doubt represent purely personal whims on the part of the builders and had no bearing on the subsequent trend in construction. On the other hand, there are features that adumbrate later developments. In only three examples (four if Kiva A of the first unit is included) was the pit portion of a dwelling encircled by a definite bench. This corresponds closely with the situation at a Modified Basket Maker site in the Chaco Canyon where 2 out of 20 structures had benches and the remainder did not. At the Long H Ranch, southwest from the Whitewater ruins, in a series of 16 pit remains, 9 were without a bench and 7 had the feature. This tends to strengthen the suggestion made in a previous discussion of the Long H group to the effect that the structures with encircling bench probably represent a later development of the pit type of house. The adoption of this structural element apparently did not occur until shortly before the transition that culminated in the circular, subterranean ceremonial chamber called kiva. The lack of a bench, however, does not necessarily mean that a structure is older than one that has such a feature, because the older forms persisted to some extent after new ones appeared. The proportion of one style to another in a series of structures or in a village probably does have significance, although how much emphasis should be placed on it is still questionable.

Two of the pit structures, 1 and 3, contained examples of what may be considered a prototype of the pilaster, as well as an illustration of the manner in which that architectural feature developed in the Southwest. In the series of houses as a whole was evidence of a shift in function in the floor basin adjacent to the fire pit; as a matter of fact it is possible to trace the origin, growth, and change of the feature in this one set of house remains. A number of the pits that probably represent the early stage of occupancy have an abraded depression in the floor adjacent to the fire pit that seems to indicate the resting place of the base end of a ladder. The wearing of a basin apparently suggested the construction of an actual box to hold the end of the ladder. In a number of the structures this takes the form of a simple concavity, with carefully plastered sides, in the floor. Then the use of stones to line the pit was introduced and the feature became a definite box. In the case of pole-and-rung ladders so much of the space would be unoccupied by the ladder ends that it offered a place where ashes cleaned from the fire pit could be deposited temporarily until they could conveniently be removed from the structure. When the advantage of this became fully apparent it may have led to the idea of removing the ladder from the pit and embedding the ends in the floor, to prevent slipping, so that the entire box could be employed as an ash basin. Whether the evolution of the ladder box-ash pit followed exactly the steps as outlined or not there is no question of the change, as that was clearly shown in the remains of the pit structures. In some cases the houses may have been equipped with a notched-log ladder rather than the pole-and-rung style, but that would have little effect on the question of a placement for the lower end. There was no evidence for the single-log type in any of the remains, although there were definite indications of the other form.

A unique feature in the pit structures at this locality was that of combining several into one larger building, as illustrated by 6 and 7, 9, 10, and 11. An interesting factor in the joining together of these dwellings was that the units that went into the make-up of the larger building were individually complete. An interpretation of the situation is that although the people were ready to combine their houses they were not yet willing to give up house characteristics that had long been present in the single dwellings. Reference was made, in this connection, to the old theory that the rectangular-roomed communal buildings of the Pueblo peoples were an outgrowth of the practice of combining a number of circular houses into one large structure. The evidence offered by other examples, the structures 15 and 16 groups and the first unit, indicates a more logical step in house development, however, and for that reason the combined pit structures, one containing two and the other three houses, are considered as a peculiar local development that did not have a direct bearing on the growth of the communal type building in general.

The superstructure for No. 12 was the only one of its kind in this district. It may represent a purely local method for covering a pit that was above the average in size, or it may be characteristic of the type of construction employed for larger structures. The latter probably is the proper answer rather than that it was a local development. A certain similarity between the framework here, especially the outer ring of supports, and some of the Plains earth lodges was mentioned. Attention should also be called to the fact that a comparable secondary outer framework was used in some of the Hohokam and Mogollon houses [93] and also was present in a large circular structure in a Modified Basket Maker village in the Chaco Canyon.[94] Since these other structures are consistently larger than the ordinary pit dwellings of the Anasazi province it is probable that the style of construction was that used when a greater area was roofed over. Due to its apparent widespread distribution and the fact that it is present in various stages in different cultural patterns it probably represents a common trait in the general pit house-earth lodge complex rather than evidence for later borrowing or influence from some specific pattern. Future work, however, will no doubt throw additional light on the subject and may give some indications of the lines along which it diffused.

The evolution of the unit-type dwelling, which has long been considered the basic component in the development of the great communal buildings that were characteristic of the Anasazi province, is well illustrated by several groups at this site. First in the series is structure 16 with its associated granaries. In structure 16 entrance was by means of a ladder placed in a small shaft that was connected to the main chamber by a covered trench or passage. The granary pits, located west of the structure, were roughly oval in form and two of them gave evidence of having been used as shelters or a makeshift habitation. The second in the series is the structure 15 group. There the side shaft and passage was too small to serve as an actual entrance and had become a ventilator. Access to the chamber was by means of a ladder through the hatchway in the roof. The granaries, located north and west of the structure, had become rectangular in form, were built in a row, and some of them gave evidence of having been lived in. Outdoor fire pits and brush shelters were associated with the granaries and a rude form of portico was erected in front of one of them. The third group is that of the first unit in the Developmental village. The pit structure retains many of the features noted in the others and probably was an actual dwelling when first completed. The granaries had become rooms, however, built in a contiguous row and some of them contained marked evidence of use as a definite habitation. The portico was retained at one end of the building and a small court with open fire pit provided at the other. The pit structure probably was used less and less for domiciliary purposes and more and more for ceremonial purposes, so that it represents a transition in function from house to kiva. Fourth in the series is the second unit in the Developmental village. Here the pit structure had become a kiva with typical characteristics and the granaries were definitely a habitation, although they occu-

---

[93] Haury, 1932, fig. 14; 1936 b, fig. 26.
[94] Roberts, 1929, pp. 78-79.

pied the same position relative to the pit remains. The last in the series is the fully developed form illustrated by the third unit with its surface dwelling, court, and subterranean ceremonial chamber. The sequence was determined by stratigraphical evidence based on material from the various refuse mounds and test sections, supplemented by that from the pillars left from the fill in various structures, and by dendrochronological dates. While there is a certain overlap in the case of structure 15 and the first unit, it is not of such a nature as to vitiate the illustration of the growth in type.

The changes taking place in the various structures can be summarized briefly by saying that the typical small house and its associated subterranean ceremonial chamber grew from a semisubterranean pit structure and its accompanying granaries. The evolution in this district includes shifts in nature and function for both the granaries and the pit structures. The former passed from roughly oval or circular forms to those with a rectangular outline; their superstructures shifted from a pyramidal to a truncated type; the walls from a sloping pole and plaster variety to vertical ones made of stone. Associated with this was the growth in masonry types. From a series of disconnected cells the granaries became a row of contiguous rooms. At each change they became shallower until their floors ultimately attained the ground level. From storage places they became habitations. In the circular structures there was progression from a side-entrance passage to the smoke-hole-hatchway mode of access. The old entrance was retained in reduced and slightly modified form as a ventilator. The truncated-pyramidal superstructure supported by upright posts was replaced by the cribbed style of roof resting entirely on the top of the bench encircling the pit, evidence of such replacement being found in Kiva B of the second unit. The bench apparently was a development out of the narrow shelf formed at the top of the pit wall when the sloping side poles of the superstructure were set back from the edge of the excavation to prevent their slipping into the chamber or damaging the sides of the room In contrast to the rising floor level in the granaries, the pit of the original domicile became deeper and deeper in the shift from dwelling to ceremonial chamber until from a semisubterranean structure it became one that was wholly below the level of the ground. After the adoption of the large communal houses, erected by combining numbers of units together, the ceremonial chamber emerged from the ground and was incorporated in the block of the building, its former subsurface characteristic being simulated by a fill of earth between the curved wall of the kiva proper and the enclosing rectangular room that made its inclusion in a building possible. The kivas along the front of one of the Great Pueblo ruins probably represent this last stage, although no definite statement can be made due to lack of investigation in the ruin.

Another unique feature at the main site consisted of a large circular adobe pavement bordered by a series of small upright stone slabs. Adjoining the circle at its northern side were traces of a three-sided structure that enclosed a form of dais opening toward the floored area. For want of a better name these remains were called a dance court. That the place actually was used for such a purpose is not known. There was no evidence for a superstructure or covering of any nature over the enclosed area, but because the general plan is suggestive of a great kiva or superceremonial chamber an explanation is proffered to the effect that it possibly functioned in a similar capacity. During Developmental Pueblo times at this location the rites and rituals that later were performed in the great kiva present at the north end of the nearby Great Pueblo ruins may have been held in the dance court. It is possible, of course, that the dance court was merely a temporary provision for the observance of communal ceremonies while the great kiva was under construction. The court is unusual, nevertheless, and thus far no other example has been described for the Anasazi province. Hough's great dance pit at Luna may be analogous in purpose, but the forms differ to a considerable extent.[95] Jeancon's dance plaza on the Piedra River in southern Colorado more nearly approximates the present example, yet it is different.[96] There does not seem to be any valid basis for the assumption, made by several visitors to the site while work was under way, that the dance court represents a variation of the so-called ball courts of regions farther to the south.

The Great Pueblo ruins in their unexcavated state suggest two large buildings and a great kiva placed so as to form a partially enclosed court in which two rectangular towers were located. Such of the masonry as is visible and the potsherd and other materials scattered over and through the refuse mounds indicate that the community had certain affinities with the Chaco Canyon pattern and that it was roughly contemporaneous with a Great Pueblo village on the Zuñi Reservation. The smaller of the two buildings seems to have been erected first, and it is possible that its original nucleus dates from about the same time as the third unit in the floor of Whitewater Valley. The larger building may have been constructed by groups withdrawing from the various scattered units in the district and joining the center on the ridge that was started when the first terraced house was erected. All indications are that these ruins fall within the eleventh century and that while their main features point

---

[95] Hough, 1919, pp. 414–415.
[96] Roberts, 1930, p. 33.

to a northern and eastern influence, there are some traces of elements reaching them from the Little Colorado region to the west and others from the south and southeast.

Dates obtained from charred beams found in different structures provide some interesting data on several aspects of the growth of the Pueblo peoples. Approximately 2 centuries are represented by the remains excavated and described in the preceding pages. This omits, of course, the Great Pueblo ruins for which no dates are available. The earliest building date is that for structure 2 and the latest that for the third unit. Timber from structure 2 gave dates 814 and 815, the latter being considered as the year for the erection of the structure because it is the latest in the remains. One timber from the kiva in the third unit recorded the cutting date as 1011 ± 2 or a maximum of 1013. A fragment from the house in the third unit is recorded as 994 ± 20, or a maximum of 1014. Using the minimum of 814 and maximum of 1014 gives exactly 200 years. The third unit was no doubt occupied for a number of years after it was completed, but from the standpoint of the evolution of the house type that is not important. The significant thing is that the unit type in the full sense of the word was fully established by 1014 in this district. During the span of 2 centuries the domicile changed completely from a simple pit dwelling and associated granaries to an above-ground house and associated ceremonial chamber. When regarded more specifically, however, the transition covered a shorter interval. Structure 3, it will be recalled, was considered as a kiva for a unit group and its building date was 867 or soon thereafter. Kiva A in the first unit in the Developmental Village contained the single date 845. There is some question about this date, but inasmuch as the latter structure gave every indication of being first a house, then a ceremonial chamber, and as an accompaniment of the change associated granaries were replaced by actual dwelling rooms, the year may not be far off if considered as representative of the original construction. This is given some support by the fact that one beam from structure 3 showed a cutting date of 842 and that a number of those in structure 12 read 844. Although the latter were no doubt reused timbers in structure 12, they show that considerable activity was taking place at about 845. On the other hand, structure 15 with its associated granaries, a group that illustrates an elementary stage in the evolution, yielded the building date of 888, although this relates to a reconstruction following a fire and not the original building of the house. In this connection it was pointed out that structure 15 possibly was the dwelling of an immigrant group coming in from the northwest and for that reason was somewhat of a laggard in development. The occupants might have been a conservative element in the community and slow to adopt new ideas. Still, on the basis of these several remains it can be said that the trend toward the unit-type dwelling had its inception shortly after the middle of the ninth century and in at least one example had attained a definite pattern by 867. The second unit in the Developmental Village produced no dates. On the basis of potsherd comparisons between it and structure 12, with its readings of 918, there is little doubt but that it closely approximates that year. The second unit was not a fully developed example of the perfected type, yet it exhibits sufficient characteristics to warrant its being considered an illustration of a crystallizing plan of construction. Thus it seems logical to conclude that the major developments took place in a span of from 50 to 60 years. The approximately 80 years elapsing between the erection of the second unit and the third unit were marked by refinements in the plan, not by any major changes. Whether the development and transition was as rapid in other sections or not still has to be determined. At present there is not enough evidence on this stage for other districts to warrant conclusions. Because of indications that the Whitewater region was influenced by the larger centers to the northeast and that it was marked in some degree by a peripheral lag, it seems that the development may have been more rapid here than would have been the case had it resulted from independent efforts. Nevertheless it is a good illustration of the extent of change that can take place in a short space of time, even among people considered to be groping their way toward a higher cultural level.

The dendrochronological dates from the individual structures suggest a number of interesting items and also raise several troublesome questions. Perhaps the most important single factor in this connection concerns the stress that should or should not be placed on the significance of a date for a ruin based on only one or two timbers. Three of the structures in the Whitewater series contained beams that covered a span of from 25 to 74 years for a single building. Those from 3 ranged over a 25-year interval, those from 15 included 31 years, and those from 12 incorporated the 74-year group. With the information available from the work at the site it is possible to conclude that this condition is due to the use of old timbers and beams salvaged from abandoned houses, but under other circumstances an entirely erroneous conception could be given by a limited set of dates. For example, if only 3 or 4 fragments of charcoal had been saved from structure 12 and, as could easily happen, they were all from the early end of the series, the implications would indeed be misleading. From such evidence the remains would naturally be placed approximately 74 years earlier than their actual date and in the present instance that length of time would more than cover the interval during which there were marked changes in the cultural pattern. When the rapidity of change is considered even the quarter of a century represented by the wood in structure 3 could make a tremendous difference in interpretations of evidence and the problem of correlations. For that reason it seems that dendrochronological dates, accurate and helpful as they are, must be used with a great degree of discretion and when only a few are available from a site they should be regarded more as an approximate indication of age rather than a definite demonstration of the precise interval of time encompassed by the remains. Even with such reservations, the years recorded will be of considerable assistance in solving numerous problems. In the present group of ruins little emphasis could be placed on the 845 from Kiva B were it not for the complementary evidence from other structures and also from various archeological manifestations that augment the dendrochronology. As it is, the correlation between the date and the structure is not above question, as was pointed out in the discussion of the second unit.

The question of how to interpret the dates from a single structure is not easily answered. From the standpoint of accepted archeological practice the latest material is the date determinant and for general purposes the mere statement that the last year recorded was such and so would suffice for the age of the house. Yet there may be something of significance in a series covering an interval of some length and proper interpretation of it may have much more value than the actual terminal date. The timbers from structure 2 show 814 and 815 and probably represent the span of a single year. The explanation that seems most logical is that the house was built in 815 from timbers cut in 814 and 815. In this case the problem is relatively simple. The house in the third unit yielded timbers with dates from 994 to 1004. The erection of the house would, according to rule, be placed at 1004, but when the series is studied it is noted that all but the 1004 beam have dates either 994 or 995. Hence it seems that the actual building date was probably 995 and that the single timber cut 9 years later represents a replacement or bit of repair work necessitated by the wear and tear of occupancy. While it is not important in this particular instance, it is not inconceivable that such a 9-year difference might have a pronounced effect on the validity of the conclusions made with respect to specific features at a site.

The 74-year span in structure 12 furnishes another example of a problem in explanation and the choice of procedure in the use of the evidence. The terminal date for the structure is 918, the earliest 844. In the discussion of the structure it was suggested that timbers from an older house, probably a smaller one occupying the same spot, were used in the construction work of 918, or shortly thereafter. This is a good explanation and likely a correct one. Examining the series of beam years, however, the student is struck by the fact that there is more to be considered than the building of a structure in 918 making use of a number of logs cut in 844. There is one cut in 845, one cut in 853, several that show 862 as the year when they were felled, another with the date 870. Now the question is, how are these to be regarded? Was the original structure built in 845 from timbers cut for the most part in 844? That seems a logical conclusion. Then, was the 853 specimen a timber replacement repairing a damaged section of the roof? Such an explanation is entirely plausible. But the 862 group is more difficult to interpret. Were extensive repairs called for at that time in the original structure, or were timbers salvaged from still another house to complete the material needed in the 918 construction? Either would be a satisfactory answer, yet there is nothing to indicate which is more likely the correct one. Again it might be asked, can not the 862 series represent the actual time when the structure was built and the 870 and 918 dates be those of repairs? Offhand the reply would seem to be yes. Further investigation, however, shows that the 870 timber was one of the main support posts for the superstructure and it probably was not a replacement or bit of repair work. Hence the erection of the structure in 862 could be ruled out and as it presumably was after 870 and 918 is the next date present that appears to be the logical one for the remains. The other features can not be wholly ignored, though, and there is still the problem of how they should be interpreted and what emphasis should be placed on them. Perhaps mention of the various possibilities is enough. The writer frankly is at a loss to know just how to use such information to the best advantage. The situation is further complicated by the fact that it frequently is necessary for the dendrochronologist to write his dates with a plus or minus sign qualification. This means that the year is as given but that several more should be added, just how many not being known, up to the limit of the qualifier. When the date is used should the qualifier be dropped consistently or should the maximum be added in every case and that made the number? A majority of the archeologists seem to be in a similar quandary and there is no standard followed in all cases. From a conservative point of view the safest plan is probably that of habitually adding the qualifier to the date.

From a comparative standpoint the dates from the Whitewater ruins indicate certain interesting factors. The earliest, 815, from structure 2 is from a house showing much less development than a pit structure in the Chaco Canyon that produced the date 777 ± 10, or a maximum of 787.[97] The structure in the local series that was more nearly comparable to that in the Chaco was No. 15 with its 888 ± 15, or a maximum of 903. Then structure 12 with 918 ± 3, or a maximum of 921 rather closely establishes the date for the second unit. In the Chaco Canyon both architecture and ceramics were much farther along by 921 than they were in this district. Pueblo Bonito had been started and types of pottery had appeared that were still unknown in the vicinity of Allantown. The maximum date for the third unit was 1014, 994 ± 20. By 1014 Pueblo Bonito was definitely a Great Pueblo center and various features characteristic of that stage were well established in the Chaco, but many of them apparently had not reached this location. The ruins at the Village of the Great Kivas on the Zuñi Reservation gave a date of 1015 ± 15, or a 1030 maximum. The general pattern at that location was Chacoan, and while not as advanced as that in the Chaco at 1030, did have some things not present in the 1014 unit on the Whitewater. However, the beginnings of the Great Pueblo stage at the main part of the site may have antedated slightly the beginnings at the Zuñi community, as was pointed out in the discussion of those structures. On the basis of this data it seems quite clear that the ruins in the Whitewater district south of Allantown represent a peripheral lag in the Chaco pattern and, despite many recent expressions of opinion to the contrary, the flow of influence was from the Chaco toward Allantown and not the reverse. The evidence indicates that the movement was slower in earlier than in later times and that when the Great Pueblo stage was reached the lag was not very pronounced. Actual dates from the large ruins here might change the picture somewhat, but the information at hand suggests the trend was as described.

Stratigraphic tests made from pillars left from the fill in various structure pits and in different parts of several refuse mounds are mainly important for a study of the ceramic sequence and for changes in artifact types. The fill in a number of the houses indicated certain intervals when the area immediately adjacent to them was unoccupied. This probably means that the people had moved elsewhere on the site or in the surrounding district rather than that the region was completely deserted. During the earlier stages of the Developmental period there was more of a tendency to shift about than was the case after the larger, more permanent type of dwelling became established. For this reason the ruins in a district suggest a larger population than actually inhabited it. In the present instance it is not improbable that the people, for one reason or another,

---

[97] Judd, 1924, house No. 2; Douglass, 1935, p. 51.

moved from the top of the ridge to the valley bottom, then back to the ridge again, or to another valley location before returning to higher ground.

Most of the burials for the various groups and units were made in the refuse mounds. In some cases the interment was in a room or beneath an occupied area, as mentioned in the discussion of the various structures. The flexed type of burial predominated and in a majority of them funerary offerings of pottery vessels and other objects accompanied the remains. Most of the skeletons were in a poor state of preservation and out of a total of 150 only 15 are suitable for anthropometric studies. The material is in the hands of Dr. T. D. Stewart, assistant curator of the Division of Physical Anthropology, United States National Museum, and a complete report on it is to be included as an appendix to the second part of the report on the Whitewater district. Burials of another type, those of turkeys and dogs, are common in the refuse mounds of the district. In a majority of cases the interment appears to have been intentional, not an accidental covering over of a dead fowl or animal, and the body frequently was accompanied by offerings of one kind or another. Potsherds rubbed down to form shallow dishes, complete miniature vessels in some graves, and corn or animal bones, according to whether it was a turkey or a dog, were the customary objects for that purpose. The location of all burials is shown on the maps of the various groups and units.

The food supply for the district consisted of corn, beans, seeds from a species of wild grass,[98] pinyon nuts, rabbits, deer, and antelope. It is questionable that the turkey was used for food. Most of the turkey bones found were parts of articulated skeletons in definite burials. Other vegetal products were no doubt utilized, but those named are the only ones that were found in the houses or refuse deposits. Every example recovered was charred, which probably accounts for the preservation. On the basis of what is indicated there is no question but what the group here had the same economic pattern as the rest of the Pueblo peoples. They were mainly agriculturalists, supplementing their diet by such hunting as the country afforded.

Estimates of population for the district are not possible because only a portion of the ruins was excavated and it is not known how many were contemporaneous or what the total number for any one stage may have been. The most that can be said is that the unit-type structures probably housed from 10 to 20, the pit dwellings 6 to 10, the smaller of the large structures from 50 to 60, the larger

---

[98] *Eriocoma cuspidata* Nutt. (*Oryzopsis hymenoides* (Roem and Schult.) Ricker), identified by Dr. Melvin R. Gilmore, Ethnobotanical Laboratory, Museum of Anthropology, University of Michigan.

from 150 to 200. As suggested in the discussion of the Great Pueblo ruins, the maximum for that community was probably about 250 people. If the Whitewater Valley proper is considered, the area within a radius of 2 miles (3.219 k) of the large ruins probably never contained more than 300 people at any one time. The average was not likely that large. Suggestions concerning the district as a whole, however, must wait until further work has produced more evidence than is available at the present time.

LITERATURE CITED

BUSHNELL, D. I., JR.
    1922. Villages of the Algonquian, Siouan, and Caddoan Tribes West of the Mississippi. Bulletin 77, Bureau of American Ethnology, Washington.

COUES, ELLIOTT.
    1897. New Light on the Early History of the Greater Northwest. The Manuscript Journals of Alexander Henry and David Thompson, 1799–1814, vols. I–III, New York.

CUMMINGS, BYRON.
    1915. Kivas of the San Juan Drainage. American Anthropologist, n. s. vol. 17, no. 2, pp. 272–282, Lancaster.

CUSHING, F. H.
    1896. Outline of Zuñi Creation Myths. Thirteenth Annual Report Bureau of Ethnology, pp. 321–447, Washington.

DOUGLASS, A. E.
    1932. Tree Rings and their Relation to Solar Variations and Chronology. Annual Report Smithsonian Institution for 1931, pp. 304–313, Washington.
    1935. Dating Pueblo Bonito and Other Ruins of the Southwest. Pueblo Bonito series, National Geographic Society, Contributed Technical Papers, no. 1, Washington.

FENNEMAN, N. M.
    1928. Physiographic Divisions of the United States. Third edition, revised and enlarged. Annals of the Association of American Geographers, vol. XVIII, no. 4, Albany N. Y.

FEWKES, J. W.
    1904. Two Summers' Work in Pueblo Ruins. Twenty-second Annual Report, Bureau of American Ethnology, pt. 1, pp. 3–195, Washington.
    1909. Antiquities of the Mesa Verde National Park: Spruce-tree House. Bulletin 41, Bureau of American Ethnology, Washington.
    1911. Preliminary Report on a Visit to the Navajo National Monument, Arizona. Bulletin 50, Bureau of American Ethnology, Washington.
    1919. Prehistoric Villages, Castles, and Towers of Southwestern Colorado. Bulletin 70, Bureau of American Ethnology, Washington.

GLADWIN, WINIFRED and H. S.
    Undated. The Red-on-Buff Culture of the Papagueria. Medallion Papers, IV, Globe, Ariz.
    1929. The Red-on-Buff Culture of the Gila Basin. Medallion Papers, III, Globe, Ariz.
    1930. An Archeological Survey of Verde Valley. Medallion Papers, VI, Globe, Ariz.
    1935. The Eastern Range of the Red-on-Buff Culture. Medallion Papers, XVI, Globe, Ariz.

GREGORY, H. E.
    1916. The Navajo Country. A Geographic and Hydrographic Reconnaissance of Parts of Arizona, New Mexico, and Utah. United States Geological Survey, Water-supply Paper 380, Washington.

GUERNSEY, S. J.
    1931. Explorations in Northeastern Arizona. Report on the Archeological Fieldwork of 1920–1923. Papers of the Peabody Museum of American Archeology and Ethnology, Harvard University, vol. XII, no. 1, Cambridge.

GUERNSEY, S. J., and KIDDER, A. V.
    1921. Basket-Maker Caves of Northeastern Arizona. Papers of the Peabody Museum of American Archeology and Ethnology, Harvard University, vol. VIII, no. 2, Cambridge.

HARGRAVE, L. L.
    1930. Prehistoric Earth Lodges of the San Francisco Mountains. Museum Notes, Museum of Northern Arizona, vol. 3, no. 5, Flagstaff.
    1933. Pueblo II Houses of the San Francisco Mountains, Arizona. Bulletin 4, Museum of Northern Arizona, pp. 15–73, Flagstaff.
    1935. Report on Archeological Reconnaissance in the Rainbow Plateau Area of Northern Arizona and Southern Utah. Based upon Fieldwork by the Rainbow Bridge-Monument Valley Expedition of 1933. University of California Press, Berkeley.

HARRINGTON, M. R.
    1927. A Primitive Pueblo City in Nevada. American Anthropologist, n. s. vol. 29, no. 3, pp. 262–277, Menasha, Wis.

HAURY, E. W.
    1932. Roosevelt 9:6, A Hohokam Site of the Colonial Period. Medallion Papers, XI, Globe, Ariz.
    1936 a. Some Southwestern Pottery Types, Series IV. Medallion Papers, XIX, Globe, Ariz.
    1936 b. The Mogollon Culture of Southwestern New Mexico. Medallion Papers, XX, Globe, Ariz.

HEWETT, E. L.
    1922. The Chaco Canyon in 1921. Art and Archeology, vol. XIV, no. 3, pp. 115–131, Washington.

HODGE, F. W.
    1923. Circular Kivas Near Hawikuh, New Mexico. Contributions from the Museum of the American Indian, Heye Foundation, vol. VII, no. 1, Hendricks-Hodge Expedition, New York.

HOOTON, E. A.
    1930. The Indians of Pecos Pueblo, a Study of their Skeletal Remains. Papers of the Southwestern Expedition, no. 4, Department of Archeology, Phillips Academy, Andover. Yale Press, New Haven.

HOUGH, W.
    1903. Archeological Field Work in Northeastern Arizona. The Museum-Gates Expedition of 1901. Annual Report of the Smithsonian Institution for 1901, Washington.
    1919. Exploration of a Pit House Village at Luna, New Mexico. Proceedings of the United States National Museum, vol. 55, no. 2280, pp. 409–431, Washington.

IRVING, J. T., JR.
    1835. Indian Sketches, taken during an Expedition to the Pawnee Tribes. 2 vols., Philadelphia.

JEANCON, J. A.
  1922. Archeological Research in the Northeastern San Juan Basin of Colorado during the Summer of 1921. State Historical and Natural History Society and the University of Denver, Denver.
  1929. Archeological Investigations in the Taos Valley, New Mexico, during 1920. Smithsonian Miscellaneous Collections, vol. 81, no. 12, pub. no. 3015, Washington.

JUDD, N. M.
  1924. Two Chaco Canyon Pit Houses. Smithsonian Report for 1922, pp. 399–413, Washington.
  1925. Archeological Investigations at Pueblo Bonito, New Mexico. Exploration and Field-work of the Smithsonian Institution in 1924. Smithsonian Miscellaneous Collections, vol. 77, no. 2, pp. 83–91, Washington.
  1926. Archeological Observations North of the Rio Colorado. Bulletin 82, Bureau of American Ethnology, Washington.
  1930. Pueblo Bonito and its Architectural Development. Proceedings of the 23d International Congress of Americanists, pp. 70–73, New York.

KIDDER, A. V.
  1924. An Introduction to the Study of Southwestern Archeology, with a Preliminary Account of the Excavations at Pecos. Department of Archeology, Phillips Academy, Andover. Yale Press, New Haven.

MARTIN, P. S.
  1930. The 1929 Archeological Expedition of the State Historical Society of Colorado in Cooperation with the Smithsonian Institution. The Colorado Magazine, vol. VII, no. 1, pp. 1–40, Denver.
  1936. Lowry Ruin in Southwestern Colorado. Anthropological Series, Field Museum of Natural History, vol. 23, no. 1, pub. no. 356, Chicago.

MAXIMILIEN (ALEX. P.), LE PRINCE DE WIED-NEUWIED.
  1843. Voyage dans L'intérieur de L'Amerique du Nord. (vol. 1 published 1840, vol. 2, 1841, vol. 3, 1843), Paris.

MILLER, C. F.
  1934. Report on Dates on the Allantown, Arizona, Ruins. Tree Ring Bulletin, vol. I, no. 2, pp. 15–16, Flagstaff.
  1935. Additional Dates from Allantown. Tree Ring Bulletin, vol. I, no. 4, p. 31, Flagstaff.

MINDELEFF, V.
  1891. A Study of Pueblo Architecture: Tusayan and Cibola. Eighth Annual Report, Bureau of Ethnology, Washington.

MORRIS, E. H.
  1919. Preliminary Account of the Antiquities of the Region between the Mancos and La Plata Rivers in Southwestern Colorado. Thirty-third Annual Report, Bureau of American Ethnology, pp. 155–206, Washington.
  1921. The House of the Great Kiva at the Aztec Ruin. Anthropological Papers American Museum of Natural History, vol. XXVI, pt. 2, New York.
  1924. Burials in the Aztec Ruin, the Aztec Ruin Annex. Anthropological Papers American Museum of Natural History, vol. XXVI, pts. 3 and 4, New York.

MORRIS, E. H.
1925. Exploring in the Canyon of Death. National Geographic Magazine, vol. XLVIII, no. 3, pp. 263–300, Washington.

PEPPER, G. H.
1920. Pueblo Bonito. Anthropological Papers American Museum of Natural History, vol. XXVII, New York.

PRUDDEN, T. M.
1914. The Circular Kivas of the Small Ruins in the San Juan Watershed. American Anthropologist, n. s. vol. 16, no. 1, pp. 33–58, Lancaster, Pa.

ROBERTS, F. H. H., JR.
1929. Shabik'eschee Village: A Late Basket Maker Site in the Chaco Canyon, New Mexico. Bulletin 92, Bureau of American Ethnology, Washington.
1930. Early Pueblo Ruins in the Piedra District, Southwestern Colorado. Bulletin 96, Bureau of American Ethnology, Washington.
1931. The Ruins at Kiatuthlanna, Eastern Arizona. Bulletin 100, Bureau of American Ethnology, Washington.
1932. The Village of the Great Kivas on the Zuñi Reservation, New Mexico. Bulletin 111, Bureau of American Ethnology, Washington.
1935. A Survey of Southwestern Archeology. American Anthropologist, n. s. vol. 37, no. 1, pp. 1–35, Menasha, Wis.
1937. Archeology in the Southwest. American Antiquity, vol. III, no. 1, pp. 3–33, Menasha, Wis.

SIMPSON, J. H.
1850. Report of an Expedition into the Navajo Country in 1849. *In* Reports of the Secretary of War, Senate Executive document no. 64, 31st Congress, 1st session, pp. 55–64, Washington.

STEVENSON, MATILDA C.
1904. The Zuñi Indians: Their Mythology, Esoteric Fraternities, and Ceremonies. Twenty-third Annual Report, Bureau of American Ethnology, Washington.

WHIPPLE, A. W.
1856. Reports of Explorations and Surveys, to Ascertain the Most Practical and Economical Route for a Railroad from the Mississippi River to the Pacific Ocean. Vol. III, Senate Executive Document no. 78, 33d Congress, 2d session, Washington.

WINSHIP, G. P.
1896. The Coronado Expedition, 1540–1542. Fourteenth Annual Report, Bureau of Ethnology, Washington.

INDEX

ALLANTOWN, ARIZ., ruins near, 1
ANASAZI:
  burial custom of, 14
  dwellings of, 14
  use of the name, 4–5
ANASAZI REMAINS, location of, 5
ANIMALS of region of ruins, 2
ARCHEOLOGY, SOUTHWESTERN, summary of status of, 4–5
ASH PITS, evolution of, 255
ASHES:
  pits for saving of, 230, 231
  use of, 200
AZTEC, N. MEX., reference to ruin at, 218
AZTEC RUINS, mention of kiva in, 247
BASKET MAKER CULTURE, development of, 7–9
BEADS, discovery of mass of, 202
BENCH:
  development of, 257
  discussion of significance of, 254
  of Kiva B, 209
  ridges of plaster on, 107–108
BINS:
  purpose of, 25
  stone slab, 25
BLOCKS, stone, purpose of, unknown, 38
BROWN, RALPH D., assistance rendered by, XI
  See also SHELTER REMAINS; SHELTERS.
BRUSH SHELTERS:
  description of, 56–57
  probable use of, 57
BURIALS:
  in and under refuse mound, 239
  in room 12, 204
  in structure 16, 154
  Mogollon, 15
  of children, 205–206
  of dogs, 186, 264
  of parts of bodies, occurrence of, 185–186
  of turkeys, 230, 264
  offerings interred with, 264
  summary of, 264
  under granaries, 158
  unusual position in, 204
  See also SKELETON.
BUSHNELL, D. I., JR., cited, 25, 104, 122

BUTCHART, RUTH R., work of, XII
CACHE found in fill, 123
CACHE PIT, jug-shaped, description of, 178
CARVING, SHELL, mention of, 14
CASA RINCONADA, mention of kiva in, 247
CEREMONIAL CHAMBER:
  evolution of, 48, 257
  See also KIVA.
CHACO CANYON:
  pit structure, date of, 263
  reference to, 218, 233, 247
  reference to masonry of, 250
CHETTRO KETTLE, mention of Great Bowl in, 247
CLANS, number of, suggested by kivas, 249
CLIMATE, description of, 4
COMPARTMENT, stone-walled, 89–90
COOLEY, HAROLD E., assistance rendered by, XII
CORNERS, reinforcement of, 199–200
COURT:
  description of, 175–176
  Unit 3, description of, 231–232
COVER STONES, use of, for ventilators, 19
CREMATION, practice of, 14
CULTURAL STAGES, determination of sequence of, 12
CUMMINGS, BYRON, cited, 233
CUSHING, F. H., cited, 97
DANCE COURT:
  description of, 126–128
  discussion of, 258
  measurements of, 129–130
  possible use of, 128
  remains covered by, 124
  suggestive of great kiva, 128
DATES:
  covered by remains, 259–263
  cultural lag shown by, 262–263
DEFLECTOR:
  example of, 24
  incorporated in fire pit, 75
  materials used for, 41
  use of, 19
  use of, in kivas, 215
DENDROCHRONOLOGY:
  as an aid to archeologists, XII
  dates obtained by, 259–260
  discussion of dating by, 260–263

DEPRESSIONS IN FLOORS:
   corresponding to kiva vaults_ 107
   problematical _____ 23, 64, 104–106
   unusual construction of_____ 122
DEVELOPMENTAL PUEBLO STAGE:
   discussion of_____ 9–10
   remains belonging to_____ 110
   ruins showing trend of____ 253–254
DEVELOPMENTAL VILLAGE, investigation of_____ 17
DOGS:
   burials of_____ 186, 264
   use of, for food_____ 176
DOUGLASS, A. E., scientific work of_____ 13
DOUGLASS METHOD of dating from tree rings_____ 30
DWELLINGS:
   construction of_____ 14
   Mogollon, dating of_____ 15
   used as turkey pen_____ 118
   See also STRUCTURES; SURFACE HOUSES.
ENCLOSURE, plaster-rimmed, discussion of_____ 236–237
ENTRANCE:
   description of_____ 151
   measurements of_____ 156
   ventilator replaced by_____ 151
FENNEMAN, N. M., cited_____ 2
FEWKES, J. WALTER:
   cited _____ 218, 250
   perforated stones found by__ 69
FILL:
   cache found in_____ 123
   conclusions drawn from_____ 112–113, 118, 163
   in kiva, study of_____ 238–239
   of Kiva A, examination of_ 184–185
   of Kiva B, significance of___ 220
   of Kiva B, study of_____ 218–220
   significance of__ 30, 42–43, 50, 71–72
   significant features of_____ 154
   stratigraphic study of_____ 27–29, 93–96, 110–112
   use made of tests of_____ 263
FINKELSTEIN, JOE, assistance rendered by_____ XII
FIRE PITS:
   association of, with dwellings _____ 172
   combined with ladder pit____ 49
   description of_____ 37, 74–75, 87
   outside, use of_____ 195
   perforated stones covering__ 71
   plastered rim of_____ 49, 69, 74, 87, 180
   secondary, discussion of_____ 49

FIRE PITS—Continued.
   slab-lined _____ 65
   surface, investigation of____ 176
FLOOR:
   of Kiva B_____ 216
   plaster ridges on_____ 180–182
   See also DEPRESSIONS; PAVING.
FOOD SUPPLY, remains indicating_ 264
GILMORE, MELVIN R., reference to_ 264
GLADWIN, W. and H. S., cited___ 15
GRANARIES:
   Basket Maker_____ 8
   construction of_____ 100–101
   contiguous rooms suggested by_____ 147
   description of_____ 134–135, 157–160, 163–164
   description of group of___ 145–149
   development of_____ 257
   measurements of_____ 135, 147–149, 159–160, 166
   or corner closets, description of_____ 203–204
   remains of_____ 100–101
   significance in group of_____ 159
   use of, as dwellings_____ 158, 159
   See also STORAGE.
GREAT KIVA:
   dance court suggestive of___ 128
   discussion of purpose of__ 247–248
   measurements of_____ 246–247
GREAT PUEBLO PERIOD:
   development of_____ 10–11
   ruins representing_____ 253
GREAT PUEBLO RUINS:
   conclusions drawn from___ 258–259
   description of_____ 244–251
GREAT PUEBLO STRUCTURES:
   dates of_____ 252–253
   measurements of_____ 247, 249, 251
GREGORY, H. E., cited_____ 1
GRUBBS, J. A.:
   acknowledgment to_____ XII
   information furnished by___ XI
HARGRAVE, L. L., cited_____ 110
HARRINGTON, M. R., cited_____ 20, 57
HARVARD UNIVERSITY, mention of_ XI, XII
HAURY, E. W., cited_____ 15, 255
HAWIKUH, reference to archeological work at_____ 71
HEMATITE, use of, in kiva floor__ 216
HEWETT, E. L., cited_____ 247
HODGE, F. W., reference to work of_____ 71, 214
HOHOKAM:
   cremation practiced by_____ 14
   cultural stages in_____ 14

INDEX

HOHOKAM—Continued.
    dwellings of 14
    use of the name 5
HOLES AND DEPRESSIONS:
    problematical 104–106
    See also DEPRESSIONS.
HOMINY, use of ashes in preparation of 200
HOOTON, E. A., cited 239
HOPI:
    cited 57, 258
    reference to kivas of 218
HOUGH, WALTER, reference to investigations of 70
IRRIGATION, progress in 14
IRVING, J. T., cited 25
JEANCON, J. A., cited 108, 233, 258
JONES, DAVID, work of XII
JUDD, N. M., cited 57, 108, 182, 218
KATCINA KIHU:
    explanation of 212
    niche compared with 68
KATCINA NICHES, discussion of .. 212
KIDDER, A. V., cited 218
KIMBALL, SOLON T., assistance rendered by XI
KING, DALE S., assistance rendered by XI
KITCHEN, outdoor 205
KIVA A:
    description of 180–188
    discussion of date of 187–188
    discussion of status of ... 186–187
    masonry in 180
    measurements of 191–194
    superstructure of 180
KIVA B:
    description of 207–218
    measurements of 223–226
KIVA, UNIT 3:
    description of 232–238
    measurements of 242–244
KIVA VAULTS, depressions corresponding to 107
KIVAS:
    Chaco, feature suggestive of . 107
    number of clans suggested by 249
    timbers in wall of 233
    See also CEREMONIAL CHAMBER.
KNEIPP, ROBERT, work of XII
LABORATORY OF ANTHROPOLOGY, Santa Fe, work of XI
LADDER BOX:
    change in function of 21
    combined with fire pit 49
    development of 255

LADDERS:
    kiva, placement of 215
    pits for 21, 49
    two-pole-and-rung type 21
    types of, in use 255
LOWRY RUIN, mention of kiva at .. 247
LUNA, mention of dance pit at ... 258
MARTIN, P. S., cited 20, 247
MASONRY:
    of Great Pueblo structures .. 250
    of Kiva B 209
    superior grade of 232–233
    use of, in pit houses 33–34
    See also WALLS.
MESA VERDE, reference to 218
METATE AND MANOS, found in position 139
MILLER, CARL F.:
    assistance rendered by XI
    cited 110, 142, 239
    work of .... XII, 30
MINDELEFF, V., cited 55, 122, 198
MODIFIED BASKET MAKER HOUSES:
    feature of 25
    horizontal masonry in 34
MODIFIED BASKET MAKER PERIOD:
    discussion of 8–9
    traces indicating 253
MOGOLLON:
    correlation of, with Anasazi . 15–16
    correlation of, with Hohokam 15–16
    cultural stages of 15
    use of the name 5
MOGOLLON CULTURE, characteristics of 15
MORRIS, EARL H.:
    cited 108, 218, 247, 248
    reference to work of 128
NICHE:
    as a feature of kivas 217–218
    between rooms 202
    kiva, discussion of opening to . 218
    suggestive of Katcina Kihu . 122
    See also KATCINA NICHES.
NUSBAUM, DERIC, assistance rendered by XII
OVEN. *See* PIT OVEN.
PECOS CLASSIFICATION, adoption of 6
PAVING, remains of 122
PERFORATED STONE SLABS, discussion of 69–71
PERIODS, CULTURE, classification of . 6–7
PIEDRA RIVER, mention of dance plaza on 258
PILASTER:
    construction of 50

PILASTER—Continued.
  evolution of _____ 35–36
  examples of development of _____ 254–255
  use of _____ 35
PIT DWELLINGS, structures comparable to _____ 19
PIT OVEN, description of _____ 55
PIT REMAINS:
  D-shaped _____ 46, 58, 102
  description of _____ 21, 58
  investigation of _____ 20
  kiva suggested by _____ 108
  significance of fill in _____ 30, 42
PIT STRUCTURES:
  changes made in _____ 257
  conclusions drawn from _____ 168–169, 254
  connected, discussion of _____ 80–81
  connected, group of, described _____ 67–80
  elaborate interior features of _____ 137–138
  partially superimposed _____ 62
  theory concerning combinations of _____ 255
  three forming one _____ 81
  three-in-one, discussion of _____ 96–98
  transition in function of _____ 256–257
  See also PIT DWELLINGS; PIT REMAINS; STRUCTURE No. 1 _____ 18
POPULATION:
  estimated, of Great Pueblo _____ 249, 250
  estimated, of Unit 3 _____ 239–240
  estimates concerning _____ 264–265
PORTICO, description of _____ 174
POSTS, bracing of _____ 35, 47
POT REST:
  description of _____ 163
  in Kiva A _____ 183
POTSHERD MATERIAL, stratigraphic test of _____ 27–28, 41–42
POTTERY:
  cultural stage determined by _____ 12
  method of making _____ 14–15
  Mogollon _____ 15
  See also POTSHERDS.
PRUDDEN, T. M., cited _____ 218
PUEBLO BONITO:
  date of _____ 263
  mention of kiva in _____ 247
PUEBLO COMMUNAL BUILDINGS, development of _____ 97
PUEBLO CULTURE, development of _____ 7, 9–11
PUEBLO GRANDE, NEVADA, reference to _____ 20

PUEBLO-TYPE STRUCTURE:
  description of _____ 248–249
  See also PUEBLO COMMUNAL BUILDINGS.
PUERCO RIVER, discussion of stream bed of _____ 2–3
REED, ERIK K., assistance rendered by _____ XII
REFUSE MOUNDS:
  conclusions drawn from _____ 252
  examination of _____ 251–252
  Great Pueblo, discussed _____ 251–252
  location of _____ 172, 194–195, 227, 245
  purpose of trenching of _____ 20
REGRESSIVE PERIOD, causes of _____ 11
REMAINS:
  southwestern, divisions of _____ 4–5
  See also RUINS.
RENAISSANCE PERIOD, development attained in _____ 11–12
RIDGES, ADOBE:
  compartments outlined by _____ 39
  on bench _____ 107–108
ROBERTS, FRANK H. H., JR., cited _____ 6, 12, 19, 20, 25, 56, 57, 67, 69, 107, 127, 182, 204, 207, 214, 218, 247, 248, 250, 255, 256, 258.
ROBERTS, LINDA B., work of _____ XII
ROOF, CRIBBED:
  explanation for _____ 49
  of kiva _____ 235
  presence of _____ 46
  significance of _____ 48
ROOFS:
  construction of _____ 48
  kiva, cribbed type _____ 235
  Kiva B, description of _____ 209–211
  use made of _____ 137
  See also ROOF, CRIBBED.
ROOMS:
  in tiers, description of _____ 248–249
  of surface structure _____ 197–206, 229–231
  rectangular block of _____ 248–249
  steps in _____ 197, 198, 201, 203
RUINS:
  location of _____ 1
  periods represented in _____ 15
  time covered by _____ 259
  unnamed _____ XII
SELENITE, use of, for windows _____ 174
SHELTER REMAINS:
  conclusions drawn from _____ 133
  description of _____ 130–132, 147, 176–177, 206
  measurements of _____ 132–133, 149, 222–223

INDEX

SHELTER REMAINS—Continued.
  problematical feature of — 131
  question concerning — 207
SIMPSON, J. H., deductions drawn from diary of — 3
SIPAPU:
  jug-shaped — 116
  occurrence of — 40, 49
  rectangular example of — 75
  symbolism of — 23
SKELETON, parts of, in Kiva A — 184–185
SLABS, STONE:
  imbedded in floor — 38, 39
  possible use of — 38
  use of, in pit houses — 33–34
SOIL, quality of, around ruins — 2
STEWART, T. D., material assigned to — 264
STONE, PERFORATED, use of, to frame aperture — 69
STORAGE:
  wall pocket for — 116–117
  See also GRANARIES; STORAGE BINS; STORAGE CIST; STORAGE PITS; STORAGE ROOM.
STORAGE BINS:
  description of — 200–201
  of Kiva B — 217
STORAGE CIST, description of — 100–101
STORAGE PITS:
  discussion of — 178–179
  jug-shaped — 232
STORAGE ROOM:
  description of — 201
  See also GRANARIES.
STORAGE STRUCTURE:
  beehive-shaped — 140
  See also GRANARIES.
STRATIGRAPHY of fill, conclusions drawn from — 96
STRUCTURE No. 1:
  description of — 21–30
  measurements of — 30–33
STRUCTURE No. 2:
  dates of — 43
  description of — 33–46
  measurements of — 43–46
  two occupations of — 34–35
STRUCTURE No. 3:
  dates of — 48, 52
  description of — 46–53
  measurements of — 52–53
STRUCTURE No. 4:
  description of — 58–62
  measurements of — 60–64
STRUCTURE No. 5a:
  description of — 62–65
  measurements of — 65–66

STRUCTURE No. 5b:
  description of — 26–65
  measurements of — 66–67
STRUCTURE No. 6:
  description of — 67–72
  measurements of — 72–73
STRUCTURE No. 7:
  description of — 73–75
  measurements of — 75–76
STRUCTURE No. 8:
  description of — 77–78
  measurements of — 78–79
STRUCTURE No. 9:
  description of — 81–84
  measurements of — 84–85
STRUCTURE No. 10:
  description of — 85–87
  measurements of — 88–89
STRUCTURE No. 11:
  description of — 89–91
  measurements of — 91–93
STRUCTURE No. 12:
  dates of — 108
  description of — 102–110
  kiva suggested by — 108
  measurements of — 113–115
STRUCTURE No. 13a:
  description of — 116–120
  measurements of — 118–120
STRUCTURE No. 13b:
  description of — 120–123
  measurements of — 123–124
STRUCTURE No. 14:
  description of — 124–126
  measurements of — 128–129
STRUCTURE No. 15:
  date of — 141–142
  description of — 135–141
  measurements of — 142–145
STRUCTURE No. 16:
  description of — 149–156
  measurements of — 155–156
  relative age of — 155
  unusual entrance to — 151
STRUCTURE No. 17:
  description of — 160–164
  measurements of — 164–166
STRUCTURE No. 18:
  description of — 166–169
  measurements of — 169–170
STRUCTURES:
  connection of — 19–20
  construction of — 18
  general characteristics of — 18–19
  interior features of — 19
  opening in wall between — 75
  problematical — 250–251
  Pueblo-type — 97, 248–249

STRUCTURES—Continued.
  unidentified, remains of 177
  use of the term 17
  See also CEREMONIAL CHAMBER; KIVA; PIT STRUCTURES; SHELTERS; SUPERSTRUCTURES; SURFACE HOUSES; SURFACE STRUCTURES.
SUPERSTRUCTURES:
  change made in 257
  construction of 104, 137
  description of 27, 102–104
  discussion of 255–256
  of Kiva B 209–211
  of three-in-one pits 97–98
  restoration of 27
SURFACE HOUSES:
  description of 53–56, 98–100
  measurements of ... 57–58, 101–102
SURFACE STRUCTURE, UNIT 2:
  construction of 196–197
  description of 196–206
  measurements of 220–222
  rooms of 196
SURFACE STRUCTURE, UNIT 3:
  description of 227–231
  measurements of 240–242
THOMAS, SIDNEY J., assistance rendered by XII
TOPOGRAPHY, of region of ruins .. 1–2
TOWERS, discussion of 250–251
TURKEY PEN, remains of 118
TURKEYS:
  burials of 230, 264
  domestication of 14
UNIT No. 1:
  description of 171–194
  surface building, measurements of 188–191
UNIT No. 2:
  description of 194–226
  number of families in 196
UNIT No. 3:
  dates of 239
  discussion of 227–240
  measurements of 240–244
UNIT-TYPE DWELLING:
  evolution of 256–258
  time involved in evolution of . 260
UNIT-TYPE STRUCTURES:
  discussion of 170–171
  general description of 171
UNIVERSITY OF ARIZONA, mention of XI
UNIVERSITY OF DENVER, mention of XI

UNIVERSITY OF MINNESOTA, mention of XII
UNIVERSITY OF OKLAHOMA, mention of XII
UNIVERSITY OF TEXAS, mention of . XII
VENTILATOR:
  construction of 50
  description of 19, 75, 83–84, 108
  development of 257
  of kiva, description of 183, 237
  origin of 25
  remodeling of 38–39
  subfloor type of 212–214
  unusual construction of 126
  unusual features of . 26, 71, 139–141
VILLAGE OF THE GREAT KIVAS, dates of 252, 263
VILLAGE REMAINS, change recorded by 171
WAINSCOTING of walls, discussion of 233–235
WALL NICHE:
  possible explanation of 68
  purpose of 83
  See also WALL POCKETS.
WALL POCKETS:
  for storage 116–117, 162
  in Kiva, use of 180
WALLS:
  construction of ... 173, 196, 198–199
  horizontal masonry in 196
  rubble finish on 196
  timbers incorporated in ... 199, 233
  wainscoting of 233–235
WATERCOURSE:
  buried 172, 195
  diversion of water from 172
WATER SUPPLY, discussion of 3–4
WEAPONS, mention of 15
WHIPPLE, A. W., cited 3
WHIPPLE RAILROAD SURVEY, reference to 3
WINDOWS, discussion of 173–174
WINSHIP, G. P., cited 233
ZUÑI:
  culinary practices at 200
  granary found at 204
  reference to Great Kivas of . 218
  reference to storage bins of . 198
ZUÑI KIVA, perforated slab used in 69
ZUÑI RESERVATION:
  baking pit found on 56
  mention of kivas on 247
  reference to masonry of 250

www.ingramcontent.com/pod-product-compliance
Lightning Source LLC
Chambersburg PA
CBHW022115080426
42734CB00006B/135